PRAISE FOR *SEARCHING FOR JESUS*

"This entertaining book, setting its scenes with plenty of local color, demonstrates just how far the modern skepticism about Jesus has overreached itself. Questions remain, but Robert Hutchinson reminds us that we do not need to be browbeaten by those who say that only negative answers are available."

—N. T. Wright, Ph.D., author of *Simply Good News* and Chair of New Testament and Early Christianity at the School of Divinity at the University of St. Andrews

"Robert Hutchinson's new book—*Searching for Jesus: New Discoveries in the Quest for Jesus of Nazareth*—is a significant and very welcomed contribution to the discussion about the 'Historical Jesus.' In his book, Hutchinson reviews recent archaeological finds and new directions in New Testament scholarship that challenge some of the older theories. He does it with great clarity and in a lively and intriguing way."

—Israel Knohl, Ph.D., Yehezkel Kaufmann Chair in Biblical Studies, The Hebrew University, Jerusalem

"*Searching for Jesus* is an excellent, informed, up-to-date review of biblical research presented in clear, engaging prose for the average reader. Again and again, Robert Hutchinson shows how recent historical and archaeological investigations have overturned many of the bias-laden and unverified conclusions of biblical scholarship in the past century. *Searching for Jesus* will teach you, challenge you, and encourage you. I highly recommend this book to anyone who is seeking the truth—about Jesus of Nazareth and about the historical accuracy of the Gospels."

—Mark D. Roberts, Ph.D., author of *Can We Trust the Gospels?* and executive director of the Max De Pree Center for Leadership at Fuller Theological Seminary

SEARCHING FOR JESUS

SEARCHING FOR JESUS

NEW DISCOVERIES IN THE QUEST FOR JESUS OF NAZARETH—
AND HOW THEY CONFIRM THE GOSPEL ACCOUNTS

ROBERT J. HUTCHINSON

NELSON
BOOKS

An Imprint of Thomas Nelson

Published in Nashville, Tennessee, by Nelson Books, an imprint of Thomas Nelson. Nelson Books and Thomas Nelson are registered trademarks of HarperCollins Christian Publishing, Inc.

Thomas Nelson titles may be purchased in bulk for educational, business, fund-raising, or sales promotional use. For information, please e-mail SpecialMarkets@ThomasNelson.com.

Unless otherwise noted, Scripture quotations are taken from the *New American Bible, revised edition.* © 2010, 1991, 1986, 1970 Confraternity of Christian Doctrine, Washington, DC. Used by permission of the copyright owner. All rights reserved. No part of the New American Bible may be reproduced in any form without permission in writing from the copyright owner.

Scripture quotations marked NRSV are taken from New Revised Standard Version Bible. Copyright © 1989 National Council of the Churches of Christ in the United States of America. Used by permission. All rights reserved.

Scripture quotations marked ESV are taken from the ESV® Bible (The Holy Bible, English Standard Version®). Copyright © 2001 by Crossway, a publishing ministry of Good News Publishers. Used by permission. All rights reserved.

Scripture quotations marked NIV are taken from the Holy Bible, New International Version®, NIV®. Copyright © 1973, 1978, 1984, 2011 by Biblica, Inc.® Used by permission of Zondervan. All rights reserved worldwide. www.zondervan.com. The "NIV" and "New International Version" are trademarks registered in the United States Patent and Trademark Office by Biblica, Inc.®

Scripture quotations marked NLT are taken from the *Holy Bible*, New Living Translation. © 1996, 2004, 2007, 2013 by Tyndale House Foundation. Used by permission of Tyndale House Publishers, Inc., Carol Stream, Illinois 60188. All rights reserved.

Scripture quotations marked RSV are taken from the Revised Standard Version of the Bible, copyright 1946, 1952, and 1971 National Council of the Churches of Christ in the United States of America. Used by permission. All rights reserved.

Scripture quotations marked NKJV are taken from the New King James Version®. © 1982 by Thomas Nelson. Used by permission. All rights reserved.

Scripture quotations marked KJV are taken from the King James Version.

Scripture quotations marked by an asterisk are the author's own interpretations.

Library of Congress Control Number: 2015943724

ISBN: 978-0-7180-1830-6 (HC)
ISBN: 978-0-7180-7797-6 (IE)

Printed in the United States of America

15 16 17 18 19 RRD 6 5 4 3 2 1

Πῦρ ἦλθον βαλεῖν ἐπὶ τὴν γῆν
"I have come to set the earth on fire."

—LUKE 12:49

For our first grandchild, Theodore,
whose name means "God's gift"

CONTENTS

Author's Note   xv

Introduction   xix

Prologue   xxix

1. Is There Eyewitness Testimony in the Gospels?   1

2. Liar, Lunatic . . . or Legend?   39

3. Are the Gospels Forgeries?   69

4. Have Archaeologists Found Jesus' House?   91

5. Did the Church Invent the Idea of a Suffering Messiah?   117

6. Just How Kosher Was Jesus?   137

7. Did Jesus Have a Secret Message?   163

8. Was Jesus a Zealot Revolutionary?   181

9. Did Jesus Plan His Own Execution?   201

10. Do We Have Proof for the Resurrection?   219

11. Jesus, God and Man   253

Epilogue   271

CONTENTS

Acknowledgments   277

Selected Bibliography   279

Notes   285

Index   337

About the Author   349

πάντα δὲ δοκιμάζετε, τὸ καλὸν κατέχετε.
"Test everything; hold fast to what is good."

—1 THESSALONIANS 5:21 NRSV

*"We must love them both, those whose opinions
we share and those whose opinions we reject.
For both have labored in the search for truth,
and both have helped us in the finding of it."*

—ST. THOMAS AQUINAS

AUTHOR'S NOTE

For more than a century, Bible scholars and university researchers have been systematically debunking much of what ordinary Christians thought they knew about Jesus of Nazareth. Every Christmas and Easter over the years, educated Christians grew accustomed to reading magazine cover stories and seeing TV documentaries purporting to demonstrate that most traditional beliefs about Jesus are not merely fairy tales but outright fabrications.

But what if a lot of what we have been told about the historical Jesus of Nazareth—many of the academic orthodoxies we've heard over the decades from university experts and media sources—turned out to be . . . *false?*

What if parts of the New Testament were actually composed by eyewitnesses to the events, perhaps even when Jesus was living in Galilee?

What if Jesus was not a Zealot revolutionary . . . or a Greek Cynic philosopher . . . or a proto-feminist Gnostic . . . but precisely who he claimed to be, the divine Son of Man prophesied in the book of Daniel, who gave his life as a ransom for many?

What if some people in Jesus' time and place knew *precisely* what that meant—and, contrary to what Christians have been told for the past two hundred years by scholars, were actually *expecting* a suffering and dying messiah who would redeem the world?

In short: What if everything the Gospels say about Jesus of Nazareth—his words, his deeds, his plans—actually turned out to be . . . true?

This is a book about new discoveries in the search for Jesus of Nazareth. It's an overview of recent archaeological finds and new developments in biblical scholarship that are calling into question much of what skeptical scholars have assumed and asserted about Jesus over the past two centuries.

It argues that many of the "scientific" or scholarly ideas about Jesus paraded in the media every Christmas and Easter are increasingly *obsolete,* based on assumptions, theories, and unproven hypotheses that are, in some cases, more than a century old and which have been superseded by more recent research.

Among the recent developments discussed in this book are:

- the 2012 announcement of the discovery of seven previously unknown New Testament papyri—one of which, from the gospel of Mark, may date to the first century;
- the 2009 discovery of a first-century stone house in Nazareth that refutes one of the key arguments used by those who say Jesus never existed;
- a young secular scholar in the UK who recently argued that the gospel of Mark was written not forty or fifty years after Jesus' death, as many scholars have claimed for at least a century, but more like five or ten;
- recent excavations in Israel that have uncovered archaeological proof of the existence of key figures mentioned in the New Testament, including the high priest Caiaphas and possibly James the Just;
- new research that suggests belief in Jesus as a divine savior arose very early, within a year or two of the crucifixion, not fifty to one hundred years later as academic researchers used to claim in the twentieth century;
- the recently discovered Hebrew-language tablet dating back to the early first century that speaks about a messiah who would suffer, die, and perhaps rise again in three days;
- Jewish experts who insist that the Gospels show Jesus was not an "illiterate peasant," as some historians and popular writers have claimed, but was likely a highly trained and knowledgeable rabbi;
- leading New Testament researchers who are now challenging the notion that Jesus was a "zealot" who sympathized with efforts to overthrow Roman rule (and who point out that Jesus' followers

were not arrested with him and were allowed to operate openly in Jerusalem for decades after his death—something that would have been impossible had the Roman authorities really believed Jesus approved of insurrection);

- a top New Testament scholar in the UK who insists that the Gospel accounts are based on eyewitness testimony tied to named individuals, not based on anonymous reports that circulated over decades as scholars once thought;

- new studies that argue the Gospels' version of the crucifixion—that Jesus was arrested on trumped-up charges of sedition because he openly challenged temple authorities—may be far more historically accurate than previously believed; and

- the growing recognition that the Gnostic Gospels the Christian church allegedly suppressed were actually written one hundred to three hundred years after Jesus, and are in some cases openly misogynistic.

In the end, these new discoveries are causing some experts to wonder if the basic portrait of Jesus in the Gospels is *far more plausible* than the elaborate reconstructions created by academic skeptics over the past 150 years.

In other words, the New Testament may be truer than we thought, and Jesus of Nazareth, rather than being smaller than the Gospels portray him, may actually be much *bigger* . . . and far more interesting.

—**Robert J. Hutchinson**
Jerusalem, July 2014

INTRODUCTION

"I truly understand that God shows no partiality,
but in every nation anyone who fears him and
does what is right is acceptable to him."

—ACTS 10:34–35 NRSV

I t's a warm, sunny day in northern Israel, and I am sitting on the railing of a fishing boat from Kibbutz Ginosar as we slowly make our way along the shoreline of the Sea of Galilee. Behind us, on the burnt-brown hills that rise up sharply from the lake, we can see the resort town of Tiberias, originally built by the first-century Jewish ruler Herod Antipas, with block after block of new condominium developments climbing like ivy up the ridges behind it. In front of us, the Sea of Galilee remains the same as I remember it when I lived here decades earlier. In fact, the Kinneret, as it is known in Hebrew, looks like it couldn't be all that much different from what it was like in the time of Jesus, although the shoreline of the lake has changed and some archaeologists claim the region was once much more lush than it is today.

The biblical village of Bethsaida, for example—the hometown of the apostles Philip, Andrew, and Peter, now being excavated by Israeli and American archaeologists—was discovered about a mile (1.5 kilometers) inland from the Sea of Galilee's current shoreline. No one realized the shoreline had changed that much. In fact, the discovery of Bethsaida happened almost by accident. On the other hand, Capernaum, Jesus' adopted hometown (Matt. 9:1), is still found right on the shoreline of the lake. A new church (nicknamed "the spaceship" because of its ultramodern design) has been built directly over a first-century house that archaeologists are confident was the home of the apostle Peter and his mother-in-law, and where Jesus stayed on occasion (Mark 1:29–30). Archaeologists have unearthed the rough stone *insula*, or housing blocks, where dozens of extended families lived, as well as a well-preserved synagogue from the fourth or fifth century AD.

Robert Hutchinson

Few pilgrims can take a boat trip on the Sea of Galilee and not be transformed by it. Very quickly, the stories in the Gospels come alive as you see where everything took place. As the old holyland joke has it, "if it didn't happen here it happened a hundred yards from here."

I walk to the stern of the boat and talk to the captain. He is a wizened old kibbutznik with skin the color of saddle leather, dressed from head to toe in royal-blue work clothes. *"Mishahu amar lee shay-ain harbay dagim be-kinneret achshav,"* I tell the captain in my rusty Hebrew. "Someone told me that there aren't many fish left in the lake."

He snorts derisively in traditional Israeli fashion.

"Whoever told you that doesn't know what he's talking about," the captain curtly replies. "As the lake recedes, the fish move into deeper water. The Kinneret is full of fish." He adds that only two hundred fishing licenses are given out at a time, and that fishing is heavily regulated to maintain the fish population.

The Sea of Galilee is a decent-sized lake, about seven miles across and thirteen miles long (thirteen by twenty kilometers), with a maximum depth of about one hundred thirty feet (forty meters). The air is warm but the winds are remarkably strong, with small whitecaps buffeting the shoreline. I can't help but think of the scene in the Gospels where the apostles are out on the lake, Jesus falls asleep, and a storm threatens to capsize the boat. At Ginosar, they've built a modern museum just to house the ruins of a first-century fishing boat, known as the Jesus Boat, discovered in the lake mud in 1986.

Looking back at the lush shoreline, I marvel at how much of the gospel story took place in this small, still quite rural area. The Mount of the Beatitudes, the traditional site of the Sermon on the Mount, looms directly above us, a small clump of trees on a brown ridge. Below that is Tabgha, the meadow area where local Christians believe Jesus multiplied the loaves and fishes. Coming to Ginosar, I passed the new development of Magdala, likely the hometown of Mary Magdalene and where a first-century synagogue was discovered in 2009. Just north of the lake, up the Wadi Kerazeh, lies the biblical town once known as Chorazin, which Jesus denounced for its rejection of his message (Matt. 11:21–24). And across the lake, the Golan Heights loom. In the northern Golan lie Caesarea Philippi and the enormous rock cliff that was once the shrine of the Greek god Pan, where the Gospels suggest Jesus proclaimed Simon bar Jonah the "rock" (Aramaic *kepha*) upon which he would build his new kingdom community.

DISCOVERING THE CARPENTER OF NAZARETH

I've been fascinated by the person and adventures of Jesus of Nazareth my entire life. I always felt that there must have been a lot more to the story than we read in the Gospels, not less. Whatever else Jesus may have been, I recognized in him a figure of enormous power and influence. When I was young, what I admired about Jesus more than anything else was his raw guts and fundamental decency. I was particularly struck by the way he stood up to an angry mob that was about to stone a woman to death for adultery. I read this passage over and over, imagining the scene in my mind. I now know that this pericope (passage) is not found in the earliest Greek manuscripts we have of John's gospel, and some translations, such as the scholarly New Revised Standard Version (NRSV), now include it only in brackets (7:53–8:11). Nevertheless, it is so characteristic of Jesus that some experts believe it reflects a genuine event that was perhaps part of the Lukan source material and added to the text of John in the early third century. There are many learned monographs written on just this subject.[1]

When I was twelve, however, I knew nothing of all that. I was just impressed by Jesus staring down the mob with the sheer force of human decency. So much of Jesus' character, as revealed throughout the New Testament, is encapsulated in this brief passage: his concern for the oppressed and scorned, his willingness to forgive "seventy times seven" times (Matt. 18:22 NKJV), his courage, his readiness to stand up against unjust authority, his defiance of legalism. This passage also had everything a young boy's imagination could want: Sex (a woman caught in the "very act" of adultery). Defiance of authority. The threat of violence. Also, it made me curious. This wasn't some boring minister droning on. Whoever this Jesus was, he was definitely *different*. What else did he say? What else did he do? I began to pay more attention, and I began to read. I wanted to know more about Jesus' life and times—how he lived, where he lived.

I turned, first, to a sensationalistic novel by a writer of historical fiction named Frank Yerby. I am not particularly proud of the fact that my introduction to critical biblical studies came through the work of a pulp fiction writer, but God works in mysterious ways, so they say, and that was how he worked in my case. The name of the novel was *Judas, My Brother*. Published in 1968, when I was only eleven, *Judas, My Brother* was part of a century-old genre that attempted to reconstruct the events of the New Testament on purely naturalistic terms and to tell the reader what "really" happened. Around the same time, Irving Wallace published the steamy novel *The Word*, about the discovery of a "lost" Gospel that would ostensibly, or so its cover jacket proclaimed, "blow the lid off orthodox Christianity." It was *The Da Vinci Code* of its day. Rather strangely for a novel, *Judas, My Brother* came with footnotes and went out of its way to ground its many dotty historical assertions on something like scholarship—or what seemed like scholarship to a bright-eyed twelve-year-old. The book relied rather uncritically on the work of the early-twentieth-century Jewish scholar Joseph Klausner, but it introduced me, for the first time, to scholarly books and ancient sources about the life and times of Jesus—including the first-century Jewish historian Josephus, the Mishnah, Emil Schürer, and even, I am amazed to see now, the respected Jewish New Testament scholar Geza Vermes.

My fascination with the character of Jesus, as well as his life and times, continued throughout high school and into college. That is probably why I never really rebelled against Christianity, as is common among teenagers.

Robert Hutchinson

The archaeological excavations are extensive at the lakeside village of Kfar Nahum, or Capernaum. According to the Gospel of Matthew, Jesus left Nazareth and made his home in this small town during the years of his ministry (Matt. 4:13).

How could you rebel against someone willing to stand up to a mob that is about to stone a woman to death? Rebelling against Jesus would be like rebelling against Oskar Schindler or Raoul Wallenberg. You might decline to follow their example, to be sure, but who would rebel against what they stood for?

My path to the academic study of the New Testament was thus the opposite of many popular writers today, such as Bart Ehrman and Reza Aslan, who embraced fundamentalist Christianity as teenagers and then lost their faith altogether when they studied the New Testament as adults. In contrast, I just accepted as a self-evident truth that at least some of the New Testament was legendary, that the tale grew in the telling, and that, as the great German New Testament scholar Rudolf Bultmann said, it was virtually impossible to know what really happened behind the preaching— the *kerygma*—of the early church.[2] I was taught in high school that the infancy narratives were *theologoumena*—legendary stories that conveyed important theological but not literal historical truths. I considered myself a faithful Christian, to be sure, and still do to this day. But the historical-critical study of the Bible that Ehrman and Aslan found so shocking in graduate school I just considered, well, standard operating procedure.

IN THE LAND OF ISRAEL

All that changed for me when I moved to Israel to learn Hebrew after college. At that time, anyone could come to Israel and study Hebrew for free, provided you were willing to work a little. In exchange for four hours of work per day, usually on an agricultural settlement known as a kibbutz or moshav, the Jewish Agency would provide professional teachers and you would receive four hours of intensive Hebrew language instruction six days a week for five or six months. I did two Hebrew courses, first level Aleph and then, a year later, level Gimel. You didn't have to be immigrating to Israel to participate; in fact, you didn't even have to be Jewish. In my class of about thirty students, however, I would say only about four or five were not making Aliyah (immigrating). The rest were Jewish, moving to Israel permanently, and the *ulpan* course was the first stage of their new lives.

For the first time in my life, the world of Jesus and the Gospels was not something I read about in books, but something I could see with my own eyes and feel etched in stones. The Bible really comes alive when you're living right where it all happened. As I wandered the stone alleys of Jerusalem on my days off, or explored archaeological ruins in Caesarea or Nazareth, I felt like I was stepping back in time. Suddenly, these ancient stories, characters, battles, place names, foods, plants, animals, genealogies, and even obscure biblical laws took on real meaning. Israelis are fanatical tourists both at home and abroad, and even the most secular of them frequently go on field trips to visit the various locations mentioned in the Bible. They often begin to explore their country while in the army and just keep it up for most of their lives. As a result, I spent a lot of time exploring the biblical sites I had once only heard about from the pulpit—Megiddo, Mount Tabor (the traditional site of the Transfiguration), Ein Gedi, Mount Carmel, the Jordan River, Tel Dan, Beit Shean, Mount Hermon. My Israeli friends and I would set out in cars, or occasionally in small buses, and explore the countryside. On my second *ulpan*, I even shipped a motorcycle to Israel from Los Angeles so I could better explore the Galilean countryside.

I quickly saw how the biblical heritage is woven into daily life in Israel through the myriad practices and traditions of Judaism, but also through the geography and the language. Even something as simple as the *Kabbalat Shabbat*, the welcoming of the Sabbath, was quite moving. I remember sitting at a big table in the *heder ha-ohel*, the kibbutz dining hall, during my first *ulpan*, while the text of Genesis 2:1–2 was read by a teenage girl (in fluent Hebrew, naturally): *"Vah-yehulu ha-shamaim veh-ha-aretz . . ."* ("Thus the heavens and the earth were finished, and all their multitude. And on the seventh day God finished the work that he had done, and he rested on the seventh day from all the work that he had done." NRSV).

Even these nonreligious, socialist kibbutzniks kept the Sabbath, honoring the ancient commandment handed down through generations for literally thousands of years. This naturally made me curious about the other commandments, all those dry and seemingly bizarre laws. One of my Hebrew teachers gave me a book about the *mitzvot*, the 613 commandments

Balage Balogh

Reconstruction of what the lakeside village of Capernaum, where Jesus lived after leaving Nazareth, looked like in the first century. The remains of stone insula, *or connected townhouses, are still visible.*

the Jewish sages find in the Torah, and I spent hours in a nearby town library reading about them—and about how they are put into practice in modern-day Israel. I learned about the Mishnah and the Talmud, the great encyclopedic commentaries on these laws, and the Shulhan Aruch. I learned that, long before there was the Way of Jesus, there was the way of *halacha*—the way of Jewish law.

When I returned to the United States, I began to read Jewish writers who were then re-examining the question of who Jesus was and what his relationship was to the various approaches to Judaism that existed in his day. I eagerly followed the twisting turns and amazing discoveries in historical Jesus research that were then unfolding. In the 1990s, as a popular religion writer, I occasionally wrote about these developments for publications such as *Christianity Today*.[3] I was particularly interested in the work of Jewish scholars writing about Jesus, such as the famous Talmud scholar Jacob Neusner,[4] because during my time in Israel I had become fascinated by the Jewish roots of Christianity. Eventually, I became so interested in the topic that I decided to pursue a graduate degree in New Testament studies at Fuller Theological Seminary, an interdenominational evangelical seminary in southern California. For eight years after I had returned to the United States, I drove thirty miles two or three times a week to attend classes in Koine Greek, exegetical method, Near Eastern studies, systematic theology, and other, even more arcane topics. My fellow students and I would struggle our way through large swaths of the New Testament, line by line in Greek, trying to untangle the meaning of these ancient texts.

Of course, all this only makes me a "semi-educated layman," as my professors used to put it, not a real expert. However, in the past few years I've been amazed to discover that leading experts in the field of historical Jesus research have been drawing startling new conclusions that are dramatically at odds with the skeptical theories I was taught in college and then in graduate school—skeptical theories that often dated to the late nineteenth and early twentieth centuries. Even more startling to me was the fact that these newer conclusions were often *not* showing up in the media—even though in many cases they were being proposed by secular experts at top universities. In the TV documentaries I watched and magazine stories I read, the reporters often seemed oblivious to these new developments and merely repeated the older, hyper-skeptical conclusions from the nineteenth and early twentieth centuries; for example, that belief in Jesus as a divine being only emerged very late as the Jesus movement spread out into the pagan Greek world. Yet every month, it seemed, archaeologists in Israel and biblical scholars at major universities around the world were announcing new discoveries that, rather than undermining the basic portrait of Jesus in the Gospels, were actually confirming it.

This book, then, is my attempt to bring some of these recent discoveries and scholarly developments to a wider audience. To do that, however, I also provide a little background on how academic New Testament scholars go about their work and how they arrived at some of the earlier conclusions that are now being questioned. By necessity, I touch briefly on and quickly summarize very complicated subjects—such as the development of source and form criticism—and I know these breezy summaries will no doubt make many professional biblical scholars, like my former teachers, shake their heads in disbelief.

Finally, a quick note on the Bible in general: In my own mind, I am writing for two groups of people: committed Christians of many denominations who have a wide variety of beliefs about how and to what degree the Bible is inspired or even inerrant; and, secondly, general readers who are interested in Jesus of Nazareth and early Christianity but who are not wedded to any previous notion that the Bible is based on real events. Writing for these two groups presents many challenges, of course, but I tried to steer a middle course and remain respectful both of Christian orthodoxy and secular skepticism. What's more, most of this book is about what secular, Jewish, and not necessarily Christian scholars and archaeologists are discovering and concluding—and how their recent research is, to a surprising degree, supporting much of what the Gospels say about Jesus of Nazareth. Thus, this book is not primarily a work of Christian apologetics as such but rather a brief overview of the changing world of New Testament scholarship.

In a very real sense, this book is also something I've been working on all my life. It is a very personal project for me. Like any modern person, I have the same natural skepticism toward the miracles in the New Testament, and the strange talk of atonement in the writings of St. Paul, as my secular, non-Christian friends. But unlike them, I have spent a lifetime thinking about what Jesus of Nazareth was trying to achieve and a decent amount of time studying some of the very best contemporary New Testament scholarship. Having been raised on that scholarship, and taught in high school and college that parts of the New Testament were legendary, I was never disillusioned or shocked. Instead, I've just been curious—and able to see how many of our older scholarly ideas about Jesus are being aggressively challenged today, often by Jewish and secular experts who don't really have an axe to grind.

I approach the effort to understand Jesus with what I hope is an open mind. Although I am a believing Christian, I have no trouble questioning many of the central assertions of historic Christianity, especially when there are good reasons for doing so. At the same time, however, I feel equally free to question the assumptions and unproven theories of contemporary New Testament scholarship, especially when there are good reasons for doing so. I view them with the same skepticism and weary familiarity with which other people view the doctrines of Christianity. What I find exciting, though, is that many of these unquestioned assumptions of New Testament scholarship are now being forcefully questioned, and we're discovering that many of them may well turn out to be false. Jesus of Nazareth may not have been an illiterate peasant who expected the world to come to an end in his own lifetime, as so many contemporary authors claim. He may have been a well-trained Jewish rabbi who had a very specific mission—a mission to save the human race from itself. And therein lies a very interesting story indeed.

PROLOGUE

Here's what our records tell us: sometime in the early decades of the first millennium, a young, charismatic Jewish rabbi from a tiny village in northern Palestine ignited a social movement that gradually spread across the entire eastern Mediterranean—an underground movement that, he said, would somehow change the course of human history.

His real name was Yeshu'a bar Yosef. We call him Jesus.

By all accounts, Jesus viewed what he was doing quite literally as a suicide mission. He told his closest associates that he did not have much time to do what he needed to do—and predicted his mission would get him killed (Mark 10:32–34).

And it did.

The movement that he was inaugurating, he said, was not about overthrowing governments. It was something far more subversive; it was about changing the entire world from the inside out.

He called this underground movement "the kingdom."

Some modern Bible scholars claim that Jesus was really a deluded fanatic who expected the world to end at any moment in a great cataclysmic disaster, with God killing the many and saving the righteous few.[1] But that's not what the texts actually say.

In the "gospel behind the gospels," the hypothetical collection of Jesus' sayings that scholars call Q, Jesus said the kingdom he was proclaiming was not about conquering armies. Rather, it was like a tiny mustard seed that is planted but then grows into an enormous tree (Luke 13:19), or like yeast that a woman takes and mixes with flour until all is leavened (Luke

13:21). It is, he said, "good news," like "treasure hidden in a field" (Matt. 13:44 NRSV). He told his disciples to pass on to John the Baptist what the kingdom is like: the "blind regain their sight, the lame walk, lepers are cleansed, the deaf hear, the dead are raised, and the poor have the good news proclaimed to them" (Matt. 11:4–6). The kingdom, he said, belonged not to soldiers and kings, but to children (Mark 10:14).

Jesus was also supremely confident, even joyful. He appears to have drawn crowds by the thousands—perhaps by the tens of thousands (Luke 6:17).

He told strange symbolic stories that lingered in his hearers' minds for years, and in some cases for the rest of their lives. They were stories about grace and forgiveness, about mercy in unexpected places, about hidden treasures and lost sheep.

And in ways few people have done before or since, Jesus reached out to the most wretched and despised people in society—the demon-possessed, the deformed, those afflicted with horrible contagious diseases, prostitutes, tax collectors, even soldiers of an occupation army. He told them all the same thing: Your faith has saved you. Your sins are forgiven. Go in peace (Mark 5:34, 10:52; Luke 7:50, 8:48, 17:19, 18:42; Matt. 9:22).

In a series of carefully calculated symbolic actions—what we might today call acts of civil disobedience—this charismatic rabble-rouser set about changing public opinion pretty much everywhere on the planet. As a result of what he said and did, people from one end of the earth to the other would one day rethink everything they had once believed.

His influence was massive, and what he said and did ended up sparking a chain reaction in human culture for the next two thousand years, changing everything from the law and marriage customs to the conduct of war. If Jesus was only a mythical character created by the Roman Caesars, as one modern writer now claims,[2] he was the most influential nonexistent person in history.

Despite what many scholars say, Jesus appears to have had some sort of detailed, well-thought-out plan. Very quickly, he recruited a number of close associates. He specifically told them that they would be building a social movement ("Follow me, and I will make you fishers of men" [Matt. 4:19 ESV]). These men, in turn, deputized others to spread his message, and his movement, throughout the immediate area. He had friends in high places, including members of the ruling Jewish aristocracy, the Sanhedrin (Mark 15:43), and perhaps even the wife of the Roman governor who would one day sentence him to death (Matt. 27:19).

And he had a method: He "chose seventy-two other disciples and sent them ahead in pairs to all the towns and places he planned to visit. These were his instructions to them . . . 'Don't move around from home to home. Stay in one place, eating and drinking what they provide. Don't hesitate to accept hospitality, because those who work deserve their pay'" (Luke 10:1–2, 7 NLT).

From the very beginning, Jesus appears to have predicted that his movement would eventually extend far beyond his own people and time. We don't know for sure if Jesus spoke Greek, the lingua franca of his age, but the documents we have portray him conversing with people from all walks of life and from many different countries. He certainly traveled far afield to the Greek-speaking, mostly pagan areas of Tyre, Sidon, and the Decapolis (Matt. 15). He spoke easily with a divorced woman in Samaria (John 4), which would be almost like an Orthodox Jewish rabbi today chatting with a Palestinian divorcée in Nablus.

Jesus predicted that his message would one day reach all corners of the globe.

And it did.

"This gospel of the kingdom will be preached in the whole world as a testimony to all nations," Matthew records him saying (24:14 NIV). Of course, some critical scholars claim that Jesus didn't make any such prediction; that this saying was created by Matthew.[3] But even if this were true, Matthew wrote no later than AD 90,[4] when the tiny Christian sect was in danger of being annihilated by homicidal Roman emperors. It didn't look like it would last until the end of the week, much less for the next two thousand years.

To me, the great mystery and ultimate proof that Jesus was far more than a teacher of timeless moral truths has been this: the trajectory of his movement through history. According to Rodney Stark, a sociologist of religion at Baylor University and author of *The Rise of Christianity*, Jesus' kingdom movement grew from about 1,000 followers in AD 40, a decade after his death, to roughly 217,000 followers at the end of the second century, to almost 34 million in AD 350, after the Emperor Constantine declared Christianity the official religion of the Roman Empire.[5] Today, roughly two billion people, or a third of the earth's entire population, call themselves Jesus' followers.[6]

Many authors say that Jesus was a false messiah, like Judas the Galilean before him and Theudas after him, because he failed in his mission to redeem Israel.[7] But if Jesus' true mission wasn't to kill all the Romans, as the later Zealots wanted and some modern writers claim, but to change the world—to spread his message of mercy and human dignity to all the ends of the earth—then you'd have to say that even on a human level he was an overwhelming success.

IS THERE EYEWITNESS TESTIMONY IN THE GOSPELS?

New Approaches to the New Testament as History

> *[M]any have undertaken to set down an orderly*
> *account of the events that have been fulfilled*
> *among us, just as they were handed on to us by*
> *those who from the beginning were eyewitnesses.*

—LUKE 1:1–2 NRSV

As an observant Jew, Jesus of Nazareth almost certainly made the arduous, three-day trip from the Sea of Galilee region to the holy city of Jerusalem many times in his life. In the first century, Jews would often make the trek three times a year, for the three major pilgrim feasts of Pesach (Passover), Shavuot (Weeks), and Sukkot (Tabernacles). According to Luke, Jesus and his parents, Mary and Joseph, went to Jerusalem for Passover "every year" (2:41). It was a daunting journey—as anyone who has hiked in the Jordan River valley can attest—and a testimony to the deep faith of Galilean Jews that they would make it regularly. On this score the gospel of John's descriptions of Jesus' travels are probably more accurate historically than those of the Synoptic Gospels (Matthew, Mark, and Luke); John describes Jesus coming and going to the Jerusalem area many times over a three-year period. Likely for simplicity's sake and to make their stories easier to follow, the Synoptics condense Jesus' itinerary into two basic phases: his ministry in Galilee and his final trip to Jerusalem, rather than including accounts of his coming and going.

A reconstruction of the Pool of Bethesda as it existed in Jerusalem in AD 65, outside the city walls. Photo of the Model of Jerusalem in the Israel Museum. Photo taken by Deror Avi.

On one occasion, according to John's gospel (5:2–10), Jesus entered Jerusalem through the Sheep Gate, near what is today called the Lion's Gate. Outside the city walls and immediately before the gate, there were two large pools of water surrounded by colonnades. One was called Bethesda or Bethzatha, where people came who wanted to be cured of various ailments: "Now in Jerusalem by the Sheep Gate there is a pool, called in Hebrew

Beth-zatha, which has five porticoes," the gospel of John explains. "In these lay many invalids—blind, lame, and paralyzed" (5:2–3 NRSV).

One of the sick people there had been ill, John tells us, for thirty-eight years. When Jesus saw the man, he stopped and asked, "Do you want to be made well?"

The man replied that he was too sick to get into the healing water of the pool. "Sir, I have no one to put me into the pool when the water is stirred up," he explained. "While I am making my way, someone else steps down ahead of me."

Jesus looked at him, then said, "Stand up, take your mat and walk" (5:7–8 NRSV). And, according to John, that is precisely what the man did.

However, it was the Sabbath, and anyone who has been to Jerusalem knows that the devout Jews of Jerusalem take the rules for observing the Sabbath very seriously. Even today, there are special "religious police" with neon vests who walk around the Western Wall Plaza and tell tourists not to take photographs once the Sabbath has begun on Friday evening.

One of the prohibited activities on the Sabbath is carrying, or, more technically, "transferring," something from one domain to another. During the time of Jesus and in the decades after, the rabbis were debating precisely what the Torah means by "work." The Torah forbids "work" on the Sabbath (Ex. 31:12–17), but does not define what "work" actually is. The rabbis came up with thirty-nine categories of creative activity that constitute work—including planting, gathering, tying, building, lighting or extinguishing a fire, cooking, and so on.[1]

Eventually it was also decided that carrying something from one dwelling to another was a type of work as well, and it was forbidden. To make life easier in communities with large numbers of Orthodox Jews, however, an ingenious solution was devised: an *eruv*. An *eruv* is an artificial "household" that is created by stringing wire or twine around a neighborhood, marking it off as a single living area. That way, children or belongings can be carried within it on the Sabbath. Today in Jerusalem, and particularly in the Jewish Quarter of the Old City, you can see discreet wires with pieces of cloth tied to them strung around the city from pole to pole, creating the *eruv*. This is the world in which Jesus lived.

"Now that day was a sabbath," John continues. "So the Jews said to the man who had been cured, 'It is the sabbath; it is not lawful for you to carry your mat'" (5:9–10 NRSV).

We will confront this highly sensitive issue of Jesus' attitude to Sabbath observance and whether that put him at odds with the mainstream Jewish community in another chapter. But for now, what is interesting is how John's account matches very closely what we now know both about Jerusalem and about the customs of the people within it.

WAS THE AUTHOR OF JOHN AN EYEWITNESS?

John's gospel is very different from the Synoptics. It exhibits what scholars call a "high Christology," which means that Jesus is portrayed more as an all-knowing God-man than as a Jewish prophet or seer. As a result, many critical scholars in past decades insisted it was written very late, perhaps in the early second century, in a largely pagan milieu, and thus cannot be

Robert Hutchinson

The remains of the Pool of Bethesda today, inside the Church of St. Anne to the right of Jerusalem's Lion Gate, show a massive pool structure thirteen meters deep.

considered historical. For a "hundred years the character of John's Gospel as a theological, rather than a historical document, became more and more axiomatic for [New Testament] scholarship," writes the respected British New Testament scholar James D. G. Dunn.[2]

And yet there are historical details found in John that are found nowhere else, either in the New Testament or in secular sources. One of the details that John gets right is the pool of Bethesda.

When you go into Jerusalem today through the Lion's Gate, the first thing you see on your right is the large complex of the Church of St. Anne, the mother of Mary, a courtyard with a crusader-era church maintained by the White Fathers of France. Inside the courtyard are the massive ruins of the very deep pools of Bethesda. In 1871, while working to restore the church, archaeologists accidentally uncovered the pools, and they spent the next century or so excavating them.

There are two pools. The first was created in the eighth century BC when a dam was built across the Beth Zetha Valley (2 Kings 18:17) that comes into Jerusalem itself.[3] The second pool was built in the second century BC to provide the temple with more water, probably for cleaning sheep for the sacrifices (hence the Sheep Gate). Eventually it became used as a kind of spa for healing.[4]

The porticoes mentioned by John are no longer there, but Saint Jerome, writing in the early fifth century from nearby Bethlehem, describes the pools precisely:

> Bethesda, a pool of Jerusalem . . . had five porticoes; [local people] show a double pool, one of which is fed with winter rainfalls; surprisingly, the water of the other appears reddish as if tainted by blood and thus attests its ancient use by the priests who, as it is said, would come here to wash the [sacrificial] victims, and this is where its name comes from.[5]

In short, John reveals an intimate knowledge of Jerusalem that led Israeli archaeologist Rami Arav and John Rousseau, a fellow of the Jesus Seminar and research associate at the University of California, Berkeley, neither conservative Christians, to conclude that "the primary author of the Gospel of John was probably *an eyewitness* to several events in the life of Jesus" and was "well acquainted with Jerusalem and its surroundings."[6]

THE GOSPELS AS HISTORICAL SOURCES

One of the first issues anyone interested in Jesus of Nazareth must confront is whether, or to what degree, the New Testament as we now have it is a reliable record of who Jesus was, what he did, and what he said. That's because the New Testament is practically our only source for information about Jesus. There is no mention of Jesus of Nazareth in any non-Christian source for nearly a century after his death around AD 30. The handful of non-Christian sources we do have—writings from Roman historians in the early second century[7] and traditions recorded in the Jewish Talmud[8]—have only a few scattered references in passing. The first-century Jewish historian Josephus, who wrote about every detail of his homeland in two enormous works of twenty-seven combined volumes, mentions Jesus only in two brief passages, and what little he does write has been so obviously tampered with by later Christian copyists that some historians (although not the majority) think those passages are outright forgeries.[9] We do know of at least thirty apocryphal gospels written about Jesus in the earliest centuries of the first millennium[10]—besides the four canonical versions found in the New Testament. But of these, we have the complete texts of only four and fragments from seven, and these apocryphal texts were by and large written hundreds of years after the canonical Gospels and likely contained little historical information, judging from the ones we have extant.[11]

As historical sources, the canonical Gospels themselves present many challenges to historians. Some experts argue that the basic outline or chronology of Jesus' adult career as presented in the Synoptic Gospels came from a single author, Mark, whom Matthew and Luke follow, often word for word. The difference is that Matthew and Luke added a lot of extra material, such as the Beatitudes, that Mark didn't include. What's more, the gospel writers plainly edited their sources, possibly to eliminate facts they didn't like or which they thought might reflect negatively on Jesus' image—for example, that he got angry (Mark 3:5) or that his healings didn't always work completely on the first try (Mark 8:22–26).

Even more important, the creators of the Gospels are plainly biased. They state flat-out that they believe Jesus was the long-awaited Jewish messiah, the Savior of the entire world, whom God raised from the dead after Jesus' ignominious crucifixion. The evangelist John tells us directly that he writes "so that you may come to believe that Jesus is the Messiah, the Son of God, and that through believing you may have life in his name" (John 20:31 NRSV). As a result, the evangelists appear to arrange their accounts to emphasize the *meaning* of Jesus' life and deeds more than strict chronology. They do not always agree on the details. They have different outlooks on who Jesus was and what he was trying to achieve. They contain what some critical scholars suspect, at least, are outright errors of fact. For example, Matthew says that Jesus was born before Herod the Great died (2:1) in 4 BC, while Luke says that he was born when Quirinius, the governor of Syria, ordered a census to take place (2:2), which occurred in AD 6. One of the gospel writers, probably Luke, appears to have gotten at least the year of Jesus' birth wrong.[12] The incidents of Jesus' life also appear to be arranged more for the editorial purposes of the Gospel authors than for accurately recording a history of his life.

Because of these challenges, early twentieth-century New Testament scholars and historical Jesus writers—such as Martin Dibelius (ca. 1883–1947) and Rudolf Bultmann (1884–1976)—tended to dismiss large portions of the New Testament as legendary, invented by the early Christian community. However, in the past few decades, as we'll see, many scholars—even Jewish or agnostic scholars working in secular universities—have begun to reevaluate this preemptory attitude. For example, a Talmud expert at the University of California, Berkeley, Daniel Boyarin, insists that many incidents, ideas, and sayings of Jesus in the New Testament that previous generations of scholars thought were simply made up by the early Christian community may actually be historical.[13] Other experts, such as the secular New Testament scholar James Crossley at the University of Sheffield in the UK, have challenged the alleged late datings of the Gospels. Still others, such as Richard Bauckham at the University of St. Andrews, are challenging the notion that the Gospels are not based on eyewitness testimony. Even many non-Christians, including Israeli archaeologists and Jewish scholars, now concede that the Gospels likely contain information that could only have come from eyewitness observers. We will look at all these new developments in later chapters.

DID JESUS OF NAZARETH EVEN EXIST?

While many modern scholars believe that some incidents in the Gospels were invented by the early Christian community, virtually all believe Jesus was a real historical person who lived in the early first century of the common era. There are some exceptions, however. In the nineteenth century, a number of rationalist philosophers—most famously the German writer David Strauss (1808–1874) and philosopher Bruno Bauer (1809–1882)—argued that Jesus of Nazareth likely never even existed at all, that the entire New Testament can be shown to be nothing but a work of creative fiction. This point of view is sometimes referred to as "Christ myth theory" or "mythicism" (as opposed to "mysticism"). Few mainstream historians take it seriously, but in recent years there has been a revival of sorts among college students, amateur historians, and a handful of academics. There are now literally dozens, even hundreds, of websites and bloggers dedicated to popularizing the Christ myth arguments—such as JesusNeverExisted. com—and that refer to Jesus as Christians' "imaginary friend." As one of the theory's chief contemporary proponents, the Canadian author Earl Doherty, puts it, mythicism is "the theory that no historical Jesus worthy of the name existed, that Christianity began with a belief in a spiritual, mythical figure, that the Gospels are essentially allegory and fiction, and that no single person lay at the root of the Galilean preaching tradition."[14]

As you might expect, Christ myth writers and bloggers are all over the ballpark in terms of their arguments. They range from the serious to the silly, from those who voice scholarly doubts about particular incidents in the Gospels to those promoting elaborate conspiracy theories—such as the idea that Jesus was invented by the Roman Caesars to help manage the restless Jewish population.[15] There appear to be four academic heavyweights of the Christ myth blogging craze: Robert Price, a former Baptist pastor with a PhD in both systematic theology and New Testament studies and the author of *The Incredible Shrinking Son of Man* (2003); Thomas Brodie, a Dominican friar with a doctor of sacred theology (STD) degree from the Pontifical University of Saint Thomas Aquinas in Rome and author of *Beyond the Quest for the Historical Jesus: Memoir of a Discovery*; Thomas Thompson, an American professor at the University of Copenhagen who earned his PhD in

Old Testament at Temple University and who is a famous pioneer in what is called biblical minimalism—the belief that most of the Bible is fictional; and Richard Carrier, a blogger who has a PhD in ancient history from Columbia University and is the author of *On the Historicity of Jesus: Why We Might Have Reason for Doubt.* Other popular mythicist writers who seem to attract a following include David Fitzgerald, author of *Nailed: Ten Christian Myths That Show Jesus Never Existed at All*; Earl J. Doherty, author of *Jesus: Neither God Nor Man*; René Salm, author of *The Myth Of Nazareth: The Invented Town Of Jesus*; and Frank Zindler, author of *The Jesus the Jews Never Knew.*

Christ myth advocates make much of the fact that there is no mention of Jesus of Nazareth in any non-Christian source for nearly a century after Jesus' death. "Virtually everyone who espoused the Christ-Myth theory has laid great emphasis on one question," writes Price. "*Why no mention of a miracle-working Jesus in secular sources?*"[16] Despite the fact that his fellow mythicists spend a great deal of time on this subject, Price concedes that the lack of corroboration in ancient secular sources is not a very good argument for the claim that Jesus never existed. That's because, as the agnostic New Testament scholar Bart Ehrman points out, we don't have archaeological or textual evidence for the existence of *most* people in the ancient world—even most famous people. Ehrman points to the example of Pontius Pilate. "And what records from that decade do we have from his reign," Ehrman asks, "what Roman records of his major accomplishments, his daily itinerary, the decrees he passed, the laws he issued, the prisoners he put on trial, the death warrants he signed, his scandals, interviews, his judicial proceedings? We have none. Nothing at all."[17]

The same is true of the Jewish historian Flavius Josephus (ca. AD 37–100). Due to his treachery and betrayal of his own people, Josephus not only saved his skin during the Jewish War but also became a personal favorite of the Roman emperor Vespasian. He lived in Rome on an official pension—and it is there that he penned his multivolume histories of his defeated people and their tragic war against the Romans. Yet despite being a personal friend of the emperor, "how often is Josephus mentioned in Greek and Roman sources of his own day, the first century CE?" Ehrman asks rhetorically. "Never."[18]

The other arguments that Christ myth writers often use—for example, that Jesus is simply a Jewish version of "dying and rising god" myths allegedly found in ancient paganism—are also now dismissed by most experts.[19] The fact that the Gospel writers modeled some of their descriptions of incidents in Jesus' life on similar episodes in the Hebrew Bible (a technique known as *midrash*) doesn't mean they didn't happen. It could just mean that the Gospel writers tried to tie these parallel incidents to ancient prophecies and may have modified some of the details in the process. As for "dying and rising gods," Bart Ehrman is particularly scathing on that point: "Even though most mythicists do not appear to know it, the onetime commonly held view that dying-rising gods were widespread in pagan antiquity has fallen on hard times among scholars," he says.[20] The same thing is true with the common nineteenth-century idea that Jesus was simply a version of the "divine man" figures seen in the ancient world, such as Pythagorean philosopher Apollonius of Tyana. It's true that, like Jesus, Apollonius had disciples, performed miracles, even supposedly raised people from the dead. He left the world and, as Ehrman puts it, "returned to meet his followers in order to convince them that he was not really dead but lived on in the heavenly realm."[21] Pretty interesting parallels, you must admit. But, as Ehrman and others point out, there is one problem with using these parallels to argue that Jesus didn't exist: Apollonius of Tyana was a real historical figure![22]

WHAT IS THE NEW TESTAMENT ANYWAY?

The New Testament is an odd collection of texts. It consists of twenty-seven separate pieces of writing, or books, comprising about 138,000 words altogether. In their final form, all were written between the years AD 40 at the very earliest, and AD 120 at the very latest. We know from the writings of Josephus, the Mishnah, and other ancient sources that Jesus, the members of his immediate family, and his closest followers all probably spoke Aramaic, a sister language of Hebrew widely used in the Near East at the time. Yet the New Testament—the record of the early Jesus movement—is written entirely in Koine or common Greek, a dialect that functioned as the lingua franca throughout the Mediterranean world. Right off the bat, that creates enormous challenges of interpretation for both historians and ordinary people in the pews.

The longest book in the New Testament, the gospel of Luke, is 19,482 words in Greek. The shortest, 3 John, is only 219 words. Four of the books, which we know as the Gospels, tell the story of Jesus of Nazareth in a very brief, impressionistic way; they are less biographies in the modern sense than theological portraits. Another book, the Acts of the Apostles, was written by the same author who wrote the gospel of Luke, and tells the story of the earliest followers of Jesus in the years after his death and resurrection. Of the remaining twenty-two books in the New Testament, twenty-one are written in the form of epistles, or public letters, and one is an apocalypse, or symbolic vision. Of the twenty-one books written in the form of letters, thirteen are presented as written by the apostle Paul; three by the apostle John; two by the apostle Peter; and one each by an author named James (believed to be James, the brother, half-brother, or cousin of Jesus); Jude, another brother of Jesus; and an unnamed author who wrote the letter to the Hebrews. Modern specialists consider many of these texts to be pseudepigraphic—that is, not written by the claimed author but by an associate or follower. Of the thirteen works ascribed to the apostle Paul, for example, at least seven are considered by many critical scholars to have been written by Paul himself (even if dictated to a *gramma-teus*, or professional scribe) while the remaining six are disputed.[23] The letters deemed written by Paul himself are Romans, 1 and 2 Corinthians, Galatians, Philippians, 1 Thessalonians, and Philemon. The earliest piece of writing in the New Testament is widely regarded by modern scholars to be 1 Thessalonians, a letter written by the apostle Paul around the year AD 52, probably when he was living in the Greek city of Corinth. Some scholars believe that Galatians was written first, perhaps as early as AD 46.[24] Embedded within all these texts, moreover, many scholars believe they can detect early sources, such as hymns and sayings of Jesus, that date back to just a few years after Jesus' execution and, in some cases, to when he was living and teaching in Galilee.[25]

THE HISTORICAL PROBLEM OF MIRACLES

One reason often given for doubting the historical reliability of the Gospels is their description of events that, from a modern scientific standpoint, could read more like legends than history. "Mark's story of Jesus is packed with preposterous stories of miracles that Jesus performs and of miraculous things that happen to Jesus," sniffs Burton Mack, a New Testament scholar at the School of Theology at Claremont.[26]

Balage Balogh

The city of Jerusalem, already a thousand years old when Jesus first visited, was one of the wonders of the ancient world. The rebuilt Temple Mount, begun by Herod the Great in 26 BC, spans 36 acres, took 18,000 workers more than 80 years to complete, and still stands today.

Scholars count at least thirty-seven specific miracles attributed to Jesus in the Gospels—twenty in Mark, twenty-two in Matthew, twenty-one in Luke, and only eight in John (where they are called "signs"). All the miracles in Mark are repeated in either Matthew or Luke except for one (the healing of a deaf mute in 7:31–37).

Yet of these thirty-seven purported miracles, twenty-five (or 68 percent) are miracles of healing that even many secular historians believe reflected, at least in part, real events—the Gerasene Demoniac, the healing of leprosy, the blind man at Bethsaida, the Syrophoenician woman, the woman with a hemorrhage, the centurion's servant, and so on.

Since the nineteenth century, some critical scholars have tried to rationalize the descriptions of Jesus' miraculous cures as reflecting the primitive understanding of medicine in the first century, even among the evangelists. The descriptions of Jesus' exorcising demons could be based on real encounters with social outcasts we would now call paranoid schizophrenics, the argument goes, so these stories in the Gospels could well be based on actual events.

Thus, of the thirty-seven miracles besides the resurrection described in the Gospels, only twelve are nonhealing miracles[27] that present a formidable challenge to modern skepticism. Of these twelve, six could well be what scholars call "doublets," that is, the same event reported twice. For example, there are two descriptions of the miraculous catching of fish: one in Luke (5:4–11) and the other in John (21:1–11), and two descriptions of the feeding of a multitude (five thousand in all four Gospels, four thousand only in Matthew and Mark). Also, the description of Jesus calming a storm (Mark 4:37–41) and walking on water (Mark 6:47–52) could also stem from the same event.

That leaves only six nonhealing miracles. Two of these even some conservative scholars concede could be legendary: Jesus cursing the fig tree and it withering (Mark 11:12–14) and the miraculous finding of the temple tax coin in a fish's mouth (Matt. 17:24–27). One miracle, Jesus turning water into wine at Cana, is found only in John (2:1–11).

The other three miracles are all raising people from the dead: the raising of the widow's son at Nain (Luke 7:11–17), the raising of Jairus's daughter (Mark 5:21–43), and the raising of Lazarus (John 11:1–44). The first two of these are often understood by contemporary scholars as more healing miracles than miracles of resurrection. That's because even the Gospel texts themselves are ambiguous. For example, when discussing Jairus's daughter, Mark quotes Jesus as saying, "the child is not dead but sleeping" (Mark 5:39 NRSV). That leaves only the miracle of raising Lazarus four days after his burial, found only in John (11:1–44). That is a full-blown, no-doubt-about-it, you-either-believe-it-or-you-don't miracle.

My point is simple: Despite what many people think, we're not talking about a lot of miracles. While modern skeptics may not believe anyone can walk on water, calm the sea, turn water into wine, or raise the dead back to life, the number of these incidents reported in the Gospels is remarkably small. For this reason, many critical New Testament scholars do not believe that the handful of nonhealing miracles in the New Testament, by themselves, provide a sufficient reason for rejecting the overall historical reliability of the Gospels—especially regarding the portrait of who Jesus was, what he said, and what he was trying to do. "In spite of my innate and well-nourished skepticism, I do not believe that the presence of miracle stories in the Gospels makes them unreliable, though it does complicate the evaluation of their reliability," writes Mark Roberts, a Harvard-trained New Testament scholar.

> If there were no miracles in the New Testament Gospels, then many scholars today as well as many ordinary folk would be much more likely to acknowledge the Gospels' historical reliability. Of course, if there were no miracles in the New Testament Gospels, if Jesus didn't heal the sick, cast out demons, and eventually rise from the dead, there would be no New Testament Gospels. In fact, there would be no New Testament at all. Jesus would have been dismissed by his contemporaries as an overly optimistic but deceived prophet who proclaimed the kingdom of God but didn't deliver on his promises.[28]

DISCREPANCIES IN THE GOSPEL ACCOUNTS OF EVENTS

Another reason critical scholars often give for doubting the historical reliability of the Gospels involves alleged discrepancies in the descriptions of events both within and between the various gospels. Debunkers of Christianity often call these "contradictions," but, as we will see, most (but not all) of the differences in the gospel accounts are better described as merely differences and not logical contradictions. For example, if one witness says she saw one bank robber and another witness says he saw two, that isn't a contradiction. The fact of there being one bank robber doesn't preclude the possibility that there were really two.

This is not a new subject by any means. Sometimes writers today give the impression that they discovered the inconsistencies in how the Gospels report events—"replete with the most blatant and obvious errors and contradictions," as Reza Aslan, author of *Zealot*, puts it[29]—but this is not the case. I have in my library an old book, *An Examination of Alleged Discrepancies of the Bible,* written in 1874. It is a remarkably sophisticated analysis of the factual, ethical, doctrinal, and historical discrepancies found in both the Hebrew Bible and in the New Testament.

Discrepancies in the Gospels fall into about six broad categories, as outlined in Craig L. Blomberg's *The Historical Reliability of the Gospels*:[30]

1. Chronological Divergences

Even a brief time spent with a synopsis of the Gospels—in which you can read the accounts side by side—reveals the problems inherent in creating a harmonized chronology of gospel events. Did Jesus cleanse the temple of the money-changers during the *last* week of his life, as the Synoptic Gospels of Matthew, Mark, and Luke report, or at the very beginning of his ministry, as in John? Or did he do it *twice,* as some apologists claim? Did Jesus' ministry last one year as in the Synoptics, or three years as in John? Even in the Synoptics, the gospel writers apparently felt free to reorder events in order to better make their theological points, or just for editorial clarity. For example, Blomberg points out, in Mark, the arrest of John the Baptist occurs in the middle of Jesus' ministry, after Jesus had already begun to send his own disciples out to the villages of Galilee (Mark 6:17). Luke, however, puts John the Baptist's arrest near the beginning of his gospel (3:1–20), at the end of his discussion of John's baptism ministry.

2. Variations in Name and Number

In the various gospel accounts of what happened after Jesus' burial, there are differences in the number of women who visit the tomb. Mark says three, Matthew says two, and Luke says at least five.[31] John says just one. Mark says there was one angel or man when the women arrived (Mark 16:5). John says there were two (John 20:12). Critics and debunkers of Christianity like to say this inconsistency proves the gospel accounts are unreliable. The same sort of variation is sometimes seen with names, although less often. In Luke, Joseph's father is called Heli (3:23). In Matthew, he is called Jacob (1:16). In Mark and Luke, Jesus exorcised the demoniac in the region of the Gerasenes; in Matthew, it is in the land of the Gadarenes (8:28).

3. Paraphrases and Composite Speeches

There are many variations in the speeches that Jesus gives throughout the Gospels. Critics claim that, once again, this means we can't know what Jesus *really* said about a given subject. The Sermon on the Mount is a classic example. In Luke 6:20, Jesus says, "Blessed are you who are poor, for yours is the kingdom of God" (NRSV). In Matthew 5:3, he says, "Blessed are the poor in spirit, for theirs is the kingdom of heaven" (NRSV). But the New Testament is written in Greek, while Jesus spoke in Aramaic. From the very beginning, therefore, it's not a question of quoting Jesus' "actual words" (what scholars call the *ipsissima verba*) but rather his "actual voice," or intent (*ipsissima vox*).[32] Furthermore, there are no quotation marks in ancient Greek. We can't know if the evangelist meant an indirect quotation, which communicates the general sense of someone's speech, or a direct quotation, which communicates their actual words. What counts, though, is the overall import of what Jesus is saying. With a few important exceptions, the "discrepancies" in how the various gospels report sayings of Jesus do not necessarily make the Gospels less reliable.

4. Apparent Doublets

As noted above, a few incidents appear to be reported more than once in some of the gospels—such as Jesus feeding five thousand and then feeding four thousand, or the miraculous catches of fish. Conservative scholars simply assume that these refer to two separate incidents, while more liberal scholars claim that the evangelists incorporated different traditions or reports in their narratives without knowing, or verifying, if the reports referred to the same incident. According to Blomberg, however, the difficulty with the theory of doublets is that in most cases the "double incident" occurs within the *same* gospel. For example, the feeding of five thousand and then again four thousand people occurs in both Mark (6:32–44, 8:1–10) and in Matthew (14:13–21, 15:32–39). Thus, it is more difficult to argue that this was unintentional or simply the result of poor editing. Moreover, Blomberg points out that the feeding of the five thousand appears to be primarily among Jews, and the Greek text uses a term for "basket" common in Palestine (*kophinos*), while the feeding of the four thousand occurs in a series of passages in which Jesus is moving among Gentiles, and the word for container used to collect the extra fish there is *spyris,* a different word.[33] Finally, other scholars, such as historical Jesus expert Richard Horsley and archaeologist Neil Asher Silberman, argue that free public banquets for the very poor were part of Jesus' *modus operandi*, and thus it is very probable that Jesus fed, miraculously or not, large groups of people on more than one occasion.[34]

5. Omissions

Again, this is something you can examine for yourself with a synopsis of the Gospels. Some evangelists did not include material in their accounts that other gospel writers did include, either deliberately for theological or editorial reasons, or perhaps because they did not have access to the same sources. Scholars who accept what is called the Four-Source theory and believe that Matthew and Luke had access to Mark's gospel point to numerous instances in which Matthew and Luke omit details found in Mark's account. For example, Luke, who tradition claims was a physician by trade, omits the negative comments about physicians found in Mark's version of the story of the woman who suffered from a hemorrhage.[35] In Mark 8:24–26, Jesus heals a blind man in two stages, or, as some might see it, two attempts. The other evangelists delete the whole passage. In Mark 3:20–21, Jesus' family tries to "restrain" him because people are saying that Jesus is "out of his mind."[36] Both Matthew and Luke do not include the passage. Once again, however, this only shows that the evangelists were actual authors who shaped their material according to their own theological agendas and purposes. If they thought an incident or saying might detract from their overall message, they, like many journalists or authors would today, simply didn't use it.

6. True Contradictions

Finally, some of the discrepancies in the Gospels do involve what appear to be actual contradictions, not merely differences over details. For example, in Mark 16:8, the evangelist writes that after the women fled from the empty tomb in terror, "they said nothing to anyone, for they were afraid" (NRSV). Yet in Matthew 28:8, it says the opposite: "They left the tomb quickly with fear and great joy, and ran to tell his disciples" (NRSV). So which was it? Did the women report the empty tomb to other people or not? Another example is the date of the Last Supper. The Synoptics say that Jesus celebrated the Last Supper on the eve of Passover and that he was crucified on the first day of Passover. In John, on the other hand, Jesus is crucified on the day of preparation for Passover (John 19:14). Many scholars think only one of these alternatives can be correct.

Of course, for the average Christian in the pew, these discrepancies don't threaten their faith nearly as much as some critical scholars seem to think they should. If anything, they strengthen their conviction that the Gospels describe real events—events about which we have divergent eyewitness reports—and are not simply fictions created out of whole cloth or, as scholars such as Robert Price claim, fictionalized retellings of stories from the Hebrew Bible (known as *midrash*).[37] As one British barrister says in his book on the resurrection, testimony that never contradicts itself is inherently suspect.[38] It means the witnesses got together to make sure they told the same story. It's when the witnesses *disagree* that you know you are closer to the truth!

TAKING A CLOSER LOOK AT THE NEW TESTAMENT

Beginning in the eighteenth and nineteenth centuries, academic scholars in Europe, especially in Germany, began to look at the biblical texts the same way they looked at any other kind of historical text. Many began with the assumptions of the Enlightenment—that the Bible was not inspired in any sense and that miracles cannot and do not happen—and they tried to figure out how the biblical texts came to be written. For a variety of reasons, the methods and initial assumptions of New Testament scholars differed from those of Old Testament scholars,[39] but the same basic approach was used.

For the New Testament, the first thing that the scholars noticed was that the gospel of John was quite different in style and content from the other three gospels, Matthew, Mark, and Luke. These three gospels are called the Synoptic Gospels from the Greek words *syn* and *optic,* which means to "see together." Whereas the Synoptics portray Jesus speaking like a prophet but also in a fairly normal way, the gospel of John presents a portrait of Jesus more as an all-knowing God-man who speaks of himself in very grandiose, even cosmic terms. As a result, the initial wave of critical scholars concentrated on the Synoptic Gospels. They arranged these three gospels in parallel columns in what are known as "synopses." (I have a copy of one of these in English and another one in Greek.) Once they started to read these gospels "horizontally" rather than sequentially—that is, compared the gospels' accounts of events line by line and word by word—the scholars began to notice some key commonalities and differences.

The first thing they noticed was that the same incidents appeared, often in the same order, in all three of the Synoptic Gospels. Frequently the wording is either very similar or exactly the same. This seems to suggest a certain literary dependence—that one or more of the evangelists used one or more of the other gospels. The question is, who used whom? According to Daniel Wallace, director of the Center for the Study of New Testament Manuscripts, there are eighteen possible combinations for this but only three plausible ones:[40]

1. **THE AUGUSTINIAN HYPOTHESIS:** Matthew wrote first, Mark used Matthew, and then Luke used Matthew.
2. **THE GRIESBACH HYPOTHESIS:** Matthew wrote first, Luke used Matthew, and then Mark used them both.
3. **THE HOLTZMANN/STREETER HYPOTHESIS:** Mark wrote first, and then both Matthew and Luke used Mark independently.

Some other scholars add a fourth possibility:

1. **THE FARRER/GOULDER HYPOTHESIS:** Mark wrote first, but Luke used both Mark and Matthew when composing his gospel.[41]

The third possibility, the Holtzmann / Streeter Hypothesis, which is diagrammed on the next page, is the dominant view today, for a variety of reasons.[42] For one thing, Mark's gospel is much shorter than the other two Synoptic Gospels, and scholars have long theorized that it makes more sense that Matthew and Luke added to Mark's bare-bones account than the opposite, that Mark abbreviated a longer version. (Sometimes Matthew and Luke do appear to delete things from Mark, but for theological reasons.[43]) In other words, it makes more sense that Matthew and Luke would *add* long speeches by Jesus, such as the Beatitudes in the Sermon on the Mount, than it does that Mark would cut them out.

Also, as Wallace points out, Mark's Greek grammar is the poorest of the three writers. There are many places in which it appears that both Matthew and Luke correct Mark, improving his Greek syntax and grammar. Mark also uses both Greek slang words and, strangely, Aramaic. (According to

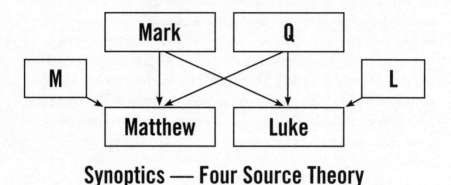

Synoptics — Four Source Theory

the second-century writer Papias, Mark was the "secretary" for the apostle Peter in Rome, so it's very possible that Mark picked up Aramaic words and phrases from him.[44]) The other two evangelists mostly omit Mark's Aramaic words and phrases. Even Matthew, who is considered the most "Jewish" of the Gospel writers, often cuts out the Aramaic words found in Mark (as do most modern vernacular translations, by the way).[45] For example, Mark quotes Jesus saying to the synagogue official Jairus's stricken daughter the Aramaic phrase *talitha kumi* (5:41), but both Matthew and Luke drop the Aramaic. Matthew doesn't have Jesus say anything to the girl (9:25), and Luke simply translates what the Aramaic means ("Child, get up!" 8:54 NRSV). Many of the incidents in Mark's version are considered what scholars call "harder" readings—that is, they contain details that can be seen as unflattering to Jesus, such as him expressing anger (Mark 3:5), not being able to work a miracle (Mark 6:5), or being thought insane (Mark 3:21). These unflattering details are all missing in Matthew and Luke, which implies that the authors deleted them from Mark's version. (By the way, what I love about historical-critical study of the New Testament is that you can see a lot of these things yourself. All it takes is a little time and a good synopsis of the New Testament—such as the one edited by Kurt Aland and published by the United Bible Societies.)

Once scholars decided that Mark was probably the first gospel to be written, and that Matthew and Luke both used his gospel when composing theirs, a lot of other things began to make sense. The experts began to see certain patterns emerge in the ways the different evangelists edited Mark, certain themes that they seemed to emphasize.

Let me give you my favorite example, which I've used in a previous book because it's so funny. According to all three of the Synoptic Gospels, when Jesus was on his way to cure Jairus's daughter, a woman who had suffered from hemorrhages for years came up to Jesus and touched him, seeking to be cured. As we've just seen, most scholars today believe Mark wrote his account first, because it's the simplest and the other evangelists appear to follow his order of events. If that's true, you can see the small but significant changes that the other two Synoptic Gospel writers made to the story if you read them side by side. The other important point to keep in mind is that, according to tradition at least, the evangelist Luke was a physician by trade.

The table below is another way to look at it, showing how Luke could have edited Mark with a modern word processor. The strikethroughs are deletions, and bold is added text:

MARK 5:25–27 RSV	MATTHEW 9:20 RSV	LUKE 8:43–44 RSV
And there was a woman who had had a flow of blood for twelve years,	And behold, a woman who had suffered from a hemorrhage for twelve years	And a woman who had had a flow of blood for twelve years
and who had suffered much under many physicians,		**and could not be healed by any one,**
and had spent all that she had, and was no better but rather grew worse.		

She had heard the reports about Jesus,		
and came up behind him in the crowd and touched his garment.	came up behind him and touched **the fringe of** his garment.	came up behind him, and touched **the fringe of** his garment.

And ~~there was~~ a woman who had had a flow of blood for twelve years, and ~~who had suffered much under many physicians, and had spent all that she had, and was no better but rather grew worse~~ **could not be healed by anyone,** ~~She had heard the reports about Jesus, and~~ came up behind him ~~in the crowd~~ and touched **the fringe of** his garment.

At first glance, the accounts seem very similar. But look carefully at the differences as New Testament scholars do. Luke's version removes the biting comments about how the woman had suffered under "many physicians," as well as the comment that she had spent all her money on them but only grew worse. If Luke really was a physician by trade, it makes sense that he would be tempted to remove such obvious denigrations of his profession. Also, you can see how Mark, whom scholars believe likely wrote for Gentile readers and probably from Rome, refers merely to Jesus' "garment." Matthew, on the other hand, who likely wrote for Jewish-Christian readers and who often tries to show that Jesus is the fulfillment of Jewish prophecies and teaching, adds the detail about the "fringe" (Hebrew: *tzitzit*) of his garment, a reference to the traditional tallit or "prayer shawl" commanded in Numbers 15 and still worn by Orthodox Jewish males all over the world.

HOW MATTHEW AND LUKE EDITED MARK

This is part of what New Testament scholars do for a living. They look closely at parallel passages like these to try to identify patterns in how the different evangelists present the same materials.

And this brings us to another testable point that anyone with a Bible and a little time on their hands can check for themselves: if Mark did write first, as many New Testament scholars believe, Matthew and Luke appear to have *added stuff* to Mark's bare-bones account!

Matthew adds material that is only found in Matthew's gospel, and Luke adds material that is only found in Luke's gospel. They seem to take the outline of Mark's account and then fill in details taken from other sources. Put another way, 97 percent of Mark's gospel is reproduced in Matthew, and 88 percent in Luke. Yet both the books of Matthew and Luke are nearly twice as long as Mark, so where did all that extra material come from?

Scholars speculate that each had a source for the material unique to each gospel, often dubbed *M* for Matthew's source and *L* for Luke's source. (And when scholars talk about the multiple "sources" confirming an incident in Jesus' life, they usually count these hypothetical sources, such as *M* and *L*, when asserting that a saying of Jesus or an incident is "multiply attested.")

But in addition to material that is unique to both Matthew and Luke, scholars noticed something else: in many cases both Matthew and Luke added the *same* material to Mark's account, often using identical words. This mostly applies to the sayings and sermons of Jesus. But they sometimes added these sayings of Jesus at different points in the narrative.

In Mark's gospel, Jesus is a man of few words. But in Matthew and Luke, Jesus gives much longer talks and sermons. Those talks and sermons are so similar—in fact, in many places identical—that scholars decided almost a century ago that both Matthew and Luke must have used the same written "sayings source," which was dubbed *Q* (short for the German word for "source," *Quelle*).[46]

Put another way, the hypothetical *Q* source is nothing more than the 230 sayings of Jesus found in both Matthew and Luke that are not found in Mark. According to the *Q* expert John S. Kloppenborg Verbin, author of *Excavating Q,* there are passages in Matthew and Luke where the sayings of Jesus agree almost 100 percent, such as Matthew 6:24 and Luke 16:13 (98 percent), and Matthew 12:43–45 and Luke 11:24–26 (93 percent).[47]

Again, the fun thing about studying the New Testament is that this is something you can check for yourself. Here is an example in both English and in Greek. If you look carefully, you can see that the two quotations differ only in a single Greek word, *oiketes* (οἰκέτης), which means "household slave." Matthew's version says "no one" can serve two masters and Luke's says "no slave." Other than that, they are identical.

MATTHEW 6:24 RSV	LUKE 16:13 RSV
"No **one** can serve two masters; for either he will hate the one and love the other, or he will be devoted to the one and despise the other. You cannot serve God and mammon."	"No **slave** can serve two masters; for either he will hate the one and love the other, or he will be devoted to the one and despise the other. You cannot serve God and mammon."
Οὐδεὶς δύναται δυσὶ κυρίοις δουλεύειν· ἢ γὰρ τὸν ἕνα μισήσει καὶ τὸν ἕτερον ἀγαπήσει, ἢ ἑνὸς ἀνθέξεται καὶ τοῦ ἑτέρου καταφρονήσει. οὐ δύνασθε θεῷ δουλεύειν καὶ μαμωνᾷ.	Οὐδεὶς **οἰκέτης** δύναται δυσὶν κυρίοις δουλεύειν· ἢ γὰρ τὸν ἕνα μισήσει καὶ τὸν ἕτερον ἀγαπήσει, ἢ ἑνὸς ἀνθέξεται καὶ τοῦ ἑτέρου καταφρονήσει. οὐ δύνασθε θεῷ δουλεύειν καὶ μαμωνᾷ.

So, if you can imagine Matthew and Luke at their writing desks, they likely had at least three sources before them—the gospel of Mark and the *Q* sayings source, versions of which they both shared, and then another written source unique to each of them (*M* or *L*). With these materials, then, Matthew and Luke wrote their own versions of the Jesus story—with their own emphases, assumptions, and editorial agendas. As you might imagine, the discovery of these powerful tools of analysis—the ability to, in a sense, look over the shoulders of the evangelists as they penned their written accounts of Jesus' deeds and sayings—filled the first generations of New Testament scholars with giddy excitement and perhaps overconfidence. Because they could see how Matthew and Luke appeared to make changes to Mark's versions of events, many of the early New Testament "critics"—such as the Germans Martin Dibelius and Rudolf Bultmann—quickly decided that the evangelists had a far more creative role in the shaping of the Gospels than merely transcribing Jesus' deeds and sayings. This led them to a belief that the evangelists didn't merely *edit* their sources for brevity and clarity but may have actually created entire incidents and speeches out of whole cloth. It is this hyper-skeptical approach to the New Testament, which has dominated much of historical Jesus research for generations, that is now being reexamined in the light of recent discoveries.

Robert Hutchinson

The narrow alleyways and staircases of Jerusalem have not changed all that much in 2,000 years. Many of the structures of the Old City, such as the eastern wall and gates facing the Mount of Olives, were built directly atop their first-century counterparts.

COULD THE GOSPELS BE EARLIER THAN WE THOUGHT?

One reason some modern scholars question whether there could be substantial eyewitness testimony in the Gospels involves their dating. Many (but not all) modern scholars believe that the gospel of Mark was likely written first, probably in Rome in the late 60s or early 70s AD,[48] followed by Luke in the mid-80s,[49] Matthew in the 80s,[50] and then by John sometime after AD 90.[51] In the past, critical scholars favored a dating of John well into the second century—AD 125, 150, or even 175—but then the discovery of a papyrus fragment with portions of John's gospel on both sides, known as P52, put an end to such extreme late datings. Many scholars accept the judgment of expert paleographers that P52 was written around AD 125, which means the original text must have been finished earlier still.

Even when I was in graduate school, this consensus dating just didn't add up for me. Here's why. The Acts of the Apostles, the sequel to the gospel of Luke, ends with the apostle Paul under house arrest in Rome in the years AD 62–64. There is no mention of any of the great events that are about to sweep up the Jesus movement in the next ten years:

- no mention of the execution of Paul and Peter in Rome (probably AD 62–64);
- no mention of the stoning of James, "the brother of the Lord," described by Josephus as occurring after the death of the procurator Porcius Festus but before Lucceius Albinus assumed the same office around AD 62;[52] and
- no mention even of the Jewish Revolt against Rome (66–70) and subsequent destruction of Jerusalem and the temple.

Granted, news traveled slower in first-century Rome than it does today. There was no Internet, and mail could take months to be delivered. But even so, the absence of any mention of the last event is the most troubling.

In AD 66, a rebellion broke out among the Jews in Palestine against Roman rule. It had been brewing for decades, and over the years there had been periodic attempts to throw off Roman rule by an assortment of Jewish messiahs, such as Judas the Galilean in AD 6. We know a lot about the Jewish War of 66–70 because one of the participants, a wealthy Jerusalem aristocrat named Yosef ben Matityahu, wrote a lengthy, exhaustively detailed account of the entire war under his Roman name, Titus Flavius Josephus (ca. AD 37–100). His work, *History of the Jewish War,* is a painstaking effort to chronicle one of the greatest disasters to befall the Jewish people in their entire history.

Josephus was not merely a historian but an active participant, having been involved, incredibly, on both sides of the conflict. According to his own account, he was drafted to be the commander of Jewish forces in Galilee and fought the Romans there for two years. Eventually, he was trapped in the Jewish hilltop fortress of Yodfat. The Roman army attacked, massacring thousands, and the few survivors fled to a nearby cave where they made a suicide pact, like the famous future suicide pact at Masada. Josephus claims he came up with the idea for how they could kill themselves: they would draw lots and kill each other. Alas, the sole remaining survivor turned out to be Josephus himself, who surrendered to the Romans and thus lived to tell the tale. Josephus went on to become a negotiator for the Romans during the long, bloody siege of Jerusalem in AD 70, in which both his parents and his wife were killed.

The Jewish War against Rome was merciless and brutal. When the Romans finally succeeded in busting through the walls of Jerusalem, they slaughtered the old and infirm and sold the children under seventeen as slaves.[53] The Roman general Titus initially sought to spare the famous and ancient temple, which was considered one of the wonders of the ancient world, but eventually Caesar gave the order that the entire city must be destroyed (save for three towers) and the temple demolished. To this day, you can still see large stones that the Roman soldiers threw into the streets from the ancient city walls, near Jerusalem's current walls, as well as the round stone "bullets," about the size of basketballs, they hurled at the besieged city from catapults. Along with the sacred vessels from the temple sanctuary, the surviving leaders of the rebellion were carried off in defeat—an event depicted in eerie detail in a carved tableau on the Arch of Titus in Rome. Historians estimate that fully 40 percent of the Jewish population in Judea may have been wiped out during the war.[54] The Roman historian Tacitus (AD 56–117) estimates 600,000 people were besieged in Jerusalem but gives no estimate for the total number killed.[55] By Josephus's account, widely believed to be exaggerated, in the end more than 1.1 million people[56] were killed during the war, most of them Jews.

In AD 70, Roman legions succeeded in conquering Jerusalem and destroying the ancient Temple and much of the city. Jewish leaders and souvenirs from the Temple, including the famous Menorah, were brought back to Rome in triumph—a victory commemorated on the Arch of Titus in Rome and still visible today.

WHY NO MENTION OF THE FALL OF JERUSALEM?

And yet *none* of this is mentioned in the Gospels.

For more than a century, critical scholars have cited passages in the Gospels where Jesus seems to be predicting the fall of Jerusalem. One of these is Mark 13:2, where Jesus refers to the temple and says, "Do you see these great buildings? Not one stone will be left here upon another" (NRSV)—and insisted that these are "prophecies after the fact" (*vaticinium ex eventu*). The idea is that the writers of the Gospels, living after the Jewish War began, simply put words in Jesus' mouth predicting the coming catastrophe—words that he didn't actually say. But that assumes that a prediction that Jerusalem was facing imminent destruction was unreasonable even in human terms. More recent scholars insist that you would have had to have been deaf, dumb, and blind not to have seen war coming in Palestine in those days. The entire country was seething with revolutionary rage against Rome and Roman collaborators. We know from Josephus that the Romans had already butchered many Jews during Jesus' lifetime.[57]

That's why, as an interested layman, I've always been skeptical of late datings of the Gospels. They seem driven as much by ideology as by textual evidence. It wouldn't bother me if the Gospels were composed very late—because, as I said, they could still be based on sources that were composed very early. But still, the declaration that the Gospels were written four, five, even six decades or more after Jesus' execution seems based on hunches more than anything else.

This is one of the many reasons that some scholars—perhaps most famously the liberal Anglican bishop John A. T. Robinson in his classic 1976 work, *Redating the New Testament*—have openly challenged the late dating of the Gospels. Despite his status as a liberal theologian, Robinson didn't buy the argument that the Gospels were written forty to one hundred years after Jesus' crucifixion. "One of the oddest facts about the New Testament is that what on any showing would appear to be the single most datable and climactic event of the period—the fall of Jerusalem in AD 70, and with it the collapse of institutional Judaism based on the temple—is never once mentioned as a past fact," Robinson wrote.[58]

In the last few years, younger scholars have also begun to question the old assumptions of New Testament scholarship regarding the dating of the Gospels. One of the more fascinating examples is James Crossley, a young British New Testament scholar at the University of Sheffield in the UK. Crossley studies the New Testament from a strictly secular perspective, and even debates Christian apologists such as William Lane Craig on such topics as the resurrection of Jesus. Yet Crossley is skeptical of late datings for the gospel of Mark. In a fascinating 2004 book, *The Date of Mark's Gospel*, Crossley defies more than a century of New Testament scholarship to argue that the gospel of Mark, far from being written in the late AD 60s or even early 70s as older scholars have long believed, could well have been written as early as the mid-30s—perhaps just five to ten years after Jesus was crucified. He insists that scholars in the past have incorrectly interpreted passages that predict the destruction of Jerusalem, such as Mark 13, as prophecies after the fact, when they make more sense as simply a realistic appraisal of the ongoing political tension that prevailed during Jesus' lifetime. For example, Crossley argues that the "desolating sacrilege" mentioned in Mark 13:14 need not be seen as a reference to the destruction of the temple in

AD 70, but could just as likely refer to events that occurred during what is known as the Caligula crisis, around AD 39–40.[59] The passage reads:

> But when you see the desolating sacrilege set up where it ought not to be (let the reader understand), then those in Judea must flee to the mountains; the one on the housetop must not go down or enter the house to take anything away; the one in the field must not turn back to get a coat. Woe to those who are pregnant and to those who are nursing infants in those days! Pray that it may not be in winter. For in those days there will be suffering, such as has not been from the beginning of the creation that God created until now, no, and never will be. (Mark 13:14–19 NRSV)

The Anglican bishop and New Testament scholar N. T. Wright and other Christian scholars make the case that this passage could well be historical on its face, simply a prediction of coming disasters that will befall Jerusalem and the people of Judea. The secular Crossley, however, joins some other scholars, such as Gerd Theissen and N. H. Taylor,[60] in arguing that this passage could reflect wars and political upheavals in Palestine in the late 30s—such as the Antipas-Nabatean war of AD 36–37 and the Caligula crisis of AD 39–40.[61] He makes the case that the "desolating sacrilege" that would be "set up" could very likely refer to the statue of the Emperor Caligula that the mad emperor attempted to have erected in the Jerusalem temple in AD 39–40. These secular scholars argue that Jesus did, in fact, predict the destruction of the temple—many people could see that war with Rome was virtually inevitable—and that the evangelist Mark, writing perhaps in the early 40s, simply made use of current political realities as he was rewriting and editing sayings of Jesus from the hypothetical sayings source *Q*. Luke, who likely was writing during or after the Jewish War of AD 66–70, modified this passage to reflect the current realities in *his* day—which were, in fact, "Jerusalem surrounded by armies" (Luke 21:20). The table on the next page shows this clearly.

As a result of these and other factors, Crossley concludes that Mark could very well have written his gospel far earlier than New Testament scholars have believed for more than a century. The arguments used for dating the gospel around the fall of Jerusalem, AD 70, "tend to be too speculative to be convincing and all too often rest upon numerous unfounded assumptions," Crossley says.[62] If he's right, and Mark was written in the late AD 30s, that means that some of the earliest source material for the Gospels was put to paper within five to ten years after Jesus' crucifixion—and not thirty, forty, or sixty years, as previous scholars believed. This strengthens the argument, therefore, that the Gospels are likely based on eyewitness testimony, even if that testimony was often rearranged according to the editorial decisions of the different evangelists.

MARK 13:14 NRSV	MATTHEW 24:15–16 NRSV	LUKE 21:20–21 NRSV
[W]hen you see the desolating sacrilege set up where it ought not to be (let the reader understand), then those in Judea must flee to the mountains.	[W]hen you see the desolating sacrilege standing in the holy place, as was spoken of by the prophet Daniel (let the reader understand), then those in Judea must flee to the mountains.	When you see Jerusalem surrounded by armies, then know that its desolation has come near. Then those in Judea must flee to the mountains . . .

EYEWITNESS TESTIMONY HIDDEN IN THE GOSPELS

The issue of eyewitness testimony in the Gospels is another area where recent scholarship is challenging the old views that were first developed in the nineteenth century and that are often paraded in the media as shocking "new" discoveries. Some critical scholars of the New Testament and popular writers seem to take as a given that it would be virtually impossible for the canonical Gospels to be based on eyewitness accounts. The standard line these critical scholars have taken is that the Gospels were written four to eight decades after Jesus' death in about the year AD 30 and "not by eyewitnesses." They very much stress the "not by eyewitnesses" part. "[A]ll of the Gospels were written anonymously, and none of the writers claims to be an eyewitness," proclaims Bart Ehrman in his entertaining and popular introduction to contemporary biblical scholarship, *Jesus, Interrupted*.[63]

The operating assumption of many critical scholars today was developed in the early years of the twentieth century by advocates of "form criticism," which subdivides the biblical texts into isolated literary units and approaches their content in light of their "form." These mostly German scholars, such as Rudolf Bultmann, believed that reports about Jesus circulated *anonymously* in the decades after his death and were only written down forty, fifty, or sixty years later, after having grown in the telling. As Ehrman puts it: "The stories were being told by word of mouth, year after year, decade after decade, among lots of people in different parts of the world, in different languages, and there was no way to control what one person said to the next about Jesus' words and deeds."[64] The implication is often that the Gospels are more myth than history, and certainly not reliable records of what actually occurred.

But this hypothesis of anonymous circulation has never been proven—only guessed at. Over the past few years, more and more scholars—including D. A. Carson, Douglas Moo, James M. Arlandson, Alan Millard, and Mark Roberts—have begun to question this century-old theory. "[G]iven the tendency of much modern scholarship to be overly skeptical," writes Roberts, who earned his PhD at Harvard, "you may be pleasantly surprised to learn that quite a few scholars believe that the gospels, if not actually written by one of Jesus's disciples, nevertheless reflect genuine reminiscences by these disciples that were preserved in their Christian communities. So the Gospel of John, for example, may not have been penned by John himself, but may incorporate John's memories and teachings."[65] In fact, a number of scholars now believe there is evidence of substantial and detailed eyewitness testimony embedded in the gospel texts—testimony that was passed on, and perhaps even written down, while Jesus was *still preaching in Galilee*. We suspect the evangelists drew upon oral and possibly *written* eyewitness sources, such as the famous hypothetical Q sayings source. The evangelist Luke says this explicitly in the opening words of his gospel:

Since many have undertaken to compile a narrative of the events that have been fulfilled among us," [note the words *many* and *compile*] just as those who were eyewitnesses from the beginning and ministers of the word have handed them down to us, I too have decided, after investigating everything accurately anew, to write it down in an orderly sequence for you, most excellent Theophilus, so that you may realize the certainty of the teachings you have received. (Luke 1:1–4)

In other words, Luke at least claims that he investigated "everything accurately anew" and drew upon the testimony of "those who were eyewitnesses from the beginning." The gospel of John makes the same explicit claim that it is based on the testimony of at least one eyewitness: "An eyewitness has testified, and his testimony is true" (19:35).

Recently, James M. Arlandson has revived an old discussion about the possibility, and even likelihood, that some of these eyewitness reports may have been *written down during Jesus' own lifetime*. Arlandson argues that at least a few of Jesus' many followers and hearers would have taken extensive written notes during his sermons and talks. In fact, given the celebrity status that Jesus appears to have enjoyed, it would have been strange if his more literate followers, such as the tax collector Matthew, had *not* taken notes. Arlandson points out that some of the Hebrew prophets had secretaries who wrote down their sayings (Jer. 36:4)—and there is no reason to think Jesus would not have been given similar treatment. In addition, Arlandson points out that the New Testament itself has references to parchment notebooks (2 Tim. 4:13) and writing tablets (Luke 1:63). He also points to the work of the Hebrew scholar Alan Millard, at the University of Liverpool in the UK, who insists that Galilee was not an "illiterate backwater," as previous generations thought, and that there was a "ubiquity of writing in first-century Palestine."[66] In his book *Reading and Writing in the Time of Jesus,* Millard insists he is not claiming that the evangelists began to write the gospels themselves in Jesus' lifetime. Rather, he argues that "some, possibly much, of their source material was preserved in writing from that period, especially accounts of the distinctive teachings and actions of Jesus."[67]

This discussion of written sources is particularly interesting in light of the discovery, in 1945, of the Gnostic or proto-Gnostic gospel of Thomas, a collection of 114 written sayings of Jesus, in Nag Hammadi, Egypt.[68] While few scholars think that the gospel of Thomas is itself the long-hypothesized sayings source called *Q*, its existence at least proves that Jesus' sayings were eventually written down and then later organized and collected. The question is: How early were they written down and by whom?

THE AGES OF POSSIBLE EYEWITNESSES

Next, let's consider the issue of the ages of any possible eyewitnesses. A witness who was twenty when Jesus died around AD 30 would be only thirty years old if James Crossley is right and the gospel of Mark was written no later than AD 40; but he would still be younger than sixty if the gospel was written between AD 65 and 70, as many scholars believe.[69] And that's assuming that the author of Mark or his sources spoke to the eyewitnesses only immediately before he composed the gospel. It is possible, even likely, that the author of Mark spent many years collecting sayings and anecdotes about Jesus' life, both written and oral, perhaps in the AD 30s and 40s. In that case, many of the eyewitnesses could have been relatively young, in their late thirties and forties, when they told their stories or showed their notes about what they saw Jesus do and say.

And now, a leading New Testament scholar at the University of St. Andrews, in Scotland, Richard Bauckham, has come forth with compelling new evidence of eyewitness testimony found in all four of the gospel texts. In his influential 2006 book, *Jesus and the Eyewitnesses: The Gospels as Eyewitness Testimony*, Bauckham argues that the accounts of Jesus' deeds and sayings were tied to named eyewitnesses who "vouched" for their accuracy.[70] Bauckham's argument has rekindled an enormous debate in New Testament scholarship and is causing some scholars to reexamine the old notion that traditions about Jesus' deeds and sayings floated around Christian circles for decades and were embellished and modified extensively along the way. As Bauckham himself concedes, his argument that "the texts of our Gospels are close to the eyewitness reports of the words and deeds of Jesus—runs counter to almost all recent New Testament scholarship."[71] Instead, Bauckham explains, a common view among New

Testament scholars today is that the followers of Jesus made up stories about his life and even some of his sayings in the years after his crucifixion. Many contemporary authors believe that "the traditions were not only adapted, but in many cases created for the use to which the Christian churches put them, in preaching or teaching."[72]

HEARING FROM THOSE WHO HEARD JESUS

Bauckham begins to refute this by noting that early Christian writers such as Papias insisted that the Gospels were based on eyewitness testimony. Papias (ca. 100) was a bishop in the Greek city of Hierapolis who belonged to the third generation of Christians. He wrote a book called *Exposition of the Sayings of the Lord*, which no longer exists but was quoted by the later church historian Eusebius. Papias claimed to have heard "Presbyter John" in person, and reported that John said the writer of the gospel of "Mark, in his capacity as Peter's interpreter, wrote down accurately as many things as he recalled from memory—though not in an ordered form—of the things either said or done by the Lord." Papias added that the evangelist Mark

> neither heard the Lord nor accompanied him, but later, as I said, Peter, who used to give his teachings in the form of *chreiai* [anecdotes], but had no intention of providing an ordered arrangement of the *logia* of the Lord. Consequently Mark did nothing wrong when he wrote down some individual items just as he related them from memory. For he made it his one concern not to omit anything he had heard or to falsify anything.[73]

Bauckham points out that this is an early and quite explicit claim that the gospel of Mark, at least, is based on the eyewitness testimony of Peter. The second-century bishop Irenaeus also recalled how he used to listen to Polycarp (69–156)—a bishop in western Turkey who was a disciple of the apostle John—when he recounted his meetings with "John and with others who had seen the Lord" and how Polycarp would relate their words from memory, the things "concerning the Lord, his mighty works and his teaching . . . as having received them from the eyewitnesses."[74] In other words, it was widely known in the early church that the stories about the deeds of Jesus and his sayings were passed down by eyewitnesses, not by an anonymous tradition, and that these named eyewitnesses lent credibility for the accuracy of the reports about Jesus that were passed along.

EYEWITNESS TESTIMONY PERMEATES THE GOSPELS

Much of Bauckham's book is a detailed analysis of the New Testament in an effort to show that this eyewitness testimony runs throughout the gospel accounts and the letters of Paul. Moreover, this testimony is carefully tied to the names of specific people. According to Bauckham, a careful reading of the gospel of Mark shows how thoroughly the Petrine perspective permeates the entire text.

Bauckham also makes a strong case that the early followers of Jesus took great care that the accounts of Jesus' deeds and his sayings were passed on accurately. "We have unequivocal evidence, in Paul's letters, that the early Christian movement did practice the formal transmission of tradition," he writes. "By 'formal' here I mean that there were specific practices employed to ensure that tradition was faithfully handed on from a qualified traditioner to others."[75] The evidence, Bauckham says, lies in the technical terms that Paul uses for handing on a tradition about a deed or saying of Jesus—the Greek word *paradidomi* for "handing on" a tradition and the word *paralambano* for "receiving" a tradition. These technical words were used in both Hellenistic schools and in later rabbinic academies to describe the process by which teachings were formally transmitted to students. What's more, Paul explicitly states that the traditions he "received" were to be maintained precisely as he passed them along. For example, in 1 Corinthians 11:2, Paul praises the members of the Corinthian community "for holding to the traditions just as I passed them on to you" (NIV). As for the content of those traditions, including the traditions surrounding the resurrection, Paul mentions repeatedly that they came from eyewitnesses. In his letter to the Galatians, for example, Paul reports that he visited Jerusalem and spent two weeks with Peter (1:18) and also met with James (1:19).[76]

GOSPELS MAY BE FAR MORE
RELIABLE THAN SCHOLARS SUSPECTED

In the end, Bauckham makes a powerful case, against at least a century of New Testament scholarship, that the Gospels are based on and incorporate the testimony of eyewitnesses who saw and heard Jesus of Nazareth while he was alive on earth. Moreover, based on a detailed analysis of the texts, he accepts that at least one gospel writer, John, was himself an eyewitness to some of the events he describes,[77] just as the gospel itself appears to claim (21:24).[78] This is particularly significant because previous generations of Christian pastors, authors, and seminary professors were taught that John's gospel was written very late, and that its "high Christology" depiction of Jesus as a kind of all-knowing God-man—a "Gnostic redeemer-myth," as Rudolf Bultmann famously called it—proves that it was fabricated by pagan Greeks and not by Jesus' actual followers.[79] But Bauckham convincingly demonstrates that this simply is not the case. For Bauckham, John was a thoroughly Jewish eyewitness follower of Jesus. In this, he follows some earlier scholars, such as F. F. Bruce, who insisted that John's gospel is so riddled with details of Palestinian geography and local Jewish customs that only an eyewitness on the ground in Jerusalem could have known them. "The evangelist was evidently a Palestinian," Bruce wrote. "Although he may have been far from his native land when he wrote his Gospel, his accurate knowledge of places and distances in Palestine, a knowledge which appears spontaneously and naturally, strongly suggests one who was born and brought up in that land, not one whose knowledge of the country was derived from pilgrim visits."[80]

Indeed, some Jewish students of the New Testament, particularly in recent decades, exhibit a far less skeptical attitude toward the Gospels as historical sources than did the first generation of "critical" scholars in Germany in the early twentieth century. For example, the famous Israeli biblical scholar David Flusser (1917–2000), an Orthodox Jew who taught at the Hebrew University of Jerusalem, often sought to correct what he saw as the distortions that the hyper-skeptical approach to the Gospels created in trying to understand who Jesus was and what he was trying to do. "The early Christian accounts about Jesus are not as untrustworthy as scholars today often think," he wrote in his classic book *Jesus*. "My research has led me to the conclusion that the Synoptic Gospels are based on one or more non-extant early documents composed by Jesus' disciples and the early church in Jerusalem . . . Thus, when studied in the light of their Jewish background, the Synoptic Gospels do preserve a picture of Jesus that is more reliable than is generally acknowledged."[81]

FOR FURTHER STUDY

Bauckham, Richard. *Jesus and the Eyewitnesses.* Grand Rapids, MI: William B. Eerdmans, 2006.

Blomberg, Craig. *The Historical Reliability of the Gospels*, 2nd ed. Downers Grove, IL: InterVarsity Press, 2007.

Bruce, F. F. *The New Testament Documents: Are They Reliable?* Grand Rapids, MI: William B. Eerdmans, 1981.

Roberts, Mark D. *Can We Trust the Gospels? Investigating the Reliability of Matthew, Mark, Luke, and John.* Wheaton, IL: Crossway, 2007.

Rousseau, John J. and Rami Arav. *Jesus and His World: An Archaeological and Cultural Dictionary.* Minneapolis: Fortress Press, 1995.

LIAR, LUNATIC . . . OR LEGEND?

Portraits of Jesus Today and Why They Are Less Plausible than the Gospels

*"Now Jesus and his disciples set out for the villages
of Caesarea Philippi. Along the way he asked
his disciples, 'Who do people say that I am?'"*

—MARK 8:27

Even after two thousand years, the ruins of the Greco-Roman city of Caesarea Philippi are still a magnificent sight. Located twenty-five miles (forty kilometers) north of the Sea of Galilee at the base of Mount Hermon, Caesarea Philippi was considered one of the most beautiful resort areas in the ancient world. After Herod the Great died in 4 BC, his son Philip made the city the capital of his tetrarchy east of the Jordan River. According to Josephus, the Roman general and future emperor Vespasian used to rest his army for weeks at a time in this area. In an arid land, this region is blessed with an abundance of water flowing from Mount Hermon and from gushing natural springs. There are still vast natural pools, waterfalls, and lush vegetation everywhere. You can also see dozens of hyraxes, the large furry mammals Israelis call *shafanim*, often mistaken for rodents but actually related to elephants.

This part of Israel was widely known as a pagan region in both the Hebrew Bible and the New Testament. In the nearby Tel Dan Nature Reserve, Israeli archaeologists have uncovered the ruins of numerous Canaanite temples. The Greeks and the Romans knew the area as Banias, or Paneas, because there was a large shrine there dedicated to Pan, the pagan god of nature, fertility, and sexual prowess. In Greek mythology, Pan was a faun with the upper body of a man and the lower body of a goat, and he was widely known as a companion and seducer of nymphs. The legend is that Pan liked to steal the clothes of women as they were bathing in the many streams and natural pools in the region. When the women came out of the water and saw that their clothes were missing, they would "panic."

Wikipedia

The ruins of the Greco-Roman resort town of Caesarea Philippi, which the Gospels say Jesus visited with his disciples, are still visible today at Banias at the foot of Mount Hermon in the Golan Heights. The large cave was a shrine to the Greek god Pan. Photo taken by Gugganij.

In the time of Jesus, Caesarea Philippi was a thriving Greek (that is, pagan) city with many magnificent buildings, including a vast colonnaded cardo, or shopping mall, as well as numerous public buildings whose ruins you can still see today. All three of the Synoptic Gospels report that, after Jesus performed the miracle known as the multiplication of the loaves, he took his closest disciples to Bethsaida, a fishing village at the northernmost tip of the Sea of Galilee and the home of the apostles Philip, Andrew, and Peter (John 1:44; John 12:21). From there, the Synoptic Gospels report, the tiny band headed north toward Caesarea Philippi, following the Jordan River due north through the Hula Valley, around the lake of the same name, to the base of Mount Hermon. It's not clear why Jesus made this trip. Some scholars speculate that at this point in his mission Jesus was on the run and the northern resort areas at the base of Mount Hermon were a good place to lie low.[1]

Whatever his reason, the Gospels report that Jesus asked his disciples a strange question on their way to the Greek city: "Who do people say that the Son of Man is?" They replied that some said he was John the Baptist; others, the messianic herald Elijah. Still others said he was "one of the prophets." And then Jesus really pressed the issue. "But who do you say that I am?" Mark and Luke report that Peter said simply, "You are the Christ," that is, the long-hoped-for Jewish messiah (Matt. 16:13–16 ESV). But Matthew fills in the story quite a bit from his sources. When Peter finished, according to Matthew, Jesus said, "Blessed are you, Simon Bar-Jonah! For flesh and blood has not revealed this to you, but my Father who is in heaven. And I tell you, you are Peter, and on this rock I will build my church, and the gates of hell shall not prevail against it. I will give you the keys of the kingdom of heaven, and whatever you bind on earth shall be bound in heaven, and whatever you loose on earth shall be loosed in heaven" (16:17–19 ESV).

EARLY DISPUTES OVER WHO JESUS WAS

Of course, one of the odd things about Christianity is that people have been trying to answer Jesus' question for more than two thousand years and have come up with a bewildering array of possible answers. We know this because we have records of the disputes over just who and what Jesus was, dating all the way back to the first century AD. Even in the New Testament itself it is clear that the followers of Jesus did not agree on this point. In Paul's first letter to the Corinthians, for example, he complains of factionalism within the early community. Some people were saying they were followers of the early Christian evangelist Apollos, and others were claiming to be the followers of Paul (1:12). The author of the Acts of the Apostles reports that the disputes got to be so heated, in fact, that the very first church council was convened in Jerusalem, probably around the year AD 50, to settle the issue (Acts 15).

Amazingly enough, the central issue of this council is still relevant today: whether Gentile followers of Jesus had to first convert to Judaism and observe all the *mitzvot* of the Torah, including circumcision. Contemporary scholars are still at odds, two thousand years later, over whether Jesus' mission was solely a reform movement meant exclusively for Jews or whether he had the broader intention that his message and movement would eventually be carried to "all nations," as was displayed in the Gospels (Matt. 28:19). The author of Acts reports that there was substantial debate over whether the Jesus movement was to be exclusively Jewish. As we know from Paul's own writings, Paul and his Gentile companion, Barnabas, argued that not only was conversion to Judaism unnecessary, but it actually undermined what the Jesus movement was all about. The council was apparently swayed when Peter arose and gave a speech that is recorded in Acts 15. He announced that it was not only Paul who was winning Gentile followers to the Way of Jesus. "Brothers, you know that in the early days God made a choice among you, that by my mouth the Gentiles should hear the word of the gospel and believe," Peter said. "He made no distinction between us and them, having cleansed their hearts by faith. Now, therefore, why are you putting God to the test?" (Acts 15:7, 9–10 ESV). James, the "brother of the Lord" (Gal. 1:19) and leader of the Jerusalem community, agreed. He proposed that the leaders of the Jerusalem community write a letter to the various Gentile communities, instructing them that they had to observe only a minimum of the Jewish law, to abstain from "things polluted by idols, and from sexual immorality, and from what has been strangled, and from blood" (Acts 15:20 ESV).

But the disputes continued. Apparently the Jewish party advocating stricter observance of the Torah within the Jesus movement was not satisfied by the decision of the Jerusalem Council, because we know from the writings of second-century church fathers that a Jewish-Christian community known as the Ebionites (from the Hebrew word *evanim*, or "poor") existed in many places after the first century and may have continued in the Middle East up until the Muslim Conquest.[2] We don't know for sure if the Ebionites are descended from the Jerusalem community itself or arose independently of it, but we first hear of what you might call "messianic Jews" in the writings of Justin Martyr,[3] born an Aramaic-speaking Gentile in AD 100 in what is today Nablus on the West Bank. The second-century theologian Irenaeus (ca. 130–202) mentions the Ebionites by name. "Those who are called Ebionites agree that the world was made by God; but their opinions with respect to the Lord are similar to those of Cerinthus and Carpocrates," he writes, referring to some early Christian heretics. "They use the Gospel according to Matthew only, and repudiate the Apostle Paul, maintaining that he was an apostate from the law. . . . They practice circumcision, persevere in the observance of those customs which are enjoined by the law, and are so Judaic in their style of life, that they even adore Jerusalem as if it were the house of God."[4]

Many modern New Testament scholars now revel in the wide diversity of early Christian groups, like the Ebionites, and celebrate their "unorthodox" beliefs.[5] A cottage industry has arisen, in fact, documenting the multiplicity of early Christian doctrines, communities, and practices. One important question is whether or not these nonorthodox groups maintained traditions and knowledge about Jesus that were lost to the mainstream Christian community. Many modern scholars doubt this[6] because most of these "unorthodox" groups arose very late, in the second, third, and fourth centuries. However, there are a handful of scholars—most famously John Dominic Crossan, a cofounder of the Jesus Seminar—who give greater weight to the writings of these unorthodox groups in many cases than they do to the canonical Gospels. In fact, Crossan in particular famously bases his case that Jesus was a Greek-style "Cynic philosopher" on what he claims are fifty-two independent sources for information about Jesus, most of which are either apocryphal texts from the second and third centuries or his own ingenious reconstructions of hypothetical texts, such as something he calls the Cross Gospel, embedded within apocryphal texts.[7]

THE QUEST FOR THE HISTORICAL JESUS

For at least a thousand years, Christians in Western Europe and in the Middle East accepted the events and sayings in the Gospels at face value. I didn't really understand what that meant until I heard a lecture recently, in Jerusalem, from a professor of Islamic studies at the University of Bethlehem. A devout Muslim, the professor is a learned man who teaches at the most prestigious universities all over the world. I asked him if, given the long history of Islamic involvement in science and mathematics, Muslims were facing the same questions about the historical reliability of the Qur'an as Christians were facing vis-à-vis the New Testament and Jews with the Torah. "Not really," the professor told me with a candor that took me aback. "For us, if it's in the Qur'an it's simply a fact."

Until two or three hundred years ago, that was the same basic attitude that many Christians had toward the entire Bible. The Bible is the Word of God, Christians believed and still believe, and God wouldn't "lie," not even about insignificant details of history, astronomy, or biology. Yet there was an awareness, even in the earliest days of Christianity, that the biblical texts should not be read simplistically and without an understanding of their context, original languages, narrative structure, different literary genres, and so on. "Without accurate research it is not possible to discover if a fact that seems historical actually happened according to the literal sense of the words or if it did not happen at all," wrote the theologian Origen (ca. 185–254) as early as the third century AD. "By keeping the commandment of the Lord to 'search the Scriptures' (John 5:39), one ought to examine with care and attention where the literal meaning is historical and where it is not. In Scripture not everything is objectively historical in the literal sense."[8]

Augustine (ca. 354–430), who was a teacher of rhetoric before becoming a bishop, agreed. "At the outset, you must be very careful lest you take figurative expression literally," he wrote in his classic work on biblical interpretation, *On Christian Doctrine*.[9] In fact, the greatest minds of Western Christendom—such as Origen, Jerome,[10] Augustine, Aquinas,[11] and

Calvin—understood that the Bible is a vast anthology that contains many different literary genres, often in the same book, and that these can be interpreted in a variety of ways. These different literary genres—including law codes, love poetry, songs, historical chronicles, prayers, parables, and so on—can't all be read in the same way. Legal codes such as those contained in parts of the Torah typically strive for precision and lack of ambiguity, while the poetry in the Song of Songs or the Psalms is often deliberately ambiguous. To treat both types of writing the same way will result in profound errors of interpretation.

When it came to the New Testament, however, with its relatively straightforward narratives of Jesus' deeds and sayings, Christian readers usually took the gospel descriptions more or less at face value. Of course, biblical scholars in the churches noted apparent discrepancies in some of the gospel accounts. For example, in the Synoptic Gospels of Mark, Matthew, and Luke, Jesus drives out the moneychangers from the temple precincts at the end of his ministry (see Mark 11:15); whereas in John's gospel (2:15), the same event seems to occur at the very beginning. Even more profoundly, the Jesus depicted in the Synoptics—a very human man who suffers pain, hunger, fear, and even doubt—differs radically from the portrait in John, where Jesus appears as a virtually omniscient, fearless divine being.

Yet these discrepancies have rarely bothered ordinary Christians. For nearly two thousand years, Christians have simply taken the various deeds and sayings of Jesus from all four gospels and put them together in an overarching narrative of Jesus' life. From the earliest days of the church, people have created harmonizations of the Gospels—from Tatian's *Diatessaron* to *The Greatest Story Ever Told* to *The Life of Christ in Stereo.* These accounts will take the account of the visit of the Magi and the slaughter of the innocents in Matthew's gospel and put them together with Luke's description of the annunciation of the angel Gabriel and the shepherds guarding their flocks, creating one combined account of the birth of Jesus. There is nothing wrong with this, as far as it goes.[12] Christians assumed that the different evangelists simply told different parts of the same story. It seemed natural, then, for authors to piece together the whole story from the different parts in order to get a better picture of what actually happened.

Yet the same effort to figure out what "really happened"—to piece

45

together the different parts of the story found in the different gospels—is what eventually gave birth to the historical-critical method and its emphasis on studying the differences in how the gospel texts present events. As we discussed in the previous chapter, when scholars began to closely compare the different gospel accounts line by line, they not only noticed discrepancies in the various accounts, but they also noticed that different events and sayings occurred at different times and in different locations in the Gospels. For example, the Sermon on the Mount in Matthew occurs on a hill; in Luke, the same sermon (or close to it) occurs on a "level place" (*tópou pedinoú*) after Jesus and his disciples "came down" from a mountain (6:17). Of course, it's likely that Jesus delivered the same sermons in many different places, so this type of discrepancy is easily explained away. But other inconsistencies of location and chronology are not so easily resolved.

Beginning with Celsus in the second century right up to Thomas Paine's *The Age of Reason* and Bart Ehrman's *Jesus, Interrupted*, anti-Christian polemicists have listed numerous supposedly irresolvable discrepancies in the gospel accounts. The reaction of many ordinary Christians to these discrepancies, however, is simply to shrug. Not knowing whether Jesus taught the Our Father as part of the Sermon on the Mount, before multitudes, as recounted in Matthew, or to his disciples alone in private, as in Luke 11, doesn't really rattle the faith of many Christians. What counts for them is the content of Jesus' message, not where he delivered a particular sermon.

In addition, many of the supposed "discrepancies" in the gospel accounts of events can be explained as being the result of literary brevity or "telescoping" on the part of one of the authors. For example, one writer may give a full account of an event, with lots of detail, and another writer may simply give an abbreviated version. Does this mean that the second writer "lied" or is unreliable? Some scholars, such as Bart Ehrman, seem to think so. But other experts disagree,[13] insisting that many discrepancies in the gospel texts can be explained as the result of literary decisions, not deception or false information. To illustrate, look at the account of what happened when Jesus' tomb was discovered empty. On the surface, there appear to be some key differences between the gospel accounts. Mark, likely the earliest gospel to be written, says that "Mary Magdalene, Mary, the mother of James, and Salome" went to the tomb to anoint the body of Jesus (16:1). Matthew says it was Mary Magdalene and "the other Mary" (28:1). Luke says that "they" went to the tomb (24:1), adding later that it was "Mary Magdalene and Joanna and Mary the mother of James and the other women with them" (24:10 ESV). John mentions only Mary Magdalene (20:1).

You can almost hear an attorney interrogating the witnesses: "So then, let me get this straight. Mark says Mary Magdalene, Mary the mother of James, and Salome went to the tomb . . . but Luke says Mary Magdalene, Mary the mother of James, and *Joanna*. Plainly, one of you must by lying!" But while the cross-examining attorney sees deliberate deception or unreliable testimony, others, with perhaps more common sense, simply see different ways of recounting the same event. Matthew and John, not expecting they would have to testify in court someday, may have decided they didn't need to list every person who went with Mary Magdalene to get their point across. Luke may have counted Salome among the "other women" mentioned by Mark. In short, abbreviation is not the same as deception and does not necessarily make a written account unreliable.

There are other differences in the various accounts of what Jesus did and said. Anyone who studies a synopsis of the Gospels can see that. Bart Ehrman titles one of his chapters "A World of Contradictions" in his 283-page book on the "hidden contradictions in the Bible," *Jesus, Interrupted*. But along with long digressions about his teenage flirtation with fundamentalism, his time at the Moody Bible Institute, and how much he resisted modern biblical scholarship, Ehrman lists very few actual contradictions. The "world of contradictions" turns out to be, in the case of the Gospels at least, about fifteen. They include differences in the accounts of Jesus' birth and genealogy, variations in the words heard at Jesus' baptism (Matthew reports the voice said, "This is my beloved son," while Mark says it was "You are my beloved son"), where Jesus went after he was baptized, whether Jairus's daughter was dead or not, how long Jesus' ministry lasted, the death of Judas, whether there was one man or two at the tomb after the resurrection, how many women went to the tomb, as above, and whether Jesus rode one animal or two during his entry into Jerusalem on Palm Sunday.[14]

The problem with debunkers of Christianity using examples like these to undermine the basic credibility of the Gospel accounts is that they assume what they must prove: that variations in different historic accounts mean that *none* of the accounts can be trusted or that they can't be trusted in the aggregate. In fact, historians without a personal axe to grind against Christianity, such as Michael Grant in his classic book *Jesus: An Historian's Review of the Gospels,* often insist that the opposite is true.[15] When you have different sources asserting the same basic outline of events, but with differences in the details, you can usually have confidence that these sources are reliable because such differences are to be expected when dealing with real events and eyewitness testimonies. As noted above, it's when accounts agree entirely that a historian suspects fraud.

THE MODERN QUEST

In a very real sense, the quest for the historical Jesus began in the Renaissance and with the dawn of the Protestant Reformation. During the Renaissance, there was a big push to return to the sources as scholars such as Erasmus of Rotterdam began to rediscover ancient books, both pagan and Christian, written in the original languages (usually Greek). But it was the Protestant Reformation that really set the stage for a historical inquiry into the origins of Christianity. The Reformers, led by the former Augustinian friar and Bible scholar Martin Luther (1483–1546), believed that the Roman Catholic Church had added numerous man-made doctrines to the plain sense of the gospel message. Eventually, they adopted the slogan *sola scriptura,* or "Scripture alone," with the concomitant belief that by studying the Bible afresh, with new eyes, they could rediscover the authentic message and teaching of the New Testament. This was the beginning of the notion that there is a distinction between the "real Jesus" and the "Christ of faith"—although the reformers themselves would not have seen it that way.

Once the genie had been let out of the bottle, and educated people began to suspect that the Jesus of history might be radically different from the Jesus proclaimed by the churches, all bets were off. Very slowly at first, but with increasing forcefulness, philosophers and writers began questioning not just the portrait of Jesus proclaimed by the various churches but, even more radically, the portrait of Jesus found in the New Testament itself.

Additionally, in reaction to the development of modern science after Galileo (ca. 1564–1642), some people began to question whether miracles actually happen—and that led to doubts about whether everything in the New Testament could be trusted. Modern philosophers, such as René Descartes (1596–1650), insisted that everything must be called into question and investigated anew.[16] Finally, a few courageous souls, such as the Deist Hermann Reimarus (1694–1768) and later David Strauss (1808–1874), uttered the unutterable: they claimed that the real Jesus must have been much different from the way he is portrayed in the New Testament. Strauss even insisted Jesus was simply a "myth," in the sense that Christians unconsciously made up most things about him,[17] but Reimarus was more radical: he insisted that the Gospels were outright frauds and the apostles deliberate deceivers.[18]

THE FIRST QUEST: A JESUS WITHOUT MIRACLES

So began a new movement that continues to this day—a movement to discover who Jesus of Nazareth really was. This effort is known as the quest for the historical Jesus—or really, the quests. That's because this project has proceeded in three very distinctive waves, from about the 1830s until today; scholars refer to these as the first, second, and third quests.

The first quest was a product of a largely discredited and obsolete nineteenth-century rationalism, yet its assumptions, methods, and conclusions are still widely seen today. Beginning in the mid-to-late nineteenth century, academic Bible scholars, full of new confidence that they were able to uncover "sources" that lay behind the Gospels—such as the Q sayings source, the M and L sources, and so on—began to think they could reconstruct a more accurate picture of Jesus than the one found in the New Testament. Many of the "shocking" and "new" discoveries you read about in weekly news magazines every Easter season are products of the first quest—and thus are 150 years old. The basic assumptions of the first quest were:

1. Miracles cannot and do not happen.
2. The Jesus of history is dramatically different from the Christ of the Gospels.
3. The message of Jesus was dramatically different from the message of the early church.

4. The Gospels can't be trusted as historical sources and, in fact, may be considered deliberate falsifications of what actually happened.

With these operating principles, which are still the operating principles of many academic New Testament scholars today, writers tried to imagine

Public domain

The French writer and historian Ernest Renan (c. 1823–1892) pioneered the popular presentation of the Historical Jesus along purely naturalistic lines. His Life of Jesus *(1863), which presented a Jesus of Nazareth without miracles or the resurrection, was enormously popular and hugely influential.*

(quite literally) what Jesus of Nazareth must have been like and what he was trying to achieve. Hundreds of popular books were written in the nineteenth century that sought to retell the Jesus story along more "scientific," naturalistic lines. The most famous and successful of these books was Ernest Renan's *Life of Jesus,* published in 1863. It went through sixty-one editions[19] in French and was widely translated into other languages. Renan was a highly educated philosopher, a popular writer, and an expert on the Middle East. He had personally visited Palestine and was a professor of Hebrew and Syriac at the Collège de France. Like so many New Testament scholars of his time, he was also culturally anti-Semitic. According to his biographers, Renan popularized the notion that Europe's Ashkenazi Jews are not really descended from the Jews of Palestine but are, in fact, Khazars, a nomadic Turkish people who supposedly converted to Judaism and adopted Yiddish as their language in the eighth century. This thoroughly discredited theory (that modern European Jews are really Khazars) has been used by anti-Semites for more than a century to put considerable distance between Jesus and mainstream Judaism because it insinuates that European Jews are not really Jews.[20]

As a thoroughly modern, "scientific" citizen of the nineteenth century,

Renan of course rejected the miracles in the New Testament out of hand, especially the resurrection. He believed that Jesus, ignorant of modern science, was a sincere but largely deluded faith healer and "thaumaturgus," who unknowingly used the power of suggestion and placebo to work what seemed, both to himself and his observers, to be genuine miracles of healing.[21] The resurrection was nothing more than a delusion experienced by hysterical women when they confronted an empty tomb, Renan contended, but he nevertheless insisted that Jesus "still presides over the destiny of the world" and that he was and is "the one who has caused his fellow-men to make the greatest step toward the divine."[22]

Renan is quite eloquent on this point. "Mankind in its totality offers an assemblage of low beings, selfishness, and is superior to the animal only in that its selfishness is more reflective," he concludes. "From the midst of this uniform mediocrity, there are pillars that rise toward the sky, and bear witness to a nobler destiny. Jesus is the highest of these pillars which show to man whence he comes, and whither he ought to tend."[23]

Critics rightly point to Renan's anti-Semitic prejudices, which infected much of New Testament scholarship in the nineteenth and early twentieth centuries and still to this day.[24] While acknowledging that Jesus was born a Jew and even claiming that "Jewish society exhibited the most extraordinary moral and intellectual state which the human species has ever passed through,"[25] Renan asserts that Jesus gradually sloughed off his Jewishness as he became, in effect, the first Christian. Basing his account largely on the gospel of John, with its easily misunderstood statements about "the Jews," Renan argues that Jesus "represents the rupture with the Jewish spirit,"[26] which he earlier describes as "intolerance."[27] "The general march of Christianity has been to remove itself more and more from Judaism," Renan explains. "It will become perfect in returning to Jesus, but certainly not in returning to Judaism."[28]

Thus, Renan's Jesus was a liberal teacher of righteousness whose work resonated with educated, science-minded, rationalistic Europeans and Americans. "Let us place, then, the person of Jesus at the highest summit of human greatness," Renan declares. "Jesus remains an inexhaustible principle of moral regeneration for humanity."[29] The first quest, therefore, let rationalists have their cake and eat it too. They could doubt all the miracles and what they saw as the other superstitious nonsense of the New Testament—including the resurrection—and yet still consider themselves as, in some sense, faithful Christians. Jesus taught a "universal and eternal religion" and a "perfect idealism" that remained vitally important. "In this sense we are Christians," Renan concludes, "even when we separate ourselves on almost all points from the Christian tradition which has preceded us."[30]

A CRISIS OF FAITH

In the wake of Renan's book, and others like it, there gradually emerged a kind of rationalistic Christianity that we now call Liberal Protestantism, exemplified in the work of such nineteenth-century theologians as Adolf von Harnack (1851–1930) and Albrecht Ritschl (1822–1889). It was largely a religion of ethics and social progress. "The kingdom of God is the divinely ordained highest good of the community founded through God's revelation in Christ," explains Ritschl. "But it is the highest good only in the sense that it forms at the same time the ethical ideal for whose attainment the members of the community bind themselves to each other through a definite type of reciprocal action."[31]

But even as many people embraced this new rationalist view of Jesus, a number of doubts arose as to its historical accuracy. One doubt, of course, was expressed by the Anglican bishop William Temple. "Why anyone should have troubled to crucify the Christ of Liberal Protestantism has always been a mystery," he famously quipped.[32]

A far more devastating critique of the rationalist view of Jesus was expressed by the German New Testament scholar Johannes Weiss (1863–1914) and then, later, by the great humanitarian, medical doctor, and New Testament scholar Albert Schweitzer (1875–1965). While scholars were correct to pinpoint the "kingdom of God" as Jesus' central message, Weiss said, they had to pay closer attention to *what he actually meant by it.* Weiss thought Jesus proclaimed a coming cataclysm in which "God will destroy this old world which is ruled and spoiled by the devil, and create a new world."[33]

Dr. Schweitzer went even further: Jesus was not a gentle teacher of ethical high-mindedness, as Liberal Protestantism had proclaimed, but an apocalyptic prophet who preached the imminent end of the world. In his classic summary of (or eulogy for) the first quest, *The Quest of the Historical Jesus*, published in 1906, Dr. Schweitzer concluded that the search for the historical Jesus had been an effort in which, in a sense, scholars peered down the long, dark well of history, and the image that they saw was nothing more than their own reflections looking back at them. "What [rationalism] is looking for is not the past, but itself in the past," Schweitzer wrote. "For it, the problem of the life of Jesus is solved the moment it succeeds in bringing Jesus near to its own time, in portraying Him as the great teacher of virtue, and showing that His teaching is identical with the intellectual truth which rationalism deifies."[34]

A few years earlier, another scholar, Martin Kähler (1835–1912), had offered an even better reason for why the quest was doomed from the start: the historical sources available are simply not sufficient for the task at hand. If you reject the Gospels from the start as unreliable, and insist that Jesus must have been radically different from the way he is portrayed in the New Testament, then you simply don't have enough information with which to construct a realistic portrait of Jesus of Nazareth, Kähler argued. "I regard the entire Life-of-Jesus movement as a blind alley," he wrote.[35] In his magisterial critique of two centuries' worth of historical Jesus research, James Dunn of the University of Durham explains why Kähler and others found the entire project of the historical Jesus "questers" to be deeply problematic: "[T]he multiplicity of different reconstructions only made faith harder and not easier. More to the point, only a few scholars have the specialist training to carry through such reconstruction. Is faith, then, to depend on the findings of a few scholars? Are critical historians to become the new priests and pope of Christian faith?"[36]

By the turn of the twentieth century, many of the leading theologians of Europe, such as Karl Barth and Rudolf Bultmann, would have agreed with Kähler's critique of the quest for the historical Jesus. They would insist that Christian faith is based on the *kerygma*, the proclamation of the church, and has little if anything to do with the tentative, uncertain research of academic history. The only Jesus people have access to, these theologians said, is the Jesus of the Gospels. Any other Jesus is just in the imagination of dreamy nineteenth-century rationalists such as Renan. In a sense, both argued that the historical details of Jesus' life are irrelevant to

Christian faith. "In history as such there is nothing so far as the eye can see which can provide a basis for faith," Barth remarked.[37] Bultmann was even more radical: "[W]e can know almost nothing concerning the life and personality of Jesus, since the early Christian sources show no interest in either, are moreover fragmentary and often legendary; and other sources about Jesus do not exist . . ."[38]

THE SECOND AND THIRD QUESTS

Thus, in the period between the two world wars, Christianity was at an impasse. Liberal Protestantism appeared bankrupt. The quest for a "scientific" portrait of Jesus was revealed as a dead end. Many theologians and Christian leaders accepted more or less as a given the same dogmatic disbelief exhibited by the rationalists of the nineteenth century—that miracles don't happen—but they lacked the cheerful optimism that science and social progress would somehow save mankind. The savage realities of trench warfare and the rise of fascism in the 1930s sowed the seeds of deep disillusion in people worldwide. There eventually arose a kind of "Christian existentialism" that put less emphasis on proving the historical facts in the New Testament and more on what it means to have faith in the first place. Karl Barth, the founder of what became known as neoorthodoxy, insisted that it is not human beings who are to evaluate God's Word but the other way around: God's Word judges human beings.

Needless to say, to many people such theological abstractions sounded dangerously close to the Christ myth theories David Strauss and others had espoused in the nineteenth century that we discussed in chapter 1. As a result, a reaction set in against the existentialist theologians of the early twentieth century, and a second and then a third quest for the historical Jesus was launched. The "new" or second quest, which began in the 1950s and 60s with students of Bultmann, such as C. H. Dodd, Oscar Cullmann, and Günther Bornkamm, was followed by a third quest, which began in the 1970s and continues today. These later two efforts to discover a "real" or historical Jesus behind the alleged inconsistencies, implausibilities, and embellishments of the gospel accounts are generally marked by a greater humility than the first quest. Their practitioners have availed themselves of all the tools of New Testament scholarship—such as source, form, and redaction criticism—and added to them a new effort to investigate Jesus within the context of Second Temple Judaism and Galilean society.

MODERN SCHOLARS DISAGREE SHARPLY ON WHO JESUS WAS

Today, studying the New Testament on the graduate level is a lot like watching the film *A Beautiful Mind* for the first time. The 2001 film starring Russell Crowe is about the life of the genius mathematician John Nash, a Nobel laureate in economics who made major contributions to the study of game theory, differential geometry, and other esoteric disciplines. In the first half of the film, viewers watch as Nash pursues graduate studies in mathematics and then is recruited by the US government for top-secret work in cryptography, the decoding of enemy communications. It's the height of the Cold War. Nash's government contact explains that the Russians are sending secret messages to their agents in the field via US newspapers. Nash's job, using his advanced skills as a mathematician, is to find the patterns in seemingly random bits of news and decode these secret Soviet messages.

As you watch the film, it all seems very plausible. Nash puzzles out elaborate mathematical formulae on blackboards and meets with his government intelligence contact; it makes perfect sense that some NSA-like organization recruited him to decode secret messages. But halfway through the film the scriptwriters reveal the truth: Nash is mentally ill—clinically insane. All the previous scenes of him doing top-secret government work— the meeting with a top intelligence officer, the decoding of messages—were not real and were all in his imagination. Nash is still brilliant, of course. He still knows more about mathematics than just about anyone on the planet, but his grasp of reality, of the big picture, simply isn't there.

Contemporary biblical scholarship can sometimes seem like this. Students follow brilliant scholars through long, complex, tortuous historical arguments—some historical Jesus books are more than eight hundred pages long—only to find, at the end, a conclusion that contradicts not only what the Gospels themselves affirm about Jesus but also what most other experts say as well.

New Testament scholars master the minutiae of ancient history. They learn ancient Greek, Hebrew, and Aramaic, sometimes even Akkadian and Ugaritic. They use computer programs to analyze the New Testament texts, trying to discern the various "strata," or stages of development, in the gospel narratives. They create hypothetical sources behind the gospel texts and then try to identify strata in those. They come up with very plausible-sounding criteria for evaluating which sayings or deeds of Jesus recorded in the Gospels are likely authentic or not—such as the famous "criterion of dissimilarity," which asserts that if a saying of Jesus too closely resembles something the early Christian community might have said, it's likely that Jesus *didn't* say it. But when they're all done, many of the theories that these scholars come up with begin to seem as plausible as John Nash's work decoding newspaper articles. That doesn't mean you should ignore their work—like John Nash, who won the Nobel Prize, they are often brilliant—but it does mean you have to exercise a little common sense when evaluating their more radical proposals.

To place things in perspective, let's run through the top eight models[39] of who Jesus purportedly was that have been proposed by elite scholars today—the big name New Testament scholars who write most of the historical Jesus books.

Model 1: Deluded Apocalyptic Prophet

This is probably the most common view of Jesus held by scholars in secular universities and in more liberal Christian seminaries. It's the view held by such luminaries as Albert Schweitzer, John P. Meier, E. P. Sanders, Paula Fredriksen, Gerd Lüdemann, and, most recently, Bart Ehrman and James Tabor. In essence, this view is that Jesus was essentially a delusional fanatic who believed that the world was about to come to a crashing halt.

"There should be little doubt that Jesus taught that the end of the age, with the appearance of the Son of Man, would occur shortly, within his own generation," Bart Ehrman writes in his 2012 book, *Did Jesus Exist?*[40] Jesus "believed that God would soon intervene in the course of human affairs to destroy the Romans, and *everyone else opposed to him,* before setting up his kingdom on earth" and awarding Jesus with the throne.[41]

Many other top scholars agree: The "good news" that Jesus proclaimed was holy war, the promise that God was about to kill all the Romans!

According to Paula Fredriksen, a widely respected Jewish New Testament scholar now at the Hebrew University of Jerusalem, what made Jesus unique in the world of Second Temple messianic pretenders and prophets was not his proclamation of the kingdom of God but his timetable. Other prophets and messiahs, at Qumran and in Galilee, said the kingdom was coming. Jesus said it was *already here*. "Jesus had stepped up the Kingdom's time-table from *soon* to *now*," Fredriksen writes in her book *Jesus of Nazareth: King of the Jews*.[42]

Of course, the central question is what Jesus meant by the "kingdom." It is by no means clear that by "kingdom" Jesus meant the end of the world. Yet that is the assumption that underlies the arguments of those who claim Jesus was an apocalyptic prophet. The kingdom of God for Jesus, according to these scholars, meant that God was about to intervene directly in human history, kill all the Romans, and establish Jesus as the ruler of the world. But that is not actually what the gospel texts say. Jesus' description of the kingdom in the Gospels does not sound at all like war or even like a political organization. It sounds more like an ideal human community—or a wedding banquet (Matt. 22:1–11). Jesus tells everyone he meets that the kingdom is "good news" (Luke 4:43), "like treasure hidden in a field" (Matt. 13:44 NRSV). When John the Baptist sends a message to Jesus from prison, asking whether Jesus is the messiah or if they should expect another, Jesus provides a description of the kingdom he is proclaiming: "The blind receive their sight, the lame walk, the lepers are cleansed, the deaf hear, the dead are raised, and the poor have good news brought to them" (Matt. 11: 5–7 NRSV). Finally, throughout the New Testament a recurring theme is that establishing the kingdom is the task of Jesus' followers. The apostle Paul tells the Romans that "the kingdom of God is not a matter of eating and drinking, but of righteousness, peace and joy in the Holy Spirit" (Rom. 14:17 NIV). In his letter to the Colossians (4:11 NRSV), Paul talks about his "co-workers for the kingdom of God," implying that the kingdom is not the Day of Judgment at the end of time but something for which Jesus' followers must "work."

Model 2: Violent Revolutionary

This is the view of Jesus espoused by Hermann Reimarus,[43] Joel Carmichael,[44] S. G. F. Brandon,[45] Robert Eisenman[46] of California State

University Long Beach, and, most recently, Reza Aslan,[47] the Muslim author of the international bestseller *Zealot*. This theory is fairly self-explanatory and builds on the claim that Jesus was an apocalyptic prophet. These writers assert that Jesus wasn't content to wait for God to intervene and destroy all the Romans; he actually wanted to kill them himself—or, at the very least, was sympathetic to those who did. For these authors, Jesus was a Jewish nationalist who wanted to overthrow the Roman occupation forces in Palestine. His original followers were more like violent Muslim jihadists than the peaceful advocates of nonviolence, brotherly love, and turning the other cheek depicted in the Gospels. In fact, they suggest the Gospels are a deliberate cover-up of what really happened between Jesus' followers and the Romans. They claim that the Gospels were written after the disastrous Jewish War of AD 66–70 to assure the victorious Romans that the followers of Jesus were no threat whatsoever because they were really a peaceful group with no interest in politics. "The author of the Markan Gospel, seeking . . . to explain the Roman execution of Jesus, presented Jesus as the victim of the hatred of the Jewish leaders," writes Brandon in his classic book, *Jesus and the Zealots*. "This Markan portrait was designed . . . to meet the needs of the Christian community in Rome, involved as it was in the aftermath of the Jewish War. It was an ad hoc presentation, being primarily concerned with showing that Jesus had been loyal to the Roman government in Judaea."[48]

Model 3: Social Reformer and Community Organizer

In this view, advocated by scholars Richard Horsley, Hyam Maccoby, and Gerd Theissen, Jesus was a prophet in the classical sense—a proponent of radical social change who wanted to overturn the unjust social structures of his age. The "sweeping program of community renewal"[49] that Jesus began in Galilee was a form of nonviolent resistance to the barbarism and economic oppression of the Roman Empire and its corrupt client-rulers in Palestine. For Horsley especially, Jesus seems to have been engaged in a very practical, this-worldly political and social struggle, but not a military one. He was a first-century "community organizer" who attempted to revitalize the villages of Galilee without actually taking up the sword.[50] "The mission of Jesus' disciples was an ambitious yet down-to-earth attempt to overturn the accepted order through a revolution in the people's behavior,"

Horsley and Neil Asher Silberman write.[51] Jesus and his followers did this by proclaiming a new movement of covenantal renewal in which villages would recommit themselves to the ideals of social justice in the Torah—and turn their backs on the pagan practices of economic exploitation and taxation foisted upon them by the Herodians (such as Herod Antipas). An important symbol of this new movement of community renewal was the series of village banquets Jesus encouraged and sponsored in which the poor and starving were invited and treated like guests of honor. "When you give a banquet," Luke quotes Jesus as saying, "invite the poor, the crippled, the lame, and the blind" (Luke 14:13 NRSV). The sharing of food, such as the multiplication of loaves and fishes, was at the center of what Jesus was doing in Galilee, these scholars claim. The ordinary people "could remain within their villages, freely and willingly sharing, rather than allow themselves to become beasts of burden to build theatres and forums, to plow and harvest fields now owned by others, or bring to the palaces of the high and mighty the first-fruits of the land," Horsley writes.[52]

Horsley, Maccoby, and Theissen do not agree with those who say Jesus was a Zealot or a Zealot sympathizer. Theissen cites the fact that none of Jesus' disciples were arrested after him as proof that the Roman authorities did not believe Jesus headed a revolutionary group. The cleansing of the temple, which advocates for the Jesus-as-Zealot model insist was an actual attack, was what the Gospels imply it was, a symbolic prophetic action.

However, others in this group agree with the Zealot advocates that the Gospels are not an accurate reflection of what Jesus was really like or intended to achieve. Horsley believes that by the time the gospels of Matthew and Luke were written in the late 80s and 90s AD, the followers of Jesus had already "sold out"[53] Jesus' radical political ideals and settled into comfortable lives of suburban domesticity—or at least what would have passed for suburban domesticity in the first century. In this sense, the gospels were distortions of what happened, just as S. G. F. Brandon claimed, designed to curry favor with the Romans and to show that they had nothing to fear from the followers of Jesus and vice versa.[54] The gospel of Luke, especially, Horsley and Brandon suggest, is actually imperial propaganda—with the major events in Jesus' life marked by the names of the Roman emperors. For the evangelist Luke, "God's blessing had been transferred from the People of Israel to the faithful Christian subjects of the Roman Empire," Horsley writes. "All the events of salvation were related to imperial chronology . . ."[55]

Model 4: Wisdom Sage

The next model of who Jesus was takes an approach almost opposite to that of the social reformer advocates. This model was famously promoted in the 1990s by associates of the Jesus Seminar, an informal group of academics, intellectuals, and New Testament scholars who met and voted on which sayings of Jesus were "authentic" and which were created by the early Christian community. The Jesus Seminar experts decided that "about 18 percent of the sayings and 16 percent of the deeds attributed to Jesus in the gospels are authentic."[56] For many of the scholars associated with the Jesus Seminar, such as Robert Funk and John Dominic Crossan, Jesus was really a "wisdom sage," an itinerent preacher of timeless moral truths similar to the Cynic philosophers in the Greek world. In our terms, this model of Jesus paints him as a kind of proto-hippie who advocated a countercultural lifestyle that eschewed economic ambition and "family values." Crossan, a cofounder of the Jesus Seminar, says this explicitly in his 1991 classic, *The Historical Jesus.* Cynics "were hippies in a world of Augustan yuppies," he writes. "Jesus and his followers . . . fit very well against *that* background."[57] Did not Jesus insist that only the Gentiles ("the nations") worried about what they would eat or what they would wear (Luke 12:30)? Did he not say in the age to come no one will marry (Matt. 22:30)? Crossan and others who share his outlook agree with the social reformer advocates that "free healing and common eating" lay at the heart of Jesus' message, but for Crossan this was less a political organizing tactic than a lifestyle choice. Jesus moved about, proclaiming the "brokerless" kingdom of God, which means, apparently, that individuals should enter into direct relationships with God and one another without a "mediator," such as the Jerusalem temple or even himself.[58]

Model 5: Charismatic Faith Healer

The fifth model of Jesus was pioneered by the late Jewish scholar Geza Vermes and by Marcus Borg, a New Testament scholar at Oregon State

University and a fellow of the Jesus Seminar. Both of these scholars believe that Jesus did not see himself in any way as the messiah, nor did he believe the world was about to come to an end. He was not an apocalyptic prophet, expecting God to kill all the Romans, and he certainly did not advocate violent revolution. Instead, in this view Jesus was primarily a *hasid*, a charismatic Jewish holy man and faith healer. Beginning with his 1973 book, *Jesus the Jew*, Vermes argues that Jesus never intended to reform Judaism and start a new religious movement: Christianity was all essentially a mistake, a misunderstanding of what Jesus was really all about. Jesus' mission, as a kind of proto-Hasidic rabbi, was solely to the house of Israel, to his fellow Jews. However, in his zeal he caused a major scene on the Temple Mount and the authorities, rightfully fearful of the crowds at Passover, had Jesus arrested. He was executed as a political troublemaker when really he was nothing of the kind. "As far as basic Jewish beliefs are concerned, the only serious clash reported in the Gospels between Jesus and the Jewish authority finds him opposing the Sadducees in their denial of the resurrection of the dead," Vermes writes.[59] He was just a sincere Jewish rabbi who got a bit carried away and, due to the turmoil of the times, paid for it with his life. Vermes agrees with Jewish writers like Rabbi Shmuley Boteach[60] that Jesus was, more or less, an ordinary Jew, but he disagrees that he was a "patriot" who wanted to liberate the Jewish people from the Romans. Borg also sees Jesus primarily as a charismatic figure but, unlike Vermes, he is willing to see him more as a religious revolutionary. Borg does not believe Jesus expected the end of the world to come in his lifetime, as so many academic scholars suggest, but he does think Jesus intended to found a subversive *religious* movement within Judaism. As he explains in his clear and concise 2008 book, *Jesus: The Life, Teachings, and Relevance of a Religious Revolutionary*, Borg believes that Jesus had an essentially spiritual message. He was a "man of the Spirit" and emphasized a spiritual approach to the Torah, one that elevated the practice of compassion and mercy above strict adherence to ritual laws of purity.[61]

Model 6: Jewish Messiah

By this point it may seem difficult to believe, but there are a few academic New Testament scholars who argue that Jesus was, in fact, what he is portrayed as being in the New Testament: the messiah prophesized in the Hebrew scriptures. Perhaps the foremost exponents of this radical, contrarian view among academics are the Anglican bishop and New Testament scholar N. T. Wright, the Catholic scholar and former Benedictine monk Luke Timothy Johnson, and Robert Stein, a professor of New Testament at Southern Baptist Theological Seminary in Louisville, Kentucky, and author of the widely studied book *Jesus the Messiah.* Of these, N. T. Wright is probably the most influential and widely known through his many books and his public position as a prelate in the Anglican Church, although Luke Timothy Johnson also has a wide following. Wright argues strenuously that many facts about Jesus can be known for certain, and, even more controversially, he is one of the few Jesus scholars who argue that Jesus set out quite deliberately to get himself killed in fulfillment of various messianic prophecies. In fact, although Wright is often considered a conservative, he admits that he follows Dr. Albert Schweitzer quite closely in his belief that Jesus was acting out a kind of messianic script and deliberately provoked his own death.[62]

Wright is rare among academic New Testament scholars in that he makes a heroic attempt to incorporate most of what the Gospels say into a grand synthesis—and thus he offers explanations for the atonement themes that permeate some of the New Testament texts. Wright is also rare because he asks if it is even conceivable that Jesus deliberately intended to die—and, if so, what he could possibly have thought his death would accomplish. Wright's proposal is that Jesus thought of his Passion as his ultimate prophetic symbolic action. Like the prophet Ezekiel, Wright says, Jesus decided he would "symbolically . . . undergo the fate he had announced, in symbol and word, for Jerusalem as a whole."[63] Like the prophets before him, Jesus was warning Israel of the consequences of compromising with paganism—only this time it was paganism's power politics—its reliance upon the sword—that was being judged.

Wright believes Jesus declared that the Way of the kingdom is one of peace, not suicidal war, and, as Israel's messiah, Jesus would "lose the battle on Israel's behalf."[64] And what would that accomplish exactly? Wright struggles to make this clear, but says that Jesus would "let them do their worst to him, believing that the dawning kingdom would see him vindicated."[65] In that sense, Jesus took upon himself the "wrath"[66]—not of God—but that which Israel's military ambitions would inevitably provoke from the Romans. Jesus "would go ahead of his people, to take upon himself both the fate that they had suffered one way or another for half a millennium at the hands of pagan empires and the fate that his contemporaries were apparently hell-bent upon pulling down on their own heads once for all," Wright concludes.[67]

As Wright makes clear in later works, such as *The Challenge of Jesus* and *Simply Jesus*, this understanding of Jesus' mission is not the same as the atonement model we will discuss next; rather, it is, in Wright's view, the "root from which that theology would have grown."[68] For Wright, Jesus' death was his own ultimate symbolic enactment, his final demonstration, of what the new covenant entails: ultimate victory from ultimate defeat, redemption through suffering.

Wright concludes:

> Instead of the insults and threats that the [earlier Maccabean] martyrs had hurled at their accusers, Jesus, as the entire many-sided early Christian tradition bears witness, suffered in silence, except for words of forgiveness and hope. This is so remarkable an innovation into the martyr-tradition that it is quite inexplicable unless it is true to the historical facts. Having been known for his remarkable compassion throughout his public work, Jesus' last great act drew into one that giving of himself for others to which the early church referred so regularly and with such awe.[69]

Model 7: Atoning Sacrifice

Another model of Jesus that is common among many Christian scholars is that he came simply to offer himself as a sacrifice on the cross to atone for the sins of the human race. In this view, Jesus' death was his primary mission, the purpose to which he had dedicated his entire ministry. One of the very earliest statements of Christian belief, found in Paul's first letter to the Corinthians and dating to the first years after the crucifixion, is that Jesus died "for" or "on behalf of" (the Greek *huper*) "our sins": "I handed on to you as of first importance what I in turn had received: that *Christ died for our sins* in accordance with the scriptures" (15:3 NRSV, emphasis added).

In the Gospels, Jesus describes his mission as one of service and "to give his life" as a "ransom": "The Son of Man did not come to be served but to serve and to give his life as a ransom [*lutron*] for many" (Mark 10:45; Matt. 20:28). A "ransom" is the price that is paid to free a hostage or kidnapping victim. Furthermore, many passages in the Gospels portray Jesus as *fore-seeing* his own execution and even, in some sense, viewing it as his destiny. In Mark 8, Jesus tells his disciples that "the Son of Man must suffer many things and be rejected by the elders, the chief priests and the teachers of the law, and . . . must be killed and after three days rise again" (v. 31 NIV). Jesus predicts his own death three separate times in the Synoptics.

Finally, Christian scholars say Jesus clearly saw his likely death as an *act of sacrifice,* quoting Jesus' words in the gospel of John: "Greater love has no one than this: to lay down one's life for one's friends" (15:13 NIV). That is also the essence of what Jesus was communicating at the Last Supper ritual—that in some way he was giving up his life to save human beings. In Mark's version, Jesus says of the cup that it is "my blood of the covenant" which is "poured out for many" (14:24 NIV). Matthew expands this slightly but significantly, adding the words "for the forgiveness of sins" (26:28 NIV).

Almost all Christian churches accept the fact of the atonement, in some sense, as part of the essence of the Christian message. Even so, many theories have been proposed over the centuries for precisely how, or in what way, Jesus' death is a saving act. Christianity's first theologian, the apostle Paul, insisted that Jesus was in some way a "sacrifice" that reconciled human beings to God. In his letter to the Romans, for example, Paul wrote that God sent "his own son in the likeness of sinful flesh to be a sin offering" (8:3 NIV), adding that God "did not spare his own Son, but gave him up for us all" (8:32 NIV). What's more, Paul repeatedly proclaimed that human beings are somehow saved by Jesus' "blood." He wrote that "we have now been justified by his blood" (Rom. 5:9 NIV), even adding that God put forth Jesus as a "sacrifice of atonement [*hilasterion*][70] by his blood" (Rom. 3:25 NRSV). Thus, whatever else Jesus understood his mission to be—proclaiming the gospel, healing the sick, inaugurating a new global movement—his earliest followers saw part of that mission as involving the voluntary sacrifice of his own life on humanity's behalf.

But how does this atoning sacrifice actually work? For the first thousand years of Christianity, the dominant view was that Jesus' death was, as Jesus himself said, a ransom or payment to free human beings from the bondage of sin. But to whom was the ransom paid? The early church fathers, including Augustine, said the ransom was paid to Satan—and thus Jesus' death freed human beings from the bondage of Satan's influence. Later, Anselm of Canterbury (ca. 1033–1109) insisted this theory gave Satan too much power, and that, in fact, the ransom was paid not to Satan but to God as a "satisfaction" of God's honor.[71] The Protestant Reformers, led by the lawyer John Calvin, modified this theory by replacing God's honor with his justice. The Reformers insisted that when the Bible says Jesus died "for" human beings' sins, it means not "on behalf of" or "for the sake of," but "in place of." In this view, the sins of the human race were and are so horrific that God's righteous wrath had to be appeased and his justice fulfilled, and so he sent his Son, Jesus, to die in our place as a vicarious sacrifice. Jesus bore the full weight of God's punishment—just as the prophet Isaiah said, "he was pierced for our transgressions . . . crushed for our iniquities" (53:5 NIV)—and thus humanity's sins have been wiped clean or are no longer counted against us. For some Christians, the view that Jesus died as a vicarious sacrifice to uphold God's justice is the very essence of the gospel message. "Few other doctrines go to the heart of the Christian faith like the Atonement," writes one pastor, Mark Dever, in an article in *Christianity Today* entitled "Nothing But the Blood." *"At stake is nothing less than the essence of Christianity."*[72]

Model 8: Founder of a Global Movement

The understanding of Jesus' mission just described above—known technically as the penal substitution theory of the atonement—has become increasingly controversial in recent years, particularly among secular New Testament scholars.[73] One reason is that nowhere in the Gospels does Jesus himself say that his *death* will save people from their sins. Instead, in the Gospels Jesus says that his "purpose" is to "preach the good news of the kingdom of God" (Luke 4:43 ESV)—and, long before he dies, repeatedly insists that people are *already* saved from their sins, that God's mercy and forgiveness extends even to the wretched outcasts of society whom the pious condemn as sinners (Luke 5:20). He tells the religious elites of his age

65

that prostitutes and swindlers are more righteous in the eyes of God than they are (Matt. 21:31). In fact, E. P. Sanders, an influential historical Jesus scholar, contends that one of the most distinctive characteristics of Jesus of Nazareth was that he appeared to offer forgiveness to "sinners" (*hamartoloi*) "*without* requiring repentance as ordinarily understood; that is, without requiring the offering of sacrifice and, in the case of an offense against another person, providing the required restitution . . . and then keeping the law obediently."[74]

Thus, some secular New Testament scholars and some churches accept the final model of Jesus as the founder of a radical social and religious movement that would eventually become the Christian church.[75] In this view, Jesus did indeed see himself as the *herald and agent* of God's rescue operation for the human race, and he accurately foretold that his mission to inaugurate this new era in human history and in mankind's relationship to its Creator would likely get him killed. In this view, Jesus did indeed sacrifice himself for humanity: he willingly gave his life as "a ransom for many" (Mark 10:45). Despite what N. T. Wright and advocates for the penal substitution understanding of the atonement claim, scholars advocating the Jesus-as-global-movement-founder model believe that Jesus' intended purpose *wasn't* to die. That was why he begged God, in the Garden of Gethsemane, to take the cup of his suffering from him. Rather, they view his death as simply the foreseeable price Jesus was willing to pay in order to complete his mission. In this view, Jesus came to inaugurate a new way of being human—the way that God intended from the beginning. This new Way, what Jesus called at the Last Supper a "new covenant" between God and the entire human race, would start small—like a mustard seed—but would eventually grow until it filled and transformed the world, like leaven in dough. Bringing the seed and leaven of this new type of human community, what he called the kingdom of God, was Jesus' mission, and he was willing to die in order to make sure the seed was planted. In that sense, advocates for the global-movement-founder model would say that Jesus did sacrifice himself in order to bring God's message of forgiveness and mercy to the world—and in that sense, he was an overwhelming success, not a failure. They claim that human beings are saved through the influence of, and by being incorporated into, the community of believers that Jesus founded, because that is where Jesus is proclaimed—where his message is heard and his saving grace accepted. "Therefore he who would find Christ must first find the Church," wrote the Protestant reformer Martin Luther. "How should we know where Christ and his faith were, if we did not know where his believers are? And he who would know anything of Christ must not trust himself nor build a bridge to heaven by his own reason; but he must go to the Church, attend and ask her. Now the Church is not wood and stone, but the company of believing people; one must hold to them, and see how they believe, live and teach; they surely have Christ in their midst. For outside of the Christian church there is no truth, no Christ, no salvation."[76]

For advocates of this model, Jesus did see himself, in some way, as the fulfillment of Israel's prophecies for a future messiah, but what he had in mind far outstripped the messianic concepts available during his time. And such concepts were only an approximation in any case. The messianic age that Jesus inaugurated is still in its earliest phases, and it's up to all people inspired by his message to help build the kingdom of God on earth. That kingdom already exists elsewhere in the cosmos, but the task for humans is to make it real on earth as well. That's the essence of the prayer Jesus taught his followers: "Your kingdom come . . . on earth as it is in heaven" (Matt. 6:10 NRSV).

In the end, of course, it's possible to affirm simultaneously several of these various models of who Jesus was and what he was trying to do; and these models reflect the beliefs of different Christian denominations. For example, many Christian denominations believe that Jesus died to save human beings from their sins, that he was the fulfillment of various messianic prophecies in the Hebrew Bible, and that he founded a global movement, called the church, to continue his work on earth. Critical scholars, for their part, often embrace more than one model as well. Scholars who believe Jesus was a violent revolutionary can sometimes also insist he was an apocalyptic prophet who saw himself as the agent for God's wrath. What is clear, however, is that all these models can't be correct. It is implausible that Jesus was both a nonviolent advocate for social renewal in Galilee and, at the same time, a revolutionary plotting the overthrow of the Roman government in Palestine. That, alone, is reason to be skeptical of skeptical scholars: their pronouncements can sometimes seem mutually contradictory. Scholars such as Bart Ehrman and James Tabor insist Jesus was an "apocalyptic prophet" who expected the world to end at any moment, while other historical Jesus experts—such as N. T. Wright, John Dominic Crossan, Richard Horsley, Luke Timothy Johnson, and Marcus Borg— insist that simply isn't true. Finally, as we will see in later chapters, many of these models are now being openly questioned due to new discoveries in archaeology and New Testament studies. In chapters 5 and 10 especially, we will see that some of these models are now obsolete, or at least not as popular as they once were in the early twentieth century.

FOR FURTHER STUDY

Beilby, James K. and Paul Rhodes Eddy, eds. *The Historical Jesus: Five Views.* Downers Grove, IL: InterVarsity Press, 2009.

Crossley, James G. *Why Christianity Happened: A Sociohistorical Account of Christian Origins (26–50 CE).* Louisville, KY: Westminster John Knox Press, 2006.

Demarest, Bruce. *The Cross and Salvation.* Wheaton, IL: Crossway Books, 1997.

Dunn, James D. G. *Jesus Remembered.* Grand Rapids, MI: William B. Eerdmans, 2003.

Ehrman, Bart D. *Jesus: Apocalyptic Prophet of the New Millennium.* London: Oxford University Press, 1999.

Theissen, Gerd and Annette Merz. *The Historical Jesus: A Comprehensive Guide.* Minneapolis, MN: Fortress Press, 1998.

Witherington III, Ben. *The Jesus Quest: The Third Search for the Jew of Nazareth.* Downers Grove, IL: InterVarsity Press, 1995.

3

ARE THE GOSPELS FORGERIES?

Scholars Discover Manuscripts of the New Testament Dating Back to the Dawn of the Jesus Movement

"I, Paul, write this greeting in my own hand, which is the distinguishing mark in all my letters."

—2 THESSALONIANS 3:17 NIV

On February 1, 2012, one of the world's leading experts on ancient New Testament manuscripts made a startling announcement that caused a stir in scholarly circles. Daniel Wallace, director for the Center for the Study of New Testament Manuscripts at the Dallas Theological Seminary, was debating Bart Ehrman on Ehrman's home turf at the University of North Carolina at Chapel Hill. The debate concerned the text of the New Testament. Ehrman and other debunkers of Christianity like to point out that we don't have the original texts of the New Testament—only copies of copies of copies of copies. And it's true: for many parts of the New Testament, the earliest copies we have were written hundreds of years after the originals. In addition, we know that these copies of copies have been repeatedly changed over the centuries—usually accidentally and with only minor significance, but occasionally deliberately. Thus, Ehrman argues, we can't *really* be sure that what we read in our Bibles about Jesus accurately reflects what the New Testament writers themselves actually wrote.

This may sound like an esoteric debate of interest only to scholars, but it's of great significance. The issues that this debate raises go to the very heart of how scholars have approached the biblical texts for the past two hundred years—and challenge some of their most closely held assumptions about how the New Testament came to be written, whether it is a reliable witness to the events it describes, and whether Christians today can trust that what they read in the Gospels accurately reflects what happened.

Both Ehrman and Wallace are internationally renowned. They have debated each other at various university campuses over the last several years. Ehrman is a former Christian who became a respected New Testament textual critic, gradually lost his faith, and now is famous for writing a series of bestselling books that reveal, in his view, shocking truths about the origins of the New Testament. He alleges that scholars and clergy alike have kept these truths hidden from the general public for decades. Wallace, for his part, has become one of the world's foremost textual critics, defending both the basic integrity of the New Testament text and the general historical reliability of the Gospels.

During his 2012 debate with Ehrman, however, Wallace pulled an ace out of his sleeve: he revealed that researchers associated with his Center for the Study of New Testament Manuscripts had recently discovered *seven* previously unknown New Testament papyri—six of which probably date from the second century (AD 100–200) and one probably from the first (that is, the seventies, eighties, or nineties). The fragments would be published at a future date, he said. If most scholars support the dating of these ancient fragments, this is a major discovery that could change, but will more likely reinforce, what historians already know about the writing of the Gospels.

According to Wallace, the discovery of these ancient papyri means that we now have eighteen New Testament manuscripts from the second century and one from the first. He estimates that more than 43 percent of all New Testament verses are found in *just these eighteen early manuscripts.* That would lend considerable weight to the argument that the official Greek text of the New Testament, relied upon for most modern Bible translations, is pretty close to the original.

The most startling of the recent discoveries, according to Wallace, is the first-century fragment; it is from the gospel of Mark, which is widely believed by scholars to be the very first gospel written. The earliest manuscript of Mark we currently have, called P45, is dated to around the year AD 250. Thus, this new find would predate P45 by 100 to 150 years. "It was dated by one of the world's leading paleographers," Wallace wrote two weeks after the debate. "He said he was 'certain' that it was from the first century. If this is true, it would be the oldest fragment of the New Testament known to exist."[1]

This could very well be a monumental discovery—yet another way in which recent scholarship is uprooting the longstanding, outlandish portraits of Jesus that took root over the past hundred years or so. The more

Robert Hutchinson

The scholars associated with the Institute for New Testament Textual Research (Institut für Neutestamentliche Textforschung), based in a modest brick building at the University of Münster, Germany, combed through 5,800 ancient Greek manuscripts of the New Testament in order to prepare an "official" text used in most modern translations.

researchers study ancient papyri in general, the more convinced they are that our versions of the New Testament are very close to what the authors actually wrote nearly two thousand years ago. Thus, the portrait of Jesus passed on in the New Testament texts was not a series of legends concocted in the first centuries of the common era, as European philosophers such as Bruno Bauer (1809–1882) and David Strauss (1808–1874) claimed in the nineteenth century, but instead reflects what his earliest followers said and wrote in the decades immediately after his crucifixion.

WHERE DOES THE BIBLE COME FROM ANYWAY?

The Institute for New Testament Textual Research is located in a plain, three-story brick building at 1 Pferdegasse Street, across the street from the Museum of Art and Culture in the beautiful German university town of Münster. Recently in Bonn on business, I couldn't resist traveling two hours north to Münster to see the institute. When I was in graduate school, I was surprised to discover that virtually all translations of the New Testament found in modern Bibles—from the New Revised Standard Version (NRSV) and the New International Version (NIV) to the Catholic New American Bible and the Contemporary English Version (CEV)—are based on the decisions made at this institute in Münster. It was founded in 1952 by a German Bible scholar named Kurt Aland (1915–1994). Aland worked with another German scholar, Eberhard Nestle, to edit an edition of the Greek New Testament (the *Novum Testamentum Graece*) that has gradually become the de facto "official" text of the New Testament. Known as the Nestle-Aland text, now in its twenty-eighth edition (abbreviated NA28), it is the same text found in the United Bible Societies edition that is used by most modern Bible translators.

For a long time, this troubled me. Did it mean that Christian faith is ultimately based on the judgments not of the pope in Rome or the World Council of Churches or the Synod of Bishops in the Lutheran Church, but on the judgments of *five or ten obscure international scholars in Germany*? After all, if it is they who determine what the text of the New Testament is—and it is this text that is used for all modern translations—then their judgments are crucial for Christian faith.

Fortunately, most people don't arrive at faith in Jesus Christ through a study of textual variants in the gospel of Luke. And as we will see, these textual variants, while of interest to scholars and specialists, do not threaten any major Christian doctrine. The basic message of the gospel as revealed in the New Testament and passed on through Christian churches was proclaimed for fifteen hundred years before scholars began discovering ancient New Testament manuscripts and the modern science of textual criticism began.

The University of Münster, which lies in the heart of the city, is one of the most famous universities in Europe. Some of the biggest names in twentieth-century theology either studied or taught here—including the founder of Protestant neoorthodoxy, Karl Barth; Karl Rahner, S.J., who dominated Catholic theology in the second half of the twentieth century; Johann Baptist Metz; and a studious German professor who one day became Pope Benedict XVI. During the Second World War, Münster was also famous as the see of Cardinal Clemens August Graf von Galen, one of the very few German churchmen, Protestant or Catholic, who had the spine to stand up publicly against the Nazis and denounce their racial and euthanasia policies from the pulpit.

In contrast to the beauty and grandeur of Münster, the institute itself is relatively modest. It looks and feels like the entrance to the classics department of a medium-sized university, relegated to whatever quarters the more affluent departments no longer need or want. Despite its modest surroundings, however, it's difficult to exaggerate the institute's importance in the analysis and translation of the New Testament. Every modern translation of the New Testament, in almost every language, is based upon a critical edition prepared by the Institute's international team of scholars, which determines as closely as possible what the original books of the New Testament said in the original Greek. Many teams working on new translations of the Bible have their own text-critical scholars, and they are free to decide for themselves which reading of a particular passage they want to use. But by and large, most modern translations follow very closely the decisions made at this German university institute.

Although the institute was only founded in 1952, scholars have been at this work now for four hundred years. The first edition of the Greek New Testament was printed in 1514 by Cardinal Francisco Jiménez de Cisneros, but publication was delayed until 1520. In the intervening years, Erasmus of Rotterdam brought out his own text of the Greek New Testament, hastily published in 1516. Scholars have been revising these texts ever since, as new ancient manuscripts are discovered and new methods developed for figuring out which variant is more authentic.

After years of relative obscurity, the work of the institute has suddenly taken on a more public role. That's because in the past few years a handful of New Testament scholars have questioned whether we can really know what the evangelists actually wrote when they wrote the Gospels, what Paul wrote when he wrote his letters, and so on.

Naturally, this cynicism has caught the attention of the media. It is similar to another small but influential voice in Near Eastern studies, those known as "biblical minimalists," who claim there is little if any evidence that the central figures of the Hebrew Bible ever existed (Moses, King David, and the like). The minimalists claim that most of what passes for history in the Hebrew Bible is, in essence, complete fiction. This, too, is not a majority view among experts in Near Eastern history, but it has received a disproportionate amount of media coverage and now has become a pop culture "meme" that frequently goes unquestioned.

During my visit to the institute, I was met by Dr. Georg Gäbel, a genial man in his early forties with a short beard and a rather scholarly looking old sweater. Dr. Gäbel's office looked like that of any academic, piled high with books and papers, so he took me down to the institute's small library so we could have some room to chat. In the hours to come, he would generously offer background to some key questions, as presented below.

WHERE DO WE GET OUR BIBLES?

Most people—even most Christians and Jews—know very little about the arcane world of biblical manuscripts. We usually get our Bibles the same way we get our food: we go to a store, pay money, and don't usually ask too many questions about where either the food or Bibles come from. In the case of the Bible, we know that different teams of scholars produce new translations every few years—such as the Contemporary English Version (CEV, 1995) and the English Standard Version (ESV, 2001)—but we usually don't ask where the translators get *their* Bibles. From which Bible do the translators, well, translate? Is there some ancient copy of the Bible somewhere, written in Hebrew and Greek, that the translators all use when they make their translations into modern English, Spanish, or French?

The answer is, actually, no—there isn't.

In the early years of the Christian movement, many different groups and individuals wrote about Jesus. But there weren't any printing presses in the first century, only hand-copied scrolls or little booklets called codices. For a written work to be "published" and read by other people, it had to be copied by hand, letter by letter, word by word. We know about dozens of works that have been lost. Eventually, the followers of Jesus recognized that some of these works were more authentic than others—for example, those allegedly written by people who knew the apostles. Some works, while *claiming* to be authored by an apostle, obviously weren't because they were full of bizarre theosophical ramblings that had nothing to do with what the earthly Jesus said and did.

The early Christian community had to decide, within the first two centuries of the Jesus movement, which of these works most accurately reflected the Christian faith and which did not. Lists of approved books were drawn up. Eventually, early theologians like Origen (184–253) and local church councils like Hippo (393) and Carthage (397) recognized the four gospels of Matthew, Mark, Luke, and John, and twenty-three other works, as "God-breathed" (2 Tim. 3:16) or inspired, and thus they became the official canon of the New Testament. This anthology of writing about Jesus was translated from the original Greek into many different ancient languages. Finally, in the early fifth century, a scholar named Jerome translated the entire New Testament into Latin; that, along with Jerome's translation of the Hebrew scriptures, became the official Bible of Christianity for more than a thousand years. It's known as the Vulgate because it was written in colloquial ("vulgar") Latin.

In the years immediately preceding the Protestant Reformation, when Greek manuscripts of the New Testament were surfacing, some scholars thought it might be a good idea to compare the official Latin Vulgate translation with the ancient Greek manuscripts they were finding. They wanted to make sure Jerome got things right, and to aid translations into vernacular languages. At the dawn of the Protestant Reformation in the early 1500s, when the cry of Christian humanists everywhere was for a return *ad fontes,* "to the sources"—not just for the Bible but for texts of Aristotle and the other ancients—the push to find better, more accurate manuscripts gained momentum.

When the Catholic priest and scholar Desidarius Erasmus of Rotterdam was compiling one of the first Greek editions of the New Testament, published

Shutterstock

The Christian humanist Desidarius Erasmus (1466–1536) published the first printed text of the Greek New Testament in 1516 based on twelfth-century manuscripts he obtained in Basel. Also known as the Textus Receptus, *Erasmus's Greek text was used by Tyndale for the first English New Testament (1526) and by translators of the King James Version (1611).*

in 1516, he sought to find as many Greek manuscripts as he could. Unfortunately, he didn't have the same resources we have today—and for some passages he was forced to translate from the Latin Vulgate back into Greek as best he could, creating versions that don't exist in *any* Greek manuscripts. As Ehrman informs us, Erasmus's Greek New Testament was largely based on a very late, twelfth-century Greek manuscript, and it was basically this text that the translators of the King James Bible used when creating their timeless English translation. This is one reason why the KJV Bible differs in many places from modern English translations, which are based on far more ancient Greek manuscripts and are thus more reliably accurate.

In the centuries after Erasmus worked, however, biblical scholars have discovered *thousands* of ancient Greek manuscripts of the New Testament, some dating back to the fourth, third, even second centuries. In a few instances, they've even discovered fragments of the gospels dating back to the early second century. We also now have two complete Greek Bibles that date to around the AD 350s—Codex Vaticanus, housed in the Vatican Library, and Codex Sinaiticus, discovered in 1844 by German biblical scholar Constantin von Tischendorf in Saint Catherine's Monastery at the foot of the mountain traditionally believed to be the original Mount Sinai, in the Sinai Peninsula.[2] These two ancient codices, or bound books, have been central to the scholarly reconstruction of the Greek New Testament and are the basis for most modern translations. Yet as old as they are, Codex Vaticanus and Codex Sinaiticus often disagree. In fact, one scholar estimated that they disagree 3,036 times—although most are small spelling differences that don't really matter much.[3] It's a fascinating story that Bart Ehrman, in his many popular books, tells well, in some detail and with a certain bombastic flourish.

WHAT EVIDENCE DO WE HAVE?

At last count, there are approximately 5,800 manuscripts of the New Testament written on scraps of parchment scrolls or bound together in little booklets, dating back to the first thousand years of Christianity. They are now housed in museums and libraries all over the world. These thousands of ancient scrolls and books were all hand copied by scribes— copies of copies of copies, as Bart Ehrman says—and their Greek texts don't always agree with each other on every line. Some words, phrases, entire paragraphs, and even entire books found in one manuscript are missing in others. They range from papyrus fragments no bigger than a credit card, dating to the AD 200s, to complete bound codices of the entire Bible from the twelfth century. As mentioned earlier, there is also a possibility that we have recently unearthed a papyrus manuscript that dates all the way back to the first century, within just a few decades of the originals (or "autographs"). Textual critics divide these 5,800 manuscripts into three basic categories: papyri, majuscules, and minuscules.

Wikipedia

The Ryland Papyrus P52, the earliest surviving piece of New Testament scripture. A fragment of a papyrus codex containing John 18:31–33 and 37–38, this papyrus was found in Egypt and has been dated to about AD 125. It currently resides at the John Rylands Library in Manchester, England.

Papyri

At the bottom of each page of the Greek New Testaments that seminary students use, such as the Nestle-Aland twenty-eighth edition, there is what's called a "critical apparatus," or series of symbols that lets students know which ancient manuscripts contain the texts that the editors used for a particular passage. The New Testament papyri are denoted by the capital letter *P* followed by a number from their order of discovery. For example, the most famous is P52, a papyrus fragment identified in 1934, with the text of John 18:31–33 on one side and John 18:37–38 on the other. Discovered in 1920 in a treasure trove of ancient documents in a garbage dump in Egypt, this incredible document lay unnoticed in the John Rylands Library at the University of Manchester until it was identified by a researcher named C. H. Roberts. Experts dated it from between AD 100 to around 150, with a consensus of around 125. Until the recent announcement by Dr. Wallace, the papyrus discovery that had critics most excited was probably P75, a codex dated between AD 175 and 225, which contains the earliest text we have of the gospel of Luke and one of the earliest of John.[4]

Majuscules (Once Called "Uncials")

These are codices of parchment (treated animal skins) bound into a book format, all written with Greek capital letters and usually without any spaces or punctuation between the words, like this passage at the beginning of the gospel of John: ΕΝΑΡΧΗΗΝΟΛΟΓΟΣΚΑΙΟΛΟΓΟΣ ("in the beginning was the Word and the Word . . ."). They date from the fourth to the tenth century and, next to the papyri, are considered the most important "witnesses" to the original or earliest Greek text. Among the most famous majuscule codices is the aforementioned Codex Sinaiticus (usually designated with the Hebrew letter aleph, א). This entire codex is now available online, and you can read for yourself the corrections scribes made to the text.[5] In the critical apparatus at the bottom of Greek New Testaments used for study, the scribal corrections are indicated with superscript letters, such as א[a] or א[b].

Other famous examples of early codices are Codex Vaticanus, dating from AD 325–350 and designated with a capital *B*; Codex Alexandrinus, dating from the fifth century and designated with a capital *A*; Codex Ephraemi, dating from the fifth century and designated with a capital *C*; and Codex Bezae, dating from the fifth century and designated with a capital *D*.

Minuscules

These are smaller codices or books made out of vellum or calfskin and dating from the ninth century onward, using a small cursive Greek script, known as minuscule, similar to that found in most Greek New Testaments today. There are at least 2,400 examples of these minuscule codices.[6] There are so many, in fact, that they are referred to just by numbers in the Greek New Testament critical apparatus—for example, 1230 or 1079.

In addition to these three categories of actual manuscripts of the Greek New Testament, there are a few other important categories of "witnesses" to the original text of the New Testament.

Lectionaries

Lectionaries are collections of scriptural passages used for public readings in churches, usually arranged for each day of the year. Textual critics use primarily the medieval Greek lectionaries (that is, where the passages are all taken from the Greek New Testament). They date from the ninth century onward and are designated by a small letter *L* followed by a number—such as l10 or l12. The editors of the Greek New Testament cite more than 200 Greek lectionaries[7] in their preparation of the official text of the New Testament, but there are actually more than 2,280 lectionary manuscripts.[8] One famous Greek lectionary, known as Lectionary 150 or Codex Harleianus, is an elaborate illuminated book dating before AD 1000 and on display in the British Library. Copied by a priest named Constantine, the lectionary is originally from Constantinople, the capital of the old Byzantine Empire.

Ancient Translations

The New Testament was quickly translated from the original Greek, in which all or most of it was written, into other ancient languages—such as Latin, Syriac, Coptic, Armenian, Ethiopic, Nubian, Gothic, Old Church Slavonic, and on and on. These translations date back to the earliest centuries of Christianity, but our copies of them are usually much later. The modern editions of the Greek New Testament cite them with lowercase initials, such as *syr* for Syriac or *vg* for (Latin) Vulgate.

Quotations from the Church Fathers

The early Christian leaders and thinkers who wrote in the decades immediately after the writers of the New Testament are called church fathers; the writers who wrote in Greek are called the Greek fathers; the ones who wrote in Latin are called the Latin fathers. The earliest of these leaders, those in the first and second centuries, are also called the apostolic fathers. Some of them met the apostles and are considered highly relevant in reconstructing what the early Jesus movement believed. These writers quote the New Testament extensively—so extensively, in fact, that textual critics claim that if every Greek manuscript of the New Testament were

42 Γενομένης δὲ ἡμέρας ἐξελθὼν ἐπορεύθη εἰς ἔρημον τόπον· καὶ οἱ ὄχλοι ἐπεζήτουν αὐτὸν καὶ ἦλθον ἕως αὐτοῦ καὶ κατεῖχον αὐτὸν τοῦ μὴ πορεύεσθαι ἀπ᾽ αὐτῶν. 43 ὁ δὲ εἶπεν πρὸς αὐτοὺς ὅτι Καὶ ταῖς ἑτέραις πόλεσιν εὐαγγελίσασθαί με δεῖ τὴν βασιλείαν τοῦ θεοῦ, ὅτι ἐπὶ τοῦτο ἀπεστάλην. 44 καὶ ἦν κηρύσσων εἰς τὰς συναγωγὰς τῆς Ἰουδαίας³.

---

³ 44 {B} εἰς τὰς συναγωγὰς τῆς Ἰουδαίας 𝔭⁷⁵ ℵ B 892 *Lect* syr^{s,h} ‖ ἐν ταῖς συναγωγαῖς τῆς Ἰουδαίας C L *f*¹ 1241 1365 cop^{sa?bo?} ‖ εἰς τὰς συναγωγὰς τῶν Ἰουδαίων W *l*¹⁸ ‖ εἰς τὰς συναγωγὰς τῆς Γαλιλαίας (*see* Mt 4.23; Mk 1.39) D Ψ *f*¹³ arm? ‖ ἐν ταῖς συναγωγαῖς τῆς Γαλιλαίας (*see* Mk 1.39 mg) A K X Δ Θ Π 28 33 565 700 1009 1010 1071 1079 1195 1216 1230 1242 (1253 αὐτῶν τῆς) 1344 1546 1646 2148 2174 *Byz* *l*²¹¹,²²⁶,²⁹⁹,⁸⁵⁴,¹⁷⁶î it^{a,aur,b,c,d,e,f,ff²,l,q,r¹} vg syr^{p,hmg} cop^{bomss} goth arm? eth geo ‖ ἐν ταῖς συναγωγαῖς αὐτῶν (*see* Mt 4.23) *l*³⁴,⁴⁸,¹²³¹ᵐ

---

41 Σὺ...θεοῦ Mt 8.29; Mk 3.11; Lk 4.34   οὐκ εἴα...εἶναι Mk 3.12   43 Καὶ...θεοῦ Lk 8.1
44 ἦν...Ἰουδαίας Mt 4.23

Robert Hutchinson

The critical apparatus at the bottom of the page in Greek New Testaments, found "below the line," provides variant readings for particular passages based on different Greek manuscripts. The job of textual critics is to determine which "reading" is likely closest to what the original authors wrote.

lost we could still reconstruct the entire text just from the quotations in the Greek fathers alone. However, according to the introduction to the Nestle-Aland text, citations from the church fathers are almost entirely taken from later printed editions that have not themselves been checked against ancient manuscripts of the writings themselves.

So how can you check for yourself to see if a given passage is in the earliest manuscripts?

For any important passage or phrase, the editors of the Greek New Testament insert a footnote and then cite the verse number in bold. Next to the verse number is a letter in brackets: [A], [B], and so forth. This is a rating system the editors use for evaluating their own judgment as to the accuracy of the reading. For example, an *A* rating [A] indicates that, in the editors' judgment, the text is "virtually certain,"[9] meaning that it's found in almost all the earliest manuscripts we have. A *B* rating [B] means there is some degree of doubt. A *C* rating [C] means there is a considerable degree of doubt, and a *D* rating means, well, who knows what the text actually is![10] Next to the letter in brackets comes the proof to back it up—a string of citations to the papyri, majuscules, minuscules, lectionaries, and so on. These are the primary sources textual critics use when attempting to reconstruct the original text of the New Testament. With such a volume of material, more than 5,800 Greek manuscripts, they further divide the manuscripts into "families" or "text types." Scholars speak of the Byzantine text, the Alexandrian text, and so on. This is far too complicated to discuss here, and it is one of the reasons why textual criticism, like higher mathematics, can drive some people insane. But at least you can get an idea about the general accuracy rating.[11]

Compared to other ancient writings, there exists an overwhelming volume of material and written "witnesses" to the New Testament text. Christian apologists have pointed out for decades just how few manuscript witnesses exist for other ancient writings. For example, we have only twenty manuscripts of the writing of Plato, with the earliest dating from the ninth century AD—or more than 1,250 years after they were written! We have only eight manuscripts from the writings of the Greek historian Thucydides, one of our principal sources for the history of ancient Greece; and only eight manuscripts of the Greek historian Herodotus, all of which date from the tenth century AD—or between 1,300 and 1,350 years after they were written. The same is true for most of our other sources for ancient history. We have only ten manuscripts of Julius Caesar's *Gallic Wars*, dating from the tenth century, or 950 years after they were written; only twenty manuscripts of the writings of Tacitus, dating from AD 1100, or a thousand years after they were written; and only seven copies of Pliny the Younger's *History of Rome*, dating from AD 850, or 750 years after it was written.[12] In contrast, we have 5,800 manuscripts of the New Testament writings—some of which date to between fifty years (or less!) and three hundred years[13] after the originals were first written. For example, if the gospel of John was written between AD 90 and 100, as many scholars believe, and the papyrus P52 dates to 125, then the copy we have was copied only twenty-five to thirty-five years after the gospel was originally written. That is a truly amazing chronological proximity to the original text!

Yet few ancient historians claim that we can't be sure what Caesar, Tacitus, Herodotus, or Thucydides wrote, even though the earliest copies of their writings in existence date a thousand years or so after the original texts were written. There is very little discussion of copyist error in the case of Thucydides or Herodotus—even though the same dynamics were no doubt present with scribes who copied these works as with those who copied the gospels. There would be the same tendencies toward routine errors, spelling mistakes, dropped words, and the like; yet most historians rely upon these documents as reflecting, with reasonable accuracy, what the ancient writers actually wrote. By contrast, a rigorous standard of scrupulosity is commonly applied to the texts of the New Testament.

DID CHRISTIAN SCRIBES CHANGE THE BIBLE?

Textual criticism is a literary discipline that seeks to establish the "official" or most accurate text of what an author actually wrote, whether that author is Ernest Hemingway, Shakespeare, Homer, or the apostle Paul. In modern times, this isn't all that difficult. We often have in hand the author's original handwritten manuscripts, corrected typescripts, proofs of corrected bound galleys, and the like. But when dealing with works from the distant past, such as those by Plato or from the New Testament, textual criticism becomes far more complex because we don't have the author's original manuscripts. "Not only do we not have the originals, we don't have the first copies of the originals," Ehrman writes. "We don't even have copies of the copies of the originals, or copies of the copies of the copies of the originals."[14]

Ehrman's basic point is highlighted in his book about textual criticism, *Misquoting Jesus*, but it has also been widely known and acknowledged by biblical scholars for centuries. He contends that the scribes who penned these "copies of copies" changed them over time, usually unintentionally (minor spelling mistakes or dropped words), but occasionally deliberately. The scribes often employed different word choices or used synonyms.

To show what this means concretely, here is an example of a passage in which there exist what scholars call textual variants. In Mark 4:19, Jesus explains to his listeners the meaning of the parable of the sower sowing his seed, about how some people hear the word of God but "the worries of this life, the illusion of wealth and the desires for other things come in and choke the word, making it unfruitful."* Well, the ancient manuscripts differ on the phrase, "illusion of wealth." Some say "love of wealth." Others say "illusion (or "deceitfulness") of wealth." Here is what it looks like in a table:[15]

MANUSCRIPT	DATE	GREEK	ENGLISH
Codex Sangallensis 48	800s	η αγαπη του πλουτου	the love of wealth
Codex Sinaiticus	300s	η απατη του πλουτου	the illusion of wealth
Codex Alexandrinus	400s	η απατη του πλουτου	the illusion of wealth
Codex Vaticanus	300s	η απατη του πλουτου	the illusion of wealth

Codex Ephraemi Rescriptus	300s	η απατη του πλουτου	the illusion of wealth
Codex Washingtonianus	400–500s	απαται του πλουτου	the illusions of wealth
Codex Bezae	400s	απαται του κοσμου	the illusions of world

If you look at the first two entries carefully, you'll see that they differ only in two Greek letters. The older codex, Sinaiticus, which dates to the early AD 300s, speaks of the "illusion" (*apate*, ἀπάτη) of wealth. The later manuscript, Codex Sangallensis 48, which dates to the ninth century, changes the Greek letter Pi in *apate* to a Gamma and the Tau to a Pi, resulting in the "love" (*agape*, ἀγάπη) of wealth. (The Greek letters Tau (τ) and the Pi (π) look almost alike and are easily confused.) Thus, it is easy to see how a monastic scribe, after five hours of copying biblical manuscripts by candlelight, could have made an error like this. Textual critics are tasked with deciding what the original reading is in this first pair; clearly it's *apate*, or "illusion," since it's found in the older manuscripts (also in Codex Alexandrinus, Codex Vaticanus, and Ephraemi Rescriptus) and the other reading looks to be merely a scribal error. Textual critics specialize in looking at thousands upon thousands of minute differences in the ancient New Testament manuscripts, just like these, in an effort to discover or at least to guess what the original authors wrote.

In a concluding, moving section of *Misquoting Jesus*, Ehrman gives a passionate defense of the text-critical guild and of the dedicated men and women, like himself, who devote their lives to this practice. He inspires readers to care about the arcane science of textual criticism—and helps them to appreciate what scholars must do to create an authoritative text:

The Bible is, by all accounts, the most significant book in the history of Western civilization. And how do you think we have *access* to the Bible? Hardly any of us actually read it in the original language, and even among those of us who do, there are very few who ever look at a manuscript—let alone a group of manuscripts. How then do we know what was originally in the Bible? A few people have gone to the trouble of learning the ancient languages (Greek, Hebrew, Latin, Syriac, Coptic, etc.) and have spent their professional lives examining our manuscripts, deciding what the authors of the New Testament actually wrote. In other words, someone has gone to the trouble of doing textual criticism, reconstructing the "original" text based on the wide array of manuscripts that differ from one another in thousands of places.[16]

THE PROBLEM OF OVERZEALOUS
SCRIBES "CORRECTING" THE TEXTS

In addition to accidental spelling or copyist errors, the "thousands of places" Ehrman speaks of include instances of well-intentioned, pious Christian scribes changing what they copied to "correct" what they believed were errors made by previous copyists, or making changes to harmonize their manuscript with other texts from the New Testament—for example, adding "Son of God" after Jesus' name (Mark 1:1) or changing "Jesus" to "Jesus Christ." Ehrman wrote an entire scholarly book on this subject, *The Orthodox Corruption of Scripture,* in which he argued that deliberate scribal modification of the New Testament was far more extensive than scholars acknowledge—and this means that we can't really be *sure* we have the New Testament as it was originally written.

Of course, all this dodges the central question: Are any presumed early copyist errors—of which we have no evidence, by the very nature of the case—significant or not? On top of this, critics such as Daniel Wallace insist that Ehrman is often guilty of the logical fallacy of assuming that if something is *possible* it is therefore *likely*—even when there is no evidence that it actually occurred.

PASSAGES NOT FOUND IN ANCIENT MANUSCRIPTS

It comes as a shock to many seminary students that a handful of the most beloved passages of the New Testament aren't found in the oldest manuscripts we have—most famously, the scene in John 7:53–8:11, where Jesus defends the woman taken in adultery against a mob about to stone her. This is, in fact, one of my favorite passages as well, and one of the reasons why I decided as a teenager that whatever Jesus was—God, man, or God-man—I wanted to be on his team.

But textual critics have known for at least a century that this passage is *not* found in the oldest copies of the gospel of John, and, as Ehrman points out, is written in a different style of Greek and uses phrases found nowhere else in the gospel. There are a handful of other passages like this, but Erhman gives only one other example: the long ending of the gospel of Mark (16:9–20).

In addition to examining these big chunks of narrative, however, textual critics also make decisions on individual words and phrases. For example, in most modern Bibles the gospel of Mark begins, "The beginning of the gospel of Jesus Christ, *the Son of God*" (ESV). Textual critics know that the final phrase, "the Son of God," is not found in many early manuscripts. Many modern scholarly translations now set off these words in brackets or have a footnote that explains that they are not in all existing manuscripts of the text. This is probably an example of a deliberate change made by Christian scribes to the original text, "correcting" it to conform to other places in the New Testament where Jesus is described as the "Son of God." There are other examples. The one that bothers me the most is the famous statement of Jesus on the cross in Luke 23:34: "Father, forgive them, for they know not what they do" (ESV). Alas, this is not found in the earliest papyri that we have. This doesn't mean necessarily that Jesus didn't say these words. It's possible that a later copyist had access to a manuscript, now lost to us, that contained the phrase and he was adding back an authentic saying of Jesus missing from the manuscript he was copying. These are the issues that make textual criticism a more exciting field than many imagine.

New Testament scholars have known about all of this for a long time. Even Saint Jerome—the original textual critic, who pored over parchment scrolls himself when he was translating the Bible from Greek and Hebrew into Latin in the 400s, the so-called Vulgate that was "the" text of the Bible in the West for a thousand years—knew that the ancient manuscripts had variant readings. He hunted down as many Greek manuscripts as he could find and even moved to Palestine, living in a cave in Bethlehem, in search of better, more accurate manuscripts.

CAN WE TRUST THE TEXT OF THE NEW TESTAMENT?

So what is the average person on the street or in the pew to make of all this? Given what we know—that we only have copies of copies of copies of the originals—can we trust that our manuscripts reflect what the New Testament writers actually wrote? And if so, why?

In interviews with Daniel Wallace at the Center for Study of New Testament Manuscripts in Dallas, Texas, and in my discussions with the staff at the Institute for New Testament Textual Research in Germany, I asked about Bart Ehrman's basic points and what all this means to the average person. The experts agree that Ehrman raises legitimate issues. They agree that our earliest manuscripts of some New Testament books were copied hundreds of years after the originals, and that there is evidence that the texts were changed over time, usually accidentally but sometimes deliberately. They even agree that the general public should know more about all this. Yet they also assert that this does not mean that we can't trust that we have more or less what the original authors wrote. There are so many manuscripts, from such a wide geographic area, that the scholars who pore over them are usually able to identify both accidental and deliberate changes. "One way we know there are mistakes is because they turn the text into nonsense in many places," Wallace told me in an interview. "For example, if you were looking at a hand-copied text of the preamble of the US Constitution and it read, 'We the People of the United States, in order to form a more perfect *onion*,' you would likely recognize right away that a mistake had occurred." Wallace added that textual critics are often able to spot errors in the New Testament manuscripts just this easily, and, when the hundreds of different manuscripts are compared, they are often able to deduce what the original reading most likely was.[17]

Christian scribes made many accidental and some deliberate changes to the Greek text of the New Testament over the centuries. But scholars insist that, with more than fifty-eight hundred Greek manuscripts available, they are able to reconstruct what the original authors likely wrote with a reasonable degree of accuracy.

Dr. Gäbel at the Institute in Münster confirmed this. He showed me an elaborate computer system, based on something called the Coherence-Based Genealogical Method (CBGM), that tracks every letter of every word in every available manuscript of the New Testament. No other book in history has been the subject of such intense, letter-by-letter analysis, he explained, with so many "witnesses." Not only are experts and computers able to compare every line of the New Testament against 5,800 separate manuscripts over a thousand-year period and track the flow of changes over time, but they are also able to compare these lines with ancient quotations from the apostolic fathers (who quoted the New Testament at length) as well as versions in different languages. All together, this level of analysis provides scholars with a great deal of confidence that they can reconstruct at least an approximation of what the original text of the New Testament actually said. In fact, Dr. Gäbel insisted that what counts is not the age of the manuscript so much as the age of the *text* written on the manuscript—just as the text of Shakespeare's plays printed in a modern paperback is actually far older than most texts printed in old, musty books from the early 1700s. The books from the 1700s may look older than the modern paperbacks, but the source texts of Shakespeare are far older in the modern paperbacks. It's the same with the texts of the New Testament.[18]

Despite Ehrman's fearsome image among evangelicals, he is what you might call a moderate among the ranks of debunkers of Christianity. In fact, he doesn't see himself as a debunker at all. He sees himself as what he is—a trained New Testament scholar, but one who is willing to say publicly and forcefully what "most" scholars allegedly know but only discuss in private. However, he is relatively conservative on the details of that scholarship, rarely advocating views not widely accepted at secular universities. More than one critic has complained, in fact, that Ehrman says one thing in his scholarly, peer-reviewed works—when he knows his academic reputation is on the line—and something quite different in his popular bestsellers.

That is one charge Daniel Wallace levels against Ehrman when it comes to textual criticism. For example, in the textbook on New Testament studies that Ehrman wrote for Oxford University Press, he writes that "we can reconstruct the original words of the New Testament with reasonable (although probably not 100 percent) accuracy."[19] This is, Wallace says, the same judgment as that of many world-renowned textual critics, including Ehrman's own mentor at Princeton Theological Seminary, Bruce Metzger, as well as Kurt Aland at the institute in Münster, Günther Zuntz, J. K. Elliott, E. C. Colwell, Gordon Fee, and many other experts. Not all these textual critics are believing Christians, by the way—and a few are self-proclaimed atheists. But when it came time for Ehrman to write his popular book on textual criticism, *Misquoting Jesus*, Ehrman sounds more like New Atheist Christopher Hitchens than the judicious scholar he is: "What we have are copies made later—much later . . . And these copies all differ from one another, in many thousands of places . . . [T]hese copies differ from one another in so many places that we don't even know how many differences there are."[20]

This suggests that we can't trust anything in our New Testaments, Wallace says. But the reality is that many top textual critics think we can trust *most* of it. In those rare places where the experts are unsure what the original wording is, Bible readers can typically find footnotes with the most likely variant readings from ancient Greek manuscripts. Wallace believes we are very close to the original text "either above or below the line"—meaning either in the "approved" text in the official Greek New Testament published by the institute in Münster—or in one of the variants found "below the line" in the footnotes.[21] Thus, the issues raised by textual criticism seem mostly like a tempest in a teapot, even for non-Christians. Ehrman himself concedes that the vast majority of variant readings in the New Testament are insignificant—mostly spelling errors and dropped words.[22] He also admits that, for the overwhelming majority of Christians, "these textual facts can be interesting, but there is nothing in them to challenge their faith."[23] In other words, there may be, as Ehrman says, many reasons to be skeptical about the claims of Christianity, but inaccurate texts of the New Testament are probably not one of them.

FOR FURTHER STUDY

Aland, Kurt and Barbara Aland. *The Text of the New Testament.* Grand Rapids, MI: William B. Eerdmans, 1987.

Comfort, Philip. *Encountering the Manuscripts: An Introduction to New Testament Paleography and Textual Criticism.* Nashville, TN: Broadman & Holman, 2005.

Ehrman, Bart D. *Misquoting Jesus: The Story Behind Who Changed the Bible and Why.* New York: HarperOne, 2007.

Mack, Burton. *Who Wrote the New Testament: The Making of the Christian Myth.* San Francisco: HarperSanFrancisco, 1995.

Wallace, Daniel B., ed. *Revisiting the Corruption of the New Testament.* Grand Rapids, MI: Kregel Publications, 2011.

4

HAVE ARCHAEOLOGISTS FOUND JESUS' HOUSE?

"Nazareth! Can anything good come from there?"
Nathanael asked. "Come and see," said Philip.

—JOHN 1:46 NIV

J esus of Nazareth was born and raised in a time of horrifying violence. Modern scholars often dismiss the gospel story of the slaughter of the innocents as mere legend, but it's virtually certain that far worse atrocities were committed around the time when Jesus was born. When Herod the Great died around the year 4 BC, a bloody revolt broke out in the Galilee region, centered in the newly founded Greek city of Sepphoris (Hebrew Zippori)—located on a hill just four miles (six kilometers) from the traditional site of Nazareth.[1] For more than two centuries, there had been genocidal clashes in Palestine between devout Jews and the Greek and Roman populations that had settled there.[2] With Herod's death, the entire countryside descended into chaos that lasted for nearly a decade. A civil war broke out between the soldiers who were loyal to Herod and those who opposed him.[3] The rebels captured Sepphoris, seized the weapons in its armory, and declared their independence.

The Romans responded with their usual efficient ruthlessness, dispatching the Roman general Publius Quinctilius Varus from Syria with three legions to put down the insurrection.[4] Varus retook the city of Sepphoris, executing the men and selling the women and children into slavery. According to the first-century Jewish historian Josephus, Varus hunted down the leaders of the rebellion—two thousand men—and crucified them all. Had Varus crucified one rebel every seventy-five yards or so, the line of crucified prisoners would have extended the entire 90 miles (140 kilometers) from Sepphoris to Jerusalem.

This was what was happening in the area when, around the same time, a young, unmarried Jewish teenager named Miriam (whose name means "bitter sea") discovered she would soon give birth to a child—and not by her betrothed. Climbing the hills above her tiny village, Mary of Nazareth could no doubt have seen the fires of Sepphoris burning in the distance and heard the anguished screams of young girls her own age as they were paraded off in chains. One ancient tradition even asserts that Mary grew up in Sepphoris, after her parents moved there during the final decade of Herod's reign, as part of a deliberate plan to "re-Judaize" the Galilee region. Mary could have watched in horror as friends of her parents were beaten, hung on poles and trees by Roman soldiers, and left to die, their eyes pecked out by crows and their flesh eaten by wild animals. Mary could have well prayed, as in the Magnificat—the prayer ascribed to her in the gospel of Luke—that God Almighty would bring "down the mighty from their thrones" and help "his servant Israel" (Luke 1:52–54 ESV). Scholars have long questioned the historicity of a "worldwide census" that, according to Luke 2:2, was the reason why Jesus was born in Bethlehem; but census or no census, the mass slaughter in Galilee in the years after Herod's death provides a plausible explanation for why Mary and Joseph may have decided to flee, even though Mary had just given birth, away from Galilee or even farther, in exile to Egypt.

AN ANCIENT LINEAGE

There is a theory, common in some messianic Jewish circles, that both Mary and her betrothed, Joseph, were members of a Jewish sect that saw itself as descended from a "branch" of the House of David, a line that was not subject to the famous curse by the prophet Jeremiah.[5] In the Hebrew Bible,

God had promised King David that his house and kingdom would endure forever (2 Sam. 7:16). Yet around the year 586 BC, the city of Jerusalem was surrounded by invading Babylonian armies who would soon sack the city, burn the famous temple of Solomon to the ground, and carry off the influential, wealthy, and strong members of the population into bondage. Jeremiah prophesied that the Davidic kings would come to an end due to their corruption and lawlessness. Speaking of the then-king Jehoiachin, Jeremiah declared in the name of God that "none of his offspring will prosper, none will sit on the throne of David or rule anymore in Judah" (Jer. 22:30 NIV). And that is precisely what happened. Jehoiachin was dragged off in bondage and, according to 2 Kings 25:27, lived as a political prisoner for thirty-seven years. The sacking of Jerusalem by the Babylonians ended the rule of the royal house of David. And yet, some of King David's descendants *still lived*. They were likely part of the Jerusalem aristocracy that was taken off in bondage to Babylon. Supposedly another branch of the royal Davidic family had emerged through one of King David's other sons, Nathan, brother of King Solomon. This branch of the family, the theory goes, closely guarded its royal heritage for hundreds of years, through exile in Babylon and eventual resettlement in the land of Israel when the Judeans were permitted to return.

The members of this extended family, possibly ancestors of Mary of Nazareth, looked forward to the coming of a messiah to redeem Israel, based on a different prophecy, one from the Jerusalem prophet Isaiah (11:1–3 NIV):

> *A shoot will come up from the stump of Jesse;*
> *from his roots a Branch will bear fruit.*
> *The Spirit of the LORD will rest on him—*
> *   the Spirit of wisdom and of understanding,*
> *the Spirit of counsel and of might,*
> *the Spirit of the knowledge and fear of the LORD—*
> *and he will delight in the fear of the LORD.*

During the reign of King Herod the Great, these messianic clansmen may have settled in Galilee, around the newly established city of Sepphoris. The word for "branch" in Hebrew is *netzser* (נֵצֶר), and this group, the theory goes, may have called itself *netzarim,* or Nazoreans, "the branches." (To this day, the word for "Christians" in Hebrew is *Notzrim.*) The tiny, isolated community they founded, near a natural underground spring at the foot of rocky, pine-covered hills just south of the Beit Netofah Valley, was called Nazareth.

Balage Balogh

An artist's illustration of what the village of Nazareth likely looked like in the first century AD, with terraced hillsides and small stone houses located in the valley below.

A DISCOVERY IN NAZARETH

Today, Nazareth is a bustling, traffic-choked Arab town of about seventy thousand people, about seventeen miles (twenty-eight kilometers) southeast of the coastal city of Haifa. Just over three miles (six kilometers) to the northwest are found the vast ruins of Sepphoris. Off in the distance, you can see the round bump of Mount Tabor rising majestically from the Jezreel Valley. The new Jesus Trail, a popular tourist attraction, originates just outside the city and winds its way northeast, past the Horns of Hattin and then downhill to the Sea of Galilee—a fairly strenuous hike of some forty miles (sixty-five kilometers).

When I went to visit Nazareth every Sunday in the late 1970s, it was still a fairly sleepy town with few tourists. Today, giant Israeli tour buses bring thousands of people a day to visit Nazareth's handful of churches and pilgrimage sites, including the Basilica of the Annunciation (the largest Christian church in the Middle East), Mary's Well (built on top of a Byzantine bath house connected to the only natural spring in the area), the Greek Orthodox Saint Gabriel Church (built on top of another part of the spring), Saint Joseph Church (built over the traditional site of Joseph's workshop) and a modern theme park called Nazareth Village where actors dressed in biblical clothing re-create what life might have been like when Jesus lived there.

To give you some idea of the flavor of the place, you have to descend into the lower level of the basilica. In the grotto beneath lie the remains of a third-century synagogue blocked off with an iron gate, in which now stands a modern-day altar. Inscribed on the altar are the words, in Latin, from the opening of John's gospel: *Verbum caro factum est.* "The Word became flesh." Except one extra word has been added to the biblical inscription on the altar: the Latin word *hic,* which means "here." As a result, the words on the altar read, *Verbum caro hic factum est.*

The Word became flesh . . . *here.*

But what many tourists don't know is that until recently there was very little archaeological or textual evidence for Nazareth in the time of Jesus. The village is not mentioned in *any* Jewish or Roman sources other than the Gospels until about the fourth century. Not one. It's not mentioned in the Hebrew Bible or in the collection of Jewish commentaries known as the Mishnah, which includes traditions dating back to the first century; nor in the voluminous works of the first-century Jewish historian Josephus (ca. AD 37–100). This seems somewhat odd in the case of Josephus, who commanded Jewish forces in Galilee in the early years of the Jewish War against Rome, which began in AD 66. He mentions dozens of small hamlets in the area, including nearby Japha, Cana, and Beit She'arim, but not Nazareth.

The earliest nonscriptural reference to Nazareth is found in the writings of the Christian travel writer Sextus Julius Africanus (ca. 180–250), quoted by the historian Eusebius (ca. 263–339), who describes the town of "Nazara." The anonymous pilgrim of Bordeaux, who visited Palestine in AD 333–334 and kept a brief journal of his travels, never mentions Nazareth in his list of the places he had visited.[6] The first non-Christian reference to Nazareth was discovered in 1962 on a grey marble fragment in an ancient synagogue in Caesarea Maritima on Israel's coast. It was dated by Israeli archaeologists to around AD 300. The writing on the fragment (and another like it) mentions various towns and villages in Galilee, including Nazareth (which allowed scholars to know, for the first time, how Nazareth was spelled in Hebrew, with the Hebrew letter tzadik, נצרת).[7]

A FIRST-CENTURY STONE HOUSE UNCOVERED

As for archaeological evidence, until very recently there hasn't been much to show those busloads of tourists. High-resolution photographs taken in the early 1900s show Nazareth as a tiny Arab village, surrounded by barren hills, with just a handful of stone houses.[8] Mark Twain, who visited in 1867, described the town as "clinging like a whitewashed wasp's nest to the hill-side."[9] In the 1950s and early 60s, workers tore down the eighteenth-century Franciscan church in the center of town to prepare the foundation of what would become the Basilica of the Annunciation, completed in 1969. Franciscan archaeologist Bellarmino Bagatti undertook an extensive archaeological survey of the site. Father Bagatti's team found Iron Age and Roman-era artifacts, including wine presses and olive presses, interconnecting passages, water cisterns, and grain silos. Some depressions in the underlying rock led the archaeologists to conclude that stone houses had been there "probably in the Roman period," and that the area around the basilica was, in fact, a small Roman-period village.[10] Excavations of Mary's Well in the late 1990s uncovered a handful of ancient coins, including ten from the Maccabean era (165–66 BC), two from the time of Herod the Great (37–4 BC) and one from the time of Archelaus (4 BC–AD 6). Digging in the grounds of the Nazareth Village project, however, revealed little except for pottery shards. All in all, not much to show.

Indeed, one of the common arguments used by people who claim Jesus of Nazareth never existed is that *Nazareth never existed!* "We *know* the Wizard of Oz is not real, since we know there never was a Land of Oz," explains atheist writer and publisher Frank Zindler, author of *The Jesus the Jews Never Knew.*[11]

Photo courtesy of the Mary of Nazareth Centre

In 2009, archaeologists discovered, beneath a building in Nazareth just meters from the Basilica of the Annunciation, the foundations of a first-century stone house dating back to the era of Jesus of Nazareth. This is the second stone house dating to that period that has been recently discovered.

But as often happens in the strange world of biblical archaeology, Nazareth's evangelistic fortunes have recently seen a dramatic reversal. That's one of the problems with the "arguments from silence" so popular among debunkers of Christianity—those who say there is "no evidence" that a particular person, place, or custom existed in the past. Just when you least expect it, evidence has a way of popping up. For example, for years biblical "minimalists" asserted that there was no evidence that a King David actually existed and thus insisted that he was a fictional character, as real as King Arthur or Odysseus. But then, in 1993, archaeologists working in the Tel Dan Nature Reserve in northern Israel uncovered a basalt stele, now on display in the Israel Museum in Jerusalem, that mentions the "House of David" by name.[12] The same type of thing is now happening with the New Testament as archaeological digs confirm the historicity of many people, places, and events in the Gospels—including the village of Nazareth itself.

Almost one year after a "mythicist" writer named René Salm published a book in 2008, *The Myth Of Nazareth: The Invented Town Of Jesus,* Israeli archaeologists made a stunning announcement: they had discovered the remains of a stone house in Nazareth, just steps from the Basilica of the Annunciation, dating back to the time of Jesus. The previous summer, construction crews had been digging the foundation of a new Christian evangelism center, the International Mary of Nazareth Center, when they discovered rough stone structures that looked centuries old. As is the custom in Israel, work was immediately halted and experts from the Israel Antiquities Authority (IAA) were called in. The team found remains of supporting walls, what looked like an underground hideout or safe room, a courtyard, and an elaborate series of cisterns that appeared designed to collect water from the roof of a dwelling. In addition, a group of grain silos was buried deep in the ground. Today, the ruins are on display on the ground floor of the International Mary of Nazareth Center, which was built by a French Catholic organization and is staffed by members of Chemin Neuf, or New Way, an ecumenically oriented religious order founded in France in 1973.

According to a preliminary report on the excavation from the IAA's chief archaeologist, Yardenna Alexandre, the ruins are of a domestic house with a few small rooms and an open courtyard dating to the late Hellenistic to early Roman period (first century BC to early second century AD). In addition, pottery shards found on the floors of the house were of common local Galilean pottery dating to the early Roman era (first century BC).[13] Also found were soft limestone cups and bowls, used for Jewish purity rites in the Roman period.[14] As a result, Alexandre concludes that the architectural remains and the various pottery shards, vessels, and coins found at the site all indicate the house was originally built in the late Maccabean era, in the first century BC,[15] when there was a deliberate effort to "re-Judaize" the Galilee region with Jewish families from the south. Alexandre also notes in her report that the discovery of the house confirmed the Franciscan archaeologist Bagatti's suspicions that depressions in the underlying rock beneath the basilica church were probably the remnants of stone houses from the Roman period. In other words: as amazing as it sounds, the cluster of ecclesiastical buildings in downtown Nazareth—the basilica, Saint Gabriel's Church, Mary's Well—almost certainly were built directly over where the village of Nazareth lay in Jesus' day. Alexandre concludes that Nazareth was indeed settled throughout the New Testament era, located in an isolated basin in the hills, far from any main road, and thus would not have been noticed by Josephus or Roman officials. She and other archaeologists believe that Nazareth's isolation spared it from the ravages of the Jewish War of AD 65–70 and perhaps of earlier Roman persecutions.[16]

Other archaeologists go even further. It turns out that the Mary of Nazareth Center site is not the only first-century house archaeologists have turned up in Nazareth. According to Ken Dark, director of the Nazareth Archaeological Project and a professor at the University of Reading in the United Kingdom, another site in Nazareth—a first-century house partly made of mortar-and-stone walls cut into a rocky hillside—could very well have been Jesus' actual childhood home. In an article published in March 2015 in the *Biblical Archaeological Review,* Dark argues that this site, first uncovered in the 1880s by nuns at the Sisters of Nazareth convent but only excavated in 2006, was revered in the Byzantine era as Jesus' home.[17] The site Dark refers to is located only yards away from the Mary of Nazareth Center site and the Basilica of the Annunciation. It's "an exceptionally well-preserved domestic building, probably a 'courtyard house' dating from about the middle of the first century," he says. Dark adds that the stone and wood structures were catalogued and recorded in 1936 by a Jesuit priest,

Henri Senès, but his research remained unpublished and unknown except to the nuns and occasional pilgrims. In 2006, when professional archaeologists began excavating the site located in the foundations of the Sisters of Nazareth convent, they were astonished by what they found. The first-century house "had been constructed by cutting back a limestone hillside as it sloped toward the wadi (valley) below, leaving carefully smoothed free-standing rock walls, to which stone-built walls were added," Dark writes. "The structure included a series of rooms. One, with its doorway, survived to its full height. Another had a stairway rising adjacent to one of its walls. Just inside the surviving doorway, earlier excavations had revealed part of its original chalk floor."[18]

Dark believes that the house was abandoned sometime during the first century and then used as a burial ground. Two empty tombs have been discovered next to the abandoned stone house. Because one of the tombs is of the *kokhim* type—a rock-cut tomb with a rolling stone for a door—this suggests it dates to the first century when such tombs were predominantly used. Centuries later, Byzantine Christians erected a church over the site to protect it, Dark adds, and then twelfth-century crusaders built a new church at this location. For further evidence that this first-century stone house could well have been Jesus' childhood home, Dark points to a seventh-century travelogue written by Adomnán, abbot of the Scottish island monastery at Iona. The account was based on a pilgrimage to Nazareth made by the Frankish bishop Arculf. According to this text, there was a church in Nazareth "where once there was the house in which the Lord was nourished in his infancy."[19]

New Testament scholars remain cautious, of course. There is "no name on the door," as one scholar puts it.[20] However, these archaeological discoveries do suggest that Nazareth was settled in the first century and, moreover, could well have been a thriving, somewhat larger community than previously supposed. Some of the remains found at these sites, such as limestone vessels, point to the presence of a conservative Jewish community, archaeologists say.[21] "Was this the house where Jesus grew up?" Dark asks finally in the *Biblical Archaeological Review* article. "It is impossible to say on archaeological grounds. On the other hand, there is no good archaeological reason why such an identification should be discounted."[22]

THE IMPORTANCE OF THE STATE OF ISRAEL

For researchers investigating the archaeological and cultural background of the New Testament, it's difficult to overstate the importance of the founding of the State of Israel in 1948. For one, an entire population of Jews (and some Christians) has grown up in the historic land, speaking fluent Hebrew. Thus they have an intimate familiarity with the Hebrew Bible and the geographical places mentioned within it that is difficult to achieve in any other way. It is one thing to travel to visit archaeological digs; it is quite another to live your entire life close by. You can gain a familiarity with the geography, wildlife, plants, and seasons that researchers in libraries back in Oxford, Rome, or New York simply do not share.

On a practical level, the founding of Israel also means that much of the biblical landscape has been heavily excavated by professional archaeologists over the past century—although Israeli archaeologists would be the first to admit that they've only scratched the surface, and that limitations of time and money mean that there is still a lot of work to be done. Still, we now know more about the archaeology of the New Testament than we have at any other time in history. Virtually every year, archaeologists and researchers working on digs all across Israel announce discoveries that are changing how scholars understand biblical places and times. This is particularly true of the New Testament.

TOP ARCHAEOLOGICAL DISCOVERIES RELATING TO THE NEW TESTAMENT

Archaeologists have been digging up the Holy Land for at least two centuries now. For people who want conclusive proof that the Bible is "true," the results have been mixed. For example, despite looking for more than a century, archaeologists have discovered little evidence of a mass exodus of nomadic people from Egypt into the Sinai Peninsula, as described in the book of Exodus. This seems odd. Anyone who has visited the Judean mountain fortress of Masada knows that we can still clearly see the remains of Roman camps at the foot of the fortress, even though they are two thousand years old. Yet nothing remains in the Sinai—"not a single campsite or sign of occupation from the time of Ramesses II and his immediate predecessors and successors," as one pair of authors puts it[23]—of a "vast multitude" wandering there for forty years. That doesn't mean there wasn't an exodus out of Egypt, of course. The exodus would have occurred more than a thousand years earlier than the Roman siege of Masada. But the lack of any visible remains does mean that some archaeologists are rethinking how the Exodus happened or, in a few cases, whether it happened at all.[24]

On the other hand, archaeologists have made hundreds of other discoveries that appear to confirm the historical accuracy of people, events, customs, and places mentioned in the Bible. The *Biblical Archaeology Review* recently published a list of more than fifty people mentioned in the Hebrew Bible, some once considered merely fictional by older scholars, who have now been confirmed by archaeological evidence as actually being historical—including five Egyptian pharaohs, eight kings of the Northern Kingdom of Israel, six kings of Judah, as well as many Assyrian, Babylonian, and Persian Kings. Three different inscriptions now confirm the existence of a historical King David. Recently, archaeologists even discovered evidence that Belshazzar, the Babylonian king who saw the "writing on the wall" mentioned in the Book of Daniel and long suspected by scholars to be fictional, probably existed.[25]

Now the same phenomenon is happening with the New Testament. Just as a new generation of mythicists has shown up to claim that the entire New Testament is a work of fiction, archaeologists are now providing substantial evidence of just the opposite. In just the past two or three decades, dozens of events, people, and places known from the New Testament have been confirmed by archaeological discoveries. Here are a few of the most significant examples.

Recent Nazareth Excavations

The 2006 discovery of a first-century stone house with underground cisterns and grain silos was only one of a number of recent discoveries in Nazareth, as mentioned above. The discoveries at the Sisters of Nazareth convent suggest that not only was the village inhabited during the lifetime of Jesus, but it was a more sprawling village than was once supposed.[26] Archaeologist Ken Dark explains:

First discovered by accident in 1884—and thereafter informally investigated by workmen, nuns and clergy, for several decades—the archaeological site at the Sisters of Nazareth convent in central Nazareth has remained unpublished and largely unknown to scholarship. However, work by the Nazareth Archaeological Project in 2006–2010 showed that this site offers a full and important stratified sequence from ancient Nazareth, including well-preserved Early Roman-period and later features.[27]

Courtesy of IAA

In 2009, Israeli archaeologists discovered one of the oldest synagogues in the world at Migdal, or Magdala, on the Sea of Galilee just south of Capernaum. Measuring 1,300 square feet (120 square meters), the synagogue was built sometime in the first century and could well have been visited by Jesus of Nazareth.

First-Century Synagogue in Magdala

In 2009, Israeli archaeologists announced that they had uncovered the ruins of a well-preserved and large first-century synagogue complex in the village of Magdala, on the Sea of Galilee, likely in use between the years 50 BC and AD 67, when it was destroyed in the first Jewish War against the Romans. Moreover, the archaeologists said, it is almost certain that Jesus of Nazareth preached in this synagogue. According to the Synoptic Gospels, Jesus "went throughout Galilee, proclaiming the message in their synagogues and casting out demons" (Mark 1:39 NRSV). Matthew 15:39 says that Jesus "sent away the multitude, got into the boat, and came to the region of Magdala" (NKJV), although some ancient manuscripts say Magadan and the parallel passage in Mark (8:10) refers to nearby Dalmanutha. Nevertheless, this well-appointed and apparently prosperous synagogue at Magdala would have been a likely location for his preaching—and this is one of the very few places in Israel where scholars can confidently say, "Jesus almost certainly stood here."[28] Located just six miles south of Capernaum, Jesus' base of operations during his ministry (Matt. 4:13), Magdala was a thriving economic center in the first century, the only town on the western side of the lake until Tiberias was founded around AD 20. Called Taricheae in Greek, Magdala was also the center of an international fish export business. According to a preliminary report from the Israel Antiquities Authority, the first-century synagogue consisted of two large rooms—a vestibule and a reading room—and one smaller room. A mosaic was on the floor and colorful frescos covered the walls. In the main room, there was a large square stone on one side of which was a relief of a seven-branch menorah, the symbol of Judaism. The archaeologists believe that the table was used as a place upon which to put the Torah scroll for public reading—much as in contemporary synagogues.[29] This mirrors very closely what the Gospels say Jesus did in a synagogue in Nazareth: "When he came to Nazareth, where he had been brought up, he went to the synagogue on the sabbath day, as was his custom. He stood up to read, and the scroll of the prophet Isaiah was given to him" (Luke 4:16–17 NRSV).

The Caiaphas Ossuary

Matthew, Luke, Acts, and John all report that a man named Caiaphas was the high priest in Jerusalem when Jesus was arrested. In John's account, the high priest reveals how much was at stake for the Jerusalem aristocracy as a result of Jesus' massive popular following. Should Jesus inspire a revolt against Rome, they feared that the Roman legions would do to Jerusalem what they ended up doing just forty years later: utterly destroy it. "You do not realize that it is better for you that one man die for the people than that the whole nation perish," Caiaphas told his associates (John 11:50 NIV). Until recently, all our knowledge of Caiaphas was from written records. But in November 1990, a dump truck driving in the hills outside of Jerusalem near Abu Tor accidentally smashed through the buried roof of an ancient tomb dating back to the first century. Inside, archaeologists discovered ossuaries, or "bone boxes." On one of the most ornate was written the Hebrew words "Yehosef bar Qafa'" (Joseph son of Caiaphas). The ossuary contained the remains of six people—two infants, a child aged two to five, a boy aged thirteen to eighteen, an adult female, and a man about sixty years old. Unlike some other ossuaries, the Caiaphas ossuary is widely considered to be authentic, and Israeli archaeologists believe that it is Caiaphas's family tomb.[30]

Israel Museum

In 1990, road crews accidentally uncovered a tomb in south Jerusalem containing twelve ossuaries, or bone boxes. One of them, containing the bones of a 60-year-old man, was inscribed with the name Yehosef bar Qayafa, or Joseph son of Caiaphas. Some archaeologists believe this was very likely the final resting place of the high priest Caiaphas.

The Crucified Yehochanan

All four of the gospels say simply that the Roman soldiers "crucified" Jesus, without specifying what that actually entailed. Yet again, it is in John's gospel that there is a telling detail that archaeology may partly confirm. In John 20, in the story of doubting Thomas, the disciple says,

"Unless I see the mark of the nails in his hands, and put my finger in the mark of the nails . . . I will not believe" (v. 25 NRSV). Some critical scholars scoffed. The Romans tied their victims to poles with rope, they said. The Romans didn't nail their hands and feet, because such a method wouldn't have supported a man's body weight.[31] Clearly, skeptics said, this is more proof that the Gospels are mere fictional accounts.[32] But then, in 1968, Israeli archaeologists excavated a burial cave in Givat Hamivtar, northeast of Jerusalem. Inside the first-century tomb they found an ossuary containing the skeleton of a man who had been crucified. The name on the ossuary was Yehochanan. But on top of the bone of his right heel was a wooden board, and through the board, and his heel, was a 4.5-inch spike. Both the heel bone and the spike are now on display in the Israel Museum. The archaeologists concluded that the executioners had affixed the board so the condemned man couldn't pull his foot off of the cross. Experts disagree about whether or not the victim's arms were also nailed to a crossbeam or simply tied with ropes.[33] The man's legs were broken, as was the usual practice, just as John specifies (19:31). And another important detail: while some scholars claim Jesus' body would have been left on the cross and eaten by dogs, not buried, Yehochanan's crucified body was buried in a rock-hewn tomb just as the Gospels say Jesus' body was.

The Jesus Boat

Jesus knew his way around boats. As Israeli archaeologist Rami Arav says, there are forty-five references in the Gospels to boats and fishing associated with Jesus. Indeed, there were far more boats on the Sea of Galilee in Jesus' day than in our own. In January 1986, two fishermen from Kibbutz Ginosar, located on the edge of the Sea of Galilee, spotted a suspicious object poking out of the lake mud. This was during a severe drought, and the waterline of the lake was lower than it had been in decades. Upon examination, archaeologists discovered the remains of a wooden fishing boat, about eight feet by twenty-seven feet, dating back to the first century.

After weeks of painstaking retrieval that required the boat to be soaked in a solution of heated polyethylene glycol (PEG), the boat was recovered and examined in detail. The hull was found to be made of oak and cedar and patched with ten other varieties of wood. The construction employed the pegged mortise-and-tenon joints common in ancient Mediterranean "shell-based" boats, with iron nails used to hold the hull to the frames. Pottery fragments, lamps, and a coin from the reign of Herod Philip (who reigned AD 29–30)[34] found inside the boat were dated to the first century, confirmed by Carbon-14 tests. Archaeologists speculated that the boat may have been sunk during a nautical battle on the lake around AD 67, the Battle of Migdal, when Roman forces attacked Jewish boats on the lake during the Jewish War of 66–70. The remains of the boat itself, along with detailed replicas and exhibits, are now on display in an ultramodern museum called the Yigal Alon Center, located just steps from the lakeshore.[35]

Berthold Werner

The Sea of Galilee Boat housed in the Yigal Alon Museum in Kibbutz Ginosar. Discovered deep in the mud of the lake in 1987, it has been reliably dated to the AD 60s.

Saint Peter's House

The Franciscan order has been in Israel longer than any other international body, since 1217. It is charged with protecting numerous holy sites throughout Israel and has legal ownership of many of them. In 1894, the order bought land on the Sea of Galilee after British and American explorers discovered the ruins of Capernaum, which the Gospels say was Jesus' adopted hometown and perhaps the center of his operations in Galilee

(Matt. 4:13). John and the Synoptics say that Jesus' disciples Peter and his brother Andrew were born in the fishing village of Bethsaida (John 1:44) but lived as adults in Capernaum (Matt. 8:14), where they were partners in a fishing business with the brothers James and John, the sons of Zebedee (Luke 5:10). Matthew 8:14 says that Jesus came to stay at Peter's house, where Peter apparently lived with his wife and mother-in-law, who was sick.

Robert Hutchinson

The first-century stone house discovered in Capernaum, Jesus' adopted hometown on the lakeshore of the Sea of Galilee, that archaeologists believe could well have been the home of the apostle Peter, and his wife and mother-in-law, and where Jesus sometimes stayed.

In the 1920s, the Franciscans discovered the ruins of a synagogue and an octagonal church on the site, but it wasn't until the late 1960s that archaeologists received the funding to fully excavate the area. What they discovered was a series of *insula*, or attached stone townhouses, common in the first century. The Byzantine octagonal church, dating to the fifth century, had been built on top of a simple stone house dating back to the first century BC. But scratched on the walls of one room, in the plaster, were Christian prayers in Hebrew, Aramaic, Greek, Latin, and Syriac. The archaeologists concluded that it was a "house church" from the first century, and very likely the home of Saint Peter. Today, a futuristic-looking Catholic Church (nicknamed "the spaceship") has been built over the site, and visitors can peer down through glass panels at the stone house in the center surrounded by the octagonal foundation of the Byzantine church.[36]

Sepphoris

The Gospels depict Jesus speaking with many non-Jewish people, including a Roman centurion whose servant was sick (Luke 7:2–3), a Samaritan woman (John 4:7–39), a Syrophoenician woman (Mark 7:25–30), and a Canaanite woman and her daughter who was possessed by a demon (Matt. 15:21–28). He also traveled to regions known as centers of paganism, such as Caesarea Philippi. Now we may know why. The capital city of Galilee in the time of Jesus was Sepphoris, a Greek-modeled city populated mostly by Jews and located on a small hill only three miles (six kilometers) from Nazareth. It was widely considered the jewel of the Galilee region and was a thriving, beautiful city of perhaps twelve thousand people that would eventually offer such Greek amenities as synagogues, a theatre, bathhouses, a gymnasium, and a long shopping street, or cardo. During the Jewish War against Rome, the residents of Sepphoris refused to participate—no doubt remembering what had happened to their town seventy years earlier when they had rebelled against Rome: the people had been slaughtered.

After the fall of Jerusalem, Sepphoris became a major center for rabbinic Judaism. Judah ha-Nasi, Judah the Prince, directed the compilation of the Mishnah (a compendium of commentary on Jewish law) from Sepphoris in AD 200. Shortly thereafter, the city became a cosmopolitan city where Jews, Christians, and pagans lived side by side. In the 1980s and 90s, stunning mosaics were discovered on the floors of villas and synagogues in the city, with inscriptions written in both Greek and Aramaic. In one particularly luxurious villa, dubbed the Dionysius villa because of elaborate mosaics on the floor depicting people feasting, there is an unusual mosaic of a beautiful woman. Known as the Mona Lisa of the Galilee, the woman has a remarkably modern appearance and seems to be looking through time, with just the hint of a smile on her face. The discovery of the ruins of Sepphoris, a city not mentioned in the Bible, has led archaeologists to conclude that Jesus likely lived and worked in a far more cosmopolitan, multicultural milieu than previously believed—and could very well have spoken some Greek and been familiar with both Greek customs and the arts of bartering and negotiation. Some theorize[37] that as a self-employed builder and head of the household after the death of Joseph, Jesus very likely would have worked on the massive building projects going on in Sepphoris and nearby Tiberias and Bethsaida—projects that could have inspired some of his most famous parables (Luke 14:28).

Wikipedia

In the ruins of a villa in Sepphoris, the large Greek-style town located close to Nazareth, archaeologists discovered in the 1980s an elaborate floor mosaic with a haunting picture of a young woman. Known as the "Mona Lisa of the Galilee," the woman provides a rare glimpse of what people in Galilee may have looked like in the time of Jesus.

Roman Inscriptions

For a book of "fiction," as some skeptics portray it, the New Testament boasts an incredibly large number of characters for whom inscriptions with their names carved in marble actually exist. In recent decades, archaeologists have discovered concrete, physical evidence for the existence of many people mentioned in the Gospels and in the rest of the New Testament. One of the earliest discoveries, and probably the most famous, was the Pontius Pilate inscription. Until 1962, there was no archaeological proof that Pontius Pilate ever existed—and anti-Christian polemicists made much of this fact. But in that year, an Italian archaeologist working at Caesarea Maritima on the coast of Israel south of Haifa—the center of government for the Roman admini- stration during the time of Jesus—found the long-sought proof. It came in the form of an inscription that mentioned Tiberieum/[Pon]tius Pilatus/ [Praef]ectus Iuda[eae], "Tiberius [the Roman emperor of the period]/Pontius Pilate/Prefect of Judea."[38] A replica is now located on the site of the Roman prefect's villa on the Israeli coast, but the original is on display in the Israel Museum in Jerusalem.[39]

And that is only the start. Over the years, archaeologists have also found inscriptions with the names of Sergius Paulus, the Roman proconsul men- tioned in Acts 13:6–12; Gallio, the proconsul of Achaia mentioned in Acts 18:12–17; and Erastus, the city treasurer in Corinth, mentioned both in Acts 19:22 and in 2 Timothy 4:20. In his letter to the Romans, too, Paul tells his readers that "Erastus, the city treasurer, and our brother Quartus, greet you" (16:23 ESV). In Corinth, archaeologists discovered a marble slab embedded near a long pavement with the words, in Latin, "ERASTUS PRO AEDILITATE S.P. STRAVIT." According to scholars, the "S.P." is an abbreviation for *sua pecunia,* "with his own money," and an "aedileship" was a governmental office, so the entire inscription reads, "Erastus in return for his aedileship laid [the pavement] with his own money."[40]

THE LAVISH PALACES OF THE JERUSALEM ARISTOCRACY

Beyond the specific archaeological discoveries listed above, there is another, even more important way that archaeology has furthered understanding of Jesus and his times. That is the ongoing revelation, through decades of archaeological spadework in Israel, of just how massive and oppressive the building projects of the Roman occupiers and their collaborating clients really were. This is one of the major points in *Excavating Jesus,* a book by John Dominic Crossan of the Jesus Seminar and Jonathan L. Reed, profes- sor of New Testament and Christian origins at the University of La Verne and the lead archaeologist at Sepphoris. Recent digs at Sepphoris, Jerusalem, and other locations around Israel, the authors claim, have revealed an utterly bifurcated society—with an ultrarich aristocracy on the one hand and a large population of peasants sliding from ordinary poverty into abject destitution on the other.[41] Archaeological excavations in Jerusalem following the Six-Day War, which uncovered luxurious palaces for the priestly aristocracy,[42] reveal just how well the rich lived in Roman-occupied Palestine, and why the vast majority of the population suffered under grinding poverty, possibly including members of Jesus' own family. Scholars such as Richard Horsley and James Tabor have done amazing work in recent years filling in the details of what caused that level of poverty—and, in the process, have provided a plausible motive for and explanation of what Jesus might have been doing when he staged a symbolic protest against the temple "moneychangers." It was not the moneychangers themselves to which Jesus objected, these scholars theorize,[43] but the elaborate system of crushing double taxation associated with the temple aristocracy and their Roman masters. When Jesus said they had made the temple a "den of thieves," he wasn't speaking metaphorically (Luke 19:46). "The Jerusalem Temple had the most lucrative system of temple commerce in the entire Roman world," Tabor writes. "As one might expect, there were certain fees and surcharges added to these services. These funds went to support the wealthy class of Sadducean priests who had their lavish homes just west of the Temple compound in the area called the 'Jewish Quarter' of the Old City today . . . To understand the economy in Jerusalem, which really was a type of 'Temple state,' one needs only 'follow the money.'"[44]

In *Excavating Jesus*, Crossan and Reed demonstrate how archaeology has revealed the lavish lifestyles of the overseers of this "temple state." The half-shekel tax, tithes, and fees for sacrificial animals were just a small portion of their revenues. Much more came from vast estates in Galilee and in the south. After the Six-Day War in 1967, Israeli archaeologists were able for the first time to excavate the palaces and mansions of the Sadducean aristocracy that had been destroyed by the Romans during the fall of Jerusalem in AD 70. The scale of the wealth astonished them: one house was about ten thousand square feet and covered with marble slabs that normally only a king could afford. Known as the Palatial Mansion, it was "representative of the residence of first-century wealthy Jewish families, for many other dwellings with mosaic floors, luxurious bathrooms, steam baths with underfloor heating, and ritualistic baths were discovered."[45]

Balage Belogh

After the Six Day War in 1967, Israeli archaeologists were able to excavate the private homes of the Jerusalem priestly aristocracy destroyed in AD 70 by the Romans. One home, known as the Palatial Mansion, was 10,000 square feet in size and had such luxuries as underfloor heating, mosaics, bathrooms, and ritual baths.

Now imagine a charismatic young prophet from Galilee overturning the tables of the moneychangers and telling the people that this was not what God wanted, threatening to stop the flow of *millions* of silver Tyrian shekels into the hands of the temple aristocracy. Now there is a motive for murder on anyone's terms. Jesus represented no military threat whatsoever, but the power of his ideas and his ideals was very real, and very threatening indeed.

One of the most radical and controversial of the current Historical Jesus scholars, John Dominic Crossan, is adamant that Jesus' symbolic protest action in the temple led to his arrest and execution. In his book *Who Killed Jesus,* Crossan does the math. In the disturbances following Herod's death, he points out, the Romans were able to loot from the temple treasury some four hundred talents of gold—when the total annual budget for all of Palestine under Herod Agrippa I (AD 41–44) was two thousand talents.[46] Earlier, in 54 BC, the Roman general Crassus was able to loot ten thousand talents from the temple.[47] Thus, Jesus' symbolic action was a denunciation of a system of taxation and fees that involved vast sums of money. Crossan writes, "My best historical reconstruction concludes that what led immediately to Jesus' arrest and execution in Jerusalem at Passover was that act of symbolic destruction, in deed and word, against the Temple. That sacred edifice represented in one central place all that his vision and program had fought against among the peasantry of Lower Galilee."[48]

JESUS' "ATTACK" ON THE TEMPLE

In the nineteenth and early twentieth centuries, New Testament scholars—from Hermann Reimarus to S. G. F. Brandon—speculated that Jesus' action in the temple may have been an actual assault, with armed followers. "The action of Jesus in 'Cleansing the Temple' appears to have been of a more symbolic character, in that it was an assault on an aspect of the sacerdotal government, and not a personal attack on members of the higher hierarchy," Brandon writes. "However, we must remember that our sources have purposely presented the matter in an idealistic manner, and that the real event must have been very different, inevitably involving violence and pillage."[49] Jesus was executed, after all, by the Roman governor and with the penalty commonly used for political insurgents, the cross. As a result, for the first half of the twentieth century, some scholars proposed that Jesus' main adversary was the Romans. Recently, Reza Aslan, in his bestselling book *Zealot,* recycles this same basic argument. But new archaeological discoveries and new directions in New Testament research are overturning these older, increasingly obsolete views. Many scholars now believe that Jesus was perhaps attacking the *temple system itself,* on both religious and socioeconomic grounds. These scholars, such as Crossan, James Tabor, and N. T. Wright, argue that Jesus performed what we might call an act of civil disobedience within the temple precincts—a symbolic protest roughly equivalent to pouring blood on draft cards—and this led the Sadducean aristocracy to plot an extrajudicial murder. They benefited from the temple system the most, so they had Jesus arrested and turned over to Pilate on trumped-up charges of being a political insurrectionist when he was nothing of the kind. Recent New Testament scholarship, such as that of Wright, is showing that the basic outline of the story as presented in the Gospels may not be that far from the truth, and it is certainly more plausible than many of the other scenarios that have been presented over the decades—for example, the idea, first put forth by S. G. F. Brandon, that Jesus and his followers led an armed assault on the temple precincts. Whatever Jesus' intention was when he took whips to the moneychangers in the temple, he clearly was making a statement of some kind. Scholars don't agree on what that statement was, but they increasingly agree that Jesus likely made some very powerful enemies as a result—enemies who had very practical reasons for wanting him silenced.

FOR FURTHER STUDY

Arav, Rami and John J. Rousseau. *Jesus and His World: An Archaeological and Cultural Dictionary.* Minneapolis, MN: Augsburg Fortress Press, 1995.

Crossan, John Dominic. *Who Killed Jesus?* San Francisco: HarperSanFrancisco, 1996.

Crossan, John Dominic and Jonathan L. Reed. *Excavating Jesus: Beneath the Stones, Behind the Texts.* San Francisco: HarperSanFrancisco, 2001.

Freund, Richard A. *Digging Through the Bible.* Lanham, MD: Rowman & Littlefield, 2009.

Geisler, Norman and Joseph M. Holden. *The Popular Handbook of Archaeology and the Bible.* Eugene, OR: Harvest House, 2013.

DID THE CHURCH INVENT THE IDEA OF A SUFFERING MESSIAH?

Jewish Scholars Take a Fresh Look at the Evidence

"Did not the Messiah have to suffer these things and then enter his glory?"

—LUKE 24:26 NIV

In 2008, Israeli officials unveiled what may turn out to be one of the most significant discoveries in biblical archaeology since the finding of the Dead Sea Scrolls in 1947: a large stone tablet, dating from the first century, on which were written in ink eighty-seven lines in ancient Hebrew script. The tablet contains the words *Ani Gabriel*, "I am Gabriel," the exact same phrase the angel told Zechariah, the father of John the Baptist, in the first chapter of Luke's gospel (v. 19). Dubbed the Gabriel Revelation, the stone tablet was discovered on the eastern banks of the Jordan River in 2000 and, after lengthy analysis by top archaeologists, is widely deemed authentic.[1] It is also part of an enormous debate now raging in New Testament scholarship.

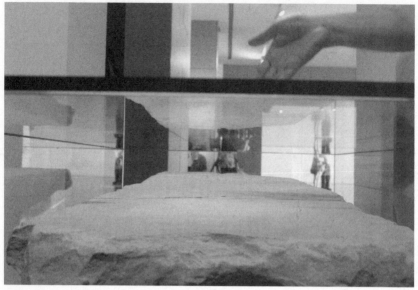

European Photo Agency

A stone tablet with ancient Hebrew writing, dating back to the first century AD, was discovered around the year 2000 near the Jordan River. Known as the Gabriel Revelation, the tablet describes an angel named Gabriel who speaks of a messiah who would suffer and die.

The Gabriel Revelation appears to describe the death of a messianic figure who lived just a few years before Jesus, who would either be *raised from the dead after three days* or who would be *granted a sign in three days.* On line eighty, the Hebrew text appears to read, "In three days, live, I Gabriel com[mand] yo[u]." But the text is faint. The word that appears to be the Hebrew imperative *hayeh* (חאיה), or "live," is smudged. Israel Knohl, a leading Israeli Bible scholar at the Hebrew University in Jerusalem who originally translated the text as "live," recently changed his mind and now says the word reads "sign" (האות). Nevertheless, he called the Gabriel Revelation "revolutionary" in its confirmation that the idea of a messiah suffering and dying was originally a Jewish concept, not a later invention of Christianity. "I believe Gabriel's Revelation . . . supports the view that the tradition of the messiah son of Joseph who is killed goes back to the late first century B.C.E. or the early first century C.E.," Knohl writes in *Biblical Archaeology Review.*[2]

Other Jewish scholars agree that the Gabriel Revelation confirms research that belief in a suffering and even dying messiah was not alien to first-century Judaism, as academic New Testament scholars have insisted for more than one hundred years. Rather it was part and parcel of the tapestry of messianic expectations that existed in the time of Jesus. As the Israeli literary critic Hillel Halkin put it while commenting on the Gabriel Revelation, "Third-day resurrection was 'in the air' of first-century Jewish Palestine, just like many other aspects of the Jesus story."[3]

Whether the excitement over the Gabriel Revelation ends up being justified or not, it is merely one in a series of new discoveries and developments that are calling into question much of what educated Christians have been told about the historical Jesus of Nazareth.

For more than a century, many academic Bible scholars have claimed that the Jews in Jesus' time had *no concept whatsoever* of a suffering messiah, let alone a messiah who would actually die. Therefore they suspected the whole idea was invented by the early Christian community and put into the mouth of Jesus decades later, by the evangelists. The Jews in Jesus' day expected the messiah to be a military leader and king, the argument goes, so obviously a suffering messiah is just a Christian apologetic device created to explain away the scandal of the cross.

This line of thinking was first pioneered in the nineteenth century by the original advocates of "higher criticism"—such as Johannes Weiss (1863–1914) and Heinrich Holtzmann (1832–1910)—and then refined in the work of Rudolf Bultmann in the early twentieth century. "[I]n the predictions of the Passion the Jewish concept of the Messiah-Son-of-Man is reinterpreted . . . insofar as *the idea of a suffering, dying, rising Messiah or Son of Man was unknown to Judaism*," wrote Bultmann, one of the godfathers of historical-critical study of the New Testament. "But this reinterpretation of the concept was done not by Jesus himself but by the Church *ex eventu*," or after the fact.[4]

For many years, Bultmann's declaration took on the character of unquestioned dogma in New Testament studies. Even today, some scholars, preachers, and Jewish writers will insist that Jesus' contemporaries expected *a conquering king*. The concept of a suffering messiah was *invented* by the early church, these scholars and writers say, by misinterpreting the prophecies in the Hebrew Bible and retroactively applying them to Jesus.

Bultmann wrote in the first half of the twentieth century, before the discovery of the Dead Sea Scrolls in 1947 revolutionized scholars' understanding of Second Temple Judaism. But other scholars, including some Dead Sea Scroll experts, continue to take the same line. "In communities ranging from the monkish Essenes at Qumran to the urbane, philosophical Diaspora Jews who followed a great Alexandrian scholar, Philo, the plain meaning of . . . the prophecies was accepted," writes David Klinghoffer in *Why the Jews Rejected Jesus.* "The Messiah would be a military and political leader."[5] More recently, Reza Aslan, author of *Zealot,* echoes this line of argument: "[T]he Jews of Jesus' time had no conception whatsoever of a messiah who suffers and dies. They were awaiting a messiah who triumphs and lives."[6] Bart Ehrman agrees. "Whatever specific idea any Jew had about the messiah (as cosmic judge, mighty priest, powerful warrior), what they all thought was that he would be a figure of grandeur and power who would be a mighty ruler of Israel," he writes in his 2014 book, *How Jesus Became God.*[7]

However, experts in Second Temple Judaism, such as Peter Schäfer of Princeton University, Israel Knohl of the Hebrew University of Jerusalem, and Daniel Boyarin of the University of California, Berkeley, all now argue that this century-old assumption—that the early Christian community made up the idea of a suffering messiah to explain away the scandal of Jesus' execution—is demonstrably false. They declare that *some* Jews in Jesus' time did very much expect a suffering messiah, perhaps even one who would die.

JEWISH SCHOLARS REEXAMINE THE EVIDENCE

When I first heard about the Gabriel Revelation, I was stunned: a Hebrew-language text from the first century that mentions the angel Gabriel? And one that mentions a messianic figure of some kind? It sounded too amazing to be true.

But it is true. Israel Knohl, the scholar who translated the ancient Hebrew tablet, is one of the most respected Bible scholars in Israel. He is the Yehezkel Kaufmann Chair of Biblical Studies at the Hebrew University of Jerusalem and a senior research fellow at the Shalom Hartman Institute in Jerusalem. He is also widely known as an authority on the concept of a suffering messiah in Second Temple Judaism, and the author of the book *The Messiah before Jesus: The Suffering Servant of the Dead Sea Scrolls.*

On a recent trip to Jerusalem, I had dinner with Knohl in the German Quarter, at a new bistro on chic Emek Refaim Street. An affable, stout fellow with a hearty laugh, Knohl was raised in a traditional Orthodox family, went to a Jewish academy (yeshiva) to study religion, and intended to study Talmud at Hebrew University. But he eventually switched to biblical studies and used the advanced skills of philological analysis that he had learned studying the Talmud to analyze the ancient biblical texts. Along the way, Knohl became fascinated by Christianity—and especially by the early connections between the followers of Jesus and various Jewish messianic groups in the Second Temple period, such as the Yahad community (widely believed to have been Essenes) at Qumran. (Archaeologists and Dead Sea Scroll scholars have long believed, based on the scrolls discovered in nearby caves, that the Qumran community was a kind of Jewish monastery made up of strict Torah-observant ascetics who had turned their backs on the temple aristocracy.)

Knohl is an Orthodox Jew. He doesn't believe Jesus of Nazareth is or was the messiah. But he does think Christians shouldn't let modern critical scholars claim that the early Christian community just made up the idea of a suffering messiah and applied it retroactively to Jesus. There were groups in Jesus' day that *did* expect a suffering, even dying, messiah, Knohl argues, and he believes that it is quite possible that Jesus himself could well have seen himself living out precisely this destiny.[8]

This undermines one of the principal claims of the older historical-critical scholarship: that much of the Gospels was *made up out of whole cloth* by the early church, and does not go back, in any way, shape, or form, to Jesus himself.

Clearly, each of the four evangelists had their own interpretation of the events of Jesus' life. As we discussed in chapter 1, they added and deleted material, inserted parenthetical comments, rearranged the incidents of Jesus' life, and likely shaped parts of Jesus' story to conform to prophecies in the Hebrew Bible. But that's not the same as saying that the evangelists made up one of the central themes of the entire New Testament, which is that Jesus somehow saw himself as fulfilling the destiny of a messiah who would suffer and die.

Knohl has been pondering these issues for decades. Did Jesus see himself as the Jewish messiah? Did he foresee his own suffering, death, and resurrection? If he did, why did he not refer to himself directly as the messiah instead of using veiled language, such as "Son of Man"? Did Jesus see himself as a divine redeemer?

Knohl notes in his classic book on the subject, *The Messiah before Jesus,*

The main tendency in New Testament scholarship for over a hundred years has been to attempt to resolve these difficulties by denying the historical reality of Jesus' claim to messiahship. Scholars of this viewpoint maintain that Jesus did not regard himself as a Messiah at all and that he was proclaimed Messiah by his disciples only after his death. Jesus, they claim, could not have foreseen his rejection, death, and resurrection, as "the idea of a suffering, dying and rising Messiah was unknown to Judaism."[9]

Courtesy the Jeselsohn Collection, Zurich, Switzerland

This is an overview of the Gabriel Revelation, dating to the early first century AD, showing the ancient Hebrew writing. Some Jewish experts say that this shows the early followers of Jesus didn't "make up" the idea of a suffering messiah to explain away the Crucifixion, as some New Testament scholars have claimed.

Knohl believes that this old scholarly view is entirely incorrect. Not only does he believe that Jesus thought of himself as the Messiah, he also thinks Jesus *expected* to be rejected, killed, and resurrected after three days. The reason: "That is precisely what was believed to have happened to a messianic leader who had lived one generation before Jesus."[10]

THE MESSIAH IN THE HEBREW BIBLE

The Hebrew word *mashiach,* which is translated as "Christ" in Greek and Latin, means simply "anointed." It comes from the Hebrew root *masah,* which means to melt oil on someone or something. In the Hebrew Bible, those who are anointed are kings, priests, and sometimes prophets. It is a symbol of a special status, the conferring of an office. Thus, throughout the Hebrew Bible, the messiah, or "anointed one," is most often a king. For example, in 1 Samuel 12:3, Saul is called the Lord's anointed (*mashiach*). Psalm 105 includes a prayer to "touch not my anointed ones (*meshachim*), do my prophets no harm" (v. 15 ESV).

At the same time, however, the Hebrew Bible contains oracles of numerous prophets concerning future Davidic kings—who are, by definition, "messiahs" in the sense that they are anointed. Some of these prophecies refer to specific situations and people in the times of the biblical prophets themselves; but the early followers of Jesus, and perhaps even Jesus himself, saw in these oracles eerie similarities to who and what he was and what he was trying to achieve. They gradually began to interpret the prophecies about a future Davidic king as referring to Jesus. For example, the prophet Micah, a contemporary of Isaiah—that is, living around 740 BC as the Assyrian Empire threatened to annihilate Jerusalem and the rest of Israel—proclaimed that a future king would come from Bethlehem to save God's people and bring peace:

> *But you, Bethlehem-Ephrathah,*
> *least among the clans of Judah,*
> *From you shall come forth for me*
> *one who is to be ruler in Israel . . .*
> *[H]is greatness shall reach to the ends of the earth:*
> *He shall be peace. (Mic. 5:1, 3–4)*

Over and over again, in fact, Israel's prophets insisted that the Jewish people look forward to a future ideal ruler who, unlike the kings of Israel, would be a true servant of God and who would establish a reign of peace on earth. These prophecies often came in times of war, when Israel was threatened by its enemies, or when it was living in exile. The prophet Jeremiah (ca. 650 BC), who witnessed the sacking of Jerusalem by the Babylonian Empire, predicted the coming of a righteous "branch" (Hebrew: *netzer*) of the House of David (Jer. 23:5–6). As the prophet watched his beloved Jerusalem burn to the ground in 587 BC, he uttered his famous oracle of the new covenant, which some scholars call "the Gospel before the Gospel":

> The days are coming, says the LORD, when I will make a new covenant with the house of Israel and the house of Judah, not like the covenant which I made with their fathers when I took them by the hand to bring them out of the land of Egypt . . . I will put my law within them, and I will write it upon their hearts; and I will be their God, and they shall be my people. . . . they shall all know me, from the least of them to the greatest, says the LORD; for I will forgive their iniquity, and I will remember their sin no more. (Jer. 31:31–34 RSV)

The prophets also speak of the future Davidic king in very universal terms, as an agent and herald of worldwide peace. The most famous example of this, used by Jesus' early followers extensively, comes from the prophet Isaiah:

> *For a child is born to us,*
> *a son is given to us.*
> *The government will rest on his shoulders.*
> *And he will be called:*
> *Wonder Counselor, Mighty God*
> *Everlasting Father, Prince of Peace. (9:6 NLT)*

Critical scholars of the Hebrew Bible often claim, of course, that Isaiah likely had in mind not Jesus of Nazareth but a successor to the Judean king Ahaz. But this objection does not bother many contemporary New Testament scholars. In their view, the early followers of Jesus discerned in the texts of the Hebrew Bible a deeper meaning, a "fuller sense" (*sensus plenior*), that the original human author may not have intended or known about, but which God *did* intend.[11] In other words, the early followers of Jesus saw these passages as "fitting" Jesus even if they knew the inspired human authors had someone else in mind, such as a future earthly king. Even more controversially, Jesus' followers saw in the prophet Isaiah's famous Suffering Servant oracles (Isa. 40–55) a fitting description of Jesus. This was despite some Jewish commentators insisting that these verses described Judah's last king, Zerubbabel, as the man who died, and the Jews' Persian occupier-king Darius as the man who would pardon them—not any future messianic king:

> But he was pierced for our transgressions,
> he was crushed for our iniquities;
> the punishment that brought us peace was on him,
> and by his wounds we are healed. . . .
> because he poured out his life unto death,
> and was numbered with the transgressors.
> For he bore the sin of many,
> and made intercession for the transgressors. (Isa. 53:5, 12 NIV)

DIVERSE VISIONS OF A JEWISH MESSIAH

It is not surprising, then, with all these various oracles and cryptic prophecies floating about in Israel's sacred books, that the Jewish people developed many different interpretations of what they all meant. The prophecies clearly pointed to some sort of idealized king, a descendent of David, who would usher in a new era of peace and righteousness—either alone or in conjunction with an idealized high priest. David Klinghoffer summarizes Israel's messianic expectation, articulated in the prophets such as Ezekiel, in the following list:

(1) gathering of Jewish exiles;
(2) the reign of a messianic king;
(3) a new covenant characterized by a scrupulous observance of the commandments;
(4) eternal peace;
(5) a new temple; and
(6) the nations recognize God.[12]

Klinghoffer argues that these criteria disqualify Jesus for any messianic claim because none of them was fulfilled during Jesus' lifetime. Christians, on the other hand, believe that Jesus never claimed his mission would be finished in his lifetime and that Jesus does meet many of these criteria, just not in the way that many people in his time expected.

What's more, some of the prophets foretold a messianic figure who would not be a conquering military leader. Zechariah, for example, predicted that the future just king would be meek and would appear "riding on a donkey" (symbolizing humility):

> *Shout for joy, O daughter Jerusalem!*
> *Behold: your king is coming to you,*
> *a just savior is he,*
> *Humble, and riding on a donkey,*
> *on a colt, the foal of a donkey.*
> *He shall banish the chariot from Ephraim,*
> *and the horse from Jerusalem;*
> *The warrior's bow will be banished,*
> *and he will proclaim peace to the nations.*
> *His dominion will be from sea to sea,*
> *and from the River to the ends of the earth. (Zech. 9:9–10)*

Some critical scholars believe the gospel writers used this passage to *make up* the story of the Palm Sunday entry into Jerusalem. It is an example of *midrash*, they say, a creative retelling of a story from the Hebrew Bible.

JESUS' PALM SUNDAY ENTRANCE INTO JERUSALEM

In Mark 11:1–10, Jesus arrives at Bethphage and Bethany, at the Mount of Olives, and sends two of his disciples into the nearby village. There they would find, he told them, a "colt" (Greek: *polos*). They were to untie it and bring it to him. Jesus added that if anyone questioned them about this, they were simply to say, "The Lord has need of it and will send it back here immediately" (ESV). Bart Ehrman points out that Matthew, always eager to find passages in the Hebrew Bible that confirm Jesus' mission, tells the same story but with a significant difference. In Matthew's version, Matthew is clearly echoing a prophecy in Zechariah 9:9 that refers to how "the king" will come humbly "mounted on a donkey, on a colt, the foal of a donkey" (ESV).

In Matthew's version of this story, Ehrman notes, Matthew clearly misunderstands the structure of Hebrew poetry and mistakenly believes that Zechariah was talking about *two different animals,* a donkey (*onos*) and a colt (*polos*), instead of just one animal (a donkey, a "colt," the foal of a donkey). Thus, he says, Matthew rewrites Mark's version to have Jesus' disciples go into the village to find "an ass tied, *and* a colt with her" (Matt. 21:2 KJV, emphasis added), specifying that they "brought the ass, and the colt, and put on them their clothes, and they set him thereon" (21:7 KJV). For Ehrman and some other critical scholars, this is proof that the whole incident never happened, that the gospel writers just made it up out of thin air.[13]

But Matthew's supposed misunderstanding of Hebrew poetry does no such thing. All this really proves is that Matthew may have modified Mark's version to make it conform better to a passage in Zechariah. That doesn't mean that Jesus didn't enter into Jerusalem in triumph or in a way heavy with messianic symbolism. What's more, the error in embellishment isn't even the main reason why Ehrman doubts the historicity of the entire episode. Ehrman's reasons for doubt center on "why didn't the authorities immediately take notice and have [Jesus] arrested both for causing a disturbance and for claiming to be the Jewish king (when only Rome could appoint the king)? Instead, according to Matthew and the other Gospels, Jesus spent an unmolested week in Jerusalem and only then was arrested and put on trial."[14]

WHY DIDN'T ROMAN SOLDIERS ARREST HIM?

Other scholars point to many possible reasons why Jesus was not arrested on the spot. For one, the "crowds" in Jerusalem (Matt. 21:9) may not have been all that large—or, even if they had been, they might simply have blended in with the enormous mass of Jewish humanity that was crowded into the holy city during Passover. For another, any soldiers standing guard may not have been paying that much attention to Jesus and his followers, or might not have understood what all the fuss was about.

Ehrman states that "it defies belief that the Roman authorities who were in town precisely in order to prevent any mob actions or uprisings would have failed to intervene if the crowds shouted in acclamation for a new ruler arriving in town."[15] While the text of Matthew does say that the whole city was in turmoil over the arrival of Jesus, it was, the texts say, because he was "a prophet," not an invading king. In addition, historians believe that, during the major pilgrim feasts such as Passover, the population of Jerusalem swelled to between 250,000 and 1 million people, while the number of Roman soldiers, who probably knew no Aramaic whatsoever, was only about fifteen hundred men at most.

How does it "defy belief" that a handful of Latin- or Greek-speaking guards at one of Jerusalem's gates would not have taken action when a large group of happy Jews, singing Hosanna in Aramaic, passed through? I was recently in Jerusalem during a time when Qassam rockets were being fired from Gaza and the Israeli police were on high alert, and yet throngs of people were entering through Jerusalem's gates with nary a glance cast in their direction. I saw a large bar mitzvah party, for example, complete with an entire band, pass through the Zion Gate while the Israeli guards stood laughing and chatting, oblivious.

Plus, the Roman soldiers would have had no clue what the Jews were even saying. Jesus' followers would have resembled many of the other groups of religion-besotted pilgrims flooding into the holy city during Passover. Ehrman concludes that "Jesus almost certainly came to Jerusalem . . . but not like this." The story of Palm Sunday, he says, "has been made up (or adopted) in order to show that he fulfilled the prophecy of Zechariah."[16]

Yet that simply doesn't follow. A far more plausible alternative is that the Palm Sunday entrance into Jerusalem did happen more or less the way the Gospels describe it. This is for one simple reason: the Gospels clearly state that Jesus *deliberately* arrived in Jerusalem in this way since he appears to have made arrangements for a colt in advance. Entering into Jerusalem on a donkey, echoing the famous prophecy in Zechariah, was a political and religious statement of what he was all about. Every Jew in Jerusalem would have suspected what Jesus was intimating if he rode through one of the city's gates on a donkey. For first-century Jews, if not for us, the symbolism was overwhelming. It would be like a US citizen walking into a political gathering with the music of "Hail to the Chief" blaring in the background. Subtle it was not. The fact that the author who wrote the gospel of Matthew, when he rewrote the passage from Mark, misunderstood the text of Zechariah and thought it referred to two separate animals—both a colt and an ass—doesn't mean the incident as described in Mark didn't happen. It just means that Matthew tried too hard to make the story fit the prophecy. Mark, likely the original source, did not.

THE MESSIAH IN THE NEW TESTAMENT

Even a cursory glance through the New Testament reveals that the early followers of Jesus believed he was the long-awaited messiah promised in the Hebrew Bible and written about in many so-called intertestamental writings, including the Dead Sea Scrolls. What exactly they understood his messianic status to mean, however, is another question.

The very first sentence of Mark's gospel begins with the declaration, "The beginning of the good news about Jesus the Messiah [*christos*], the Son of God" (NIV).[17] When Jesus asked Peter point-blank who Peter thought he was, the fisherman replied, "You are the Messiah" (Mark 8:29 NRSV). And when Jesus stood before the high priest at his trial and was asked if he was, in fact, the Jewish messiah, the "son of the Blessed One," Mark does not have Jesus dodge the question. "I am," said Jesus. "And you will see the Son of Man sitting at the right hand of the Mighty One and coming on the clouds of heaven" (Mark 14:61–62 NIV).

The other Synoptics follow suit. In Acts, the author has Peter proclaiming at Pentecost, "Therefore let all Israel be assured of this: God has made this Jesus, whom you crucified, both Lord and Messiah" (2:36 NIV). And of course the gospel of John is even more explicit: "These [signs] are written that you may believe that Jesus is the Messiah, the Son of God, and that by believing you may have life in his name" (20:31 NIV).

But what sort of messiah do the authors of the Gospels and the other New Testament writings envisage? In chapter 2, we touched upon the fact that many critical scholars believe that Jesus was a deluded End Times fanatic who eagerly looked forward to God obliterating the enemies of

Israel in his own lifetime; that he was an avenging agent, or even a catalyst, of God's wrath. Yet in the gospel of Mark, Jesus asks rhetorically, "Why then is it written that the Son of Man must suffer much and be rejected?" (9:12 NIV). In the Synoptics, Jesus predicts his own death three times and repeatedly warns his disciples that the Son of Man will suffer (Mark 8:31).[18] When the apostles begin to bicker among themselves about who is the most important among them, Jesus tells them that they are not to lord it over their fellows the way the Gentile high officials do. Instead, he says, whoever wants to become great among them must be the servant of all—"just as the Son of Man did not come to be served, but to serve, and to give his life as a ransom for many" (Matt. 20:28 NIV).

The apostle Paul, too, discusses the suffering that Jesus Christ, "Jesus Messiah," had to endure: "For just as we share abundantly in the sufferings of Christ, so also our comfort abounds through Christ" (2 Cor. 1:5 NIV). He tells the Philippians that he wants to "know Christ—yes, to know the power of his resurrection and participation in his sufferings, becoming like him in his death" (Phil. 3:10 NIV).

THE MESSIANIC HOPES IN THE DEAD SEA SCROLLS

Israel Knohl and other Jewish scholars argue that ideas about a suffering messiah and resurrection were already in the air when Jesus was proclaiming the arrival of the kingdom of God. They were not invented by the early Christian community as an apologetic device after the fact, as many New Testament scholars claimed in the twentieth century. They were found even in the Yahad community at Qumran. Knohl explains that hymns found among the Dead Sea Scrolls refer to an earlier messiah, a leader of the community at Qumran, who described himself as sitting on a heavenly throne.

> [Who has been despised like [me And who] has been rejected [of men] like me? [And who] compares to m[e in enduring] evil.
>
> Who is like me among the angels? [I] am the beloved of the king, a companion of the ho[ly ones].[19]

This hymn, known as the Self-Glorification Hymn among Dead Sea Scroll scholars, is clearly an echo of the "Suffering Servant" in Isaiah. "In view of the close connection we find in the Dead Sea literature between the coming of the Messiah and the forgiveness of sins," Knohl concludes, "one may suppose that the speaker in the first hymn . . . was regarded by his community as someone who through his sufferings had to atone for the sin of all the members of his sect."[20]

Knohl argues that the messianic interpretation of Isaiah 53—that is, of a messianic figure who would suffer and, through his suffering, redeem the people—was not invented by the Christian community. Rather, it was already a part of the teachings of esoteric Judaism, lived out by such religious sects as the Essenes, as early as the second half of the first century BC. "In view of these facts," Knohl says, "we should consider the possibility that the depiction of Jesus as a combination of the 'son of man' and the 'suffering servant' was not a later invention of the Church."[21]

And that's not all. Knohl also points to an obscure ancient prophecy, a lost pseudepigraphical book known in scholarly circles as the Oracle of Hystaspes, as further proof that many Jews in the time of Jesus expected a suffering and dying savior. The oracle was supposedly delivered by a king of the Medes who lived before the Trojan War. In fact, scholars have identified the author as a Jew writing about the Jewish people sometime in the early first century of the common era. The oracle is mentioned by Justin Martyr (ca. 100–165) and portions are preserved by the Christian writer Lactantius (ca. 240–320). The Oracle of Hystaspes predicts the coming of two kings. One, a false prophet, will call himself God and be worshipped as the son of God—which Knohl claims was Caesar Augustus, the *divi filius*, or "son of God." But there will also come a great prophet "to turn men to the knowledge of God" and who will "receive the power of doing wonderful things." The evil king, who calls himself the "son of God," will wage war against the prophet of God:

He shall fight against the prophet of God and shall overcome and slay him, and shall suffer him to life unburied; but *after the third day he shall come to life again*; and while all look on and wonder, he shall be caught up to heaven.[22]

Knohl believes that the prophet referred to both in the Self-Glorification Hymn and in the Oracle of Hystaspes was a real historical person—whom he tentatively identifies as the Essene leader Menahem, a counselor of King Herod and described at length by Josephus. Knohl believes Menahem was killed in Jerusalem during the civil war that arose after King Herod's death in 4 BC and was likely one of the two thousand Jewish leaders crucified by Quintilius Varus, Augustus' governor in Syria.[23]

Like Jesus, this earlier messiah saw himself as the Suffering Servant mentioned in Isaiah, an agent of God Almighty who would usher in a new age of redemption in which all sins would be wiped away. Like Jesus, this earlier Essene messiah found himself rejected by the Pharisees . . . and was killed in Jerusalem. His Essene followers then searched the Hebrew scriptures for prophecies of the humiliation and death of the messiah. In this way, Knohl says, what he calls "catastrophic messianism" was born, one in which the "humiliation, rejection and death of the Messiah were regarded as an inseparable part of the redemptive process." His conclusion: "We have clear evidence that the idea of a suffering Messiah already existed one generation before Jesus," he writes. "Jesus' messianic mission was therefore a journey towards a known suffering and death."[24]

DANIEL BOYARIN AND THE JEWISH GOSPELS

If Israel Knohl's intention was to rekindle interest in the diversity of Jewish views on the messiah, he succeeded. In recent years, there have been a number of new studies focused on Jewish attitudes toward a suffering messiah, from both Christian and Jewish scholars. In fact, the recent research has even triggered a feud of sorts between two famous academics—Peter Schäfer of Princeton University and Daniel Boyarin of the University of California, Berkeley. Schäfer is a Christian who argues that Christianity helped give birth to Judaism; and Boyarin is an Orthodox Jew who argues that Judaism and Christianity were siblings who grew up together. Both agree that in the time of Jesus and for quite a while afterward, the borderlines between what we now know as Judaism and Christianity were, in Boyarin's phrase, quite porous.

Daniel Boyarin is the Taubman Professor of Talmudic Culture at the

University of California, Berkeley, and author of the provocative 2012 book *The Jewish Gospels: The Story of the Jewish Christ*. He has long been considered a maverick of sorts, and is briefly the subject of the award-winning Israeli film *Footnote*.[25] While Israel Knohl's research focuses on the concept of the suffering messiah in the Dead Sea Scrolls, Boyarin directs most of his attention to some Jewish apocalyptic texts that are part of what scholars call the "pseudepigrapha" or "intertestamental" works—that is, Jewish works written in the two centuries immediately before the New Testament was completed. In particular, Boyarin looks carefully at the term *Son of Man* in the Book of Similitudes in First Enoch (first century BC) and Fourth Ezra (AD first century).

Boyarin argues that New Testament scholars in the twentieth century made two big mistakes when it came to understanding the central ideas of the New Testament, both of which occurred because of a faulty knowledge of Second Temple Judaisms. Both these errors, he asserts, were due to anachronistically projecting the ideas and beliefs present in the Talmud, codified centuries after Jesus' era, back onto the era of the Second Temple when Jesus rode into Jerusalem. The first mistake occurred when New Testament scholars decided that the Jews in Jesus' age would never have tolerated the concept of a divine-human redeemer and that this idea, of Jesus as a kind of Jewish God-man, plainly was a *pagan* concept introduced into Christianity as the Jesus movement spread out into the Gentile world. According to Boyarin, this is completely false. An analysis of intertestamental Jewish texts plainly shows, he argues, that the Jews in Jesus' time were experimenting with esoteric ideas of "binitarianism," or the notion of two divine figures of equal substance and power (such as an older and younger God, Father, and Son).[26]

The second major mistake that twentieth-century New Testament scholars made, Boyarin suggests, was claiming that the Jews in the time of Jesus had *no concept whatsoever of a suffering messiah*. Jewish scholars, too, contributed to this false idea, Boyarin says.[27] He points to the pioneering work of the Israeli scholar Joseph Klausner in his classic book, *The Messianic Idea in Israel*, as proof. "According to Klausner's generally held view, the idea of messianic suffering, death, and resurrection came about only as an apology after the fact of Jesus' death," Boyarin writes.[28] To explain the scandal of Jesus being executed as a common criminal, in other words, the early followers of Jesus invented the idea of a suffering messiah and then went looking through the Hebrew Bible to find passages, such as Isaiah 53, to serve as proof texts supporting their invention.

The notion that Jesus' followers designated him as a suffering messiah after the fact is still repeated with dogmatic certitude in many universities and seminaries today. It is also, Boyarin claims, completely false. These uncomfortable facts have been uncovered and documented by modern messianic Jews.[29] Until very recently, Jewish commentators always understood the Suffering Servant passages of Isaiah 53 to refer to the messiah, Boyarin adds,[30] not as metaphors for the people of Israel as is often claimed. "This commonplace view," Boyarin says—that the early Christians distorted Isaiah 53 from its original meaning—"has to be rejected completely," adding "[t]he notion of the humiliated and suffering Messiah was not at all alien within Judaism before Jesus' advent, and it remained current among Jews well into the future following that—indeed, well into the early modern period."[31] This can be plainly seen in the Talmud, the great encyclopedia of Jewish commentary of biblical law. In Tractate Sanhedrin of the Babylonian Talmud, Boyarin says, it is asked what the name of the Messiah is or will be. The answer "the leper" is given, the text says, because he, the messiah, "has borne our disease, and suffered our pains, and we thought him smitten, beaten by God and tortured"—a quotation from Isaiah 53:4.[32] Passages in the Talmud such as these, Boyarin concludes, show "both the vicarious suffering of the Messiah and the use of Isaiah 53 to anchor the idea."[33]

Boyarin concludes *The Jewish Gospels* with a radical challenge to the older, increasingly problematic scholarship of the twentieth century—which reflexively posits that, when in doubt, the early church must have made it all up. Boyarin doesn't believe there are many good reasons for holding this simplistic, dismissive attitude among scholars. His research "challenges the notion that the New Testament itself is an appropriation, or—even better—a misappropriation of the Old."[34]

The ideas that many modern scholars think are most characteristically Christian are really Jewish through and through. "[T]he notion of a dual godhead with a Father and a Son, the notion of a Redeemer who himself will be both God and man, and the notion that this Redeemer would suffer and die as part of the salvation process" all have "deep roots in the

Hebrew Bible" and "may be among some of the most ancient ideas about God and the world that the Israeli people ever held," Boyarin asserts.[35] In other words: The early Jesus movement didn't have to put words into Jesus' mouth, after the fact, supporting the notion that the messiah would have to suffer "many things." This view was common knowledge, at least in certain circles in Jesus' lifetime. The preemptory approach typical of early twentieth-century German New Testament scholarship went too far and, in doing so, misunderstood what the New Testament was actually saying and how it came to be written.

These ideas are like heresy in the sheltered world of contemporary New Testament scholarship and have ignited fierce debate. Peter Schäfer, a German-born professor of religion and until recently professor of Judaic Studies at Princeton University, wrote a scathing review of *The Jewish Gospels* in 2013 in the pages of *The New Republic*. Schäfer's complaint doesn't appear to be with the substance of Boyarin's analysis of the suffering messiah per se, but with something else. He faults Boyarin for not citing the antecedents of his research more thoroughly and acting as though the "discovery" of the suffering messiah in the Second Temple era was entirely his own. But more importantly, Schäfer is reacting to the view, common among some Jewish scholars, that sees in Jesus *nothing really new.*

One of the ways some Jewish scholars, such as Schmuley Boteach, approach Jesus is to assert that he fit in completely with the Jewish world of his day, and that any tension between Jesus and the "scribes and Pharisees," as seen in the Gospels, was simply made up by the early church to reflect the situation that existed fifty to one hundred years after the crucifixion. Schäfer perceives a bit of this dynamic in Boyarin's work, as though Jesus and the movement he founded was just one of the many strands of Judaism current in his day. After years in which scholars portrayed Jesus as essentially hostile toward Judaism, Schäfer says, "the pendulum has swung far in the opposite direction, with scholars outdoing each other in proving the Jewishness of Jesus and the New Testament, and arguing that there is nothing in Jesus' message as reflected in the New Testament that oversteps the boundaries of what might be expected from the Judaism of his day."[36] Boyarin denies this, however. He claims, instead, that Judaism and Christianity in a sense grew up together, and as siblings often do, eventually went their separate ways.[37]

FOR FURTHER STUDY

Boyarin, Daniel. *The Jewish Gospels.* New York: The New Press, 2012.

Knohl, Israel. *The Messiah before Jesus: The Suffering Servant of the Dead Sea Scrolls.* Berkeley: University of California Press, 2000.

Neusner, Jacob. *A Rabbi Talks with Jesus.* New York: Doubleday, 1993.

Schäfer, Peter. *The Jewish Jesus: How Judaism and Christianity Shaped Each Other.* Princeton, NJ: Princeton University Press, 2012.

Stein, Robert H. *Jesus the Messiah.* Downers Grove, IL: IVP Academic, 1996.

6

JUST HOW KOSHER WAS JESUS?

What It Meant to Be Jewish in Jesus' Day

*"Do not think that I have come to abolish the law or
the prophets; I have not come to abolish but to fulfill."*

—MATTHEW 5:17 NRSV

Jesus of Nazareth lived in a disorienting age, in some ways very much like our own. Everything in his homeland was in flux. Traditional beliefs and practices were under assault. The ordinary people, suffering under brutal military occupation and crushing taxation, were exposed to a cornucopia of bizarre and conflicting ideas. Palestine was a crossroads through which passed all sorts of exotic people and beliefs. According to Josephus, the Jerusalem aristocrat born in AD 37/38 who chronicled the tragic war of his people against the Roman empire, there were four major sects, or what he calls "philosophies," common among people in his era: the Pharisees, Sadducees, Essenes, and what he calls the Fourth Philosophy, or Zealots.[1] In the time of Jesus, all these groups were in the minority, numbering only a few thousand adherents each, all trying to win converts to their unique ways of understanding the Torah. Most ordinary people, the people of the land, hewed to the traditions of their forefathers as best they could without formally joining any of these sects.

The Sadducees, as we know from both Josephus[2] and the New Testament (Mark 12:18), accepted only the written Torah, the first five books of the Hebrew Bible, as God's inspired teaching. They also denied the existence of the afterlife. The esoteric Essenes, austere and celibate Jewish monks who rejected the entire temple system, lived in desert communities apart from the people and practiced rituals of purification. The Pharisees, who evolved gradually into orthodox rabbinic Judaism, believed in an oral tradition that created a "fence around the Torah" to make it impossible, they believed, for any written commandment to be violated. The Pharisees believed in a multitude of extra laws (*gezeirot*) and practices designed to protect the 613 biblical commandments. For example, as we mentioned in chapter one, the Pharisees eventually enumerated the thirty-nine categories of forbidden activities on the Sabbath in order to protect the commandment against "work" on the Sabbath. The Zealots, who were also strict in their loyalty to Torah law, believed it was their moral duty before God to overthrow the Romans and to reestablish a Jewish kingdom in the land.[3]

In AD 66, the Zealots and other Jewish nationalist groups succeeded finally in launching their longed-for holy war against Rome. After four years of bloody conflict, the war resulted in the temple being destroyed, much of Jerusalem being burned to the ground, the Jewish aristocracy being hauled off to Rome in chains as slaves, and as many as one million Jews being slaughtered.[4] In the aftermath of this national conflagration, perhaps the greatest tragedy to befall the Jewish people up to that point in their history, Jewish leaders needed to regroup and strategize. The Pharisees had the most practical program to offer: a way of life based on Torah study, not sacrifices in a no-longer-existing temple. It was centered around the new institution of the synagogue.

Both the Mishnah (the earliest part of the Talmud) and the New Testament reflect the debates, before and after Jesus, about how all this would work out in practice. Jews debated whether and to what degree the innovations of the Pharisee program contradicted the plain meaning of the written Torah text. The debates between Jesus and the Pharisees could get heated, as the New Testament plainly shows. "Woe to you, blind guides,"

Matthew records Jesus declaring. "You say, 'If anyone swears by the temple, it means nothing; but anyone who swears by the gold of the temple is bound by that oath.' You blind fools! Which is greater: the gold, or the temple that makes the gold sacred?" (23:16–17 NIV). In the past, many Jewish and critical scholars have claimed that these acerbic comments really reflected the debates the followers of Jesus were having later with the Pharisees in the AD 70s, 80s, and 90s as Christianity took root, not what Jesus himself said to the Pharisees in the AD 20s.[5] Supposedly, these arguments and debates in the Gospels about various points of Jewish law were, once again, simply fabricated by the early church to emphasize how distinct the Jesus movement was from Judaism. But now, some Jewish scholars are reconsidering and wondering whether the debates in the New Testament make sense and could very well be historically accurate records of Jesus' own teaching.

Shutterstock

KOSHER JESUS: JESUS AS A LOYAL PHARISEE

A recent advocate of an older scholarly view of Jesus—that he was a loyal Pharisee completely in harmony with the religious establishment of his day—is Rabbi Shmuley Boteach, the bestselling author of many books on

Judaism and married life, including *Kosher Sex: A Recipe for Passion and Intimacy* (1999), *Shalom in the Home* (2007), *The Kosher Sutra* (2009), and *Renewal: A Guide to the Values-Filled Life* (2010). A self-admitted self-promoter[6] who calls himself "America's rabbi," Boteach is one of the most famous rabbis in the world, a spiritual adviser to the late Michael Jackson, and a media phenomenon in his own right. He is also an Orthodox rabbi in the Chabad-Lubavitch Hasidic tradition and the father of nine children, and he hosted two seasons of the TV show *Shalom in the Home* on TLC, where he dispensed advice on building strong families.

In 2012, Boteach decided to wade into the complex world of historical Jesus studies and published a new book about the Jewishness of Jesus of Nazareth, which he titled *Kosher Jesus*. He argued that Jesus was "a Jewish patriot murdered by Rome for his struggle on behalf of his people" and should be embraced rather than scorned by the Jewish community. "Just as Christians would greatly benefit from a deeper understanding of Jesus the man, Jews need to accept that they have something to learn from Jesus as well," Boteach declared.[7]

According to Boteach, Jesus was an extraordinary but very mainstream Jewish man in the first century who, in a sense, said and did nothing to which observant Jews today could object. He *did* think he was the messiah, but that wasn't *that* unusual in the first century and certainly would not make him an apostate in and of itself. Josephus mentions[8] a half dozen people, before and after Jesus, who led rebellions and had messianic aspirations. What Jesus certainly did not think of himself as being, according to Boteach, was "divine" in any way, shape, or form. As Boteach puts it:

> Jesus lived, taught, and died as a Jew. He defined himself and his Jewishness in much the same way as today's Torah-observant Jews. He conducted himself as a devout rabbi and Pharisee. He wore a Jewish head covering, prayed in the Hebrew language, ate only kosher food, honored the Sabbath, had the mezuzah parchment on the doorposts of his home, lit a Chanukah menorah, wore the tzitzit-fringes, donned tefillin daily, waved an *esrog* and *lulav* on Sukkot, ate matzo on Passover, and studied the Torah regularly. He enjoyed the selfsame relationship with God shared by all Jews.[9]

Of course, up to that point few Christians would disagree. Most understand that Jesus was Jewish, followed the traditions of his people, made pilgrimages to Jerusalem to observe the feasts, and did everything that was required of him. But to make his case that Jesus was just like any other good Jewish man of his day, Boteach must ignore much of what the New Testament says about Jesus' deeds and teaching, mirroring the approach of the revisionist scholars of the twentieth century and some historical Jesus scholars today. Boteach holds that Jesus' followers in general, and the New Testament in particular, *misrepresented* much of what Jesus said, did, and believed. "The early Christians, led by Paul, needed to promote the idea that Jesus was a religious reformer rather than a political rebel," Boteach writes. "After all, they couldn't upset Rome, which already looked disdainfully on the fledgling Church. The gospels were therefore edited to purge Jesus of all anti-Roman vitriol, and Jesus' story was edited to reflect a conflict between himself and the Jews."[10]

One of these deliberate misrepresentations, he says, is the New Testament's depiction of some Jewish leaders calling for Jesus' arrest and execution. Clearly, the accusation that "the Jews" killed Christ has resulted in untold miseries for the Jewish people over the last two thousand years. Boteach insists that the Gospels' depiction of the involvement of Jewish leaders in Jesus' arrest is completely false. Jesus "fought Roman paganism and persecution of the Jewish people, and was killed by Pontius Pilate for his rebellion against Rome, the Jews having had nothing whatsoever to do with his murder," he writes in a column in *The Jerusalem Post*.[11] This is also the view put forth by many other Jewish writers on Jesus in the twentieth century, such as the Anglo-British Jewish writer Hyam Maccoby[12] and the early pioneer of Jesus studies in Israel, Joseph Klausner[13] (1874–1958) of Hebrew University of Jerusalem.

WHAT THE TALMUD SAYS ABOUT JESUS

The problem is, the view that Jesus had no conflicts with the religious authorities of his day and was executed solely by the Romans because he was a revolutionary contradicts much of what both Jewish and Christian sources say about Jesus. The earliest traditions about Jesus recorded in the Talmud, the encyclopedia of Jewish commentary on biblical law compiled between AD 200 and 500, say that Jesus was *not* a "Torah observant teacher," as Boteach claims, but an *apostate*—and that some Jewish leaders had a hand, at least, in securing Jesus' execution by the Romans. In Tractate Sanhedrin of the Babylonian Talmud, it is written that "Yeshu ha-Notzri" was executed "because he has practiced sorcery and enticed Israel to apostasy."[14] The first-century Jewish historian Josephus wrote that Jesus died "when, upon the accusation of the principal men among us, Pilate had condemned him to a cross."[15] Boteach knows about this objection, of course. He even addresses it in an appendix.[16] However, his way of handling the Talmudic evidence is to claim that the "Yeshu" in the Talmud is not Jesus of Nazareth but *another* Jesus, a student of Rabbi Yehoshua ben Perachyah, who began predicting the Temple's destruction in AD 64, about thirty years after Jesus of Nazareth was crucified. This is an old argument, apparently first made by the Talmud scholar Yechiel ben Joseph, during a disputation in Paris in 1290.[17] Nevertheless, many modern historians do believe that the Yeshu in the Talmud refers to Jesus of Nazareth because, in some manuscripts, he is even called Yeshu ha-Notzri, which means "Jesus the Nazarene" in Hebrew.

Boteach bases much of *Kosher Jesus* on the writings of the controversial Anglo-Jewish scholar Hyam Maccoby, famous for his theory that the apostle Paul was the real founder of Christianity.[18] Maccoby, who died in 2004, believed that Paul was a Gentile convert or a Gentile masquerading as a Jew who injected all sorts of pagan ideas he learned from Greek mystery cults into the original Jesus movement. Many of Maccoby's ideas on the historical Jesus, however, were pretty much in line with the "Jesus Was a Deluded Apocalyptic Prophet" concept that was fashionable in the early twentieth century and made popular by Dr. Albert Schweitzer in his classic 1911 book, *The Quest of the Historical Jesus*. According to Maccoby and Boteach, Jesus was a loyal, Torah-observant Pharisaic Jew who never challenged Jewish law in the least. He was not exactly a Zealot revolutionary, but he did believe he was the messiah, expecting God to intervene and save Israel from the Roman occupation. This belief was contradicted, however, when Jesus was unexpectedly arrested and executed by the Romans for sedition. However, his followers maintained his Torah-based community in Jerusalem, under his brother James the Just, with many believing that Jesus had been raised from the dead. For Maccoby and Boteach, this strictly orthodox Jewish sect, the followers of the rabbi Jesus, had nothing to do with the pagan religion, Christianity, created by the false Jew Paul. Paul "radically shifted Jesus' message away from politics and toward religion," Boteach writes. "Whereas Jesus preached to reinforce Judaism, Paul preached to abrogate it. Jesus came to rebel against Rome. Paul, the Roman citizen, absolves the Romans from killing Jesus and blames the Jews instead. Jesus loved his people and devoted himself to their welfare. But Paul made Jesus and the Jews into bitter enemies . . ."[19]

JESUS WAS A HIGHLY TRAINED RABBI, NOT AN ILLITERATE PEASANT

One point Boteach makes is that Jesus was obviously not, as Reza Aslan and many others claim, an "illiterate peasant" who knew little about Jewish law and scriptures. Boteach points out that, in the first century and afterward, it was quite common for learned rabbis to work at manual labor. "The Talmud documents numerous examples of sages who had 'bluecollar' professions so as to avoid financial dependence on their community of students," he writes.[20] Boteach points to the example of the great sage Hillel, who worked as a bricklayer or stone mason (similar to Jesus' profession, described in the New Testament as a *tekton*, or "builder"). Rabbi Yochanan (100–150), one of the sages of the Mishnah, was a shoemaker. Christians would point to Paul's profession as a tent maker.

Not only was Jesus a rabbi, Boteach adds, he was a deeply learned, well-versed student of Jewish holy texts. This can be seen by the way Jesus used sophisticated Pharisaic rules of interpretation. There are, Boteach explains, seven rules in all. The first and most important is *kal ve-chomer*, or "light and heavy." This means, Boteach says, that if a principle applies in a "light," or simple, example then it will also apply in a "heavy," or more complex, one. He quotes a famous Jewish scholar, David Biven, on how the Talmudic sage Rabbi Meir used *kal ve-chomer* analysis for a passage in Deuteronomy: "If the Scripture has thus spoken: 'I agonize over the blood of the wicked,' how much more so over the blood of the righteous that is shed?'"[21] This type of reasoning can be found throughout Jesus' recorded teachings, according to

Boteach. Whenever in the Gospels Jesus uses the words, "how much more so," Boteach explains, that demonstrates a classic *kal ve-chomer* type of reasoning. Here is an example from the gospel of Matthew: Jesus said, "If you, then, though you are evil, know how to give good gifts to your children, *how much more* will your Father in heaven give good gifts to those who ask Him?" (7:11 NIV, emphasis added). Boteach's conclusion: "None but a well-trained Pharisaic rabbi would draw so reliably and so heavily on the knowledge of his rabbinic predecessors in such a textbook way. And we can only conclude that Jesus was exactly that—a classically trained rabbinic scholar."[22]

Jesus' sophisticated knowledge of Torah and the rules of interpretation can also be seen in his alleged disputes with the scribes over Sabbath keeping. Boteach argues that far from flouting the Torah, Jesus' arguments show a highly sophisticated, nuanced understanding of the issues being debated in his day. Boteach asserts that "we can accept as fact" the description in the New Testament that Jesus "defied the rules of the Sabbath and allowed his apostles to do likewise."[23] But, he adds, this isn't as simple as it seems. When Jesus defends the plucking of grain by his followers on the Sabbath (Mark 2:23), in apparent violation of the Sabbath, he echoes the story from the first book of Samuel in which the starving David and his men, on the run from Saul, eat the holy bread in the Tabernacle even though they are not priests and such actions are normally forbidden (1 Sam. 21:6). This follows the established rabbinic principle, Boteach says, that the preservation of human life takes precedence over all else, even adhering to the laws in the Torah. Since Jesus and his men were starving, he claims, they were more than justified in violating the Jewish prohibition against work on the Sabbath since they needed to preserve their lives.

On another occasion, when Jesus is criticized for healing a crippled man on the Sabbath (John 5:1–47), Jesus quotes a legal precedent, preserved in the Talmud, to prove that his action is justified. Boteach explains that the Torah commands that a male child be circumcised on the eighth day after birth, but if that day happens to fall on the Sabbath, the circumcision is still allowed even though it is "drawing blood." The Talmud draws from this exception the notion that medical procedures can and must be done on the Sabbath. According to Tractate Yoma, "if circumcision, which concerns one of the 248 members of the body, overrides the Sabbath, shall not a man's whole body override the Sabbath?"[24] Boteach then points to the *nearly identical reasoning* used by Jesus for his justification of healing a crippled man on the Sabbath, recorded by John: "Now if a boy can be circumcised on the Sabbath so that the Law of Moses may not be broken," Jesus says, "why are you angry with me for healing a man's whole body on the Sabbath?" (7:23 NIV). Once again, this suggests that Jesus may not have been an "illiterate peasant"—as many contemporary authors claim[25]—but *a highly trained rabbi* fully conversant with the complex legal and religious debates in his day.[26]

THE ORTHODOX ESTABLISHMENT: JESUS WAS *NOT* KOSHER!

The Gospels portray Jesus as being a very divisive figure who attracted numerous followers but also ignited heated opposition. The publication of Boteach's *Kosher Jesus* proved that this is still the case. Rabbi Yitzchok Wolf of Chicago declared that even the title *Kosher Jesus* is *apikorsus,* a Hebrew word that means something like heretical. "This book poses great danger to the thousands of unsuspecting Jews who are approached daily by Jews for J with the sole purpose of getting them to embrace Christianity," the rabbi wrote in an e-mail to an Orthodox Jewish website. He refused, as many Orthodox Jews do, even to use the name "Jesus" in his writing and instead called him "Yoshke," a Yiddish diminutive of Yehoshua, a variation of Jesus' name. "To Jews for J this book will now become the Jewish Rabbinical textbook urging embracing Yoshke as an authentic Jew, urging us to be inspired by him, G-d forbid."[27] Rabbi Jacob Immanuel Schochet, a prominent Canadian writer for the Jews for Judaism organization, declared that the book "poses a tremendous risk to the Jewish community" and proclaimed that it was "forbidden for anyone to buy or read this book, or give its author a platform in any way, shape or form to discuss this topic."[28]

Clearly, some Jews today do not accept Boteach's argument that Jesus is an inspiring figure, a "Jewish patriot" whose life and teachings are worth a second look. What many Jews and Christians outside Israel are unaware of, though, is that there exists a hardcore extremist fringe among religious Jews that can be almost as mean-spirited as their extremist Christian counterparts. While most people in the Jewish Quarter of Jerusalem are warm and friendly, visitors to Jerusalem will sometimes see *haredi* (ultra-Orthodox) men actually *spitting* on Christian pilgrims, especially on Christian monks and nuns dressed in habits. But these extremists are equal-opportunity bigots because they also throw rocks at their fellow Jews who don't follow the Torah as scrupulously as they think necessary, for example by driving on the Sabbath.[29] There is also a quasi-terrorist group called *Tag Mehir,* or Price Tag, that vandalizes Christian houses of worship and monasteries in Israel, for example by spray-painting on doors and walls slogans such as "Death to Christians," "Jesus is dead," and "Mary was a prostitute."[30]

Plainly, the historic misunderstanding between Christians and Jews persists. Much to his credit, Boteach has spoken out courageously against this kind of religious extremism, even in Israel. "A battle is being waged for the soul of Judaism between a lunatic fringe who are slowly encroaching on the mainstream—as we have seen recently with religious men spitting on little girls in Beit Shemesh, Israel—and those who believe Judaism must always be informed, educated, open and loving," Boteach wrote in *The Jerusalem Post* in 2012. "But the religious middle risks being cowed into submission by the crazies. And I love Judaism in general, and Chabad in particular, too much to ever allow ignorant hate-mongers to overrun it, which is why I have fought back against these hateful attacks."[31]

OTHER SCHOLARS ON THE JEWISH JESUS: "NOT A PHARISEE"

Other Jewish experts in the Second Temple period are insisting that Jesus *did* fit into the religious milieu of his age—not because he was kosher but precisely because he was wasn't, or at least not in the way that later rabbinic Judaism defined it. Jesus was kosher in a more ancient, more radical way, these scholars suggest, and he was definitely *not* a Pharisee. In recent years, some Israeli scholars are rejecting the "Jesus as Pharisee" model as a hopeless anachronism—the projection back on Jesus and his time of the ideals, practices, and beliefs of rabbinic Judaism that hadn't even been fully formed in Jesus' time—or at least, wasn't yet the standard way of being Jewish for most people.

What the latest research is suggesting is that when Jesus came on the scene there existed as yet no "Judaism" as such but rather many diverse

"Judaisms."[32] In this view, Jesus and the voice of the early Christian movement were part of a larger debate about what it meant to be faithful to the God of Abraham, what it meant to live up to the "instruction" of the Torah. The followers of Jesus were active participants in those debates. When they were over, two or three hundred years after Jesus' crucifixion, two new religions were born—one that we now call Judaism and the other Christianity. Up until then, however, the lines between messianic Jews, Pharisees, Essenes, and other groups were not so easily drawn.

As Daniel Boyarin, author of *The Jewish Gospels*, explains it, Jesus rejected many of the "innovations" the Pharisees proposed to serve as a "fence around the Torah" and which supposedly were derived from the oral tradition given to Moses at Sinai.[33] It is precisely the debates about this "oral tradition" that were collected and codified in first the Mishnah (ca. AD 200) and then, later, in the Palestinian (ca. 400) and Babylonian (ca. 500) Talmuds. "Far from being a marginal Jew, Jesus was a leader of one type of Judaism that was being marginalized by another group, the Pharisees, and he was fighting against them as dangerous innovators," Boyarin writes.[34] Thus, Boyarin, who is an expert in the Talmud, takes precisely the *opposite* view of Shmuley Boteach, who claims Jesus was a faithful Pharisee. In Boyarin's view, early Christianity, far from being a radical reform movement against Judaism, was actually "a variation within Judaism, and even a highly conservative and traditionalist one." Put another way, he adds, "Jesus was a staunch defender of the Torah against what he perceived to be the threats to it from the Pharisees." It was the Pharisees, Boyarin argues, who were the "reform movement."[35]

AN EYEWITNESS REPORT HIDDEN IN MARK'S GREEK VOCABULARY?

This can be seen in the controversy over hand washing before eating. Boyarin draws on the work of a young Israeli Talmud scholar at Hebrew University of Jerusalem, Yair Furstenberg, who has studied the controversies between Jesus and the Pharisees closely. What Boyarin and Furstenberg both argue is that the classic understanding of twentieth-century New Testament scholars—that the gospel writer Mark was a Gentile who knew almost nothing about Jewish law and tradition—is almost certainly incorrect. In fact, Furstenberg and Boyarin claim, Mark's descriptions of Jesus' debates about dietary laws reveal that both Jesus and Mark knew *exactly* what they were talking about. This can be seen even in the Greek text itself, Boyarin says. In Mark 7:3, most English translations, such as the NIV, depict the narrator explaining that "the Pharisees and all the Jews do not eat unless they give their hands a ceremonial washing." But the Greek words translated "ceremonial washing" (*pugme nuphontai*) literally mean "wash with a fist"—an obvious reference, Boyarin says, to the Jewish custom of pouring water with a special two-handed cup over the loose fist of one hand and then switching hands to wash the other.[36] Even today, all over the Western Wall plaza in Jerusalem, visitors will notice special fountains for hand washing with two-handed cups affixed to the fountains with strings and people "washing with a fist." Not only is the gospel of Mark very early evidence of a Jewish practice known only from much later sources, Boyarin adds, but it also reveals an *eyewitness knowledge* of Jewish ceremonial practices on the part of the evangelist.[37] "If Mark was

Shutterstock

Water fountains in Jerusalem for Jewish ceremonial hand-washing with the special two-handed cups used for the purpose. A Jewish Talmud expert says that embedded within the Greek text of the gospel of Mark, lost to readers who read Mark in modern languages, is a tantalizing clue that the evangelist may have witnessed this ancient Jewish custom.

such a close observer and manifests such intimate knowledge of pharisaic practice, then my assumption as I read the passage is that he knew of what he spoke all the way down," Boyarin writes. "This suggests strongly that his perspective (as well as that of his Jesus) is firmly from within the Jewish world—nearly the opposite of what has been usually said of Mark."[38]

As for the substance of the dispute, Mark has Jesus arguing with the Pharisees and "teachers of the Law" about eating food with unwashed hands. The Pharisees ask Jesus, "Why do your disciples not live according to the tradition of the elders, but eat with defiled hands?" (Mark 7:5 NRSV). Jesus replies:

> "You have a fine way of rejecting the commandment of God in order to keep your tradition! For Moses said, 'Honor your father and your mother'; and, 'Whoever speaks evil of father or mother must surely die.' But you say that if anyone tells father or mother, 'Whatever support you might have had from me is Corban' (that is, an offering to God)—then you no longer permit doing anything for a father or mother, thus making void the word of God through your tradition that you have handed on. And you do many things like this." (Mark 7:9–13 NRSV)

The gospel then records that Jesus "called the crowd" to him and re-iterated his main point: "Listen to me, all of you, and understand: there is nothing outside a person that by going in can defile, but the things that come out are what defile" (Mark 7:14–15 NRSV).

"I CAME NOT TO ABOLISH THE LAW AND THE PROPHETS"

Boyarin and Furstenberg argue that Jesus wasn't abrogating the Torah with this declaration but he was actually upholding it! The Torah commands, they say, that someone is rendered ritually impure *not* through eating forbidden foods, such as pork, but through things that come *out* of the body, specifically blood, semen, and gonorrhea.[39] The only food that renders a body impure, Boyarin notes, is carrion. The new rules about hand washing that the Pharisees were "trying to foist on"[40] the people were contrary to what the Torah actually says. In other words, these contemporary Jewish scholars say that Jesus was actually correct: the Pharisees *were* changing the rules of the Torah. The "tradition of the elders," or oral Torah, was "human precepts being taught as doctrines." Thus, while Boyarin doesn't say this, it is possible that some Pharisees were using their own new rules to avoid caring for elderly parents. "Once again, Jesus and Mark have got it exactly right in terms of the Torah and the oral traditions exemplified by the Pharisees and other innovators," Boyarin concludes.[41]

Thus, Boyarin, Furstenberg, and other Jewish scholars represent a more nuanced, sophisticated understanding of how Jesus fit into his religious milieu, especially compared to Boteach's argument that he was simply like an Orthodox Jew of today plopped back into first-century Palestine. According to their more recent scholarship, which contradicts the views of Klausner, Maccoby, and earlier Jewish authors, Jesus *did* protest against the innovations of the Pharisees just as the Gospels say he did; he raised legitimate objections to the practices and reasoning of the Pharisees. As it turned out, however, what the Pharisees advocated—a set of new rules that would create a "fence around the Torah"[42]—eventually became the normative rabbinic Judaism that endures to this day. As a result, the answer to the question of just how kosher Jesus was is, well, *very* kosher—but not kosher in the way the Pharisees believed Jews should be, and probably not kosher in the way Orthodox Jews today believe Jews should have been. This gives new understanding to what Jesus said in Matthew 5:17–20 (NRSV):

> "Do not think that I have come to abolish the law or the prophets; I have come not to abolish but to fulfill. For truly I tell you, until heaven and earth pass away, not one letter, not one stroke of a letter, will pass from the law until all is accomplished. Therefore, whoever breaks one of the least of these commandments, and teaches others to do the same, will be called least in the kingdom of heaven; but whoever does them and teaches them will be called great in the kingdom of heaven. For I tell you, unless your righteousness exceeds that of the scribes and Pharisees, you will never enter the kingdom of heaven."

Daniel Boyarin and other Talmud experts thus take Jesus at his word: he was defending the ancient written Torah, and the moral principles embedded within it, against the innovations and, in some cases, casuistry of what became rabbinic Judaism. "Jesus speaks from the position of a traditional Galilean Jew, one whose community and traditional practices are being criticized and interfered with from outside, that is, from Jerusalem, by the Judaeans . . ." he concludes. "Jesus accuses these Pharisees of introducing practices that are beyond what is written in the Torah, or even against what is written in the Torah."[43] Thus, these seemingly academic disputes reveal another important way in which new research is overturning outlandish portraits of Jesus. They reveal that the arguments between Jesus and the Pharisees in the Gospels could well be historical—and were not necessarily made up by the early church to reflect later debates between the Christian and Jewish communities.

WHO REALLY KILLED JESUS?

There is no more painful dispute in New Testament studies today than the question of who killed Jesus of Nazareth. Was Jesus arrested and executed *solely* by the Roman authorities who viewed him as a violent or potentially violent revolutionary—with Jewish leaders, such as the high priest, having no complicity in his death whatsoever? Are the Gospels' descriptions of Jesus being interrogated by members of the Sanhedrin completely fabricated and unhistorical? Or do the Gospels accurately describe Jesus being executed on trumped-up charges—arrested by the temple aristocracy, who were fearful that he might spark riots or even a rebellion, and who handed him over to the Romans for execution?

The answer to this question shapes many other issues—such as whether or not Jesus' teaching was in harmony with the dominant strands of religious belief held by Jewish leaders in his day, and whether he was actually a violent would-be revolutionary. More important, it affects Christian-Jewish relations on both a personal and a corporate level. For Jews, the question of who killed Jesus is not an abstract academic question but a painfully personal one. Two thousand years of Christian anti-Semitism has been based on the perception of Jews as "Christ killers." Gospel texts such as Matthew 27:25, with the words "his blood be on us and on our children" (NRSV), have been used to justify every act of anti-Jewish savagery up to and including the Holocaust.[44] It is understandable, then, that many Jewish writers today, including Shmuley Boteach, insist that no one but the Romans had a hand in Jesus' execution.[45] But that doesn't make it true.

As David Klinghoffer documents in his book *Why the Jews Rejected Jesus*, Christians resist the claim that only the Romans were responsible for Jesus' death—not because they want to keep blaming "the Jews," but because it contradicts what the Gospels say. Those who, like Boteach, assert that only the Romans were involved in Jesus' arrest and execution also usually maintain that Jesus was *guilty* of the crime for which he was executed[46]—that is, that he *really was* leading or at least supporting a rebellion against Rome. However, such an outlook clearly contradicts the portrait of Jesus in the Gospels: that of an innocent victim wrongly accused of the crime for which he was executed.

Klinghoffer argues, moreover, that "to say that Jewish leaders were instrumental in getting Jesus killed is *not* anti-Semitic."[47] If that were true, he explains, then many of the greatest Jewish thinkers and sages of all time—up to and including the great medieval philosopher Moses Maimonides—were also anti-Semitic. That's because Maimonides accepted the testimony of the Talmud, quoted above, that "Yeshu" was executed for practicing magic and leading the people astray.[48]

In fact, Paula Fredriksen, one of the leading Jewish scholars of early Christianity and author of *Jesus of Nazareth: King of the Jews,* concedes that much in the gospel accounts, far from being the invention of the early church, could well have happened as written. While admitting that no one can know for sure what happened during Jesus' arrest, trial, and execution, Fredriksen says that it's quite possible that the high priest Caiaphas "was the one who decided that Jesus' death was the only effective way to deflate the wild hopes growing among the city's pilgrims,"[49] just as the gospel of John says Caiaphas tells the Sanhedrin: "It is better for you that one man die for the people than that the whole nation perish" (11:50 NIV).

JERUSALEM COULD EXPLODE IN VIOLENCE AT ANY MOMENT

With between 250,000 and 1 million pilgrims pouring into the crowded city for the annual Passover feast[50] and the arrival of a famous "prophet," the situation certainly must have appeared highly volatile to both Jewish officials and the small Roman garrison stationed in the city. When you add to that Jesus' action on the Temple Mount, and the possibility that hundreds, perhaps thousands, of his followers were loudly shouting "Hosanna" and proclaiming him messiah and "king," it is easy to imagine both Jewish and Roman leaders being on edge. That is why the description in the gospel of John of the nervousness among Jewish leaders (John 11:50) that Jesus might deliberately or accidentally trigger a riot that would lead to a violent Roman reprisal seems plausible to many scholars, including Fredriksen.

The Romans had reason to be nervous. Their fragile control over Jerusalem depended on people fearing their main army, of perhaps twenty thousand troops, stationed a three-days' march away in Antioch.[51] In Jerusalem itself, though, the Romans maintained a force of only about 1,500 "auxiliary" (mostly non-Roman) soldiers to keep the peace, a garrison that could easily have been overwhelmed by an enraged Jerusalem population. We know this is true because when the Jewish War finally did break out in AD 66, that is precisely what happened: according to Josephus, the Roman troops stationed in Jerusalem's Antonia fortress were slaughtered to a man, even when promised "safe passage" by the Jewish Zealot leaders.[52] Thus, when the gospel of Luke says that the political leaders "feared the people" (20:19 ESV), they had good reason.

It's also quite possible that if Jewish leaders did decide to have Jesus executed to spare the city possible riots, the scene in the Gospels of Pilate resisting this effort does not necessarily have to be viewed as an anti-Jewish invention, as some scholars claim. Boteach and others argue that Pilate, the Roman governor, whose ruthlessness and hatred of the Jews are well documented, would never have deferred to a Jewish crowd or sought to spare a Jewish criminal.[53] Such scenes, these writers say, are clearly inventions designed to attach maximum guilt for Jesus' death to "the Jews," and they were created to curry favor with the Romans after the Jewish War of AD 66–70. That's certainly plausible. But it is just as credible that the gospel accounts are *accurate*—and that Pilate sought to free Jesus not out of compassion or out of deference to Jewish leaders, but precisely to show that he wasn't taking orders from anyone. As for a crowd shouting "crucify him," Fredriksen believes it is quite possible that a substantial number of people in Jerusalem could have been violently opposed to Jesus and his message. "Is the hostile crowd solely the (apologetic) invention of the evangelists?" she asks. "We cannot know for certain, but logically it need not be. The presence in the city during the holiday of a crowd violently opposed to Jesus, as well as a crowd energetically enthused, in fact sharpens Pilate's decision: by one act, he can appease one while simultaneously deflating the other. Other reconstructions are less plausible."[54]

In other words, it's possible that the gospel accounts of who killed Jesus—the Romans at the instigation of a handful of Jewish leaders—are historically far more accurate than previous scholars have wanted to admit. The very fact that Pilate did not act against *any* of Jesus' other followers, even the apostles, suggests that he did not believe that Jesus was an insurrectionist or the leader of a violent revolution. The Romans did not hesitate to crucify thousands if they suspected them of rebellion. Josephus reports that the Roman governor crucified two thousand men during the rebellion that broke out after Herod's death in 4 BC.[55] The fact that Pilate didn't move against any of Jesus' followers supports the depiction in the Gospels that Jesus was killed as a scapegoat, an innocent man whom even the authorities didn't believe was guilty of the crime for which he was condemned. This is no doubt the origin, in later Christian writing, of portrayals of Jesus as the "lamb of God" who sacrificed his own life for the sake of his mission (John 1:29). As John's gospel has Jesus put it, "No one has greater love than this, to lay down one's life for one's friends" (15:13 NRSV).

Of course, even if some first-century Jewish leaders did conspire to get rid of Jesus by creating trumped-up charges of sedition, just as the Gospels claim, that in no way implies that "the Jews" or the Jewish people as a whole bear any responsibility for his death. That assertion is simply absurd: that is why many major Christian churches have strenuously repudiated any notion of collective responsibility for Jesus' death as flat-out anti-Semitism.[56] As the assembled bishops of the Catholic Church declared during the Second Vatican Council, "What happened in [Jesus'] passion cannot be charged against all the Jews, without distinction, then alive, nor against the Jews of today."[57]

WHY THE JEWS REJECTED JESUS

All this raises another important question: If Jesus did fit into his religious milieu—either as a loyal Pharisee as Boteach says, or as a critic of the Pharisees as Boyarin and recent scholars claim—*why did the Jewish people reject Jesus?*

One answer is that they didn't—at least not at first. The overwhelming majority of Jesus' followers, before and immediately after his death, were Jews. His mother and other relatives were all Jews. All the apostles were Jews. Most of the writers of the New Testament were Jews, including Paul. Indeed, the Jesus movement was thoroughly Jewish. What's more, there is substantial evidence that Jewish followers of Jesus endured for *centuries* after the fall of Jerusalem,[58] perhaps even up to the Arab conquest, in such groups as the Ebionites and the Nazarenes. However, it's also true that there is ample evidence in the New Testament of early and profound opposition to Jesus and his message among many Jews. The apostle Paul, despite describing himself as a loyal Pharisee, "zealous for the traditions of my ancestors" (Gal. 1:14 NRSV), nevertheless recounts numerous instances in which he was berated, even beaten by Jews outraged by what he was teaching. "Three times I was beaten with rods, once I was pelted with stones," he writes to his friends in Corinth (2 Cor. 11:25 NIV). As a result, it's not surprising that many Jewish writers such as Boteach point to the apostle Paul as the reason Judaism was so hostile toward the Jesus movement. Jesus' teaching was problematic; but Paul's teaching, proclaiming Jesus not just as the Messiah but as the "Lord," in whose name "every knee should bow, in heaven and on earth and under the earth" (Phil. 2:10 NIV), was flat-out idolatry. Even Jewish writers who are respectful of Jesus, such as Boteach and Maccoby, are often derisive in their attitudes toward Paul, whom they claim misrepresented his Jewish credentials and was certainly not as learned as he claimed to be. "First, it's unlikely Paul was a Pharisee or that he studied with Gamliel, the most advanced Pharisaic teacher of the time," writes Boteach. "The Pharisees were great scholars . . . Yet as Hyam Maccoby points out, Paul is not only not a great scholar, he seems incapable of even reading Hebrew."[59]

In the end, the chief objection to Jesus among the Jews, then and now, comes down to one simple, obvious reality: his claim, or the claim of his followers, that he was the promised Jewish messiah. For most Jews, past and present, this was and is absurd on its face. By definition, the messiah is to inaugurate a new age of peace when the Jews will end their exile and rule again in the land. But Jesus did not bring a new age of peace for the Jews. The Jews did not end their exile. In fact, the Jews ended up being slaughtered by the Romans and dispersed over the world even more. Hence, they believe, Jesus was and is not the messiah.

What is the Christian response to this? The traditional Christian response is that Jesus did or, more precisely, *is* fulfilling the messianic prophecies, but in a different way than the Jews in his time expected. The messianic age that Jesus proclaimed as the kingdom of God arrived, but it is still being worked out in time, through the ongoing activity of God through his people, both Jews and Gentiles. Jesus came to set the kingdom in motion and to extend the covenantal promises of God to all human beings. As one messianic Jewish leader explains, to say that the messianic age hasn't arrived is like walking into a baseball game at the third inning and saying the game hasn't been won yet. It's still going on!

A more liberal Christian view would be that the concept of messiah was only an *approximation* of what Jesus was all about, a title Jesus accepted reluctantly (and, in Mark, often discouraged his disciples from using). For example, when Jesus asked his followers who they thought he was, Peter replied, "You are the Messiah" (Mark 8:29). But according to Mark, likely our earliest gospel, when Peter did so, Jesus "sternly ordered them not to tell anyone about him" (8:30 NRSV). Some critical scholars, such as William Wrede (1859–1906), used to say that the "messianic secret" motif was invented by Mark to explain away the embarrassing fact that Jesus didn't actually claim to be the messiah. But today some scholars argue that Jesus' reluctance to use that title on some occasions may be historical. In other words, the traditional Jewish understanding of the messiah fit, more or less, with how Jesus saw his mission, but not entirely. Jesus no doubt knew that many Jews (but not all) expected the messiah to be a conquering military leader, a king in the political sense, and that was not what he was about. Jesus, his followers, and perhaps other groups of Jews in the first century held other ideas of what the messiah was—ideas that the messiah would not kill all the Romans but instead would save the world from itself by revealing who God really is. The gospel of John conveys this point explicitly. When Pilate asks Jesus if he is a king, John has Jesus reply, "My kingdom is not from this world. If my kingdom were from this world, my followers would be fighting to keep me from being handed over to the Jews. But as it is, my kingdom is not from here" (John 18:36 NRSV). When Pilate presses him and asks him a second time if he is a king, Jesus says, "You say that I am a king. For this I was born, and for this I came into the world, to testify to the truth. Everyone who belongs to the truth listens to my voice" (John 18:37 NRSV). Thus, the traditional Jewish concept of the messiah was only an approximation, like saying the kingdom of God is "like" a mustard seed (Matt. 13:31). Jesus is "like" what Isaiah is talking about in his oracles of the Suffering Servant, and in other messianic prophecies, but that doesn't mean those prophecies encompass all that Jesus was or define exactly his own understanding of his mission.

As the followers of Jesus continued after his death to reflect on the meaning of the revelations they had received from him through his life and teaching, they inevitably came to understand the Hebrew scriptures differently than did the rabbinic teachers who taught in the wake of the Jewish War. And after the fall of Jerusalem in AD 70, ordinary Jewish families worked to rebuild their lives in a world in which the temple no longer existed, and thus began to follow the program that the Pharisees laid out for them. Eventually there were contentious clashes between the two communities—and a legacy of violent anti-Semitism arose with which the Christian churches are only now coming to terms.

A JEWISH SCHOLAR'S LIFELONG SEARCH FOR JESUS

As we can see from all the different Jewish views on Jesus we've looked at in this chapter, the academic study of how Jesus of Nazareth fit in among the Jews of his time is in flux. Attitudes are changing; new perspectives are emerging. Yet old prejudices endure for both Christians and Jews. Many basic questions are still hotly disputed. In a way, we're still asking the same questions our forefathers and foremothers were asking in the first century. Was Jesus a loyal Jew as Shmuley Boteach claims, a radical reformer, or some combination of both?

A Jewish writer who is uniquely qualified to moderate these questions is Amy-Jill Levine, University Professor of New Testament and Jewish Studies at Vanderbilt University Divinity School and author of the modern classic *The Misunderstood Jew: The Church and the Scandal of the Jewish Jesus.* Levine was raised in a predominantly Catholic neighborhood of North Dartmouth, Massachusetts, and has spent most of her life teaching

Christian divinity students at Vanderbilt Divinity School "in the buckle of the Bible Belt."[60] Levine writes humorously of her desire, as a child, to have her first Holy Communion just like the other kids in her neighborhood, and of her secret ambition to be pope. "You can't," her mother explained to her dryly. "You're not Italian." Her liberal Jewish parents allowed her to attend Catholic catechism lessons with her friends, alternating with her twice-weekly Hebrew School classes. Less humorously, Levine relates an incident when she was about seven in which a friend on the school bus told her that she had killed Jesus. "I did not," Levine objected. "Yes, you did," her friend responded. Her friend explained that "the Jews" were responsible for the death of Jesus and, since she, Levine, was a Jew, that included her.[61] Thus began Levine's quest, going on forty years now, to learn everything she could about Jesus and his relationship to the Jewish people. Earning a PhD in New Testament at Duke University is perhaps taking things a bit far, but you do what you have to do.[62]

Levine, like many Jews, knows that Christians are often interested in Judaism only to the extent that it sheds light on Jesus or on life in first-century Palestine. Few Christians know much about Judaism at all, but what little they do know is usually gleaned from studying the Hebrew Bible or the descriptions of Jewish ideas and practices in the New Testament. Christians do not show much interest in Judaism after the time of Jesus, or in the Talmud or Rashi, or in current Jewish religious practices and ideals, or in the great heroes of Jewish history for the past two thousand years, such as Maimonides, Nahmanides, the Ba'al Shem Tov, Isaac Luria (an authority on Kabbalah mysticism), Theodor Herzl, and so on. One of Levine's bugaboos is the way in which Christians, and particularly professors in liberal Christian divinity schools, subtly but systematically denigrate Judaism in an effort to say how Jesus was unique. In a post-Holocaust world, Christians don't typically attack contemporary Judaism directly, of course, but rather belittle the Pharisees and allegedly war-mongering Jewish nationalists in first-century Judaism. She points out that many Christians don't seem to realize, however, that the Pharisees are the intellectual grandfathers of modern Judaism, so attacking the ideas and ideals of the Pharisees is pretty close to attacking the ideas and ideals of contemporary Judaism. Even the notion that the Jews in the time of Jesus were looking forward to a "warrior messiah" who would defeat Rome, she says, can be spun to say that the real reason the Jews rejected Jesus is because he taught the way to peace and the Jews wanted war.[63]

This annoys Levine to no end because, first, there are passages in the Gospels that seem somewhat militaristic themselves, such as Jesus telling his disciples he came not to bring peace but the sword (Matt. 10:34); but, more important, the Judaisms in Jesus' day had a variety of approaches to the Roman occupation, including classic demonstrations of what modern people call nonviolent resistance. Levine doesn't describe this in detail, but when Pilate faced a large Jewish mob protesting his decision in AD 26 to bring Roman standards into the holy city, which would violate the commandment against graven images, Pilate surrounded the crowd with armed soldiers. The Jews responded by kneeling and baring their throats, demonstrating that they were willing to die for their beliefs. Pilate backed down. (A massacre of unarmed men would look bad, even in Rome.) Thus, Levine believes it is unfair to characterize the Jews in the time of Jesus as inherently militaristic or bloodthirsty. "As long as Christian teachers and preachers continue to suggest that Judaism is a militaristic, warmongering system missing a concern for shalom and that Christianity is the system of peace, devoid of any sense of militarism, violence, or revenge, anti-Jewish teachings will continue," she writes.[64]

THE POLITICALLY CORRECT JESUS OF THE ACADEMICS

The politically correct academia in which Levine works also likes to highlight Jesus' unusual openness to women—in contrast to the misogyny that allegedly characterized Jewish purity laws. In addition, Levine says, Jesus' alleged universalism and openness to people of all cultures (*alleged* because some scholars claim that Jesus saw his mission as being solely for the benefit of the "the lost sheep of the house of Israel" [Matt. 10:6 ESV]) is invariably contrasted to the "xenophobia" and clannishness of Judaism. Levine joins Boteach in simply asserting as fact that "Jesus upheld the Law . . . and expected his followers to do the same."[65] She claims that at least some of the disputes over the interpretation of the Torah found in the Gospels are merely "an invention that met the needs of the growing gentile church"[66]—specifically, the idea that Jesus voided the Sabbath, declared all foods clean, and otherwise dismissed the Torah.[67] As we saw earlier in this chapter, whether or to what degree Jesus ignored or reinterpreted the Torah commandments is now being debated by some Jewish scholars.

Nevertheless, what Levine seeks is a way for Christian scholars to highlight the uniqueness of Jesus without automatically belittling Judaism or even the intellectual ancestors of modern Judaism, the Pharisees. It is by no means clear, however, how that should be done. When teachers present the history of the Protestant Reformation, which was, of course, a critique of Catholicism as it existed in the sixteenth century, they invariably highlight the differences between the views of Martin Luther and his followers and those of the Catholic hierarchy. The challenge for historians is how to do this in an intellectually honest way that doesn't misrepresent the views of either Luther and his followers or of the Catholic Church in that period. Yet to say that Luther had no bone to pick with the Catholic hierarchy at all—whether justified or not—would not be historically accurate.

As someone who has spent time in both Christian and Jewish communities, I can say that stereotypes and false information abound on both fronts. I am routinely flabbergasted by how little I and my fellow Christians know about Jewish history and current Jewish customs, and by the open hostility that many Christians still display toward Judaism— usually veiled in criticisms of modern-day Israel or Zionism. Yet I am also regularly shocked by the brazen insults that some Jews hurl at Christians, particularly in the media, and how little understanding many Jews have of Christianity beyond Christmas trees and Easter bunnies.

Levine's prescription for improving this situation, of course, is more honest conversation—such as that initiated by Boteach and Boyarin. She has many other recommendations, some of which are a tad unrealistic ("If possible, learn Hebrew and Greek and read the primary texts in the original").[68] She recommends that Christians and Jews attend one another's services—also not always an easy thing to do without good friends to smooth the way. (I had the strange experience of visiting a synagogue in Jerusalem when some elderly American Jews came up to me and, mistaking me for a member of the congregation, shyly asked, in Hebrew, if it would be okay for them to visit the synagogue. Even these Jewish tourists felt a little out of place and unsure if they would be welcomed.) Levine thinks Christians and Jews should not give up on one another but should "listen with each other's ears."[69] "Jews need to hear the sincerity in the Christians' message," she writes. "Christians need to respect the integrity of the Jewish position."[70] Levine's final thought is that Jesus of Nazareth should or could be a point of unification rather than division: "[I]f the church and synagogue both could recognize their connection to Jesus, a Jewish prophet who spoke to Jews, perhaps we'd be in a better place for understanding."[71] That would be nice, but, as Shmuley Boteach discovered when he suggested Jews embrace Jesus as a fellow Jew, it isn't easy.

FOR FURTHER STUDY

Boteach, Shmuley. *Kosher Jesus.* Jerusalem: Gefen Publishing, 2012.

Boyarin, Daniel. *The Jewish Gospels.* New York: The New Press, 2012.

Brown, Michael. *The Real Kosher Jesus.* Lake Mary, FL: Frontline, 2012.

Klinghoffer, David. *Why the Jews Rejected Jesus.* New York: Doubleday, 2005.

Levine, Amy-Jill. *The Misunderstood Jew: The Church and the Scandal of the Jewish Jesus.* New York: HarperCollins, 2007.

Silver, Abba Hillel. *Where Judaism Differed.* New York: Macmillan, 1956.

DID JESUS HAVE A SECRET MESSAGE?

The False Promise of the Gnostic Gospels

The knowledge of the secrets of the kingdom of heaven has been given to you, but not to them.

—MATTHEW 13:11 NIV

On a bright spring day likely in the year 28 or 29 of the common era, a large, boisterous crowd gathered on a hillside meadow near the Sea of Galilee, about halfway between the small fishing village of Capernaum and the sulfur springs just outside the village of Tabgha. The lake, which the local people called the Harp Sea, and which is still known in modern Hebrew as the Kinneret,[1] glistened in the distance. On the side of the hill there was a cave, now called Mughara Ayub, mentioned by the fourth-century pilgrim Egeria in her diary.[2] The people came from all over the area. The young and old, the pious and the merely curious, they poured into the area from towns and villages in lower Galilee, from Ituraea and Trachonitis in the northeast, the Ten Cities beyond the Jordan, even from as far away as Caesarea on the coast. It's likely the event had been announced and planned months in advance. According to the gospels of Mark and Luke, a "great multitude" (Luke 6:17 NRSV) gathered from Galilee but also from as far away as Judea and Jerusalem.

To an educated Roman riding up from his seaside villa near Caesarea or a Greek trader from Sepphoris, the people must have seemed a motley bunch. Most were Jews, but there were probably also a few Gentiles, even a Roman or two. Observers would have heard the Galilean dialect, the slurred language of the local people, but also a smattering of Greek. We don't know how many people actually arrived, but it could well have been thousands, perhaps even tens of thousands.[3] Modern archaeology has revealed that most people in the region lived in small villages of perhaps four hundred people each, but many bustling towns existed as well, even a few full-blown cities.[4] Bethsaida, for example, a fishing village on the northeast corner of the lake now being excavated by Israeli and American archaeologists, held perhaps two thousand people.[5] In nearby Sepphoris, a newly rebuilt showcase of Greek architecture and culture about four miles (six kilometers) or so from the village of Nazareth, there had been a recent population boom with perhaps six thousand to twelve thousand people living then in the city.[6] Tiberias, Herod Antipas's first-century pagan capital on the lake, still popular today as a lakeside resort, was about the same size.[7]

THE FIRST TRUE PROPHET IN FOUR HUNDRED YEARS

Rumors travel quickly in this part of the world, and the people must have been full of excitement. The entire area had been buzzing for months about a new prophet—the first real prophet to appear in the land in four centuries. Unlike the lawyer-scribes from Jerusalem and the rich Pharisees in the towns, the new prophet was a local, a young Galilean man from the tiny village of Nazareth. We have no idea what he looked like, but we suspect that he must have been a fairly impressive man: probably strong, from hard work with his hands, dark brown from the sun, someone who could command rough-hewn strangers to follow him. There was something vaguely wild about this new prophet—a subversive, dangerous quality. The people were "astonished" at his teaching because he spoke "with authority" (Luke 4:32). Men and women alike were clearly drawn to him. Even Roman soldiers, the Gospels report, were impressed. The crowds grew so large that he eventually had to address them from boats anchored off the lake's shoreline (Mark 4:1).

Most of what we know about the Sermon on the Mount, Jesus' magisterial summary of his mission and message, is found in Matthew and Luke, both presumably drawing upon material in the much older and now-lost sayings source called Q.[8] As we saw earlier, in chapter 1, some scholars hypothesize that, given the size of the crowd, it's almost certain that some people wrote down what they heard—either during the event itself or from memory shortly thereafter.[9] (Scholars count at least twenty-seven examples of Jesus' Aramaic dialect in his recorded sayings.) Mark, likely the first gospel to be written, does not present the sermon in a single unit like Matthew and Luke but quotes individual snippets of it (for example, the saying of not putting a light under a bushel basket in Mark 4:21). This suggests that there were independent traditions of Jesus' sayings derived apart from the Q source.

A MANIFESTO OF MERCY

The Sermon on the Mount is a manifesto, a thrilling message of hope and redemption directed primarily toward the dispossessed and reviled members of Jesus' society—what were called the *am ha-aretz,* the people of the land. It is a work of singular genius that any politician, in any era, would do well to study. The New Testament scholar Robert Stein counts more than two hundred examples of sophisticated literary devices embedded in Jesus' sermons, including both synonymous and chiasmic parallelisms, hyperbole, riddles, paradoxes, irony, and counter-questions.[10] Jesus both flatters and challenges his audience—"You are the salt of the earth; but if salt has lost its taste, how can its saltiness be restored?" (Matt. 5:13 NRSV)— virtually daring his listeners to join him in an underground movement of spiritual and social renewal. In Luke's version of the Beatitudes, Jesus addresses the crowd directly—and adds parallel warnings for each of his promises of hope.

"Blessed are you who are poor,
> *for yours is the kingdom of God.*
"Blessed are you who are hungry now,
> *for you will be filled.*
"Blessed are you who weep now,
> *for you will laugh.*

"Blessed are you when people hate you, and when they exclude you, revile you, and defame you on account of the Son of Man. Rejoice in that day and leap for joy, for surely your reward is great in heaven; for that is what their ancestors did to the prophets.

"But woe to you who are rich,
> *for you have received your consolation.*
"Woe to you who are full now,
> *for you will be hungry.*
"Woe to you who are laughing now,
> *for you will mourn and weep."*

(LUKE 6:20–25 NRSV)

RADICALIZING THE TORAH

Jesus tells his hearers that he did not come to abolish the Law and the Prophets—meaning the teachings of the Torah they live out in their daily lives—but to "fulfill" or radicalize them (Matt. 5:17). In Matthew, he then proceeds to give a series of concrete examples of what he is talking about: violence, adultery, divorce, oaths, and retaliation. In each example, Jesus contrasts what the people "have heard" they should do—referring, astonishingly, to the Torah itself—with his own, new, more radical teaching. Imagine hearing a preacher today say, "The Bible says . . . *but I say to you . . .*" "Speaks with authority" is clearly an understatement.

For example, Jesus says, "You have heard that it was said to your ancestors, 'You shall not kill; and whoever kills will be liable to judgment.' But I say to you, whoever is angry with his brother will be liable to judgment, and whoever says to his brother, 'Raqa,' will be answerable to the Sanhedrin, and whoever says, 'You fool,' will be liable to fiery Gehenna" (Matt. 5:21–22).

Jesus is challenging his audience to recognize the principles of mercy inherent in the Torah and to apply them in an even more demanding way in their daily lives. He says,

> "You have heard that it was said, 'You shall love your neighbor and hate your enemy. But I say to you, love your enemies, and pray for those who persecute you, that you may be children of your heavenly Father, for he makes his sun rise on the bad and the good, and causes rain to fall on the just and unjust. For it you love those who love you, what recompense will you have? Do not the tax collectors do the same? And if you greet your brothers only, what is unusual about that? Do not the pagans do the same? So be perfect, just as your heavenly Father is perfect." (Matt. 5:43–48)

It's a pretty shocking program by anyone's standards.

Jesus challenges the assembled crowd not to worry about money—for no one can serve two masters, God and mammon—and insists that they should focus their attention on the kingdom of God first (Matt. 6:24). In this one instance, Jesus does sound remarkably like a Greek Cynic philosopher such as Diogenes, as the New Testament scholar John Dominic Crossan observes.[11] Jesus says, "Therefore I tell you, do not worry about your life, what you will eat [or drink], or about your body, what you will wear"—a painful acknowledgment, as New Testament scholar Richard Horsley has written, that this is precisely what Jesus' hearers *were* worrying about, eating and having adequate clothing (Matt. 6:25).[12] Jesus continues:

> "Is not life more than food and the body more than clothing? Look at the birds in the sky; they do not sow or reap, they gather nothing into barns, yet your heavenly Father feeds them. Are not you more important than they? Can any of you by worrying add a single moment to your life-span? Why are you anxious about clothes? Learn from the way the wild flowers grow. They do not work or spin. But I tell you that not even Solomon in all his splendor was clothed like one of them. If God so clothes the grass of

the field, which grows today and is thrown into the oven tomorrow, will he not much more provide for you, O you of little faith?" (Matt. 6:25–30)

Powerful words, guaranteed both to thrill his listeners and to make them very uncomfortable. Paradoxically, while Jesus calls his listeners to embrace a more radical observance of the Torah, he insists that they are not to use this as an excuse to judge and condemn those who fail to live up to this higher standard of conduct. While historically both Judaism and Christianity have been known, at least on some occasions, to judge people for their transgressions, in the Sermon on the Mount Jesus advocates the opposite:

"Stop judging, that you may not be judged. For as you judge, so will you be judged, and the measure with which you measure will be measured out to you. Why do you notice the splinter in your brother's eye, but do not perceive the wooden beam in your own eye? How can you say to your brother, 'Let me remove that splinter from your eye,' while the wooden beam is in your eye? You hypocrite, remove the wooden beam from your eye first; then you will see clearly to remove the splinter from your brother's eye." (Matt. 7:1–5)

"RED LETTER" CHRISTIANS

The Sermon on the Mount is, of course, only one of dozens of passages in the canonical Gospels where Jesus communicates his message. For centuries, scholars have studied the words of Jesus—roughly two thousand words out of the hundred thousand words in the New Testament—seeking to gain a clearer idea of what Jesus' message was. More recently, a group of evangelical scholars have started an informal, nondenominational movement—known as the Red Letter Christians—to focus on Jesus' words as they ponder what his message means in a contemporary political context. In many Bibles, of course, the words of Jesus are printed in red letters.

Even a cursory glance at the actual "red-letter" words of Jesus in the Gospels reveals that his teaching centered around what he called the "kingdom" or "reign" of God. The very first words of Jesus recorded in the gospel of Mark make this clear: "This is the time of fulfillment," Jesus says. "The kingdom of

God is at hand. Repent, and believe in the gospel" (Mark 1:15). Sometimes he says the kingdom is almost here; other times, that it's here already. Jesus adds that he must preach in the villages near Capernaum because "for this purpose have I come" (Mark 1:38). Preaching the good news of the kingdom was, according to Jesus' own words, the purpose for which he came.

And what exactly is this good news, or gospel, of the kingdom that Jesus is preaching? It was *not* that the world was about to come to an end and that the overwhelming majority of people would soon be cast into a burning lake of fire for all eternity, as scholars in the early twentieth century insisted. The Gospels certainly portray Jesus as foreseeing a time of great tribulation and suffering for his hearers; and, like Jeremiah before him, he predicted that if the Jewish people chose the sword over trust in God then it would result in a national catastrophe. But his message can't really be reduced to a warning of divine wrath: that was John the Baptist's message ("Who warned you to flee from the coming wrath?" Luke 3:7).

Instead, Jesus taught a far more disturbing, subversive, and ultimately threatening message. He said that all people, even the most wretched and lost—prostitutes and con artists and even Roman soldiers—are embraced by God's mercy and forgiveness. In Luke, this even includes the Roman soldiers who nailed Jesus' hands to the cross (Luke 23:34).[13] Every Jewish prophet for eight hundred years, including John the Baptist, had proclaimed God's wrath.[14] Jesus proclaimed God's mercy.

Jesus told his listeners that God cherishes not only the pious and the observant keepers of the religious law, but even, and maybe even especially, the wretched outcasts of society who didn't even know what all the rules were, let alone how to keep them. "I tell you . . . there will be more rejoicing in heaven over one sinner who repents than over ninety-nine righteous persons who do not need to repent," he said in Luke 15:7 (NIV). It is not how many of the 613 commandments they keep that matters the most to God, Jesus said, although he upheld the commandments given by Moses. What counts most for God is a merciful, contrite heart, one that trusts in God and reaches out to people suffering in society. "Woe to you, scribes and Pharisees, you hypocrites," Jesus thundered one day. "You pay tithes of mint and dill and cumin, and have neglected the weightier things of the law: judgment and mercy and fidelity" (Matt. 23:23).

Indeed, Jesus reserved some of the harshest words in the Gospels for the outwardly pious. He appears to have had a real dislike for ostentatious displays of religious piety, telling his followers to wash their faces when fasting (so as not to look somber) and, when giving alms, not to let their right hands know what their left hands were doing (Matt. 6:17, 3). He mocked the pious who blow trumpets before them in public assemblies. "You are like whitewashed tombs," he told members of the religious elite in his day, "which appear beautiful on the outside but inside are full of dead men's bones and every kind of filth. Even so, on the outside you appear righteous but inside you are filled with hypocrisy and evildoing" (Matt. 23:27–28).

We have heard this teaching for so long that its shock value is lost to us. But hear it again: "Truly I tell you, the tax collectors and the prostitutes are going into the kingdom of God ahead of you" (Matt. 21:31 NRSV). Imagine if someone today walked up to the pope, or the archbishop of Canterbury, or the latest TV evangelist, and said, "In God's eyes, the drug addicts and hookers on skid row are more likely to go to heaven than you are."

THE GNOSTIC GOSPELS: A NEW AGE JESUS

The message of Jesus as portrayed in the canonical gospels has been proclaimed by the various Christian communities for more than two thousand years. For centuries, the message was proclaimed orally to illiterate peasants, depicted in passion plays, and portrayed in stained-glass windows. But we know from the letters of the apostle Paul that very quickly, within decades of Jesus' crucifixion, different groups started seeking newer, more esoteric teachings of Jesus—teachings that would not be quite so demanding and that allowed them a little more freedom.

In Paul's letters to the Corinthians, we learn that Paul's message of the cross—which is Jesus' message of self-sacrifice and mercy—was being "updated" by some early followers in Corinth so that, for example, some members of the community were visiting prostitutes (1 Cor. 6:16). There also are hints in Paul's writings that some early Christian groups were dabbling in the theosophical speculations that would, a century or more later, characterize the religious sects known as Gnostic.

This trend continued for centuries. Some of the alternatives to the Jesus movement portrayed in the New Testament involved messianic Jewish groups such as the Ebionites and Nazarenes, who saw Jesus as the Jewish messiah but believed in maintaining scrupulous Torah observance. Other groups went in the opposite direction, toward a more Hellenized, even occult version of Christianity that involved various gods, "emanations" of God, and so on. Historians know about many of these Gnostic groups through the writings of the early church fathers, such as Irenaeus (ca. 130–202) and Origen (ca. 182–254). In most cases, however, the writings from these various alternative Christian sects were not preserved, either as a result of deliberate censorship by the "winning" group, orthodox Christians, or simply because the alternative sects died out and no one remained to preserve and pass down their writings. Thus, of the more than thirty alternative texts identified as "gospels" of Jesus Christ—such as the gospel of the Hebrews, the gospel of Cerinthus, the gospel of Judas, the gospel of Thomas, and so on—only four complete texts and seven fragments remain.[15]

THE LOST GOSPEL OF THOMAS DISCOVERED

In 1945, a few years before the Dead Sea Scrolls were discovered in the cliffs above the Dead Sea near Qumran, scholars made a less significant but still amazing discovery near the village of Nag Hammadi, in Egypt. An Egyptian farmer found a hidden cache of twelve leather-bound papyrus codices, or books, that contained no fewer than fifty-two separate Gnostic treatises dating back to the fourth, third, and even second centuries. All the texts were written in Coptic, an Egyptian dialect written with Greek letters. The most famous of the texts was the gospel of Thomas, a collection of 114 sayings of Jesus that resembled the long-hypothesized but never proven "sayings collection" scholars call Q. Due to bickering and haggling over the various codices among the Egyptian owners—typical of the often-shady dealings in the biblical antiquities market—the texts weren't actually translated and disseminated until decades after their discovery. The biblical scholar James Robinson at the Institute for Antiquity and Christianity at the Claremont Graduate University in Claremont, California, finally brought out an English-language translation of these texts in 1977, launching a virtual industry in the study and popularization of lost Gnostic writings.

A portion of the Nag Hammadi Codex, the end of the Apocryphon of John and the beginning of the Gospel of Thomas. These Gnostic texts, written in Coptic and dating to the second and third centuries, were discovered in 1945 in the Egyptian town of Nag Hammadi.

In 1979, Elaine Pagels, an expert on comparative religion and now a professor at Princeton University, published *The Gnostic Gospels,* an analysis of the Nag Hammadi texts. This brought the existence of alternative versions of Christianity in the early centuries of the common era to the attention of the general public. However, misinformation about the texts abounded. Feminist and New Age groups were led to believe that the Gnostic Gospels were somehow more "woman friendly" than the allegedly patriarchal writings of orthodox Christianity—an amazing claim for anyone who has actually read the surviving Gnostic texts. For example, the gospel of Thomas, considered to be one of the very few Gnostic texts with a possible claim on historically authentic material about Jesus, ends with Simon Peter saying, "Let Mary leave us, for women are not worthy of life." Jesus replies that he will "make her male, so that she too may become a living spirit resembling you males. For every woman who will make herself male will enter the kingdom of heaven."[16]

Eventually, many people came to view the existence of "lost gospels" as proof of a vast early Christian conspiracy, with the Christian church systematically suppressing the truth about Jesus and his early disciples, censoring alternative accounts of Jesus' life and teaching because these texts didn't reflect the "dogma" (primarily the alleged sexism) of the institutional church. Even such a careful scholar as Elaine Pagels couldn't resist taking this line in *The Gnostic Gospels*. "For nearly 2,000 years, the Christian tradition has preserved and revered orthodox writings that denounce the gnostics, while suppressing—and virtually destroying—gnostic writings themselves," she wrote.[17]

So, is there truth to the charge? Did the Christian church "suppress" lost facts about and sayings of Jesus? It's possible but not very likely. It's possible to see what these lost texts were probably like by studying the few that have been found, such as the ones at Nag Hammadi. Every single apocryphal gospel extant can now be easily read in translation in new editions widely available to the general public. These include anthologies such as *The Nag Hammadi Library*, edited by James Robinson; *The Complete Gospels*, edited by Robert J. Miller; *The Other Gospels: Non-Canonical Gospel Texts*, edited by Ron Cameron; and *Lost Scriptures: Books That Did Not Make It Into the New Testament*, edited by Bart Ehrman.

IN SEARCH OF LOST SAYINGS OR DEEDS OF JESUS

For decades now, scholars have been poring over every word of every "apocryphal" (noncanonical) text available, as well as quotations from the early church fathers, desperately searching for an authentic lost saying (*agrapha*) or a new fact about Jesus. The results, however, have been disappointing. A handful of scholars, most notably John Dominic Crossan of the Jesus Seminar, do believe that some of the earliest Gnostic or proto-Gnostic texts contain some historically valuable information about Jesus; but most do not. The consensus seems to be that the Gnostic texts merely restate sayings by Jesus already found in the much earlier canonical Gospels and modify them to fit their own philosophical speculations. This means that study of the Gnostic texts teaches us a lot about Gnosticism but very little new about Jesus or his message. These lost, apocryphal gospels were written, by and large, centuries after the canonical Gospels. They were the creation of various Gnostic sects that were largely hostile toward Judaism and the ancient Hebrew understanding of creation as something good. Instead, the various Gnostic religions viewed the material world as evil, the handiwork of a malevolent demigod. The Gnostics appear to have taught that the purpose of existence was to free oneself from this evil material world and ascend to a primordial spirit world where the "true God," a pure Spirit, dwells. As noted before, one of the primary characteristics of Gnosticism is an obsession with elaborate theosophical speculations, which the writers of Gnostic texts often then put into the mouth of Jesus.

Indeed, anyone who spends much time perusing these lost gospels looking for new or intriguing information about Jesus is quickly disappointed. With the exception of the gospel of Thomas, which does have a few interesting tidbits, most of the texts strike modern readers as simply bizarre. They are mostly long, rambling monologues filled with theosophical speculations about emanations from the godhead. Most have none of the vivid, real-life detail found in the Gospels or in Jesus' parables.

Here are a few examples.

From the Gospel of Philip (ca. third century):

> "They err who say, 'The Lord first died and then he arose.' First he arose, and then he died. If someone does not first achieve the resurrection, will he not die? So truly as God lives, that would . . . [text uncertain]. No one will hide an extremely valuable thing in something of equal value. However, people often put things worth countless thousands into a thing worth a penny. It is this way with the soul. It is a precious thing which came into a worthless body."[18]

From the Gospel of Mary:

"The Savior said, 'All natures, all formations, all creatures exist in and with one another, and they will be resolved again into their own roots. For the nature of matter is resolved into the [roots] of its nature alone. He who has ears to hear, let him hear.'"[19]

The church historian Eusebius, writing around AD 324, declared these noncanonical books to be "spurious writings [that] are to be rejected as altogether absurd and impious . . . adduced by the heretics under the name of the apostles, such as the gospels of Peter, Thomas, Matthew, and others beside them or such as the Acts of the Apostles by Andrew, John, and others."[20] He added the self-evident observation that in these noncanonical gospels "the character of the style itself is very different from that of the apostles, and the sentiment and purport of those things that are advanced in them, deviating as far as possible from sound orthodoxy, evidently proves they are fictions of heretical men."[21] The Gnostic Gospels are useful for scholars because the more you study these second-, third-, and fourth-century texts, the more obvious it is how dramatically they differ from the texts of the New Testament. But they really aren't that helpful for ordinary people who want to know what Jesus was all about. After three centuries of relentless scholarly digging, more and more scholars are concluding that our best resource for learning about Jesus and his message is still, by far, the canonical books of the New Testament. We all wish we could find a treasure trove of new materials—authentic lost gospels, perhaps a letter Jesus wrote to Peter,[22] even a collection of Jesus' sayings in Aramaic. But as of yet, nothing like that has turned up. The closest is the gospel of Thomas—and yet, even in that case, most scholars believe it was written after the canonical gospels and is simply a modification of them. Until these new textual discoveries surface, we will have to content ourselves with the New Testament. For better or worse, it's our best source for knowledge of who Jesus was and what he was trying to accomplish.

THE REAL "SECRET" TEACHING OF JESUS

If there is a secret teaching of Jesus, there is one place it might be found: in the collection of mind-altering, spirit-enhancing stories we call the parables.

In the Gospels, Jesus himself explained why he was speaking in these cryptic riddles. When his followers ask him directly why he spoke in parables, Jesus replied enigmatically: "To you it has been given to know the secrets of the kingdom of heaven, but to them it has not been given. For to those who have, more will be given, and they will have an abundance; but from those who have nothing, even what they have will be taken away. The reason I speak to them in parables is that 'seeing they do not perceive, and hearing they do not listen, nor do they understand'" (Matt. 13:11–13 NRSV). What Jesus appears to be saying is that people who already understand what his message is all about will "get" his parables, while those who do not understand his message will view them simply as moralistic tales.

Some scholars believe that while Jesus of Nazareth may not have invented the literary form known as the parable—that is, a very short story or extended metaphor meant to convey a larger spiritual truth—he certainly perfected it.[23] There are a handful of antecedents to Jesus' parables in the Hebrew Bible. One example is the prophet Nathan's story about the rich man who steals a poor man's only lamb (2 Sam. 12:1–9). But even these antecedents lack the universality of Jesus' parables since they typically are not meant to apply to more than a single example (in Nathan's case, to David stealing Uriah the Hittite's only wife when he already had at least seven others and many concubines of his own). What's more, Jesus' parables are characterized by a brevity, forcefulness, and sheer brilliance of analogy that have rarely been equaled. They are like thought bombs that send out shock waves through time, haunting people's dreams, changing the way people view the world.

If you count as parables only the actual stories that Jesus tells, and not simple analogies or allegories, such as "I am the Vine" verses in John (15:5), there are at least thirty-seven parables related in the four canonical Gospels.[24] Of these, thirteen are found in more than one gospel, thirteen are only in the gospel of Luke, nine are only in Matthew, one only in Mark, and none in John. Versions of fourteen of these parables are also found in the extracanonical gospel of Thomas in addition to two parables that are unique to Thomas. In addition, there are also three other parables attributed to Jesus, not found in the canonical Gospels, recorded in the Apocryphon of James—a second-century text found in the Nag Hammadi library that relates "secret" teachings of Jesus to Peter and James. Altogether, parables make up fully one-third of all Jesus' sayings in the Gospels, more than half of both Matthew and Luke.[25]

DIFFERENT TYPES OF PARABLES

In terms of themes, the parables often can be categorized and interpreted in a variety of ways. But many scholars divide the parables into basic groups such as:[26]

1. six parables about the kingdom of God;
2. nine parables about the "end of the age";
3. three parables about loss and redemption;
4. three parables about the effectiveness of prayer;
5. five parables about sin and repentance;
6. seven parables about the last judgment;
7. three parables about mercy to fellow human beings; and
8. parables about various topics, including such favorites as the parable of the talents and the wise and foolish builders.

Scholars have long marveled at the concise brilliance of Jesus' simple stories. The parable of the prodigal son, for example, is able to convey Jesus' radical teaching on the unconditional mercy of the Creator God, even for the most wretched and debased of his creatures, in just a few short, dramatic sentences (Luke 15:11–32). Jesus often got his message across by putting a "twist" in his story that upended conventions. For example, Amy-Jill Levine points out that, in the parable of the prodigal son, Jesus' Jewish listeners would have smiled at a story about "two sons," an older and a younger. They knew these all by heart: Cain and Abel, Isaac and Ishmael, and Jacob and Esau. But in Jesus' story, it is the younger son, not the elder, who is irresponsible. The errant son returns, and the father brings out the fatted calf. Even the seething resentment of the "good son" conveys Jesus' psychological acuity. Jesus knew his followers well.

The parable of the good Samaritan conveys the essence of Jesus' challenge to love your neighbor as yourself, with a brilliant choice of characters that is lost on most people today (Luke 10:25–37). In Jesus' time, the

Samaritans and Jews despised one another, much as the Palestinians and Israelis do today. Thus, in Jesus' story, which was told to Jews, the man who does the good deed and helps out when no one else will was a Samaritan, or what to an Israeli might mean a Palestinian. The priest and the Levite (or, in modern terms, the rabbi and the head of the synagogue) both walk by, but it is a Palestinian man who stops, bandages the victim's wounds, and brings him to an inn. Again, with just a little twist in the story, the device of having the Samaritan/Palestinian be the "hero," Jesus was able to shock his listeners and make them think about what he was really saying.

The same can be said about the parable of the two debtors (Luke 7:36–50). One man owed a lender fifty denarii, another five hundred. Since neither could pay, the lender forgave them both. Who would love him more? In Jesus' time, a silver denarius was roughly equal to one day's pay.[27] So one man owed nearly two months' wages, another man more than a year and a half's. In our terms, that's like one man owing, say, $10,000 and another man owing $100,000. Again, it's the telling details that made Jesus' parables linger in people's minds, changing their hearts in a dramatic, lasting way.

Another example, sometimes not seen as an actual parable, is the parable of the sheep and the goats (Matt. 25:31–46). In the parable, Jesus talks about the end of days when the Son of Man will judge "the nations" and will separate people as a shepherd separates sheep and goats. To those on his right, the King will say,

> "Come, you who are blessed by my Father; take your inheritance, the kingdom prepared for you since the creation of the world. For I was hungry and you gave me something to eat, I was thirsty and you gave me something to drink, I was a stranger and you invited me in, I needed clothes and you clothed me, I was sick and you looked after me, I was in prison and you came to visit me." (Matt. 25:34–36 NIV)

Of course, the people thus invited object and say, "Lord, when did we see you hungry and feed you, or thirsty and give you something to drink? When did we see you a stranger and invite you in, or needing clothes and clothe you? When did we see you sick or in prison and go to visit you?" And then, Jesus says, delivering the punch line, the king will respond, "Amen, I say to you, whatever you did for one of these least brothers of mine, you did for me" (Matt. 25:37–40).

Strangely, many Christian denominations take this parable literally and use it to justify doctrines such as supralapsarianism, the notion that God created most human beings knowing that he would damn them for all eternity with no possibility of salvation. Modern scholars such as Bart Ehrman also take this parable literally to justify their portrait of Jesus as an apocalyptic prophet who expected the end of the world in his lifetime.[28] What Jesus is *really* talking about, however, is not doomsday (the putative subject of the parable) but what he expects from his followers—what his vision of the kingdom actually entails. With this simple story, Jesus is communicating his knowledge that God's concern extends to the most wretched of his creatures . . . and that human beings will be held accountable for how they treat the poorest and most despised.

In short, through his cryptic riddles and strange stories, Jesus invited his hearers to participate in a new spiritual and social movement based on a renunciation of ambition for worldly success in favor of serving one another, and on a restored trust in God. This call for a new way of life would require Jewish hearers to modify some of their interpretations of what the "fence around the Torah" required, and for the Gentiles to learn an entirely new way of living. A life of mercy and forgiveness would mean declining to divorce your wife when you tire of her, feeding the hungry, visiting the imprisoned, and clothing the naked. It would require sacrifice and maybe even suffering.

Here's how Brian McLaren sums up "the secret message of Jesus" in his wonderful book of the same name:

> If you are part of this kingdom, you won't slit Roman throats like the Zealots. Instead, if a Roman solider backhands you with a blow to the right cheek, you'll turn the other in a mind of nonviolent and transcendent countermove. . . . If you are part of this kingdom, you won't curse and damn the notorious sinners and scoundrels to hell; instead, you'll interact with them gently and kindly, refusing to judge, even inviting them to your parties and treating them as your neighbors—being less afraid of their polluting influence on you than you are hopeful about your possible healing and ennobling influence on them.[29]

FOR FURTHER STUDY

Bruce, F. F. *The Hard Sayings of Jesus.* Downers Grove, IL: InterVarsity Press, 1983.

Ehrman, Bart, ed. *Lost Scriptures: Books That Did Not Make It Into the New Testament.* London: Oxford University Press, 2003.

Jeremias, Joachim. *The Parables of Jesus.* New York: Scribner's, 1954.

McLaren, Brian. *The Secret Message of Jesus.* Nashville, TN: Thomas Nelson, 2006.

Miller, Robert J., ed. *The Complete Gospels: Annotated Scholars Version.* San Francisco: HarperSanFrancisco, 1992.

Pagels, Elaine. *The Gnostic Gospels.* New York: Vintage Books, 1979.

Wills, Garry. *What Jesus Meant.* New York: Penguin, 2006.

$\begin{array}{c|c|c} & 8 & \end{array}$

WAS JESUS A ZEALOT REVOLUTIONARY?

The Revival of a Very Old Idea

As Jesus was leaving the temple, one of his disciples said
to him, "Look, Teacher! What massive stones! What
magnificent buildings!" "Do you see all these great
buildings?" replied Jesus. "Not one stone here will be
left on another; every one will be thrown down."

—MARK 13:1–2 NIV

There are many time portals in the land of Israel, eerie and ancient places where you can almost gaze back across the ages. One of them is Caesarea Maritima. Built by Herod the Great on Israel's central coast, it was one of the most beautiful cities in the ancient world—a planned Greco-Roman town with luxurious villas, paved seaside promenades, public pools, enormous statues, and a vast deep-water harbor extending eight hundred feet out into the Mediterranean that welcomed ships from all across the Roman empire. Figs, oranges, dates, and pomegranates grew in abundance.

Balage Belogh

The Roman military administration in Palestine was based in the seaside town of Caesarea Maritima, built by Herod the Great. Many of the key structures, including the Roman amphitheatre, horse-racing hippodrome, and palace of Pontius Pilate are still visible today.

Incredibly, large portions of the city remain as they were two thousand years ago. At the northern end, a remnant of Herod's colonnaded sea wall extends into the Mediterranean, creating a sheltered cove of turquoise water and white sand beaches that reminds travelers of the Greek islands. Standing on this promontory and perusing the coastline, the city's vast ruins lie before you. The Roman aqueduct, which brought fresh water from Mount Carmel ten miles to the north, still stands. The oblong hippodrome, or horse-racing arena—*hippo* is the Greek word for horse—extends along the beach and once held ten thousand spectators. The towering Greek-style amphitheatre facing the Mediterranean has been completely reconstructed. According to the Christian historian Eusebius, who resided in Caesarea, it was in this very amphitheatre that Christian "atheists" were executed in the second century. Finally, just steps from the water, the ruins of a lavish villa can be seen. Originally built by Herod, this vast palace held a freshwater, Olympic-sized swimming pool, still visible, and it is here that the Roman governor Pontius Pilate resided during his ten-year rule.

The Romans took over military control of Judaea in AD 6 following the disastrous and cruel reign of Herod the Great's son Archelaus, mentioned in the gospel of Matthew (2:22). Pilate, the fifth prefect of Judaea and successor to Valerius Gratus, arrived from Rome in AD 26, likely just before Jesus of Nazareth began his public ministry. Until 1962, there was no archaeological proof that Pilate even existed—and so, nineteenth-century "mythicists" could conclude that he, too, was just a fictional character, like Jesus himself, created by the authors of the Gospels. But as we saw in an earlier chapter, archaeologists excavating the ruins at Caesarea discovered a limestone block near the amphitheatre with a Latin inscription dedicated to Pilate. The original block is now displayed in the Israel Museum in Jerusalem, but a replica stands near the Roman governor's residence. This was the first confirmation that Pilate was actually a higher-ranked "prefect," not a procurator. The inscription reads:

...]S TIBERIVM [Tiberius]
... PON]TIVS PILATVS [Pontius Pilate]
... PRAEF]ECTVS IVDA[EA] [Prefect of Judaea]

We know very little about Pilate. Yet from the handful of ancient writings about him, it appears he was a particularly harsh and vindictive governor—so much so, in fact, that he was eventually relieved of his command by the emperor Tiberius himself. The Jewish philosopher Philo (25 BC–AD 50) recounts how Jewish leaders in Jerusalem eventually wrote to Emperor Tiberius to complain about Pilate's "corruption . . . cruelty, and his continual murders of people untried and uncondemned, and his never ending, and gratuitous, and most grievous inhumanity."[1] Roman governors before Pilate made some allowances for Jewish religious beliefs—for example, by not bringing any Roman standards bearing the likeness of the emperor into the holy city of Jerusalem. The Romans did this to avoid violating the Jews' ancient prohibition against graven images.

In contrast, Pilate seems to have decided as a matter of policy that no such allowances should be made. One of his first acts as governor of Judaea was to send troops to Jerusalem carrying the offensive Roman standards and to have these set up in the city. This triggered a near-riot. According

According to the first-century Jewish historian Josephus, the relatively small Roman garrison in Jerusalem—much like this recreation in Jordan—had good reason as the Gospels say to "fear the people." When the Jewish War against the Roman occupation broke out in AD 66, Jewish Zealot forces slaughtered the entire Roman garrison in Jerusalem's Antonia Fortress to a man.

to Josephus, a "vast multitude" of Jews flooded into Caesarea, protesting Pilate's brazen violation of Jewish customs.[2] The protests continued for nearly a week as apparently thousands of outraged Jews descended upon the city. On the sixth day, Pilate agreed to a hearing in the "open place" in the city, near his official residence and where his judgment seat was located. However, using what was apparently one of his favorite tactics, Pilate ordered his soldiers to secretly surround the Jewish crowds, keeping their weapons hidden. At the appointed time, Pilate appeared on the dais to hear the latest Jewish petition against the Roman standards. He gave a quick signal, and suddenly his soldiers drew their weapons. Pilate then announced that if the Jews did not cease their protest immediately, his soldiers would execute them all on the spot.

Pilate no doubt was confident he had the upper hand. In those days, Roman brutality usually prevailed. But then something unexpected occurred. The Jews suddenly dropped to their knees, bared their throats, and announced that they would rather die than permit the violation of their ancient laws. The Roman governor hesitated. He knew that a mass execution of thousands of unarmed men would not be viewed favorably by the emperor. As a result, Pilate reluctantly backed down and ordered that the Roman standards be withdrawn from Jerusalem.

But Pilate was stubborn—and apparently held a grudge. His next provocation was to march into the temple treasury in Jerusalem and carry off the temple funds held there. Pilate needed money to build a new aqueduct for Jerusalem, and he decided to help himself to the vast sums in the temple treasury as previous Roman rulers had done before him. According to Josephus, "tens of thousands" of Jews again caused a near-riot in Jerusalem over this desecration of the temple, surrounding Pilate's headquarters and causing a loud clamor.[3] Once again, Pilate responded by secretly sending his soldiers, dressed like Jews, to attack the protestors—and this time many of the Jews were slaughtered.[4]

Not only was Jesus almost certainly aware of this incident, it appears he commented on it. The gospel of Luke recounts how some of Jesus' hearers asked him about "the Galileans whose blood Pilate had mingled with their sacrifices" (13:1 NRSV), a reference, many historians believe, to the bloody retaliation Pilate exacted against the Jewish protesters in Jerusalem.[5] "Do you think that because these Galileans suffered in this way they were worse sinners than all other Galileans?" Jesus asked in Luke's account. "No, I tell you; but unless you repent, you will all perish as they did" (Luke 13:1–3 NRSV).

THE JESUS OF THE ACADEMICS: DELUDED END-TIMES FANATIC

As we saw in an earlier chapter, some academic New Testament scholars today, perhaps even the majority, claim that Jesus was an "apocalyptic prophet" who believed the world was coming to an end in his lifetime. According to this view, Jesus believed that God would soon intervene directly in history, slaughter all the Romans, and reestablish the kingdom of Israel as the ruling power on earth with himself as king. It was the view of Jesus pioneered by the great German-French New Testament scholar and medical doctor, Albert Schweitzer. In his classic survey of failed nineteenth-century attempts to create historically credible "lives of Jesus," *The Quest of the Historical Jesus* (1904), Schweitzer proposed that Jesus was, for lack of a better term, a delusional fanatic. Schweitzer portrayed Jesus as an end-times prophet who believed that he could somehow force God's hand and trigger the hoped-for apocalyptic cataclysm by deliberately baiting the Jewish and Roman authorities into condemning him to death. This would, in effect, force God to act. For Schweitzer, Jesus was clearly wrong about the imminent end of the world and died a failed and disappointed messianic pretender when he tragically discovered on the cross, too late, that God had abandoned him to his fate (hence Jesus' anguished cry recorded in Mark 15:34, "My God, my God, why have you forsaken me?").[6]

Many New Testament scholars still advocate this older, bleak view of Jesus as a tragically misguided prophet who failed in his mission. Some sugarcoat this vision, to be sure.[7] Other scholars, however, are more blunt. Bart Ehrman cheerfully outlines the full implications of this view of Jesus as a deluded end-times fanatic. "There should be little doubt that Jesus taught that the end of the age, with the appearance of the Son of Man, would occur shortly, within his own generation," Ehrman writes.[8] This is because, Ehrman says, in the "earliest sources"—meaning the hypothetical sayings source Q and the unique Lukan and Markan source material—Jesus speaks frequently about the coming end of the age.

And what exactly would the end of the age entail? According to Ehrman, that's easy: it means death to the pagans! Jesus "believed that God would soon intervene in the course of human affairs *to destroy the Romans, and everyone else opposed to him,* before setting up his kingdom on earth" and awarding Jesus with the throne.[9]

For Ehrman, that was Jesus' core message. His "good news" was that God would soon kill all the Romans and anyone else who opposed Jesus. But over time, Ehrman argues, the Christian community deliberately "de-apocalypticized"[10] Jesus, as in the gospel of John, when it became clear that Jesus was flat-out wrong about the world coming to an end. "[O]ver the course of time, the disciples did die and Jesus' own generation came and went," he continues. "And there was no cataclysmic break in history, no arrival of the Son of Man, no resurrection from the dead."[11]

For Ehrman, moreover, Jesus was not merely a deluded end-times fanatic; he was also not a particularly noble or high-minded one. Like many of the historical Jesus scholars, Ehrman believes Jesus was far *less* noble than he is portrayed as being in the Gospels. For Ehrman, Jesus taught the Sermon on the Mount and his other ethical instructions merely as a ticket into heaven. "Jesus is often thought of as a great moral teacher, and I think that is right," he says, not all that convincingly. "But it is important to understand *why* he insisted on a moral lifestyle guided by the dictates of love." Jesus' ethical teachings were not aimed at making people or society better, he adds. Rather, "they were designed to convince people to behave in appropriate ways so that when the Son of Man came, they would be among the elect and brought into the kingdom instead of being destined for either eternal torment or annihilation."[12]

The New Testament scholar James Tabor, a colleague of Ehrman's at the University of North Carolina, agrees. He states unequivocally that Jesus was looking forward to seeing blood filling the streets. "The difference between Martin Luther King, Jr., Mahatma Gandhi, and others who have practiced 'passive resistance' in our own day is that Jesus and his movement expected and welcomed a very 'violent' apocalypse in which heads would topple and blood would fill the streets," Tabor writes in his popular blog. He continues:

> John, Jesus, and James all believed fervently that a new age or era was imminent and that there was to be a great reversal that God would bring about in their lifetimes. All the apocalyptic literature that we have from this period is violent to the extreme. Think of the "body count" in the book of Revelation alone. There is also a strong element of "rejoicing" on the part of the "saints" who see the Beast/Babylon go down. This is what [New Testament scholar Robert] Eisenman has rightly objected to in his insistence that the Jesus/James movement was not some quietist movement that had withdrawn from society into a contemplative Pythagorean or Buddhist-like aversion to this world.[13]

THE VIOLENT WORLD OF FIRST-CENTURY PALESTINE

Clearly, Palestine in the time of Christ was a far cry from the image people have today of a pastoral land with shepherds tending their sheep on the hillsides and fishermen casting their nets in the Sea of Galilee. In reality, Palestine appears to have been, at least intermittently, a fairly brutal and violent place in the first century. In Jesus' parables, bandits and robbers prey on innocent travelers (Luke 10:30). Slavery was practiced, even in small towns (Mark 12:2). There was fierce ethnic hatred: between the Jews and the Samaritans (John 4:9), the Greeks and the Jews (Mark 7:25–27), and the Romans and everyone else (John 11:48).

Historians such as Richard Horsley and John Dominic Crossan have spent decades studying the overall military and economic contexts in which Jesus and the apostles moved. They both conclude that the people of Palestine were under increasing economic stress as taxes were vastly increased, massive debts and conscripted labor became more common, and the Roman military administration, under inept and brutal procurators, terrorized the population. In their book *Excavating Jesus*, Crossan and Jonathan Reed document the economic exploitation that existed under the Herodian and then direct Roman rule in this era.[14] Recent archaeological digs have revealed seaside and mountaintop villas of enormous luxury existing side by side with bone-crushing poverty, entire families crowded together in mud-and-stone huts. Visitors to Sepphoris and Caesarea Maritima today can see the magnificent, intricately patterned mosaics on the floors of some of these villas, tour the still-stunning Roman theatres, and marvel at the public baths with the cold, warm, and hot pools.

To finance these marvels, the Herodian and Roman administrations stole agricultural lands from small local farmers and created vast estates and, in some cases, built up thriving commercial enterprises for themselves. In their book *The Message and the Kingdom*, Richard Horsley and Neil Asher Silberman document how the landed aristocracy in Galilee transformed fishing on the Sea of Galilee from a small-time, local and seasonal occupation into, in effect, an international big business. Roman entrepreneurs developed fish preservation techniques, such as pickling, that allowed them to begin exporting "Made-in-Galilee" fish products throughout the Roman Empire. "Urban populations throughout the Roman Empire grew to love the spicy, smelly fish sauces called *garum*, and stews of salted fishheads and chopped pieces called *salsamentum*, both of which were highly valued as everyday condiments and all-purpose medicine," Horsley and Silberman write.[15] By the time Jesus was about twenty years old, the lakeside town of Magdala had become such a famous center of this industry that it was called Taricheae, or "Town of the Salt-Fish." Even today, there is a nearby restaurant on the edge of the Sea of Galilee that serves the local tilapia, which the Israelis call *amnon* but which is also called "Saint Peter's fish."

To capture the hatred of the local Galilean people toward the affluent city-dwellers in Sepphoris, Crossan and Reed quote a passage from Josephus's autobiography in which the Jewish general describes his assault on the "neutral" city during the start of the Jewish War: "The Galilaeans, seizing this opportunity, too good to be missed, of venting their hatred on one of the cities which they detested, rushed forward, with the intention of exterminating the population, aliens and all."[16] Luckily, most of the inhabitants had fled from the rampaging mob, and Josephus describes how he attempted to quell the blood-lust of the local people.

SIX CENTURIES OF MILITARY OCCUPATION

For nearly six centuries, the Jewish homeland had been under direct or indirect military occupation—first by the Babylonians and then by the Persians, "Greeks" (both Greco-Egyptian and Greco-Syrian), and finally the Romans. The occupiers had little regard for Jewish religious sensibilities, building pagan temples, nude baths and gymnasia, theatres, brothels, and other foreign institutions. For a brief period of roughly a century, an independent Jewish kingdom arose under the Maccabees, between 140 and 63 BC, but that quickly deteriorated into internecine feuds until the Roman general Pompey was virtually invited to invade the country.[17] Crossan and Reed note, however, that Roman rule must have been particularly harsh because while there had been only one revolt that we know about during the five hundred years of Persian and Greek rule, there were four major revolts in the first two hundred years of Roman-occupied Palestine, each increasingly disastrous and lethal for the Jewish people. The final two revolts, in AD 115–117 and 132–135, resulted in Jerusalem being leveled, rebuilt as a pagan city, Aelia Capitolina, and Jews forbidden to enter on pain of death.[18]

Robert Hutchinson

From atop the final Zealot stronghold of Masada, near the Dead Sea, visitors can plainly see the remnants of the Roman perimeter wall and camps at the base of the mountain fortress.

THE POLITICS OF JESUS

Given the ruthlessness of Roman rule in general and of Pilate's rule in particular, it's not surprising that over the years some writers have concluded that Jesus sought to overthrow the Romans by force and free his people from their tyrannical power. Clearly, the ordinary people in Galilee and much of Palestine were seething with hatred toward their Roman masters and the collaborationist temple aristocracy in Jerusalem, which amassed vast fortunes from the tithes and fees paid by ordinary Jews. Rebellion was in the air and would break out sporadically throughout Jesus' lifetime and beyond. This is why, every now and then, a writer appears who claims that Jesus was not the peaceful teacher portrayed in the Gospels but really a violent Zealot revolutionary whose aim was to overthrow the Roman occupation government.

The first writer to suggest this appears to have been the German deist and rationalist philosopher Hermann Samuel Reimarus (1694–1768). In his *Fragments*, published anonymously after his death, Reimarus claimed that Jesus' followers perpetrated a vast fraud by transforming him from a very this-world Jewish messiah who claimed to be a Davidic king into a spiritual savior of mankind. "[The apostles] had hitherto been constantly looking forward to worldly grandeur and advantages in the kingdom of Jesus, which were put an end to by his death," Reimarus wrote. "Upon this failure they brought out a new creed of Jesus as a spiritual, suffering Saviour, which until some time afterwards had never entered their heads, and . . . then set themselves up as messengers and preachers of this gospel."[19]

For centuries, few took Reimarus seriously. However, in 1967 a British scholar of religion named S. G. F. Brandon (1907–1971) wrote *Jesus and the Zealots: A Study of the Political Factor in Primitive Christianity*. Brandon argues that Jesus was a Jewish nationalist, a Zealot who launched a violent assault on the corrupt Jerusalem temple aristocracy that collaborated with Rome. The "cleansing of the temple" scene in the Gospels, according to Brandon, was not a symbolic spiritual protest as Christians have long believed but an actual *attack* in which hundreds, perhaps thousands, of Jesus' followers participated, all clamoring that Jesus be made king of Israel. That was why, he explains, Jesus was executed by Rome with the charge posted above his head, "Jesus of Nazareth, King of the Jews." This violent, albeit primarily religious mission may have occurred simultaneously with a far more serious uprising by Zealot forces against the Romans or Roman sympathizers, Brandon suggests, and two of these men, possibly led by Barabbas, were executed side by side with Jesus on Calvary. In fact, Brandon says, this is virtually self-evident from the Gospels alone: "[T]he most certain thing known about Jesus of Nazareth," Brandon writes, "is that he was crucified by the Romans as a rebel against their government in Judaea."[20]

WERE THE EVANGELISTS TRYING TO COVER UP WHO JESUS REALLY WAS?

Of course, this suggests that the Gospels are a complete whitewash of what really happened—an attempt to make Jesus and his movement palatable to skittish Roman rulers after the Jewish Revolt of AD 66–70. This can be seen, Brandon claims, by a number of inconsistencies in the Gospel narratives. For one thing, Mark portrays Jesus as an innocent victim of scheming Jewish leaders, falsely accused of sedition and executed by the Romans;

yet the evangelist also admits that Jesus' popularity with the crowds was so great that Jewish leaders feared to arrest him publicly (12:12), and had to send an armed party to do so—and at night (14:32–51). This proves, Brandon argues, that Jesus was actually the leader of a violent opposition movement. Moreover, the fears of the Jewish leaders were apparently justified because their attempts to arrest Jesus were met by armed resistance. One of the "bystanders," whom John identifies as Peter, cut off the ear of the high priest's servant.[21]

Brandon didn't persuade many mainstream historians. However, over the years a few scholars have echoed some of his views. Recently, Robert Eisenman, director of the Institute for the Study of Judeo-Christian Origins at California State University, Long Beach, has argued that the early followers of Jesus were part of a violent "Opposition Alliance" that included the Zealots, Essenes, and other Torah-observant nationalistic Jewish groups "involved in and precipitating the Uprising against Rome in 66–70 CE."[22] Eisenman is known for his contrarian dating of the Dead Sea Scrolls, which he believes were written much later than the scholarly consensus agrees. Most controversially, Eisenman believes that James the Just, the "brother of the Lord" and one of the leaders of the early Jesus community in Jerusalem, was likely the mysterious "Teacher of Righteousness" mentioned in the Dead Sea Scrolls. Eisenman thinks that the original followers of Jesus were zealous Jews, very like or identical to ascetic and extremist Essenes, who were later marginalized and replaced by the followers of the gentile form of Christianity created by Paul of Tarsus. It was Paul, Eisenman believes, who changed Jesus' message from one of violent revolt against Rome to a universal religion of peace and love.[23]

JESUS AS AN ADVOCATE FOR JIHAD

The most recent champion for the view that Jesus was a "radical Jewish nationalist who challenged the Roman occupation and lost"[24] is Reza Aslan, a Muslim professor of creative writing at the University of California, Riverside, and author of the 2013 bestseller *Zealot: The Life and Times of Jesus of Nazareth*. Aslan was once a Christian himself, having converted, he says, during high school. However, as he learned more about the New

Testament, Aslan became disillusioned with his teenage faith and, before entering college, rediscovered his Muslim roots.[25] Aslan insists, however, that his book *Zealot* is not an attack on Christianity. "My mother is a Christian, my wife is a Christian," he said in a TV interview. "My brother-in-law is an evangelical pastor. Anyone who thinks this book is an attack on Christianity has not read it yet."[26]

While *Zealot* may not be an attack on Christianity per se, it is definitely an attack on traditional understandings of who Jesus was and what he was trying to achieve. Presenting details of the Jewish-Roman conflict in the years after Jesus' crucifixion, Aslan paints a convincing portrait of Palestine in the midst of an escalating rebellion that would eventually lead to all-out war. He does a good job of describing the rise of Jewish terrorists known as the Sicarii, the forerunners of the Zealots, who would assassinate Roman collaborators with daggers and in broad daylight—including the high priest Jonathan in AD 56.[27] In this way, Aslan tells a story similar to that of Brandon, Eisenman, and, to some extent, James Tabor. Drawing upon Josephus, Aslan shows that there were many devout Jews in Jerusalem in the 50s and 60s—whom we today would call "zealots" or extreme nationalists—who advocated violence against Rome, even outright terrorism. From there, Aslan spends most of his book trying to tie Jesus to these violent extremists and to show that he shared in their outlook and ambitions. Like Brandon, Aslan argues that the New Testament is a cover-up of what Jesus was really like.

Unfortunately, *Zealot* is a rather confusing book that frequently contradicts itself. Aslan is clearly aware that few New Testament scholars accept the view that Jesus was a revolutionary who advocated violent resistance against Rome. As a result, he covers his bases and writes that "Jesus was not a member of the Zealot Party that launched the war with Rome, because no such party could be said to exist for another thirty years after his death" and adds that "[nor] was Jesus a violent revolutionary bent on armed rebellion." Yet despite this concession, Aslan characterizes Jesus' proclamation of the kingdom of God as "a call to revolution, plain and simple," and asks, "what revolution, especially one fought against an empire whose armies had ravaged the land set aside by God for his chosen people, could be free of violence and bloodshed?"[28]

For Aslan, there was a fierce rivalry between Paul and his Gentile followers and the violent messianic Jews, the original followers of Jesus, who clustered around James, "the brother of the Lord," in Jerusalem. These rival views of what the Jesus movement was all about would have competed for dominance, but, unfortunately for the Jewish Christians, the war against Rome for which Jesus had allegedly long hoped finally occurred, only with disastrous results. In AD 62, shortly before the war broke out, James was himself arrested, charged with blasphemy by the High Priest Ananus, and stoned to death. Although Paul, too, had been arrested shortly before, because he was a Roman citizen he was shipped off to Rome to stand trial and met his death there. But Paul's version of the Jesus movement, which was rapidly gaining adherents among the Gentiles, would ultimately be victorious. According to Aslan, that's because the original followers of Jesus, the Torah-observant Jewish holy warriors in Jerusalem, died in the great conflagration that was the Jewish war against Rome. While ancient sources say that the Jesus community in Jerusalem fled to Pella, beyond the Jordan, before the war began, Aslan doesn't believe it. "[T]hey maintained their presence in the city of Jesus' death and resurrection, eagerly awaiting his return, right up to the moment that Titus's army arrived and wiped the holy city and its inhabitants—both Christians and Jews—off the face of the earth," he writes.[29]

With the Jerusalem mother church annihilated, the only Christian communities left were those founded by Paul, Aslan argues, and the only writings available were his letters. Thus, Pauline Christianity, with its alleged denigration of the Jewish Law and its false depiction of Jesus as a spiritual teacher of peace and love, triumphed. The real Jesus, the "radical Jewish nationalist who challenged the Roman occupation and lost" was, unfortunately, "lost to history."[30]

JESUS AS A PEACEMAKER, NOT A REVOLUTIONARY

The key problem with this revisionist portrait of Jesus and his followers as bloody-minded fanatics anxious for war against the Romans is that it finds little support in any early historical sources, including the New Testament, Josephus, the Jewish Mishnah, and even the writings of Roman historians.

In none of these sources is Jesus portrayed as a violent rebel or revolutionary.

In the Jewish Talmud, Jesus is described, as we saw in a previous chapter, not as a rebel but as someone who "practiced magic and led Israel astray,"[31] although some scholars argue that the "Yeshu" described there does not refer to Jesus of Nazareth. In the Gospels, Jesus not only preached personal nonresistance to evil ("If anyone strikes you on the right cheek, turn to him the other also," [Matt. 5:39 RSV]), he also *practiced* it. According to all four gospels,[32] when Jesus was arrested, his disciples immediately leapt to his defense, even cutting off the ear of the high priest's slave. However, Jesus promptly admonished them, insisting that "all who take the sword will perish by the sword" (Matt. 26:52 NRSV). In one of the earliest writings in the New Testament, Paul's letter to the Romans, likely written around AD 56, the apostle communicates Jesus' message to the Romans: "Do not repay anyone evil for evil . . . If it is possible, as far as it depends on you, live at peace with everyone . . . Do not take revenge . . . if your enemy is hungry, feed him . . . Do not be overcome by evil, but overcome evil with good" (Rom. 12:17–21 NIV). Clearly, this does not sound like the message of a first-century advocate of holy war.

Later Christian and pagan sources also portray Jesus and his followers as having *renounced* violence. In 1 Peter 2, the author insists that Jesus left "you an example for you to follow in His steps . . . while being reviled, He did not revile in return; while suffering, He uttered no threats" (vv. 21 and 23 NASB). Early Roman writers such as Suetonius (ca. 69–122) characterize the followers of Jesus as superstitious bumpkins, perhaps even troublemakers, but not as serious threats.[33] The Greek satirist Lucian (ca. 115–200) writes that the followers of Jesus, whom he calls "poor wretches," have "convinced themselves first and foremost, that they are going to be immortal and live for all time, in consequence of which they despise death and even willingly give themselves into custody." What's more, Lucian mocks, "their first lawgiver persuaded them that they are all brothers of one another."[34] Recently some authors have argued that the claim the early Christians were absolute pacifists is probably overstating the case because we know that there were Christians serving in the Roman army even before the age of Constantine. In fact, the earliest church building discovered in Israel, dating to the late second century AD and first uncovered in 2005 in Megiddo, contains an inscription describing how a Roman officer named Gaianus donated money to build the floor mosaic in the memory "of the God Jesus Christ."[35]

CHRISTIANS WIDELY KNOWN FOR THEIR OPPOSITION TO VIOLENCE

Nevertheless, the followers of Jesus were widely known for their *opposition* to violence and killing. One of the very first post–New Testament Christian writings, the *Didache* or *Teaching of the Twelve Apostles* (ca. AD 100), insists that followers of Jesus shall "not kill a fetus by abortion, or commit infanticide" (2:2), a common practice among pagans.[36] In his *Dialogue with Trypho,* Justin Martyr (100–165) writes that "we who were filled with war, and mutual slaughter, and every wickedness, have each through the whole earth changed our warlike weapons—our swords into ploughshares and our spears into implements of tillage."[37] Irenaeus of Lyon (130–202) agrees. "For the Christians have changed their swords and their lances into instruments of peace, and they know not how to fight," he writes.[38] Tertullian (ca. 160–220) insists that Christians should refuse to attend gladiatorial combats and should not serve in the army. "Will it be lawful for [a Christian] to occupy himself with the sword, when the Lord declares that he who uses the sword will perish by the sword?" Tertullian asks. "And shall the son of peace, for whom it will be unfitting even to go to law, be engaged in a battle? And shall he, who is not the avenger even of his own wrongs, administer chains and imprisonment and tortures and executions?"[39] Hippolytus (170–235), in his book *The Apostolic Tradition*, appears to acknowledge the presence of some Christians in the Roman legions. Yet in such cases, he insists that the Christian solider must avoid killing. "A military man in authority must not execute men," Hippolytus writes.[40] The Roman Christian writer Lactantius (250–325), who became an advisor to the emperor Constantine, agrees. In his *Divine Institutes,* Lactantius denounces capital punishment and gladiatorial combat, insisting that "it is always unlawful to put to death a man."[41]

JESUS' FAME SPREAD LIKE WILDFIRE

What's more, if Jesus really were just another failed Jewish revolutionary—another would-be messiah who "challenged Rome and lost"—then why is he remembered at all? There were *many* failed military messiahs in the decades before and after Jesus—Judas the Galilean, Menahem, Simon bar

Kochba—yet few people today except ancient historians know who they were. In contrast, two thousand years later, everyone all across the globe knows about Jesus of Nazareth.

Jesus' fame, in his age as in our own, spread like wildfire precisely because he was truly *something radical and new*—a prophet like nothing Israel had ever seen—proclaiming a message that no one had ever heard before. Contrary to what the "apocalyptic Jesus" scholars of the nineteenth and twentieth centuries claim, Jesus' radical new message was *not* that God or the Zealots would soon kill all the Romans and fill the streets with blood. Rather, it was that the kingdom of God was already here: God was *already* working his purposes in and through the weakest and most despised members in society, and this meant that the Romans and their empire would eventually pass away—which, by the way, they did.

Of course, the Romans were not passing away fast enough for the Jewish people—and in that sense, Jesus was not the sort of messiah for which many had hoped. But the kingdom of God that Jesus proclaimed would arrive in power before some of his hearers had died (Mark 9:1) *did* arrive in power. The movement that Jesus inaugurated and proclaimed expanded rapidly throughout the Mediterranean world. From Rome and other major cities of the empire, such as Antioch and Alexandria, the kingdom movement swept through the Roman provinces, and eventually changed the world far more than a successful overthrow of Pontius Pilate's Roman auxiliaries ever could have.

A REVOLUTION OF PEACE

As British New Testament scholar and historical Jesus expert N. T. Wright argues in his seminal work *Jesus and the Victory of God,* Jesus was about as far from being a violent revolutionary as a person could possibly be. He certainly did not believe the world was coming to an end. "Jesus did not expect, or proclaim, the end of the space-time universe," Wright writes. "Nor did he take the normal option of the military revolutionary."[42] Instead, Wright explains, Jesus "announced the end of the present evil age" and the reconstitution of the people of God in such a way that the temple in Jerusalem was no longer necessary. For Wright, Jesus was a prophet but not one who claimed God was about to annihilate the Romans. Rather, he was announcing that the corrupt Jerusalem collaborationists, the wealthy temple aristocracy, were under judgment. Jesus proclaimed a message of repentance and social solidarity similar to that of the prophets before him, and he was about to meet the same fate. Unlike "the other kingdom announcers of his time from Judas the Galilean to Simeon ben Kosiba, Jesus declared that the way to the kingdom was the way of peace, the way of love, the way of the cross," Wright concludes. "Fighting the battle of the kingdom with the enemy's weapons meant that one had already lost it in principle, and would soon lose it, and lose it terribly, in practice."[43]

In other words, what Wright, Crossan, and other recent scholars are saying is that the view of Jesus as an "apocalyptic prophet" who yearned for holy war gets things precisely backward. Jesus was not preaching about the coming holy war, as modern revisionists claim. He was desperately warning against it! "Jerusalem, Jerusalem, you who kill the prophets and stone those sent to you," Jesus lamented in Luke. "How often I have longed to gather your children together, as a hen gathers her chicks under her wings, and you were not willing" (13:34 NIV).

WHY WERE JESUS' FOLLOWERS NOT CRUCIFIED AS WELL?

Finally, it's clear from both the New Testament and the writings of Josephus[44] that the Roman authorities permitted Jesus' followers to operate openly in Jerusalem for decades after his death—which would have been virtually unimaginable if the Romans had truly believed that Jesus' followers were violent insurrectionists. Had they believed that, there would almost certainly have been *a thousand crosses* on Golgotha, not just three. As noted earlier in chapter 4, the Roman general Varus crucified two thousand Jewish rebels in the uprising that occurred after Herod the Great died in 4 BC.[45] According to Josephus, the Romans crucified five hundred rebels a day during the siege of Jerusalem at the end of the Jewish War, around AD 70. We have no records of the followers of Jesus leading revolutionary movements after his death or participating in the revolt against Rome. Rather, the early Christians were known for their opposition to violence.

For these reasons and others, few mainstream New Testament scholars today accept the view that Jesus advocated violent resistance to Rome. In fact, the evidence points in precisely the opposite direction: that Jesus saw himself in the tradition of the biblical prophets, such as Jeremiah and Isaiah, and predicted that the attempts of extreme Jewish nationalists to overthrow the Romans with military force would end in disaster. Jesus was insisting that if they chose the path of violent resistance to the Roman Empire, then Jerusalem and the temple itself would be destroyed. His proclamation of the kingdom of God was not a call for Jews to become terrorists against Rome but to become a "light to the nations" (Isa. 49:6)—to transform the world through an active campaign of free healing, table fellowship, and solidarity with the abandoned and despised. The soup kitchens, hospitals, and prison visits that have characterized Christian outreach since the very beginning are more what Jesus had in mind than violent revolution. In other words, the portrait of Jesus emerging from recent research—by scholars as diverse as N. T. Wright, John Dominic Crossan, and Richard Horsley—is closer to how Jesus is portrayed in the Gospels: a man who launched a spiritual movement to transform the world through acts of mercy and forgiveness, not violent revolution.

FOR FURTHER STUDY

Aslan, Reza. *Zealot: The Life and Times of Jesus of Nazareth.* New York: Random House, 2013.

Brandon, S. G. F. *Jesus and the Zealots.* New York: Scribner's, 1967.

Crossan, John Dominic. *God and Empire: Jesus Against Rome, Then and Now.* San Francisco: HarperSanFrancisco, 2007.

Hanson, K. C. and Douglas E. Oakman. *Palestine in the Time of Jesus: Social Structures and Social Conflicts.* Minneapolis, MN: Augsburg, 1998.

Wright, N. T. *Jesus and the Victory of God.* Minneapolis, MN: Fortress Press, 1996.

Yoder, John Howard. *The Politics of Jesus,* 2nd ed. Grand Rapids, MI: Wm. B. Eerdmans, 1994.

DID JESUS PLAN HIS OWN EXECUTION?

How the 2006 Publication of the Gnostic Gospel of Judas Revived an Old Idea

But Jesus asked him, "Judas, are you betraying the Son of Man with a kiss?"

—LUKE 22:48 NIV

The arrest of Jesus of Nazareth in the Garden of Gethsemane, at the foot of the Mount of Olives, is described in all four canonical Gospels. Matthew and Luke follow Mark's outline quite closely, adding some details, and, in Luke's case, deleting others. All four Gospels also describe the violence of Jesus' arrest, and how "one of the bystanders" leapt to Jesus' defense with a sword, cutting off the ear of the high priest's slave (Mark 14:47). The gospel of John, as usual, names names: it was Simon Peter who drew his sword, and the name of the slave was Malchus (John 18:10).

According to Mark and the Synoptics, Jesus' arrest was planned in advance. Two days before the start of Passover, the "chief priests and scribes" were seeking a way to arrest Jesus "by stealth" and put him to death (Mark 14:1 NRSV).

But they feared the people, according to the texts, and did not want to arrest Jesus during the festival lest they accidentally spark a riot. All four Gospels describe how Judas left Jesus and the other disciples as they were coming into Jerusalem, and how he met with the chief priests and agreed to betray Jesus for money. Only Matthew adds that it was for thirty pieces of silver (27:9).

After the Last Supper, Jesus and his followers sang a hymn, perhaps one of the Hallel psalms sung at Passover, and then left the room where they had eaten and proceeded to the Mount of Olives, to a place called Gethsemane. In Hebrew and Aramaic, *Gethsemane* means "oil press," and it was presumably an olive orchard that also had olive-pressing equipment, such as the large, round, rock wheels on display today on Mount Tabor. Only John calls it a "garden," but he also doesn't name it Gethsemane (18:1). In any event, it wasn't a long walk from the gates of Jerusalem to the garden. Even today you can reach the Garden of Gethsemane by walking out the Lion's Gate, near the pools of Bethesda, down the Jericho Road across the Kidron Valley to the foot of the Mount of Olives. It's a ten-minute walk. The entire area is terraced and still covered with gnarled olive trees.

Shutterstock

Of all the places mentioned in the Gospels, the Garden of Gethsemane, located at the base of the Mount of Olives across the Kidron Valley from Jerusalem's eastern wall, is one of the locations that is probably very similar today to what it looked like in the time of Jesus.

Again, all four Gospels portray Jesus as somehow knowing what suffering lay in store for him. Separating from the main group of disciples, Jesus led Peter, James, and John to another part of the garden. Then he left them, walked on a little farther, and fell to the ground. All the Synoptics portray Jesus begging for his life in prayer to God. Only Mark, traditionally the companion of Peter, adds the detail about Jesus addressing God as "Abba," the Aramaic word (still used in Israel today) for father. "Abba, Father, all things are possible for you," Jesus prayed. "Remove this cup from me. Yet not what I will, but what you will" (Mark 14:36 ESV).

When Jesus returned to where he left Peter, James, and John, he found them all asleep. Mark and Matthew show Jesus' frustration—"Could you not keep watch for one hour?" he asks in disbelief—an embarrassing detail that Luke, as usual, omits (Mark 14:37; Matt. 26:40).

Finally, Jesus announced that his time is up. "The hour has come," he said. "The Son of Man is betrayed into the hands of sinners . . . my betrayer is at hand" (Mark 14:41–42 NRSV).

The Synoptics report that Judas was "with" the crowd that came to arrest Jesus, and that he had arranged, in advance, to give a signal identifying Jesus—a kiss (Mark 14:44).

THE GOSPEL OF JUDAS VERSION

In 2006, the world heard about another version of what happened in the Garden of Gethsemane that night more than two thousand years ago—supposedly Judas Iscariot's version. Amid much fanfare, the National Geographic Society announced that a large portion of an ancient second-century gospel had been rediscovered: the long lost gospel of Judas. Until 2006, most experts only knew about the gospel of Judas from the writings of the second-century bishop Irenaeus of Lyon (ca. 130–202), who wrote about the gospel of Judas in his work, *Against Heresies.* Irenaeus described heretical groups that believed in an ultimate God beyond the creator of this evil world. These groups, Irenaeus said, claimed Jesus revealed this teaching solely to his closest and most trusted disciple, Judas Iscariot. They "declare that Judas the traitor was thoroughly acquainted with these things, and that he alone, knowing the truth as no others did, accomplished the mystery of the betrayal," Irenaeus wrote. "By him all things, both earthly and heavenly, were thus thrown into confusion. They produce a fictitious history of this kind, which they style the gospel of Judas."[1]

In a TV special, books, and articles in *National Geographic* magazine, the National Geographic Society trumpeted the discovery of an ancient Coptic manuscript of the gospel of Judas, reliably dated to around AD 220 to 340.[2] Allegedly discovered near the village of Beni Masar, Egypt, in the early 1970s, the manuscript's "provenance," as scholars call it, was somewhat dubious. In other words, that means no one knew exactly where the ancient manuscript originated and whether it was obtained legally or not. It was first seen by experts in the early 1980s, when three biblical scholars traveled to Geneva, Switzerland, to meet an Egyptian antiquities dealer who was selling some ancient manuscripts, including a very ancient one written in Coptic. The experts had been authorized to offer a maximum of $50,000 for the documents, but the Egyptian dealer insisted on a minimum of $3 million. Unable to reach an agreement on price, the would-be buyers

Kenneth Garrett / National Geographic Creative

A scholar works at reconstructing the papyrus fragments of the lost Gospel of Judas, a Coptic manuscript that has been dated to around the year AD 280. First discovered in the 1970s, the manuscript was finally translated and published in 2006 and contains a Gnostic interpretation of Jesus' teachings.

left—and that was the last anyone heard about the gospel of Judas for nearly twenty years. Before they parted, however, the scholars examined enough of the deteriorating Coptic manuscripts to see the name "Judas" prominently in the texts. The Egyptian antiquities dealer spent the next seventeen years trying to sell his priceless collection but, since no one could verify where the manuscripts had originated, museum curators were wary of spending much money on them. Finally, a woman named Frieda Nussberger-Tchacos, a Zurich-based Egyptologist and antiquities dealer, agreed to buy the Coptic manuscript for a sum in the mid six-figures. Nussberger-Tchacos quickly had the Coptic manuscript examined by experts at Yale University and learned that she had, in fact, bought the only known copy of the long-lost gospel of Judas, written in the mid-second century.

When Nussberger-Tchacos was unable to sell the manuscript on her own, she joined forces with a Swiss attorney named Mario Roberty, who runs an organization called the Maecenas Foundation for Ancient Art in Basel. Nussberger-Tchacos and Roberty sold the translation rights for the manuscript to the National Geographic Society. That was the media event that occurred in 2006—the official release, in many different languages, of an authorized translation of the Coptic gospel of Judas. Unfortunately, due to the deterioration the manuscript suffered while it was hawked all around the world, by this time the gospel was in more than one thousand fragments.[3] Indeed, according to the first Coptic expert who examined it, the gospel of Judas originally consisted of thirty-one pages, but now only thirteen remain.[4]

JUDAS TELLS HIS VERSION

As presented by the National Geographic Society, the gospel of Judas reveals a very different version of what happened in Gethsemane than what is portrayed in the four canonical Gospels. According to this version, Jesus planned his own execution and elicited the assistance of his closest disciple, Judas Iscariot, to help him. Thus, in this account Judas was not a traitor, as the canonical Gospels affirm, but a hero. He alone of all the disciples truly understood who Jesus really was and what his authentic teaching was all about.

The gospel claims to be "the secret account of the revelation that Jesus spoke in conversation with Judas Iscariot during three days before he celebrated Passover."[5] It begins with a scene in which Jesus happens upon his disciples praying over bread, obviously a reference to the Christian rite of the Eucharist. Jesus laughs derisively at them because they falsely think that it is through such rites that "your god"[6] will be praised.

In the gospel of Judas, the disciples worship a lower god, the creator of the world, but Jesus knows the highest God who exists above and beyond the material universe. As Judas says in the gospel, Jesus comes from "the immortal realm of Barbelo."[7] Throughout the text, Jesus delivers bizarre, complicated soliloquies about cosmology that are the hallmarks of Gnosticism. He explains that the true God is a "great invisible spirit," a cloud of light.[8] "[Come], that I may teach you about the things . . . [that] no person will see," Jesus declares in the gospel of Judas. "For there is a great and infinite realm, whose dimensions no angelic generation could see, [in] which there is the great invisible [Spirit]."[9] And from this invisible spirit, this luminous cloud, emerge seventy-two "luminaries" or angels who themselves made 360 additional luminaries . . . and then there are twelve aeons and six heavens for each aeon, so there are seventy-two heavens . . . and for each five firmaments so that there are 360 firmaments, and so on.[10] The magazine and newspaper articles about the gospel of Judas usually exclude mention of this bizarre material. They concentrate, instead, on how the gospel of Judas reveals the "diversity" of Christian beliefs that existed in the early years of the church before the heavy hand of orthodoxy allegedly suppressed them.[11]

In the manuscript, Jesus eventually explains to Judas that his mission is to "sacrifice the man that clothes me."[12] For this, Judas will be "cursed" but in the end he will "come to rule over" the other disciples.[13]

The gospel of Judas then ends abruptly. It says only that the high priests "murmured" because Jesus went into a "guest room" for prayer. It adds that "some scholars" were there to watch closely so they could lay hold of Jesus as he was praying. These scholars were "afraid of the people" because Jesus was regarded by them all as a prophet.[14]

The scholars approach Judas and ask him what he's doing there since he is one of Jesus' followers.

Then the gospel ends. "He answered them in accordance with their wish," it concludes. "And Judas received some money and handed him over to them."[15] And that's it.

After the National Geographic Society's initial publicity campaign, some scholars began to ask questions. April D. DeConick, a professor of biblical studies at Rice University, even questioned the accuracy of the translation and the motives of the society itself for promoting it. In DeConick's retranslation, Judas is not a hero but a demon. The most egregious error DeConick found was the passage where the National Geographic translation said that Judas will "ascend to the holy generation." What the text actually says, according to DeConick, is that Judas "will *not* ascend to the holy generation."[16] The National Geographic translators left out the word *not*, an error they now acknowledge.[17]

"Admittedly, the society had a tough task: restoring an old gospel that was lying in a box of its own crumbs," DeConick wrote in an op-ed article in the *New York Times*. "It had been looted from an Egyptian tomb in the 1970s and languished on the underground antiquities market for decades, even spending time in someone's freezer. So it is truly incredible that the society could resurrect any part of it, let alone piece together about 85 percent of it."[18]

DeConick also attributes a certain amount of political correctness to the society's big push to rehabilitate Judas. Not only does it stick a thumb in the eye of orthodox Christianity by questioning the official version of the Bible, but it also implicitly makes amends for the way the Christian churches have allegedly used Judas as a stereotype.

"Judas is a frightening character," she writes. "For Christians, he is the one who had it all and yet betrayed God to his death for a few coins. For Jews, he is the man whose story was used by Christians to persecute them for centuries. Although we should continue to work toward a reconciliation of this ancient schism, manufacturing a hero Judas is not the answer."[19]

Indeed, for all the excitement about the discovery of an authentic lost gospel from the second century, and for all the hype about "alternative" Christianities suppressed by the Christian church, in fact there is much less here than meets the eye. Many New Testament scholars concede that there is virtually nothing in the gospel of Judas of historical value—although scholars of Gnosticism, such as Elaine Pagels, are quick to insist that isn't the point.[20]

Like other Gnostic texts, the gospel of Judas reveals the beliefs of religious sects in the second century, sects that used Jesus as the spokesman for their theosophical musings about the origins of the cosmos and humanity's place within it, Pagels explains. She says that these texts show that there was a diversity of "Christianities" in the early centuries of the first millennium—just as there was also a diversity of "Judaisms." "All these recently discovered texts show that the early history of Christianity is much more engaging and diverse than I'd ever imagined," Pagels told an interviewer. "They show that the teaching about Jesus dying for your sins—because God cannot forgive sins without sacrificing his only Son—is not the only way to be a Christian."[21]

Eventually, some or most of these alternative versions died out or were suppressed as the followers of Jesus came to recognize that the Jesus portrayed in the canonical Gospels, who fed the hungry and cured the blind, was the Jesus who spoke to their hearts. The Jesus who spoke of the "aeons" and laughed at his disciples for worshiping their Creator just didn't ring true.

THE PASSOVER PLOT

The notion that Jesus somehow instigated his own arrest and execution is not a new idea. There are even hints of it in the Gospels. In places, Jesus appears to be following a script given to him in advance. He tells his followers, much to their horror, that his destiny is to "go to Jerusalem and undergo great suffering at the hands of the elders and chief priests and scribes, and be killed" (Matt. 16:21 NRSV). Moreover, it appears that he was warned repeatedly about the plots against him—"Some Pharisees came and said to him, 'Get away from here, for Herod wants to kill you'" (Luke 13:31 NRSV)—and ignored them. Jesus had opportunities, up to the last moment, to escape. Yet he appeared to wait for those scheming against him to do what he knew they would do. According to the Synoptic Gospels, Jesus told his closest followers, "one of you will betray me" (Mark 14:18).

In 1965, an eccentric British writer, New Testament scholar, and "Hebrew Christian" named Hugh Schonfield wrote a bestselling book, *The Passover Plot*, which alleged that Jesus planned his own arrest. According to

Schonfield, Jesus planned to survive the crucifixion and thereby to escape from the hands of both the Romans and his enemies among the Jewish aristocracy. His intention was to be arrested on the morning before the Sabbath so that the Roman soldiers would, according to Jewish custom, be forced to take him down from the cross before sundown. According to Schonfield's hypothesis, the "drink of wine" that John's gospel records (19:29) being offered to Jesus was actually a potent narcotic designed to render Jesus unconscious and simulate death. The idea was that Jesus' friend and secret follower, Joseph of Arimathea, would take him down from the cross, pretend to bury him in the tomb, and then nurse him back to health. But the plan backfired. Quite unexpectedly, a Roman soldier thrust his spear through Jesus' side to make sure he was dead. In Schonfield's view, Jesus could well have survived the crucifixion itself but likely succumbed from the lance wound later. His followers had removed him from the original tomb, in an effort to revive him, but after he died they buried him reverently in a more permanent tomb at a different location.[22]

A slightly different version of this theory, known as the swoon hypothesis, is that Jesus planned his arrest and *successfully* faked his execution. This theory follows Schonfield's basic outline but claims that Jesus took the narcotic drug, which successfully simulated death, and was *not* killed by the thrust of the soldier's spear into his side. Rather, the thrust into his pericardial cavity, causing "blood and water" to flow, supposedly relieved pressure on his heart and may have helped save his life.[23] He was taken down from the cross, unconscious, bloody but still breathing, and secretly nursed back to health by Joseph and Nicodemus, a trained physician. In the coolness of Joseph of Arimathea's tomb, Jesus was revived. When the women visited the tomb, they indeed found it empty—and the young man or young men who greeted them, who worked for Joseph of Arimathea, were telling the simple truth when they announced that Jesus is alive! [24]

There have been many variations on this idea over the centuries. The Lutheran rationalist theologian Heinrich Paulus proposed one version as early as 1828 in his book, *The Life of Jesus*. The theory was revived by Michael Baigent, Richard Leigh, and Henry Lincoln in their 1982 bestseller, *Holy Blood, Holy Grail*,[25] which some writers see as the inspiration for Dan Brown's bestselling 2003 novel, *The Da Vinci Code*. Supporters of the swoon theory claim that six hours is not normally enough time for someone to die by crucifixion, which often took days, and point out that in the gospel accounts even Pilate expresses surprise when told that Jesus had already died.[26] On the other hand, many commentators, including some debunkers of Christianity, doubt that a barely breathing crucifixion survivor would inspire faith in anyone as a "resurrected son of God."

DID JESUS PLAN OR FORESEE HIS OWN DEATH?

Beyond these wild and wooly speculations, which few mainstream historians take seriously, there lies an even bigger question. If Jesus did not plot to *survive* the crucifixion but, as the Gospels say, anticipated it—even if he begged God to spare him from it—what did he think would be accomplished by it? What purpose did he believe his death on the cross would serve?

In the past few years, a number of secular New Testament scholars have focused an enormous amount of attention on the subject of Jesus' mission and intention. What was Jesus trying to achieve in going up to Jerusalem? Was he surprised when he was arrested? Or did he deliberately goad the authorities in an effort to have himself arrested, even executed, in fulfillment of messianic prophecies? Scholars are all over the ballpark on this topic. Those who believe Jesus was an apocalyptic prophet who expected God to intervene and kill all the Romans, such as Bart Ehrman, do think that Jesus was surprised—that he died on the cross not only a failure but also in despair, having been literally abandoned by God.

The handful of writers who believe Jesus was a revolutionary Zealot do not think he intended to die—at least not voluntarily. They think Jesus intended to kill, not be killed![27] In contrast, the wisdom-sage scholars, such as John Dominic Crossan and the Jesus Seminar, see Jesus as a nonviolent martyr who stood up to the most powerful empire in history—and knew it would likely cost him his life.[28] Those who believe Jesus was an advocate for radical social change hold the same view. The scholars who do believe Jesus *intended* to die, including Anglican bishop N. T. Wright, are those who also believe that Jesus saw himself as Israel's suffering messiah. Those who claim Jesus was a charismatic holy man, such as Geza Vermes, face the problem that nothing they say Jesus advocated would make anyone upset, let alone want to execute him. Vermes believes that Jesus was the victim of a tragic misunderstanding, that he was not really challenging authority in any real way but the religious leaders in Jerusalem mistook his purely religious actions as politically motivated. Thus, Jesus was killed due to a mistake. "He died on the cross for having done the wrong thing (caused a commotion) in the wrong place (the Temple) at the wrong time (just before Passover)," Vermes concludes.[29]

SO WHY DID JESUS DIE?

Beginning with the apostle Paul, Jesus' followers asked why Jesus, the messiah sent from God, was killed. Why did he die? What was the purpose of his death? Why did God permit it? In Mark's gospel, Jesus himself says that he came to give his life "as a ransom" (10:45), so the question quickly became, *Well, a ransom to whom?*

As we saw in chapter 2, in the early years of the Christian community, some theologians, including Augustine, answered that the ransom was paid to Satan, that Jesus' death freed mankind from the bondage of sin. Others said that the ransom was paid to God. Eventually, the Protestant Reformers taught the notion of penal substitution; the idea was that humanity's disobedience to God's law demanded nothing less than the death penalty—and Jesus voluntarily agreed to sacrifice himself and accept the punishment in humanity's place. Jesus bore the full weight of divine wrath over human sin and, although innocent, sacrificed himself as a substitute. God poured forth his righteous anger for the sins of the human race on his Son, Jesus, who died in our place. One contemporary writer goes so far as to say that God *hated, cursed, and damned* Jesus, who became a "concentrated monumental condensation of evil" in God's sight because of all the sins of the elect that he took upon himself.[30]

The problem for many secular and some Christian New Testament scholars is that none of this vengeful-God theory can be found in the Gospels or in any of the teachings of Jesus. As we saw in chapter 2, the nucleus of the idea for penal substitution exists in the writings of Paul[31] and in the New Testament book of Hebrews, but not in the sayings attributed to Jesus himself.

"In the judgment of the majority of mainline scholars, atonement theology does not go back to Jesus himself," claims historical Jesus expert Marcus Borg. "We do not think that Jesus thought that the purpose of his life, his vocation, was his death. His purpose was what he was doing as a healer, wisdom teacher, social prophet, and movement initiator. His death was the consequence of what he was doing, but not his purpose. To use recent analogies, the deaths of Mahatma Gandhi and Martin Luther King Jr. were the consequences of what they were doing, but not their purpose. And like them, Jesus courageously kept doing what he was doing even though he knew it could have fatal consequences."[32]

So what do secular New Testament scholars propose as an explanation for Jesus' apparent acceptance of his own death?

ANOTHER VISION OF HOW JESUS SACRIFICED HIMSELF

What the Gospels do say is that Jesus plainly foresaw his own death and believed he was obeying God's will by carrying forth his mission even though it would almost certainly result in his execution. The Gospels insist that Jesus knew that going up to Jerusalem, entering the city on a foal to fulfill the messianic symbolism in Zechariah, and having a final symbolic confrontation with the temple authorities would likely result in his being tortured and killed. Plus, he knew firsthand what that meant. As had most Jews in Palestine under Roman rule, Jesus had almost certainly seen men crucified in his lifetime, perhaps even some claiming to be a messiah, such as Judas the Galilean. If he had chosen to, Jesus could have avoided stirring up trouble. He could have likely slipped away at night from the Garden of Gethsemane. Certainly, in that sense, scholars such as Borg say Jesus did sacrifice himself, allowing himself to be killed. He sacrificed his own life in fulfillment of his mission.

Imagine hiking on a mountain trail, and, in defiance of all the posted warnings, climbing up a dangerous rock cliff exceeding your abilities. You have been warned repeatedly not to do this, but you do it anyway. You end up trapped on a narrow ledge, your life in mortal danger. There is no way you can get down—no way you can save yourself. Eventually, a search-and-rescue team comes out looking for you, and a young ranger, an expert climber, scrambles up the sheer rock cliff to save you, even though it is extremely dangerous. He ties a rope around your waist and lowers you down the cliff. He saves you!

But while he is doing so, some loose rocks fall, striking him in the head and killing him instantly. In a very real sense, this young ranger sacrificed his own life to save yours. In a very real sense, he died in order to save you from your own stupidity and arrogance. But was it his *death* itself that saved you . . . or was his death simply *the price he was willing to pay* to climb the rock face to save you? In his letter to the Corinthians, Paul uses a similar metaphor. "You are not your own," he tells the Corinthians. "You were *bought at a price*" (1 Cor. 6:19–20 NIV, emphasis added).

This is how some secular scholars today believe that the early Christian church began to speak of Jesus as the "lamb of God" who sacrificed himself on humanity's behalf. For scholars such as Borg, this doesn't mean that the basic insight underlying the notion of atonement—that in a very real sense Jesus died for mankind's sins—isn't true. It just means that after reflecting on the meaning of Jesus' life and death following the resurrection, his followers came to see Jesus' actions as the ultimate sacrifice. Like the squad of soldiers in the film *Saving Private Ryan* who risk their lives at Normandy in an effort to save Matt Damon and bring him home alive, so, too, the Gospels portray Jesus as being on a similar "suicide mission" to somehow rescue the entire human race. The post-resurrection symbol of Jesus as the Passover Lamb—whose blood signaled the angel of death to "pass over" the homes of the Israelites in Egypt—was never meant to imply that God demanded *a human sacrifice* to appease his righteous anger against the human race. But this kind of misinterpretation happens, some secular and Christian scholars say, when a metaphor is absolutized into a doctrine.[33]

Scholars such as Borg seek to reconcile the penal substitution theory of atonement with what Jesus himself taught about the infinite mercy of God and the good news of his kingdom. According to Borg, the notion that "Jesus died for our sins" was originally a "subversive metaphor," what he calls a "proclamation of radical grace."[34] The problem for him, and some other contemporary New Testament scholars, is when this subversive metaphor distorts our understanding of who God is and what God wants for us. In the past, some Christian thinkers have interpreted the idea of atonement to mean that God desires to *damn* humanity rather than, as the New

Testament claims, for "everyone to be saved and to come to knowledge of the truth" (1 Timothy 2:4). In the telling image of the early American preacher Jonathan Edwards (1703–1758), we are all like spiders hanging over a raging fire . . . "sinners in the hands of an angry God."[35] But Jesus employed a different metaphor for what God is all about and what his kingdom means.

THE WOMAN AT BETHANY

The story of Jesus being anointed by oil in Bethany is told in all four Gospels. In Mark 14, it occurs right before the preparations for the Last Supper and Judas's betrayal of Jesus, during dinner in the house of Simon the leper. Luke 7:37 adds that the person with whom Jesus dined was a Pharisee, and John—who says this incident occurred six days before the Passover—implies that it happened at the home of Lazarus, whom Jesus had raised from the dead. John adds that the person who anointed Jesus' feet was Mary, sister of Martha and Lazarus (12:1–11).

When I was in college, I had a professor who wrote a book just on this one scene in the Gospels because it contains one of Jesus' most radical teachings—so radical, in fact, that my professor said that even Luke didn't quite get the point of the story. As the Synoptics tell it, Jesus was eating dinner when "a woman" approached him with an alabaster flask of ointment, pure "nard" (Mark 14:3). She broke open the flask and poured the contents over Jesus' head. Nard, also known as spikenard, is a thick, aromatic essential oil, the color of amber, widely used in the ancient Near East and still used today in Indian Ayurvedic medicine. Known in Hebrew as *shebolet nerd*, it was used as incense on the altar of incense in the temple in Jerusalem. As the Gospels make clear, nard was also extremely expensive. Mark and Matthew report that some of Jesus' disciples grumbled to themselves about the expense, with Mark adding that one of them claimed such a luxury could have been sold for more than "three hundred denarii" and the money given to the poor (14:5). A denarius was a common Roman silver coin that was widely considered worth about one day's work for a common laborer or solider. That means that the flask was roughly worth a year's wages. John adds that the name of the money-conscious grumbler was none other than

Judas Iscariot—and that Judas complained, not because he cared for the poor, but because he was a thief and wanted the money (12:4–6).

At this point Luke diverges from the other gospel writers with a slightly different emphasis. In Luke's version, the woman doing the anointing was "a sinner," and she anointed not Jesus' head but his feet. She was sobbing; she knelt at Jesus' feet, wet them with her tears, and dried them with her hair. When the owner of the house, a Pharisee in Luke's version, noticed what the woman was doing, he announced that if Jesus really were a prophet he would have known "who and what sort of woman" it was who was touching him (Luke 7:39).

And then Jesus spoke up and delivered one of the most radical teachings of the New Testament—one that many Christians, still today, refuse to accept.

Jesus answered him, "Simon, I have something to tell you."

"Tell me, teacher," he said.

"Two people owed money to a certain moneylender. One owed him five hundred denarii, and the other fifty. Neither of them had the money to pay him back, so he forgave the debts of both. Now which of them will love him more?"

Simon replied, "I suppose the one who had the bigger debt forgiven."

"You have judged correctly," Jesus said.

Then he turned toward the woman and said to Simon, "Do you see this woman? I came into your house. You did not give me any water for my feet, but she wet my feet with her tears and wiped them with her hair. You did not give me a kiss, but this woman, from the time I entered, has not stopped kissing my feet. You did not put oil on my head, but she has poured perfume on my feet. (Luke 7:40–46 NIV)

And at this point, there is some ambiguity in the Greek text of Luke. Some experts say that Luke himself missed the point of the story, and that the Greek favors a translation that says, "He who loves little is forgiven little."[36] But that contradicts what the story conveys. Therefore, other translations, such as the Revised Standard Version, translate the sentence, "He who is forgiven little, loves little" (7:47): "Therefore I tell you," Jesus continued, "her sins, which are many, are forgiven, for she loved much; but he who is forgiven little, loves little."

Then Jesus turned to the woman and said, "Your sins are forgiven . . . Your faith has saved you; go in peace". (Luke 7:48, 50 RSV). The people at the table were shocked because, presumably, only God could forgive violations of his commandments.

Jesus' teaching of radical forgiveness has scandalized the pious for two thousand years and still does to this day. The entire point of Jesus' mission was to proclaim the dawn of a new era in history, when God's life-changing forgiveness would be poured out across the entire world—first to the "lost sheep of the house of Israel" (Matt. 10:6), then to the lepers (Matt. 10:8) and prostitutes (Matt. 21:31), Samaritans (John 4:39–41) and people of the land (Matt. 11:5)—and eventually reaching every nation on earth (Matt. 28:19). As "historical Jesus" scholars such as Borg and E. P. Sanders note, that energizing acceptance, which Christian theology calls grace, was announced and practiced by Jesus *before* he was arrested and executed. "Your sins are forgiven," Jesus told the woman in Bethany. "Your faith has saved you."

As a result, in recent years many secular and Christian New Testament scholars have concluded that,[37] in the Gospels at least, it is not Jesus' *death* that brings God's forgiveness. After all, God did not ask for or need a human sacrifice. In the Gospels, Jesus insists that God offers his forgiveness freely to all who ask for it ("Repentance and forgiveness of sins is to be proclaimed in his name to all nations, beginning from Jerusalem," Luke 24:47 NRSV).

In a sense, therefore, it was the mission to proclaim God's forgiveness that indirectly got Jesus killed. Jesus announced a new age, a messianic era, in which people would no longer worship God in the temple, with its onerous taxes and fees, but in spirit and in truth. That message made a lot of wealthy aristocrats very upset; their vast incomes depended upon the tithes and sacrifices poor people paid. Jesus was willing to proclaim his dangerous, subversive message about God's forgiveness in the very heart of his society, the temple itself. That was why, as the Gospels report, the authorities began to plot his death.[38] Thus, in this view, Jesus died because he believed his mission was to proclaim the truth of who God is and what he really wants from human beings, even at the cost of his life. "What if forgiveness, rather than being a pansy way of saying it's OK, is actually a way of wielding bolt cutters and snapping the chain that links us?" asks the evangelical rabble-rouser Nadia Bolz-Weber. "In all fairness, I should remind you that this is just the kind of thing that got Jesus killed. He was going around telling people they were forgiven. He went about freeing people, cutting them loose. And that kind of freedom is always threatening, and yet it's what we all want for ourselves."[39]

FOR FURTHER STUDY

Borg, Marcus. *The Heart of Christianity: Rediscovering a Life of Faith.* New York: HarperOne, 2004.

Crossan, John Dominic. *Who Killed Jesus?* New York: HarperCollins, 1996.

Krosney, Herbert. *The Lost Gospel: The Quest for the Gospel of Judas Iscariot.* Washington, DC: National Geographic, 2006.

Meyer, Margin. *Judas: The Definitive Collection of Gospels and Legends About the Infamous Apostle of Jesus.* New York: HarperCollins, 2007.

DO WE HAVE PROOF FOR THE RESURRECTION?

Discovery of First-Century Jerusalem Tombs Reignites Debate

When they saw him, they worshiped
him; but some doubted.

—MATTHEW 28:17 NRSV

The Church of the Holy Sepulchre, located in Jerusalem's Old City, is perhaps the ugliest church in Christendom. It is a musty wreck of a building, a two-story limestone structure ravaged by earthquakes, fires, crusades, decay, and seventeen centuries of internecine squabbling among its various ecclesiastical caretakers. The current church building is maintained by six apostolic churches with ancient roots in the Holy Land: the Roman Catholics, Greek Orthodox, Armenian Orthodox, Syrian Orthodox, Copts, and Ethiopians. The original, far larger church, known as the Martyrion, was dedicated on September 17, 335, inside the Roman city of Aelia Capitolina, built on the ashes of vanquished Jerusalem.[1] Following the final, catastrophic Jewish war against the Romans, led by the messianic leader Simon bar Kokhba in AD 132–135, the entire area was demolished and paved over with stones, and an elaborate temple of Aphrodite was constructed on the site, a deliberate affront to Christian sensibilities. Two hundred years later, newly Christianized Romans, led by a Bishop Makarios, excavated the area to build a church over the site of Jesus' crucifixion. After pulling away tons of debris, they found a rocky hill that, according to the fourth-century historian Eusebius (ca. 263–339), they believed was Golgotha, where Jesus of Nazareth was hung on a short wooden stake to die.[2] The rocky hill is still there, immediately to the right as you enter the church, although it is now covered by a steep set of steps and, on top, an altar.

The Crusader façade of the Church of the Holy Sepulchre in Jerusalem. The original church was dedicated in AD 335, destroyed by Persians in 614, and then rebuilt in the Middle Ages. Many archaeologists believe it could well stand over the original site of Jesus' crucifixion on a rocky hill known as Golgotha, located just outside Jerusalem's first-century walls.

According to Eusebius, the Roman builders also discovered a site they believed was the tomb where Jesus' body was laid after he died. This site is now covered by an ornate marble shrine about twenty feet square, known as the Aedicule and maintained by the Greek Orthodox church. Near the Aedicule there are underground chambers in which are found rectangular niches, called *kokhim,* dating back to the first century and on which were laid human bodies after death. Incredibly, given the state of the church and its odd history, many (but not all) archaeologists believe that this location is very likely the spot where Jesus was executed.[3] That's because until the year AD 41, this area was likely located just *outside* of Jerusalem's city walls. (The Gospels imply that Jesus was executed "outside" the city.) In that year, or about a decade after the crucifixion, a new wall was built farther out to the west to incorporate into Jerusalem developed areas just outside the existing walls. The area where the Church of the Holy Sepulchre now stands was outside the original wall but inside the area enclosed by the newer wall. The alternative tomb site on Nablus Road to the north, known as the Garden Tomb and popular with some evangelical pilgrims, originally dates from the late Iron Age, and was not a "new tomb" as both the gospel of Matthew (27:60) and John (19:41) say Jesus' tomb was. Therefore it is deemed by many experts to be an unlikely candidate for the tomb of Jesus.[4]

Every year at Easter, the resurrection of Jesus is commemorated by the ritual of the Holy Fire, dating back to the time of the Martyrion, the original church built by Constantine. On the night before Orthodox Easter, the Church of the Holy Sepulchre is pitch black with barely a sound. Around midnight, however, a mysterious blue fire is said to miraculously ignite inside the Aedicule, above the marble slab on which Jesus' body was laid. This light, symbolizing the light of Christ, is then carried to every nation in which Orthodox churches exist. Specially chartered and outfitted aircraft stand by in Ben Gurion Airport in Tel Aviv to fly the Holy Fire to various Orthodox nations. This ritual is so old that Egeria, a Christian pilgrim from Spain, mentions it in her diary written in 385. It's so old that a medieval pope, Pope Gregory IX, in 1236 banned the Franciscans living in the Holy Land from participating in the ritual, which he considered fraudulent.

Every year on Holy Saturday night, the ceremony of the Holy Fire is repeated as it has been since the Church of the Holy Sepulchre was first built in Jerusalem in AD 331, over the site of what was believed to be the rock of Golgotha.

THE FOUNDATION OF CHRISTIANITY

For two thousand years, the belief that Jesus of Nazareth was raised from the dead and appeared alive to his friends and disciples after his execution on a Roman cross has been the foundation of Christianity. The resurrection was the ultimate proof that Jesus was, in fact, who his followers had claimed he was—the messiah long predicted in the Hebrew Bible, a world savior who came to rescue humanity from itself. "Whatever they may think of the historical resurrection, even the most skeptical scholars admit that at least the belief that Jesus rose from the dead lay at the very heart of the earliest Christian faith," the Christian philosopher William Lane Craig notes. "In fact, the earliest believers pinned nearly everything on it."[5] But for just about the same amount of time, many people have thought the very idea absurd. If there is one thing life teaches human beings, it's that there is nothing more final than death. Once people die, they stay dead, never to be heard from again. Within twenty years of Jesus' crucifixion, in fact, Greek converts to the Jesus movement were openly denying the reality of the resurrection. We know this because the apostle Paul writes to the follow-ers of Jesus living in the cosmopolitan city of Corinth to explain that, no, they were not mistaken, what he and the other apostles were proclaiming is that "Christ has indeed been raised from the dead, the firstfruits of those who have fallen asleep" (1 Cor. 15:20 NIV). Without the resurrection, Paul tells them, their newfound faith is meaningless. "If the dead are not raised, then Christ has not been raised either," Paul continues. "And if Christ has not been raised, your faith is futile . . . If only for this life we have hope in Christ, we are of all people most to be pitied" (15:16–17, 19 NIV).

This widespread and ancient disbelief in the reality of the resurrection has endured throughout history. For the past two to three hundred years, New Testament scholars have struggled to explain what the resurrection could have been. Was it a deliberate hoax? A crazy rumor that spread when Jesus' tomb really was found empty? Could it have been a mass halluci-nation? A private vision that was shared as if fact? Or perhaps just a story fabricated by the evangelists or the apostle Paul? Yet if the resurrection did *not* occur more or less the way it is described in the New Testament, then how can the rapid rise of the Jesus movement be explained? What caused the followers of Jesus to adopt their new, bold, and courageous faith if Jesus died like every other man—and stayed dead? Did the disciples gather together in an upper room at Pentecost and simply decide to go out and *pretend* Jesus had risen? *How likely is that?*

One thing is clear: over the past twenty years, many New Testament scholars, archaeologists, and researchers have not been content with the rationalistic proposals made by theologians in the nineteenth and twenti-eth centuries to explain away the resurrection. Many top New Testament researchers—some Christians, others agnostic—have tackled the ques-tion of the resurrection with new enthusiasm. Surprising new theories are being proposed—some more credible than others. In 2007, for example, a mathematical physicist named Frank Tipler proposed, in a book called *The Physics of Christianity*, that Jesus' resurrection could be explained using physical principles derived from quantum mechanics.[6] As we'll see in this chapter, new research is being done on such subjects as Roman crucifix-ion practices in Palestine, attitudes toward life after death in Jewish and pagan communities, burial practices in Jerusalem in the first century, and the precise location of Jerusalem's outer walls in the AD 30s (to better determine the location of Golgotha and Jesus' tomb). Once again, new discoveries and approaches are contradicting some of the assumptions common in twentieth-century New Testament scholarship—and convincing some secular researchers that something shocking and unusual happened when Jesus died, something that transformed a handful of terrified and demoralized Jewish villagers into energized and courageous evangelists for a new global movement.

A SHOCKING DISCOVERY IN SOUTH JERUSALEM

In 2007, a Canadian filmmaker named Simcha Jacobovici and James Cameron, the Hollywood director who created such blockbusters as *Avatar* and *Titanic,* released a documentary film that made an astonishing claim:

James Tabor

The cemented-over opening to a first-century tomb next to apartment houses in the Talpiot suburb area of southern Jerusalem. Filmmakers James Cameron and Simcha Jacobovici and New Testament scholar James Tabor (shown) claim that this site is the actual location of the family tomb of Jesus of Nazareth—a claim dismissed by one of the Israeli archaeologists who discovered it in 1980.

archaeologists had discovered the lost tomb of Jesus of Nazareth and his entire family beneath an apartment building in East Talpiot, a southern suburb of Jerusalem. What the two filmmakers were referring to is a pair of intact first-century tombs that were first uncovered in 1980 and 1981 by Israeli archaeologists—tombs that contained numerous ossuaries, or Jewish "bone boxes," some of which contained human remains. For roughly the entire first century, more affluent Jews in Palestine practiced a two-stage burial. In the first stage, the deceased person was typically placed on a slab or shelf in a rock-hewn tomb, the entrance sealed with a stone slab, and the body left to decay in the dry heat of Palestine for one year. At the end of that time, the family would return, open the tomb, and then place the remains in a small limestone chest, or ossuary, for more permanent burial. This was done mostly to save space and because tombs were expensive. The limestone ossuaries typically were as long as the longest bone in the body, the femur, or thigh bone, or about twenty inches; and perhaps twelve inches high. Stone ossuaries were only used in Israel between 20 BC and AD 70, and more than two thousand limestone ossuaries have been discovered to date. Of these, slightly more than a quarter, about 650, have inscriptions on them.[7] Many are on display on the grounds of Dominus Flevit, the church complex on the Mount of Olives and above the Garden of Gethsemane where tradition says Jesus wept for Jerusalem (*Dominus Flevit* means "the Lord wept" in Latin). According to archaeologist and biblical scholar James Tabor, forty of the ossuaries at Dominus Flevit have inscriptions with names such as Lazarus, John, Joseph, Martha, Miriam, Matthew, Salome, Yeshua, and even Simon bar Jonah, "the precise Aramaic name of Jesus' disciple Peter."[8]

EXPERTS DISAGREE ON WHETHER OSSUARIES ARE AUTHENTIC

In 1990, archaeologists even discovered the ossuary of Joseph Caiaphas, the high priest mentioned in the Gospels. The ossuary is widely believed to be authentic and is now on display in the Israel Museum in Jerusalem.[9] Another ossuary, with the inscription, "James, Son of Joseph, the Brother of Jesus,"[10] is considered authentic by some archaeologists and a well-crafted forgery by others. Some archaeologists believe that the ossuary and the words "James, Son of Joseph" inscribed on it are authentic, dating back to the first century, but that the words "brother of Jesus" were added later by a master forger. Still others argue that the ossuary itself dates from the first century but that both inscriptions are forgeries. (That was the conclusion reached in 2003 by the Israeli Antiquities Authority based on its analysis of the patina of the inscription and other factors.[11]) Other experts, including Hershel Shanks[12] of the *Biblical Archaeology Review* and the evangelical New Testament scholar Ben Witherington III,[13] believe that the ossuary and its inscriptions are likely genuine.

In the first of the Talpiot tombs, found in 1980 beneath an apartment building in south Jerusalem, other ossuaries were discovered inscribed in

Hebrew with names that Christians would readily recognize—including Yeshua bar Yehosef (Jesus, son of Joseph); Maria (the Latin form of the Hebrew name Miriam); Yosa (perhaps Jose, the name of one of Jesus' relatives); Yehuda bar Yeshua (Judah, son of Jesus); and Mariamene Mara (supposedly Mary Magdalene). The filmmakers and some of the experts featured in their documentary, *The Lost Tomb of Jesus,*[14] concluded that Jesus of Nazareth was buried in this tomb along with members of his family, including possibly his mother, Mary; his brothers; and Mary Magdalene. Their theory is that Jesus was initially buried in a new tomb owned by the wealthy Joseph of Arimathea, just as the gospels recount—and that women disciples of Jesus did come to that tomb and discovered that the body of Jesus was missing. But later, according to Jacobovici, Jesus' body was removed from its temporary burial spot and moved to a permanent location in a quiet area south of Jerusalem (ostensibly the tomb found in 1980 beneath the apartment building).[15]

Israel Museum

Inside a first-century tomb in Talpiot, a suburb of Jerusalem, archaeologists discovered in 1980 ten ossuaries, or burial boxes. One has scratched on its surface, near the top, the inscription in Aramaic, Yeshu'a bar Yehosef, Jesus son of Joseph.

WHAT HAPPENED TO THE REMAINS?

As if this theory weren't shocking enough, in 2012 Jacobovici teamed up with New Testament scholar James Tabor of the University of North Carolina and released another controversial documentary and companion book, *The Jesus Discovery*, that made an even more astonishing claim. Tabor and Jacobovici claimed that the ossuary with the words "Yeshua bar Yehosef," now on display in the Israel Museum in Jerusalem, almost certainly held the bones of Jesus of Nazareth. Further, Tabor claims that the belief of the original followers of Jesus was that Jesus was raised in a "spiritual body" after his death, not a physical body, and that therefore this alleged discovery does not contradict traditional Christian faith.[16] Because the Jewish religious authorities in Israel are very protective of human remains found in the Holy Land, all the bones found in the ossuaries were removed under mysterious circumstances sometime in the 1980s or 1990s and presumably buried.[17] No one appears to know what happened to the bones found in these ossuaries. Yet Tabor and Jacobovici were able to order DNA tests on bone chips they found still left in the Yeshua and Mariamene ossuaries and obtained what they claim were "readable DNA results for both samples."[18] These tests allowed them to reach the astonishing conclusion that they had possibly identified DNA samples from Mary Magdalene, whom they identified as the wife or concubine of Jesus, and the mother of "their son," Judah, the name on one of the ossuaries.[19]

Tabor and Jacobovici also found, they said, the first physical evidence of belief in the resurrection. On one of the ossuaries in the Patio Tomb, known by archaeologists as Talpiot B, there was a crude drawing of a fish with scales and what looks like the stick figure of a man in his mouth. Tabor and Jacobovici believe this is the "Sign of Jonah," the early Christian metaphor for Jesus' death, burial, and resurrection. They also found an inscription, written in Greek, with what appears to be, they claim, a reference to resurrection beliefs. The authors propose as a translation of the inscription, "Divine or Wondrous Jehovah Lift Up."[20]

What have other experts made of these extraordinary claims? Alas for Tabor, Jacobovici, and debunkers of traditional Christianity everywhere, not too much. In 2013, one of the Israeli archaeologists who discovered the two first-century tombs in East Talpiot, Professor Amos Kloner of Bar-Ilan University, publicly dismissed the claims and theories of Jacobovici and Tabor as "sensationalistic" and "lacking any factual or scientific foundation." "Their movie is not serious," Kloner told *National Geographic News.* "They [say they] are 'discovering' things. But they haven't discovered anything. They haven't found anything. Everything had already been published. And there is no basis on which to make a story out of this or to identify this as the family of Jesus."[21]

Earlier, Israeli experts at the Israel Antiquities Authority had challenged assertions that the first tomb was, as Jacobovici and James Cameron asserted, the "Jesus family tomb." The names inscribed on the ossuaries were extremely common in the first century, the experts asserted,[22] roughly the equivalent of John and Joe in English—although Tabor vigorously disputes this with statistical evidence.[23] The East Talpiot tombs are merely two out of thousands of tombs that existed in Palestine in that era, the IAA experts added, and there is no evidence whatsoever that the tombs can be linked to Jesus of Nazareth or to his "family." As for evidence of the "resurrection faith" found in the other tomb, the Sign of Jonah ossuary and inscription, Kloner believes that the "fish" is really a Greek amphora and that the inscription was merely a warning to trespassers not to disturb the bones in the ossuary.

ARCHAEOLOGISTS DISPUTE CLAIMS OVER TALPIOT TOMBS

Nor was Kloner alone in his criticisms. One of Tabor's colleagues at the University of North Carolina, Professor Jodi Magness of the department of religious studies at Chapel Hill, also denounced the filmmakers and Tabor for their alleged discoveries, on the website of the American Schools of Oriental Research (ASOR). "As usual, the arrival of the Easter season this year is heralded by a sensational archaeological claim relating to Jesus," Magness wrote. "In March 2007, we learned from a TV documentary and accompanying book that the tomb of Jesus and his family had been discovered in Jerusalem's Talpiyot [sic] neighborhood. The producer was undeterred by the fact that not a single archaeologist—including the tomb's excavator—supported this claim. . . . Now the same producer has identified remains of early Christian followers of Jesus in a tomb nearby. What is the basis for this new claim? Photos taken by a robotic arm that was inserted into the tomb supposedly show a graffito depicting a whale incised on an ossuary, and an inscription containing the Tetragrammaton [the name of God in Hebrew] and the word 'arise' or 'resurrection.'"[24]

Magness has long been critical of Tabor and Jacobovici's claims for the Talpiot tombs. In a book published in 2011, *Stone and Dung, Oil and Spit: Jewish Daily Life in the Time of Jesus,* she argues that such rock-cut tombs were used only by the upper classes in Jerusalem and so the humble family of Jesus, assuming they relocated to Jerusalem after his crucifixion, could not have afforded this type of tomb. Moreover, if a rich patron had bought a tomb for Jesus' family—for his mother, Mary; James the Just; or other relatives—then surely the location of that tomb would have been revered over the centuries in the same way that the site of Golgotha, now the Church of the Holy Sepulchre, has been revered consistently since the fourth century at least.[25]

Still, not everyone dismisses the possibility that the Talpiot tombs are in some way related to Jesus. In 2008, the eminent New Testament scholar James Charlesworth, editor of the Hebrew Bible pseudepigrapha and an expert on the Dead Sea Scrolls, organized a conference at Princeton University to debate the Talpiot tombs controversy. According to *Time* magazine, opinions at the conference among experts "ranged from 'no way' to 'very possible.'" Charlesworth himself told the magazine that, while he had reservations, he couldn't "dismiss the possibility that this tomb was related to the Jesus clan."[26] However, after the conference, a group of seventeen archaeologists and Near Eastern Studies experts wrote a statement in which they declared "that the majority of scholars in attendance—including all of the archaeologists and epigraphers who presented papers relating to the tomb—either reject the identification of the Talpiot tomb as belonging to Jesus' family or find this claim highly speculative."[27]

To anyone following this story closely, it is a strange tale of intrigue, competing egos, and big money. Critics assert that the entire controversy demonstrates more than anything else how biblical archaeology has been corrupted by Hollywood. Because cash-strapped archaeologists now depend upon funding from such groups as the National Geographic Society and the Discovery Channel, they are under increasing pressure to announce ever-more-sensational "discoveries" to justify their big budgets. Indeed, the claims and counterclaims made by the archaeologists and filmmakers are more of a story than the discoveries themselves. In 2013, Jacobovici filed a $1 million libel lawsuit against an American-Israeli museum curator named Joe Zias, originally from Michigan but who spent twenty-five years working at the Israel Antiquities Authority (IAA), for critical comments Zias allegedly had made about Jacobovici's most recent films.[28] Criticizing movies for being sensationalistic is not normally considered actionable, but Jacobovici claimed that Zias crossed the line into actual libel by publicly accusing him of falsifying evidence.

THE CONTROVERSY OVER THE CRUCIFIXION

Another front in the ongoing debate over the resurrection concerns Jesus' crucifixion and whether or not his body would have been taken down from the cross and buried in a tomb, as the Gospels claim, or would have been allowed to decay on the cross for days and then thrown into a shallow, anonymous grave. For many years, some scholars, most famously John Dominic Crossan of the Jesus Seminar, have claimed that the gospel stories about the empty tomb are complete fabrications, invented by the early church. In his 1991 book, *The Historical Jesus,* Crossan argues that Jesus was likely removed from the cross by his executioners and his body tossed unceremoniously into a shallow grave reserved for criminals. He notoriously proclaimed that Jesus' body was likely eaten by wild dogs. Crossan points out that the Romans ran an execution factory, having crucified two thousand Jews during the uprising of 4 BC and, during the siege of Jerusalem, up to five hundred a day, according to Josephus. Yet of all those untold tens of thousands of crucified prisoners, he says, we have physical remains of only one—Yehohanan son of Hagakol, whose anklebone embedded with a nail was found in an ossuary in 1968.[29] This proves to Crossan that crucified bodies in Jesus' time were disposed of by the state and not buried by family members. In fact, Crossan claims that the family and disciples of Jesus faced the horror of not knowing what happened to his body. "If, as I maintain, Jesus' followers had fled upon his arrest and knew nothing whatsoever about his fate beyond the fact of crucifixion itself, the horror was not only that he had been executed but that he might not even have been decently buried," he writes.[30]

Balage Belogh

Many archaeologists believe that Golgotha was likely a rocky hill just outside of Jerusalem's western wall in the time of Jesus, as shown in this reconstruction. In the late 30s or early 40s, a new western wall was built to incorporate newly developed areas into the city, which would have put this location inside of Jerusalem's walls.

Other scholars doubt that Jesus was taken down from the cross at all. The Romans did not permit the burial of crucified criminals accused of crimes against the state, they say. The whole point of crucifixion was to function as a deterrent against future offenders. The visible presence of decaying corpses left hanging on crosses for days and even weeks very effectively struck terror in the hearts of would-be Jewish rebels. Recently, Bart Ehrman took up this argument in his 2014 book, *How Jesus Became God: The Exaltation of a Jewish Preacher from Galilee.* "For years I had thought that whatever else we might think about the stories of Jesus' resurrection, we could be relatively certain that immediately after his death he was given a decent burial by Joseph of Arimathea and that on the third day some of his female followers found his tomb empty," Ehrman writes. "I no longer think that these are relatively certain historical data." Instead, Ehrman now follows Crossan in arguing that "we do not know, and cannot know, what actually happened to Jesus' body."[31] Ehrman points to evidence from Roman authors about how crucified criminals were allowed to hang on a cross for days. "[A]s far as we can tell from the surviving evidence, what *normally* happened to a criminal's body is that it was left to decompose and serve as food for scavenging animals," he says.[32] Ehrman dismisses claims by Christian scholars that the Jews were granted an exception to this general Roman custom by countering that, from what we know about Pilate from the writings of Josephus, he was not the sort of Roman to grant exceptions—*ever.*[33]

WHY EXPERTS SAY JESUS WAS GIVEN A PROPER BURIAL

On the other hand, many scholars, and not merely Christian ones, insist that Jesus' body was almost certainly taken down from the cross and buried, in deference to the Jewish holiday of Passover. For one thing, we know from the first-century Jewish historian Josephus and other writers that the Jews had a particular abhorrence of leaving dead bodies exposed because of ritual impurity. "The Jews are so careful about funeral rites that even those who are crucified because they were found guilty are taken down and buried before sunset," Josephus wrote.[34] (Rapid burial, in fact, remains the Jewish practice to this day.) Josephus recalls seeing three of his friends crucified during the siege of Jerusalem and how he begged the Roman general Titus for permission to take them down from the cross, and it was granted. Such permission was apparently common, even routine. In fact, as Christian author Timothy Paul Jones points out, it was the law.[35] According to a summary of the Roman legal code called the *Pandectae,* "The bodies of those who are condemned to death should not be refused their relatives . . . At present, the bodies of those who have been punished are only buried when this has been requested and permission granted; and sometimes it is not permitted, especially where persons have been convicted of high treason. . . . The bodies of persons who have been punished should be given to whoever requests them for the purpose of burial."[36]

New Testament scholars who support the gospel versions of Jesus' burial, such as Craig Evans, Daniel Wallace, and N. T. Wright, say that writers such as Crossan and Ehrman err when they extrapolate from what the Romans did during the siege of Jerusalem in AD 68–70—during a bitter and brutal war to the death against the Jews—and project that behavior backward forty years earlier to the time of Jesus. Moreover, it makes sense that the pragmatic Romans would have generally honored Jewish burial customs, especially during a solemn festival such as Passover when at least 250,000 Jewish pilgrims crowded into Jerusalem's narrow streets and the Romans had probably fewer than 1,500 troops available to maintain order. Roman officials did not want to trigger a riot needlessly—and Josephus relates how Pilate, despite his disdain for the Jews, *did* back down and honor Jewish religious sensibilities by removing Roman standards from the city when he met determined resistance from the Jews.[37]

Jewish law expressly forbade that the bodies of executed criminals be allowed to go unburied overnight. "When someone is convicted of a crime punishable by death and is executed, and you hang him on a tree, his corpse must not remain all night upon the tree; you shall bury him that same day, for anyone hung on a tree is under God's curse" (Deut. 21:22–23 NRSV). That's why, as the Gospels relate, the Romans regularly broke the legs of their victims, to hasten death by suffocation so that the bodies could be buried before nightfall. What's more, the only archaeological evidence we have of any crucified man in Palestine, that of Yehohanan son of Hagakol, was found precisely because he *was* taken down from the cross and given a proper burial, with his remains placed in a rock-cut tomb. For these and other reasons, many scholars reject Crossan and Ehrman's claim that Jesus was likely never given a proper burial. Instead, contemporary historians and archaeologists—such as Shimon Gibson,[38] Jodi Magness,[39] James Dunn,[40] N. T. Wright,[41] Raymond Brown,[42] E. P. Sanders,[43] James Tabor,[44] Michael Grant,[45] and Craig Evans[46]—believe that Jesus was indeed given a proper burial. The evidence "strongly encourages us to think that in all probability Jesus was indeed buried and that his corpse and those of the two men crucified with him would not have been left hanging overnight and perhaps indefinitely, or at most cast into a ditch or shallow grave, exposed to animals," New Testament scholar Craig Evans argues. "Quite apart from any concerns with the deceased men and their families, the major concern would have to do with the defilement of the land and the holy city."[47] Evans adds that assuming some members of the ruling Jewish establishment did have a hand in Jesus' execution, as both the Gospels[48] and Josephus[49] seem to relate, they would not have wanted to seem indifferent to Jewish prohibitions against defilement during the Passover. "That Jesus was buried is historically certain," concludes the renowned Catholic New Testament scholar Raymond Brown, in his authoritative two-volume work, *The Death of the Messiah.* "That Jewish sensitivity would have wanted this done before the oncoming Sabbath (which may also have been a feast day) is also certain, and our records give us no reason to think that this sensitivity was not honored."[50]

The archaeologist Jodi Magness, who teaches at the University of North Carolina, agrees. She believes the Romans likely did permit burial of crucifixion victims in deference to Jewish law, particularly before large pilgrim feasts such as the Passover; and she rejects Crossan and Ehrman's assumption that if burial had been allowed for crucifixion victims then we should have far more archaeological evidence of crucifixion. Rather, she argues that most burial sites in Jerusalem have been disturbed and, moreover, we only know about Yehohanan son of Hagakol because of a fluke: the piece of wood that remained affixed to his ankle bone. As a result, Magness concludes that "the Gospel accounts of Jesus' burial are largely consistent with the archaeological evidence" and with what we know of Jewish law in this period.[51] The Israeli archaeologist Shimon Gibson also concurs. "The idea that an executed Jew would have been chucked into a common burial pit after being removed from the cross is unlikely," Gibson says. "It may have been the normal practice for criminals of the lower classes and for slaves elsewhere in the Roman Empire, but it is unlikely to have been practiced in Jerusalem because of Jewish religious sensibilities. The truth is the Roman authorities would have wanted to keep the Sanhedrin and locals agreeable."[52]

THE FOUR PROVEN OR MINIMAL FACTS ARGUMENT

This debate, while ongoing, does illustrate both the strengths and weaknesses of the "four proven facts" argument for the resurrection of Jesus, which was recently proposed by Christian scholars such as William Lane Craig, Gary Habermas, and Michael Licona. The philosopher William Lane Craig regularly employs the "four proven facts" argument in his debates with various debunkers of Christianity, including Bart Ehrman. Habermas and Licona present one version of it in their 2004 book, *The Case for the Resurrection of Jesus.* In a different way, Anglican bishop and historian N. T. Wright goes into great detail about each of the facts in his magisterial, 738-page investigation, *The Resurrection of the Son of God*, although he carefully distances himself from the "four facts" approach and has his own complex series of arguments. In essence, all these authors argue that certain facts about Jesus' final days can be established historically and that, when a reasonable person contemplates these facts without biases, the most plausible conclusion is that Jesus of Nazareth really did rise from the grave. This is what Craig and others mean when they say they have strong historical evidence for the resurrection of Jesus. As presented by Craig during his debate with Bart Ehrman on the resurrection, the four facts are as follows.[53]

Fact 1: After his crucifixion, Jesus was buried by Joseph of Arimathea in a tomb.

Craig points to the fact that the burial of Jesus is attested to in all four Gospels and in the writings of Paul, and that scholars believe the sources for these reports are extremely early—dating from only five to seven years after the crucifixion. He also adds that it is unlikely that the benevolence of the Jewish aristocrat Joseph of Arimathea was merely a Christian invention since the early Christian community carried hostility toward Jewish leaders who, they thought, had engineered a judicial murder of Jesus. They would not have credited a member of the Sanhedrin with Jesus' burial without good reason. That is why even critical scholars such as John A. T. Robinson of Cambridge University assert that the burial of Jesus in the tomb is "one of the earliest and best-attested facts about Jesus."[54]

Fact 2: On the Sunday after the crucifixion, Jesus' tomb was found empty by a group of his women followers.

Craig argues that the empty tomb also is attested to by multiple independent sources. He adds that if the church had made up the story of the empty tomb, the followers of Jesus would not have presented women as the first people to have discovered it. That's because, according to Craig, women in New Testament times were considered to be unreliable witnesses and could not even testify in Jewish law courts. The evangelical scholar Ben Witherington III points to additional embarrassing details included in the initial reports about the empty tomb stories that point to them being authentic eyewitness accounts—for example, Mary Magdalene's questionable past

(Luke 8:2) and her suggestion, in John's gospel, that Jesus' body may have been stolen from the tomb (20:2). Thus, the empty tomb should be deemed authentic under the criterion of embarrassment (that the Christian community would not make up details that could actually undermine their case).

Fact 3: On separate occasions and under diverse circumstances, different individuals and groups of people experienced appearances of Jesus alive from the dead.

Craig argues that the appearance narratives in the Gospels provide multiple, independent attestations. He points to the famously skeptical German New Testament critic Gerd Lüdemann who concludes that "[i]t may be taken as historically certain that Peter and the disciples had experiences after Jesus' death in which Jesus appeared to them as the risen Christ."[55]

Fact 4: The original disciples suddenly and sincerely came to believe that Jesus was risen from the dead despite their having every predisposition to the contrary.

Craig claims that the Jews in Jesus' time expected the messiah to be a conquering hero who would redeem Israel. What's more, while some Jews in this period did believe in a general resurrection of the dead at the end of the world, they had no concept of anyone rising from the dead to glory and immortality before the final judgment. Thus, the disciples of Jesus must have sincerely believed Jesus had risen from the dead, Craig argues, or they would not have been willing to die for the truth of that belief. He quotes the Catholic New Testament scholar Luke Timothy Johnson that "some sort of powerful, transformative experience is required to generate the sort of movement earliest Christianity was."[56]

Therefore, Craig argues—along with Habermas, Licona,[57] and Wright[58]—that the best explanation is that Jesus of Nazareth actually rose from the dead just as the New Testament claims.

There are many attractive features to the "four proven facts" argument in supporting the traditional understanding of the resurrection—but also some weaknesses. It does help explain the rise of the Jesus movement in the wake of Jesus' shameful and degrading execution. Craig is no doubt correct that the naturalistic explanations for the resurrection of Jesus proposed by twentieth-century academics—from the swoon theory of *The Da Vinci Code* to the mass hallucination theory—now seem implausible and have less support among academic historians and scholars. However, the weakness of the four-facts argument is that many historians simply do not accept all the facts as facts. Some scholars, such as John Dominic Crossan, do not believe that Jesus was buried in a rock-cut tomb, as the Gospels relate, nor do they accept the reality of a tomb being discovered empty. Some scholars still claim that these are stories invented by the early Christian community, legends added to the gospel accounts decades after the crucifixion.

An even more contentious question for scholars, however, is, what exactly do we *mean* when we say Jesus "rose" from the dead?

DID THE STORY GROW IN THE TELLING?

One claim by New Testament scholar James Tabor, which he makes independent of his archaeological research, is that Christianity has misinterpreted what the early followers of Jesus believed about the resurrection of Jesus. Tabor claims that the early disciples of Jesus did not believe in a bodily resurrection, as has long been thought, but in a spiritual one. Tabor believes that the early followers of Jesus could well have known where Jesus' bones lay buried and, at the same time, strongly affirmed their belief that Jesus "was raised." That's because "being raised" and physical burial were not, according to Tabor, mutually exclusive or contradictory for them. "Discovering the remains of the body of Jesus is no threat to the original resurrection faith of Jesus' followers; it is actually an affirmation of that faith," Tabor asserts in *The Jesus Discovery*.[59] "Jesus' first followers believed that Jesus had been 'raised from the dead,' but as we see in the Greek inscription in the Patio tomb, they believed in his exaltation in heaven." Tabor adds: "Affirming the resurrection of the dead, before the theologians elaborated the notion, meant that one affirmed that Jesus was 'raised up' or 'lifted up' into the holy realms. It was an affirmation of triumph and glory, not a statement about the revival of a physical corpse."[60]

This is an old argument that has some support from critical scholarship of the New Testament texts but also some strong, surprising resistance.

Many interested students, when they research the resurrection, simply gather together all the passages in the New Testament in which the resurrection is mentioned and then try to harmonize the various accounts. New Testament scholars such as Bart Ehrman will point out that the Gospels do not agree on all the details—for example, were the women at the empty tomb greeted by one man sitting inside the tomb as in Mark, one angel sitting on the tomb entrance stone as in Matthew, two men as in Luke, or two angels as in John? But a more sophisticated objection is found when you look at the resurrection accounts *chronologically,* in the order in which they were written. When you do that, you see that the first descriptions of what happened were extremely vague, with the resurrection presented as an accomplished fact but with no detail. However, the later accounts of the resurrection, found in the gospels of Luke and John, had much more detail and an emphasis on the physical body.

EARLIEST ACCOUNTS HAVE VERY FEW DETAILS

Scholars disagree about which books of the New Testament are the earliest. Some claim that Paul's letter to the Galatians might have been written first, perhaps as early as the late AD 40s. Others insist that this honor goes to his letter to the Thessalonians, more reliably dated to around AD 50. Still others propose that the letter of James was written first. But regardless of which book is the earliest, what is striking is that the greatest purported miracle in history—the resurrection of Jesus from the dead—is *barely mentioned at all* in these texts and, when it is mentioned, it is only in passing as a simple fact. Writing to the Thessalonians, Paul gives thanks for their faith and says that all the believers in Greece report how the Thessalonians "turned to God from idols to serve the living and true God, and to wait for his Son from heaven, whom he raised from the dead" (1 Thess. 1:9–10 NIV). In his long, detailed letter to the Galatians that is full of theological complexities, Paul mentions the resurrection specifically only twice. The first time is in the beginning, when he says that he was made an apostle not through human beings but "through Jesus Christ and God the Father who raised Him from the dead" (Gal. 1:1). The second is when he describes his past as a persecutor of the Jesus movement, which ended when God "was pleased to reveal his Son to me" (Gal. 1:15–16). That's it. It's not until the first letter to the Corinthians that we get our earliest reports about what the resurrection actually entailed. Probably composed around AD 55 from the Greek city of Ephesus (in other words, about twenty-five years after Jesus' crucifixion), the letter refers to reports that Paul received two or three years after the events:

> What I received I passed on to you as of first importance: that Christ died for our sins according to the Scriptures, that he was buried, that he was raised on the third day according to the Scriptures, and that he appeared to Cephas, and then to the Twelve. After that, he appeared to more than five hundred of the brothers and sisters at the same time, most of whom are still living, though some have fallen asleep. Then he appeared to James, then to all the apostles, and last of all he appeared to me also, as to one abnormally born. (1 Cor. 15:3–8 NIV)

Critical scholars point out how vague even this detailed enumeration of "appearances" is. What does Paul mean when he says that Christ "appeared" to Cephas and the others? In what way did he appear? Physically? In a vision? Paul doesn't say. However, later in his letter Paul insists to the Corinthians that whatever the resurrection is, it's real and a basic component of the apostolic teaching. Apparently, even at this early date, some followers of Jesus were denying the reality of any resurrection. As a result, Paul discusses what the resurrection is in more detail—but again, mostly in an abstract, theological way. He doesn't discuss the resurrection of Jesus in particular but rather resurrection in general.

> But someone will ask, "How are the dead raised? With what kind of body will they come?" How foolish! What you sow does not come to life unless it dies. When you sow, you do not plant the body that will be, but just a seed, perhaps of wheat or of something else . . . So will it be with the resurrection of the dead. The body that is sown is perishable, it is raised imperishable; it is sown in dishonor, it is raised in glory; it is sown in weakness, it is raised in power; it is sown a natural body, it is raised a spiritual body. (1 Cor. 15:35–38, 42–44 NIV)

But what is this "spiritual body"—and is it the same as, part of, or a transfigured version of the physical body? Or does it replace the physical body? This same pattern is followed through the rest of the non-Gospel books of the New Testament. The resurrection of Jesus is assumed as a fact, its implications are discussed, but there is *almost no specific detail about what actually happened.* For example, the author of 1 Peter says that God "[i]n his great mercy he has given us new birth into a living hope through the resurrection of Jesus Christ from the dead" (1:3 NIV), but it doesn't mention what that resurrection was. The letter of James doesn't mention the resurrection at all. Paul famously writes to the Romans that belief in the resurrection of Jesus will save them: "If you declare with your mouth, 'Jesus is Lord,' and believe in your heart that God raised him from the dead, you will be saved" (10:9 NIV). But he doesn't tell them what the resurrection was or how they can know that it actually occurred.

DID MARK END HIS GOSPEL WITH JUST THE EMPTY TOMB?

That leaves the Gospels and Acts. As we've discussed, many scholars believe that Mark was the first gospel to be written, probably sometime in the AD 60s but perhaps much earlier, and that it served as the rough "template" for Matthew, Luke, and perhaps, to a lesser extent, John. And as is well known, Mark originally ends not with a resurrection appearance of Jesus but with the discovery of an empty tomb and the appearance of a "young man" dressed in a white robe. As Mark tells it, on the day that Jesus was crucified, a member of "the council," Joseph of Arimathea, courageously went to Pontius Pilate and asked for the body of Jesus (Mark 15:43). According to Mark, Pilate was surprised that Jesus had already died; but upon verifying that he was dead, Pilate agreed to release the body to Joseph. The text says simply that Mary Magdalene and "Mary the mother of Joses" watched where Jesus was laid (15:47 ESV).

The final chapter of Mark, chapter 16, relates what happened when three women arrived at the tomb with spices to anoint the body of Jesus. They came early "when the sun had risen," on the first day of the week (v. 2 ESV). They were saying to one another, "Who will roll away the stone for us from the entrance of the tomb?" (v. 3 ESV). But when they looked up, they

Shutterstock

Some Christian apologists claim that certain facts about Jesus' death can be proven historically, and one of the most important is that the disciples discovered an empty tomb on Easter morning. This tomb in Israel is a reconstruction of what a first-century tomb in Palestine looked like.

saw that the large stone was already rolled back from the tomb entrance. Upon going inside, they saw a young man sitting on the right side, dressed in a white robe. They were astonished. The young man said, "Do not be alarmed. You seek Jesus of Nazareth, who was crucified. He has risen; he is not here. See the place where they laid him" (v. 6 ESV). Then the young man instructed the women to go tell the disciples. "He is going before you to Galilee. There you will see him, just as he told you." The passage ends with the words: "And they went out and fled from the tomb, for trembling and astonishment had seized them, and they said nothing to anyone, for they were afraid" (vv. 7–8 ESV).

Many scholars believe that this is where the gospel originally ended, on this somewhat jarring note. However, another ending to the gospel, dating from at least the early second century, was soon appended to the text and includes additional details and three appearances of Jesus—one to Mary Magdalene, one to two unnamed disciples "walking along on their way to the country," and one to the eleven remaining apostles while they were at table. But these appearances seem like an afterthought and are only afforded a sentence or two each at the end of Mark. For the appearance to Mary Magdalene, the text says only that Jesus "appeared" to Mary, that she went and told his companions that "he was alive and had been seen by her," and that they "would not believe it" (Mark 16:11 ESV). The appearance to the two disciples in the country is also described with just two sentences. Jesus "appeared in a different form" to the two disciples, and they then returned and told the others, "but they did not believe them either" (vv. 12–13 NIV). Finally, Jesus appeared to the apostles while they were "at table," and told them to "go into the whole world and proclaim the gospel to every creature." And then, after he spoke to them, the text says that he "was taken up into heaven and took his seat at the right hand of God" (vv. 14–19). There is no mention of the Ascension on the Mount of Olives recounted in Luke.

All in all, Mark's gospel is a pretty spare account of the greatest miracle in history. Even if Mark did not end his gospel at 16:8, with the women running terrified from the empty tomb, the description of the resurrection appearances is very short, just 161 words in Greek. The text simply says Jesus "appeared" to Mary, the two disciples on the road and to the eleven, and doesn't mention of what those appearances consisted (vv. 9, 12, 14).

MATTHEW, LUKE, AND JOHN ADD DETAILS

It's not surprising, then, that the evangelists Luke and John (much less Matthew) fill in some details, presumably from their own sources and other traditions. Most of what we know about the resurrection appearances comes from Luke and John, both probably writing in the AD 80s and 90s—or at least a full fifty years after Jesus' crucifixion. Luke and Matthew track Mark's account fairly closely, adding some details and changing others. John includes a story about Peter running to see the empty tomb for himself (20:3–4). John also includes an appearance of Jesus to "Mary of Magdala," and says that Jesus was apparently so ordinary looking that Mary *mistook him for a gardener* (v. 15). Luke alone includes the story of Jesus' appearance to the men in Emmaus (unless these were the same two men mentioned in Mark); and Luke alone tells the story of Jesus appearing to the disciples, showing them his hands and feet, and, strangely, asking for something to eat (24:36–43). John alone has the story of doubting Thomas, in which Jesus admonished Thomas to put his fingers in the marks of the nails, and his hand in his side (20:24–29). In Luke and John's gospels, Jesus appeared to the disciples in Galilee, on the shore of the lake, and tells them where to catch fish—and John even relates the exact number of fish the disciples caught, 153 (21:11). Only Luke includes the scene of the Ascension of Jesus into heaven (24:50–53), while John has a final declaration that what he is describing comes from an eyewitness, the "disciple whom Jesus loved" (21:20).

All these later anecdotes appear designed to stress the *bodily* nature of the resurrection, which tends to undermine Tabor's claim that the "earliest followers of Jesus" believed in a purely spiritual, not physical resurrection.[61] If that were true, then why did the evangelists feel the need to buttress descriptions of the resurrection as a physical event, involving Jesus' physical body? They may have felt that the vague spiritual descriptions in Mark and Paul—of Jesus being "raised"—had perhaps given the wrong impression. What's more, Christian scholars point out that a late dating of Luke and John does not mean, in and of itself, that they cannot contain reliable eyewitness reports— just as World War II veterans in the 2000s could recall battles sixty years earlier as though they were yesterday. On the other hand, even in these later accounts of the resurrection, there are details that undermine a purely physical understanding. In Matthew 28:17, for example, at the so-called Great Commission, the text says that the eleven apostles went to the mountain to which Jesus had instructed them. "When they saw him, they worshiped him; but some doubted" (NRSV). They "saw" the risen Jesus, but they doubted.

Another example: the appearance of Jesus to the disciples on the Sea of Galilee in John's gospel is not straightforward. According to tradition, it occurred at Tabgha, a beautiful natural cove on the Sea of Galilee where the Church of the Primacy of Saint Peter now stands. John 21 recounts how Jesus "revealed" or "manifested" (*ephanerosen*) himself to the disciples Peter, Thomas called the Twin, Nathaniel from Cana, the sons of Zebedee, and two unnamed others. Peter announced that he was going fishing. They went out all night but caught nothing. Finally, near dawn, Jesus stood on the shore but "the disciples did not know that it was Jesus" (John 21:4 NRSV). John relates that the man on the shore asked the disciples if they had caught any fish and they replied that they had not. "Cast the net to the right side of the boat, and you will find some," the man told them (v. 6 NRSV). The disciples did this and they caught so many fish that they couldn't pull the net back into the boat. That's when "the disciple whom Jesus loved" announced to the group, "It is the Lord!" Peter jumped into the water and swam ashore, but the other disciples stayed in the boat. When they reached the shore, the man had a charcoal fire burning, cooking fish and bread. He told them, "Come, have breakfast." And then the text says: "None of the disciples dared to ask him, 'Who are you?' because they knew it was the Lord" (v. 7–12 NRSV). And then John adds, "This was now the third time that Jesus appeared to the disciples after he was raised from the dead" (v. 14 NRSV).

You can just hear hard-nosed historians analyzing this passage: *So, at first they don't even recognize this man as Jesus. The man never says he's Jesus. The disciples don't dare ask him if he's Jesus. But they're sure it's Jesus anyway!*

Robert Hutchinson

Tabgha, a natural cove on the Sea of Galilee near Capernaum, is the traditional site where Jesus appeared to his disciples after his resurrection and cooked them some fish (John 21:1–24). The appearances in John and Luke emphasize the bodily character of the resurrection.

THE VISIONS OF PAUL, ANANIAS, STEPHEN, AND PETER

Finally, there are Jesus' appearances to Paul, Ananias, Stephen, and Peter described in Acts. They are all clearly described as visions, not the sight of a physical body. In Acts 7, right before he is stoned to death, Stephen has a vision of Jesus. The text says he "gazed into heaven and saw the glory of God, and Jesus standing at the right hand of God" (7:55 ESV). Acts 9 describes how someone named Saul, breathing "murderous threats" against the disciples, went to the high priest and asked for letters authorizing him to arrest any followers of "the Way" in Damascus and bring them back to Jerusalem in chains (vv. 1–2). But as he was nearing Damascus, a "light from heaven" flashed around him, and Saul heard "a voice" that said to him, "Saul, Saul, why do you persecute me?" Saul asked who it was, and the voice said, "I am Jesus, whom you are persecuting. But get up and enter the city, and you will be told what you are to do" (vv. 3–6 NRSV). The text adds that the men accompanying Saul at the time were speechless because, although they, too, had heard the voice, they saw no one (v. 7). Later, in Damascus, a disciple named Ananias also received a message from Jesus. Some of the earliest and best manuscripts of the Greek text just say "the Lord said to him," but later manuscripts add the words "in a vision" (*en oramati*), which is what is implied. "Get up and go to the street called Straight and ask at the house of Judas for a man from Tarsus named Saul," Jesus told Ananias. "He is there praying, and in a vision he has seen a man named Ananias come in and lay hands on him, that he may regain his sight" (Acts 9:10–11). Finally, in Acts 11, Peter, "while in an ecstasy (*ekstasis*)," had a vision of a great sheet, filled with all sorts of animals, being lowered from heaven. He heard a voice, presumably Jesus, which said, "'Rise, Peter; kill and eat" (vv. 5–7 ESV).

Again, there is no mention whatsoever, in any of these texts, of Jesus appearing in his physical body. Stephen saw Jesus "in heaven." Paul and his companions only heard a voice, and the text says that Jesus "said" to Ananias that he should go to the street called Straight. Peter only heard a voice. All these passages lend weight to the argument of James Tabor and others that the early descriptions of the resurrection of Jesus in the New Testament are of some kind of "spiritual" appearance, not an encounter with his once-dead physical body. In those instances in which the texts do describe a normal-looking human being, such as the passage in John 21 or the appearance on the road to Emmaus in Luke 24, at first the disciples did not recognize Jesus. Instead, they spoke to him as though he were someone else. But then the "Jesus in disguise" did something, such as breaking the bread in the story of Emmaus, and then "their eyes were opened and they recognized him" (Luke 24:31). In other passages, what is being described does not seem like the seeing of a physical body. In Acts 1:3, Luke says that Jesus "presented himself alive to them by many proofs." Presented himself alive by many proofs? What does that mean?

SO WHAT REALLY HAPPENED?

For skeptics today, Christian and non-Christian, untangling all this is difficult. Much writing on the resurrection is ambiguous, seemingly designed to sound orthodox without being too credulous. Christian writers especially don't want to go too far out on a limb when discussing the resurrection, and, with a humility that comes from long experience, want to "think with the mind of the church." On the other hand, the cocksure rationalism of those who deny the resurrection flat-out seems too confident by half, asserting as fact what can only be, by definition, a conjecture.

The honest truth is that *we really don't know what happened*. The Christian churches have historically understood the resurrection of Jesus to involve some form of bodily existence—even while conceding that it was not the "resuscitation of a corpse" but the exaltation of Jesus into some other realm of existence. Yet the Apostles' and Nicene Creeds are as vague as the New Testament's earliest texts—affirming only that Jesus "rose again," and not specifying what that actually *means*. Even the catechetical documents of many churches are surprisingly ambiguous, perhaps reflecting the ambiguity in the New Testament itself. The Catechism of the Catholic Church, for example, says that "Christ's Resurrection was not a return to earthly life . . . In his risen body he passed from the state of death to another life beyond time and space."[62] On the other hand, the Catechism does affirm that whatever the general resurrection is, it does involve our *physical* bodies. Quoting from the Council of Lyon II, the Catechism affirms that "we believe in the true resurrection of this flesh that we now possess."[63] The problem for modern skeptics, of course, is that we know of no other examples of anyone—outside of the accounts in the Bible[64]—returning to life after having been dead for days. (Recent and widespread reports of Near Death Experiences, or NDEs, are of course not real deaths, even when a heart temporarily stops beating for some minutes.) That is precisely why Jesus' resurrection is such a shocking and life-changing claim: it's a singularity.

DOUBTING THOMAS AND THE MYSTERY OF FAITH

Near the end of the gospel of John, there is a final appearance of Jesus to the disciples. In this incident, all the apostles saw Jesus except Thomas, who had been absent when Jesus appeared to the others. When Thomas returned, the disciples told him that they had seen Jesus alive, but he replied that "unless I see the mark of the nails in his hands and put my finger into the nailmarks and put my hand into his side, I will not believe" (John 20:25). A week later, the disciples are gathered again, but this time Thomas was with them. Although the doors were locked, Jesus entered somehow and stood in their midst. He said to Thomas, "Put your finger here and see my hands, and bring your hand and put it into my side, and do not be unbelieving, but believe." Thomas replied, "My Lord and my God" (20:27–28). Christians have traditionally interpreted this passage as proof that the resurrection of Jesus was physical, that Jesus was raised bodily from the grave. But what is interesting is what Jesus says next. "Have you come to believe because you have seen me?" he asks Thomas. "Blessed are those who have not seen and have believed" (John 20:29).

This, of course, includes everyone. Everyone is in the situation of "not seeing." John is asserting that Jesus is asking the world to believe in him, in his continuing life and presence in the world, even though the world does *not* see him. Is that a reasonable thing to do, today, in the twenty-first century? Many people doubt it, even many Christians. I doubt it. Jesus' earliest followers doubted it, some even after having seen him alive with their own eyes ("When they saw him, they worshiped him; but some doubted," [Matthew 28:17 NRSV]). In fact, the Gospels repeatedly state that Jesus' closest followers doubted the reality of the resurrection ("But when they heard that he was alive and had been seen by her, they would not believe it," [Mark 16:11 NRSV]). But that doesn't mean Christians should abandon hope in the resurrection. Doubt and hope are not mutually exclusive. In fact, they usually go together. If you have no doubts, then you probably don't need hope.

I have been pondering the issues surrounding the resurrection appearances of Jesus for more than thirty years, ever since I first read the Swiss theologian Hans Küng's classic, *On Being a Christian,* in college. Küng was the first writer I ever encountered who squarely faced the questions raised by the New Testament texts, and who didn't flinch from asking tougher and tougher questions. He was critical of both the pat answers of Christian orthodoxy *and* the equally pat answers of twentieth-century rationalists. When I learned Greek and studied the New Testament systematically in graduate school, I found that the issues Küng raised were only sharpened. I learned to see for myself just how vague the early descriptions of the resurrection actually are in the New Testament, and to see how, over time, there was an increased emphasis on the physical to supplement a previous emphasis on the spiritual. I even learned how to track this textually, to see how over the decades scribes inserted words and phrases in the different early manuscripts of the Greek text to emphasize the physical *even more.*

REAL ENCOUNTERS WITH THE RISEN JESUS ALIVE

Küng represents a middle ground between the assumptions of orthodox Christianity and the simplistic, dismissive rationalism of some contemporary New Testament scholars. For Küng, the notion that the followers of Jesus merely experienced a life-changing "insight" that they should champion Jesus' cause, even after his death, is an inadequate explanation for the rise of Christianity.[65] Küng holds out for something more like a mystical encounter with the risen Christ, some "proof" that Jesus did not die and "stay dead," but he admits that, from our vantage point two thousand years later and given the paucity of our evidence, we can never really know what that proof was. "The reality of the resurrection itself therefore is completely intangible and unimaginable," Küng writes. "Resurrection and raising are pictorialgraphic expressions; they are images, metaphors, symbols, which corresponded to the thought forms of that time and which could of course be augmented, for something which is itself intangible and unimaginable and of which—as of God himself—we have no sort of direct knowledge."[66]

In other words, Christians, at least, have to live with this ambiguity, this lack of certainty. That is why Christian faith is faith and not scientific knowledge. Despite the best efforts of Christian historians such as N. T. Wright, scientific proof for the reality of the resurrection remains elusive. As the author of the Johannine epistles told his community, what we are after death "has not yet been revealed" (1 John 3:2 NRSV). But Christians believe, as do many Jews, that part of whatever comes after death includes some sort of bodily existence similar to but also different from what we live on earth. "The resurrection faith is not an appendage to faith in God, but a radicalizing of faith in God," Küng concludes. "It is a faith in God which does not stop halfway, but follows the road consistently to the end. It is a faith in which man, without strictly rational proof but certainly with completely reasonable trust, relies on the fact that the God of the beginning is also the God of the end, that as he is the Creator of the world and man so too he is their Finisher."[67]

In the end, Christians possess this radical hope in the One God of Israel, proclaimed and revealed by Jesus of Nazareth, and they believe that the mysterious power who created the universe will somehow shepherd billions of human lives through death into a new, transformed existence. Christians believe, despite all evidence to the contrary, that death is not the end of life but the beginning—for Jesus of Nazareth but also for humanity as a whole. One major but not sole reason for that hope is what happened to and with Jesus of Nazareth. For Christians, what happened to Jesus was the "firstfruits" (1 Cor. 15:20) of the general resurrection at the end of days— and they have traditionally relied upon the reports of the appearances of Jesus "alive" after death as proof that it is real. If those reports are less convincing today for some people, or contain what some scholars believe are legendary embellishments, then we are merely in the same situation the vast majority of Jesus' earliest followers faced after Good Friday. A very limited number had profound, life-changing experiences that "Jesus lives"—Paul says about five hundred—but the majority of his followers did not. They relied solely on the testimony of others and whatever confirmation of that testimony they could see in their own lives and experiences.

Clearly, however, something extraordinary and transformative occurred in Jerusalem two thousand years ago—something that terrified and then inspired a group of ragtag disciples to risk everything in order to spread Jesus' message across the globe. And one of the differences between the historians and scholars of today and those of the late nineteenth and early twentieth centuries is that even many secular, agnostic, and atheist scholars now accept that something extraordinary happened to Jesus' earliest followers—something that led them to believe Jesus had come back to life after death. Some of the world's most skeptical New Testament scholars now affirm this, including agnostics such as Bart Ehrman,[68] Jesus Seminar skeptics such as Robert Funk,[69] and secular historians such as Marcus Borg[70] and E. P. Sanders.[71] "There can be no doubt, historically, that some of Jesus's followers came to believe he was raised from the dead—no doubt whatsoever," Bart Ehrman concludes. "Jesus's followers—or at least some of them—came to believe that God had done a great miracle and restored Jesus to life."[72]

As William Lane Craig has documented so thoroughly,[73] none of the alternative explanations for what happened with the resurrection adequately explain all the historical evidence—not even the theory of real but entirely spiritual visions of Jesus alive on the part of the disciples. James Tabor's new theory that reports of the empty tomb were based on real events—that Jesus' body was whisked away from temporary burial near the site of today's Church of the Holy Sepulchre to a permanent tomb in south Jerusalem—is entirely conjectural, with little support even among secular archaeologists. Even the analysis of how the accounts of the resurrection changed over time as the New Testament was written, as outlined above, does not really explain several key points. Why did the evangelists incorporate reports of physical manifestations of Jesus' body, as in the account of doubting Thomas, if those reports were not based on actual experiences? Would they have done this if Jesus' followers believed, as Tabor claims, in a merely "spiritual" resurrection? Is it historically credible that Jesus' followers would proclaim that Jesus is alive and risen after death—if the followers themselves and the people to whom they were announcing this shocking news all knew that Jesus' bones lay buried in a tomb in south Jerusalem?

As for the possibility of deliberate fraud, the secular historian E. P. Sanders has written that the evidence for such actions on the part of the evangelists or early disciples is less than convincing: "I do not regard deliberate fraud as a worthwhile explanation," Sanders writes. "Many of the [disciples] were to spend the rest of their lives proclaiming that they had seen the risen Lord, and several of them would die for their cause. Moreover, a calculated deception should have produced great unanimity."[74] As a result, Sanders believes it is a "fact" that the disciples did have genuine resurrection experiences, although he adds that "what the reality was that gave rise to the experiences I do not know."[75]

Finally, even if you concede that Paul's Damascus-road experience of Jesus alive was entirely visionary, that does not adequately explain the persistence of post-resurrection appearance reports among the other followers of Jesus in many different sources—in Mark, in both the Matthean and Lukan source material, and in John. For these and other reasons, some of the most hardheaded and skeptical of Christian thinkers today continue to affirm that the disciples of Jesus encountered him alive after death—and that this involved some kind of physical, bodily (albeit transformed) existence. Scholars and theologians continue to debate what the nature of these bodily appearances were—what Paul meant in 1 Corinthians 15 by a "spiritual body," for example[76]—but many affirm that these appearances provided the earliest witnesses with an overwhelming conviction that Jesus did not stay dead, but lives, now and forever. This conviction became the essential component of the early faith of the Jesus movement and the basis for Christian hope for the future. As Paul told the Thessalonians in what is probably the earliest written document we have of Christian belief, "For since we believe that Jesus died and rose again, even so, through Jesus, God will bring with him those who have died" (1 Thess. 4:14 NRSV).

FOR FURTHER STUDY

Craig, William Lane. *Reasonable Faith: Christian Truth and Apologetics* 3rd ed. Wheaton, IL: Crossway Books, 2008.

Johnson, Luke Timothy. *Living Jesus.* San Francisco: HarperSanFrancisco, 1999.

Küng, Hans. *On Being a Christian.* New York: Doubleday, 1976.

O'Collins, Gerald, S. J. *Jesus Risen.* New York: Paulist Press, 1987.

Spong, John Shelby. *Resurrection: Myth or Reality?* San Francisco: HarperSanFrancisco, 1994.

Tabor, James D. and Simcha Jacobovici. *The Jesus Discovery.* New York: Simon and Schuster, 2012.

Wright, N. T. *The Resurrection of the Son of God.* Minneapolis, MN: Fortress Press, 2003.

JESUS, GOD AND MAN

An Early Jewish—Not a Later Gentile—Belief

At the name of Jesus every knee should bow, in
heaven and on earth and under the earth.

—PHILIPPIANS 2:10 NIV

Until 2010, tourists couldn't visit the traditional site on the Jordan River where Jesus was said to have been baptized by John the Baptist. Known as Qasr el Yahud, or the "castle of the Jews" (due to the presence of a twelfth-century crusader church nearby), the area had been off limits since the 1967 Six-Day War. Back then, two rows of electrified barbed-wire fences, topped with concertina wire and still visible today, lined both sides of the river. Thousands of land mines were buried in the hot sand. Tourists and pilgrims who wanted to be baptized in the Jordan River were directed instead to Yardenit, an area just south of the Sea of Galilee. Yet today, the site on the Jordan River south of Jerusalem is now one of the most popular pilgrim destinations in Israel, after Nazareth and Bethlehem. Both Jordan and Israel have designed special areas for pilgrims that offer wooden platforms and steps down into the river where the faithful can be baptized—although guards on both sides of the river, usually just a brown muddy creek about thirty feet wide, keep a wary eye on visitors. The barbed-wire fences remain, and signs warn visitors not to wander off; there are still land mines.

Robert Hutchinson

Qasr el Yahud, the traditional site on the Jordan River, south of Jerusalem, where Jesus was baptized by John the Baptist. The site has been off-limits ever since the 1967 Six-Day War but, since 2010, is now open to the public and is the third most popular pilgrim destination in Israel.

All four Gospels report that Jesus of Nazareth was baptized by John in the Jordan River. What's more, all four report a strange supernatural occurrence associated with the baptism. According to Mark, likely the earliest account, when Jesus came up out of the water, "he saw the heavens being torn open and the Spirit descending on him like a dove," and then a voice came from heaven that said, "You are my beloved Son; with you I am well pleased" (1:10–11 ESV). Matthew tracks Mark almost exactly except he changes "you" to "this"—"this is my beloved Son"—in effect having the heavenly voice address the bystanders and not merely Jesus (3:17). Matthew

254

also includes a scene in which John tries to beg off from baptizing Jesus, saying that he, John, should be baptized by Jesus and not the other way around (3:14). Some scholars believe this scene in Matthew reflects later controversies in the early church between the followers of Jesus and a small group still loyal to John the Baptist, since Matthew emphasizes John's secondary role to that of Jesus.

James Dunn and other contemporary scholars point out that the notion that Jesus is in some unique way God's son permeates the entire synoptic tradition, and should not be seen as merely a post-resurrection development or invention. This idea may well go back to the traditions that arose when Jesus was still alive in Galilee. This can be seen, Dunn points out, even in the hypothetical sayings source scholars call *Q*, which likely contains some of the oldest and most reliably authentic of the sayings of Jesus in the Gospels.

In Matthew 11:27, which corresponds to Luke 10:22, Jesus proclaims, "All things have been handed over to me by my Father, and no one knows the Son except the Father, and no one knows the Father except the Son and anyone to whom the Son chooses to reveal him" (ESV). This *sounds* like the gospel of John, Dunn says, yet it comes from *the oldest stratum in the Gospels,* the hypothetical sayings source *Q.* It suggests that Jesus himself might have used language that implied he possessed a unique status before God—and a unique authority from and intimacy with God.[1]

THE OLD, OLD VIEW: IS BELIEF IN JESUS AS A GOD-MAN A PAGAN GREEK IDEA?

If New Testament scholars of the nineteenth and twentieth centuries knew anything, they knew this: the early, mostly Jewish followers of Jesus saw him as a powerful rabbi, perhaps a prophet, and maybe even as the long-awaited messiah.[2] The one thing the followers didn't see him as was God.

Over and over again, like a Buddhist mantra, the experts repeated this idea. If a scene in the Gospels or a saying of Jesus reflected a "low" Christology, in which Jesus was seen as an ordinary man, then the scholars said that it was obviously authentic and belonged to the earlier stage of the Jesus tradition. If, on the other hand, a deed or saying of Jesus implied a "high" Christology—that is, pointed to Jesus as some sort of divine being, "exalted at the right hand of God" (Acts 2:33)—then that was said to be obviously fabricated by the early Christian community, not authentic, and could be dated reliably to a time when the Christian community was made up mostly of pagan Gentiles, say around AD 100. The basic assumption underlying this scholarly bifurcation was, reasonably enough, that Jews were supposedly strict monotheists and pagans were polytheists. Jews would never have accepted the notion of Jesus as a quasi-divine being because they believed in only one God. On the other hand, the pagan Gentiles worshiped many gods, had traditions in which humans became gods and gods became humans, and therefore would more easily swallow a doctrine that claimed Jesus was divine or semidivine. Makes sense, right?

But during the last decades of the twentieth century, something remarkable and unexpected happened in New Testament studies. Scholars became more skilled at identifying the various "strata" of the New Testament—the chronological layers that made up the various books. They even began to think they could identify layers in *hypothetical* sources, such as the sayings source *Q*. They would speak confidently of Q^1, Q^2, and so on as they attempted to reconstruct how Jesus' sayings were passed on orally and then in writing. By studying the forms and sources of the various New Testament books, scholars thought they could detect traditions and sayings that went back to the very earliest stages of the Jesus movement—even to times before Jesus was crucified. But as they pored over these very early traditions, creeds, hymns, sayings, and stories, scholars made an astonishing, even unsettling discovery: it was the very *earliest* stages of the Jesus tradition, not the latest, that spoke of Jesus in grandiose terms as a kind of Jewish God-man. Contrary to everything they had been taught and believed, it looked as though it had been the *Jewish* followers of Jesus who proclaimed him "son of God" and "standing at the right hand of God," not the pagan Gentile followers who joined the movement in the final decades of the first century. As we will see in a moment, the *earliest* creedal statements of who Jesus was, almost certainly composed in Aramaic by Jesus' Jewish followers just a few years after his crucifixion, spoke of Jesus as the "son of God" before whom every knee must bend.

This revelation has caused a revolution in New Testament scholarship—one that is only now being fully absorbed and assimilated. Some scholars and college professors today still repeat the same old assumptions that they learned back in graduate school—that it was the pagan Greeks and Romans who created the "divine man myth," not the Jewish followers of Jesus from Galilee. As the New Testament scholar Larry Hurtado points out, even such famous scholars as Burton Mack of the Jesus Seminar continue to argue for a dichotomy between the "Christ cult" that arose in Greek-dominated Syria and the original Jewish followers of Jesus in Palestine, who purportedly viewed him only as a learned rabbi.[3] That view, however, has been almost entirely abandoned by leading experts in early Christian traditions. Even the skeptic Bart Ehrman, in his 2014 book, *How Jesus Became God,* was forced to concede, after examining the latest research, that belief in Jesus as a quasi-divine being arose *very early* in the Jesus movement, not later as previous generations of scholars asserted so confidently.[4] The reason for this, according to Ehrman, is that critical scholars have studied the "creeds" that are embedded in the New Testament texts—emblematic descriptions and affirmations about Jesus that date back to the very first years after Jesus' crucifixion. These creeds suggest quite clearly that Jesus' followers came to believe that Jesus was "appointed" Son of God at his resurrection. This isn't the same belief as expressed in the first verse of the gospel of John—that Jesus was *born* the incarnate Word—but it is a belief in Jesus' divine status that arose very, very early. As an example, Ehrman points to the creed found at the very beginning of Paul's letter to the Romans. Writing to the Roman Christians, Paul says he is a "slave" of Jesus Christ,

> *who . . . was declared to be Son of God with power*
> *according to the spirit of holiness*
> *by resurrection from the dead. (1:3–4 NRSV)*

According to Ehrman, the tradition embodied in this formalized affirmation "appears to be one of the oldest statements of faith that survives in our earliest Christian writings."[5] He points to the use of the phrase "spirit of holiness," likely an Aramaic expression, instead of the normal Greek wording, Holy Spirit. This suggests that this description of Jesus could well go back to the days of Jesus' original, Aramaic-speaking followers and not just to the urbane Greek-speaking believers who wrote the Gospels. "From this creed one can see that Jesus is not simply the human messiah, and he is not simply the Son of Almighty God," Ehrman concedes. "He is both things, in two phases; first he is the Davidic messiah predicted in scripture, and second he is the exalted divine Son."[6]

THE DEVELOPMENT OF JEWISH CHRISTOLOGY

As with so many areas of Jesus research, scholars are finally taking a long, hard look at what Jews in Jesus' time *actually* said and believed. They are no longer assuming that the ideas and beliefs expressed by Jewish rabbis in the Talmud, compiled five or six centuries later, accurately reflected what people believed when Pontius Pilate was governor of Judea. (Imagine trying to deduce the beliefs of, say, the American colonists in the early 1700s by only reading the Twitter feeds of early twenty-first-century New Yorkers, and you get some idea of the challenges facing past scholarship.) The scholars are now studying a far greater range of materials than in previous centuries—not merely the Dead Sea Scrolls, which were discovered in 1947 but only made widely available to scholars beginning in the 1990s—but also many other ancient sources. The Nag Hammadi library texts, found in 1945, have given scholars access to a wide range of Gnostic literature. Even more important, scholars now assiduously study dozens of texts known as the pseudepigrapha, which date back to the centuries immediately before and after Jesus (200 BC to AD 100). This has opened up new veins of research into the many diverse Jewish sects that walked the narrow streets of Jerusalem during Jesus' day. This research is revealing why it is actually possible that Jewish followers of Jesus viewed him as not merely a divine being, like an angel, but somehow part of God himself. Among the scholars who are pioneering this new research are Larry Hurtado, emeritus professor of New Testament language, literature, and theology at the University of Edinburgh; Richard Bauckham, formerly professor of New Testament studies at the University of Saint Andrews in Scotland; and James Dunn, professor of divinity at the University of Durham. Also contributing to this new research are two experts in Second Temple Judaism, Peter Schäfer of Princeton University and Daniel Boyarin of the University of California, Berkeley.

JEWISH VIEWS ON THE GODHEAD

Both Boyarin (an Orthodox Jew) and Schäfer (a secular scholar) argue that Jewish views of the nature of God in the Second Temple period could very well have accommodated views of Jesus as being either semidivine or even divine. Schäfer concentrates on the Jewish Talmud and so-called inter-testamental writings, such as the Ethiopic Book of Enoch, to show that ancient Judaism had strange traditions about heavenly beings—which we call angels but other societies might have called minor gods—and even had speculations about how human beings could become divinized. In his book *The Jewish Jesus,* Schäfer discusses at length the unusual traditions surrounding the biblical character of Enoch, who becomes the highest angel in heaven, known as Metatron. The Jewish Third Book of Enoch even refers to Metatron as "*YHWH ha-qatan,*" the smaller or lesser God.[7]

Boyarin, the Talmud scholar, on the other hand, focuses most of his attention on the figure of the Son of Man in the book of Daniel, an apocalyptic work in the Hebrew Bible written around 167–64 BC by an anonymous author.[8] Some writers suggest that the term "Son of Man," used in all four Gospels as well as in Paul's letter to the Romans, the book of Hebrews, and Revelation, is simply an expression that means "man." In modern Hebrew, for example, son of man, *ben-adam,* is simply another way of saying "a man" or a human being. *Kol ben-adam,* every son of Adam, is how you say "everybody" in Hebrew today. But Boyarin, along with many New Testament scholars, believes that the New Testament writers were referring to the book of Daniel and the way the author uses "son of man" in that text. At least 150 years before Jesus was born, the Jewish author of Daniel described a human figure in a way that seems incongruous with a strictly monotheistic rabbinic Judaism:

> In my vision at night I looked, and there before me was one like a son of man, coming with the clouds of heaven. He approached the Ancient of Days and was led into his presence. He was given authority, glory and sovereign power; all nations and peoples of every language worshiped him. His dominion is an everlasting dominion that will not pass away, and his kingdom is one that will never be destroyed. (Dan. 7:13–14 NIV)

Boyarin notes that a plain reading of this text shows that the Son of Man figure is in some sense divine yet in human form, will be "worshiped," will be given power and dominion over all the kingdoms of the earth, and could even be seen as a younger-appearing divinity than the Ancient of Days (the term for God in the text). Clearly, what this passage in Daniel reveals is a second divine figure who reigns alongside the Ancient of Days—and, Boyarin says, the notion of a "more than singular God" was thus "already an intra-Jewish controversy long before Jesus."[9] Therefore, when Jesus refers to himself in the Gospels as the Son of Man—as in Matthew 9:6, "But that you may know that the Son of Man has authority on earth to forgive sins"*—the Jews in Jesus' day would have immediately understood the reference to the divine figure in the Book of Daniel and would not have thought he meant "human being." This can be easily seen, for example, in the scene at the end of Mark's gospel where the high priest asked Jesus directly if he was the messiah. "I am," Jesus replied, "and you will see the Son of Man seated at the right hand of Power, and coming with the clouds of heaven" (14:62 ESV).[10] Once again, for Boyarin, this means that the notion that Jesus participates in the very nature of God himself did not originate with the pagan Greeks, fifty or one hundred years after Jesus' death, but from within Judaism itself. "[T]he ideas about God that we identify as Christian are not innovations but may be deeply connected with some of the most ancient of Israelite ideas about God," he writes.[11] "I submit that it is possible to understand the gospel only if both Jesus and the Jews around him held to a high Christology, whereby the claim to Messiahship was also a claim to being a divine man," Boyarin adds. "Were it not the case, we would be very hard-pressed to understand the extremely hostile reaction to Jesus on the part of Jewish leaders who did not accept his claim."[12]

DID JESUS THINK HE WAS THE SON OF MAN?

What Boyarin, Schäfer, and other recent scholars of Second Temple Judaism are pointing out is that the idea of a divine Son of Man was in the air when Jesus brought his radical message of the kingdom of God to Galilee and Jerusalem. What's more, it is not implausible that Jesus did see himself, in some way, as being the Son of Man described in Daniel, as having a messianic destiny far greater than the liberal scholars of the nineteenth century imagined. The Catholic New Testament scholar Raymond Brown counts eighty instances of use of the title Son of Man in the New Testament, and all but two are self-designations by Jesus.[13] Thus, Jesus' followers were already preconditioned to see him as a quasi-divine figure before his arrest and execution. Later, when they began having experiences of him alive after death—however that is understood—it would not take them very long to connect the dots and make the claim that Jesus was, in fact, the exalted divine figure described in the book of Daniel—the Son of Man.

HOW EARLY DID JESUS' FOLLOWERS COME TO SEE JESUS AS DIVINE?

The scholarly question, then, is no longer *could* this happen in a Jewish context. More and more New Testament experts believe that it could. The question now, therefore, is, *when* did Jesus' followers make this connection? *How early* did they come to believe in Jesus as divine?

Increasingly, the answer in scholarly circles is *very* early, perhaps within a year or two after the crucifixion. After he investigated the development of Jesus devotion in the New Testament, the German scholar Martin Hengel famously proclaimed that more happened in the development of Christianity's understanding of Jesus in the eighteen years between the crucifixion and the apostle Paul's first letter "than in the whole subsequent seven hundred years of church history."[14] The New Testament scholar Larry Hurtado claims that the evidence that Hengel produced[15] means "the timespan in which the most crucial development took place is more accurately about a couple of years *at most*."[16] This means that, contrary to what historical Jesus experts have said for more than a century, belief in Jesus as in some sense divine arose almost immediately.

How we do know this? Hurtado suggests one speculative but plausible piece of evidence: the irrational vehemence with which the apostle Paul, before his conversion, persecuted the early followers of Jesus. According to the account in the Acts of the Apostles 9:1–3, verified in Paul's own writing (Gal. 1:11–16), Paul did everything in his power to arrest and bring to trial Jesus' early followers, even traveling as far as Damascus to hunt them down

The Alexamenos graffito is a mocking inscription found on a wall on the Palatine Hill in Rome, dated to around the year AD 200. The Greek text reads, "Alexamenos worships god," and depicts Jesus on a cross with the head of a donkey. It is the earliest known drawing of the crucifixion.

in foreign lands. The question is, why? Having once followed a failed messiah made you a dupe, not a criminal, say some Orthodox rabbis.[17] So why did Paul and the Jewish authorities take such drastic, swift action against the early Jesus community? Hurtado's theory is that this extreme hostility was triggered by "outrageous, even blasphemous claims and devotional behavior concerning Jesus."[18] Yet Paul's own conversion occurred within no more than three years of Jesus' crucifixion, and that means that these "blasphemous claims and devotional behavior" must have existed prior to that—in other words, *within a year or two* after Jesus' death.

And that's not all. Hurtado and another noted New Testament scholar, Richard Bauckham, also point to the very earliest Christian writings, written as early as AD 50 to 60, that *already presuppose* a cultic worship of Jesus dating back to the first years after his crucifixion. In his 1998 book, *God Crucified*, Bauckham points to texts such as Paul's first letter to the Corinthians, written around AD 55, in which Paul explains the fundamental belief of the community: "For us there is one God, the Father, from whom are all things and for whom we exist, and one Lord, Jesus Christ, through whom are all things and through whom we exist" (8:6 ESV). As Bauckham comments, a higher view of Jesus than this is "scarcely possible," and yet it is found in the earliest, not the latest, Christian documents.[19]

Paul's letter to the Philippians was written about AD 62 while Paul was in prison, probably in Rome, yet it refers to a creed or hymn some scholars date all the way back to the 40s and which may have been originally in Aramaic . . .

> [T]hough he was in the form of God,
>> did not regard equality with God
>> as something to be exploited,
> but emptied himself,
>> taking the form of a slave,
>> being born in human likeness.
> And being found in human form,
>> he humbled himself
>> and became obedient to the point of death—
>> even death on a cross.
>
> Therefore God also highly exalted him
>> and gave him the name
>> that is above every name,

so that at the name of Jesus
 every knee should bend,
  in heaven and on earth and under the earth,
and every tongue should confess
 that Jesus Christ is Lord,
  to the glory of God the Father.
(PHIL. 2:6–11 NRSV)

Ironically, Hurtado says, the more grandiose conceptions of Jesus that arose later aren't the ones that set apart the early Jesus movement from Judaism. The exalted claims about Jesus' preexistence, his participation in the creation of the world, his sitting at the "right hand of God," titles such as Son of God—all those have parallels, as Boyarin and others have shown, in ancient Judaism.[20] What has no parallel, according to Hurtado, is the devotional practices that are in evidence throughout the early strata of the New Testament—such as singing hymns about Jesus, the invocation of Jesus, prayers offered "through" Jesus or in his name, the use of his name in baptism, prophecy uttered in his name, and more. "These practices, both individually and collectively, are without precedent or parallel in Roman-era circles of Jews," he explains. Nevertheless, the evidence shows "they arose among *Jewish* circles in the earliest years of the Christian movement."[21]

Thus, Hurtado, Bauckham, and many other contemporary New Testament scholars now argue that the belief in Jesus as a quasi-divine being arose so early, and so quickly, that it cannot be seen either as an evolutionary development or due to pagan religious influence. "What we have suggested in the evidence is a more explosively quick phenomenon, a religious development that was more like a volcanic eruption," Hurtado writes.[22]

In fact, Hurtado is locked in a fascinating debate with another famous British scholar, James Dunn, over just this point. Dunn agrees with most experts that belief in Jesus as divine was an early Jewish, not a later pagan, belief, but he disagrees about when Christians actually began to *worship* Jesus as God. Dunn thinks that occurred later, toward the end of the first century.[23] Hurtado, on the other hand, thinks it occurred almost immediately—and that you can't explain the texts we have just seen without accepting that fact. What's more, Hurtado concedes that this elevation of

Jesus to divine status *was* shocking—and, contrary to Boyarin and others, can't really be explained as a mere extension of esoteric Jewish beliefs about a dual godhead. "[T]he worship of Jesus is both remarkable and without real analogy in the ancient setting," Hurtado concludes. "Indeed, it is rather clear that many contemporary Jews who did not share the faith of these early circles of Christians regarded this elevation of Jesus as completely inappropriate, even blasphemous."[24]

So, what gave rise to this shocking, sudden, "inappropriate" belief? The answer increasing number of scholars offer is not surprising: the resurrection. However the resurrection is conceived—as a physical transfiguration of Jesus' actual body or as a spiritual vision of Jesus alive—its undoubted reality among the early, very Jewish followers of Jesus caused them literally to bend their knees at his name. This outraged many Jews, such as Paul himself, and may well have been the reason that the first Christian martyr, Stephen, was stoned to death. According to Acts 7:56, when Stephen addressed the Sanhedrin in Jerusalem, he proclaimed that he had had a vision in which he saw "the heavens opened and the Son of Man standing at the right hand of God." The authorities were enraged by this proclamation, the text says; they cast Stephen out of the city and stoned him to death. All this happened among Jews, in Jerusalem, around the year AD 34 or 35—*perhaps just a year or two after Jesus' crucifixion.*

What all this means is that the story presented in the Gospels and in the Acts of the Apostles, even if colored by what some scholars claim are legendary elements, could be much closer to what actually happened than they or we ever realized. Soon after Jesus of Nazareth was crucified, his very Jewish followers not only began insisting that he was alive again, after death, but they began to use language about him that was similar to the language Jews used about God himself. If this is true, then the old hypothesis that has dominated New Testament scholarship for a century—that the Jewish followers of Jesus viewed him as a rabbi and prophet, and it was the pagan Greeks who came up with the idea of Jesus as the divine "son" of God—is simply *false.* It's quite possible and even likely that the early followers of Jesus actually believed what the Gospels say they believed—that Jesus of Nazareth was raised to life and, more than that, is now "standing at the right hand of God" (Acts 7:56). In addition, more and more experts are suggesting that the Gospels contain within them early, eyewitness testimony from people who saw Jesus firsthand. As the Israeli scholar David Flusser put it, the Synoptic Gospels "preserve a picture of Jesus that is more reliable than is generally acknowledged."[25] Thus, at the very least we should view with new skepticism the certitudes about Jesus that scholars have been propounding for decades, and begin looking at the New Testament again with new eyes.

CONCLUSION . . . AND THE BEGINNING

One of my favorite sites in Jerusalem is the Upper Room, also known as the Cenacle, the traditional site of the Last Supper. Unmarked by any sign, it's located on a Jerusalem rooftop above King David's tomb, near the Zion Gate. The building in its present form dates to the 1300s when it was rebuilt by the Franciscans.[26] However, archaeologists insist the foundations go back all the way to the second century and may be from one of the earliest churches in the holy land, said to have been built in AD 130.[27]

Shutterstock

The traditional site of the Upper Room on Mt. Zion, where Jesus celebrated the Last Supper and his followers gathered at Pentecost, is found on the second floor of a crusader-era structure built in the 1300s. Some archaeologists believe the current building may have been constructed over the remains of a small synagogue church, mentioned by early Christian pilgrims, dating back to AD 130.

As I was finishing the research for this book, I decided to visit this ancient holy place. I had been there many times before, but this time was different. It was the feast of Pentecost, the Jewish festival of Shavuot observed fifty days after Passover and that commemorates the giving of the law at Sinai. It was during Pentecost, according to Acts, that Jesus' disciples received the gift of the Spirit and began proclaiming the gospel.

As I stood in the Upper Room, marveling at its medieval arched ceiling and wondering if this could possibly be the actual location of the Last Supper, it struck me how long I had been on my own personal quest for the historical Jesus. The first time I visited this room, I was only twenty-two. For more years than I care to count, then, I have been searching for Jesus, visiting ancient sites, struggling with difficult ancient languages, studying the works of historical Jesus scholars. I also reflected that, while I have had many questions about this or that doctrine of Christianity, I have never wavered in my loyalty to Jesus of Nazareth—who he was and is, what he stands for, what he asks of us.

I do not believe Jesus was a deluded fanatic who thought the world was about to come to a crashing halt in his lifetime. While this now century-old idea remains popular in many university Near Eastern studies programs, I believe it has been effectively refuted by the most renowned historical Jesus scholars of the past twenty years—scholars such as N. T. Wright, John Dominic Crossan, Geza Vermes, Richard Horsley, Marcus Borg, and many others. It remains popular with non-Christian and former Christian scholars because it says, in essence, that Jesus was crazy—and died a tragic failure. I don't think Jesus was either.

I also don't think Jesus was a "zealot" sympathetic to Jewish nationalists who wanted to wage a holy war against Rome. For one thing, this is so out of character with the Jesus in the New Testament—basically the opposite of how he is portrayed in the Gospels and all the other writings—that only a fanatical conspiracy theorist could accept it. What's more, recent scholars, particularly John Dominic Crossan and N. T. Wright, have debunked this theory as well on purely historical grounds. As we've seen earlier, the Romans did not arrest any of Jesus' followers after his crucifixion. In fact, they allowed them to operate freely in Jerusalem for decades afterward. This simply wouldn't have happened if the Romans had even suspected that Jesus' followers were violent rebels who posed a threat to Roman rule.

So if Jesus wasn't a prophet announcing the end of the world or an extreme Jewish zealot plotting a rebellion against Rome, who and what was he then?

I believe that the historical Jesus was very close to being what the New Testament describes him as being: a fiery, courageous, charismatic populist who drew crowds by the thousands—even tens of thousands—and who briefly electrified all of Palestine with his strange and exhilarating announcement of God's kingdom in their midst. What's more, I think the evidence is compelling that Jesus set out quite consciously to launch a movement that would change the world. He recruited followers whom he told would be "fishers of men," and challenged them to take his message and his movement to every nation on earth. Jesus predicted that some who followed in his footsteps would be killed (John 16:2), even crucified (Mark 8:34) . . . but he promised he would be with them in spirit "until the end of the age" (Matt. 28:20).

Did Jesus see himself as Israel's messiah? Of course, it depends on what you mean by messiah. Recent scholarship has established that Jews in the early decades of the first millennium had many different ideas about the messiah. Some, perhaps most, thought the messiah would be a military hero who would rescue the Jewish people from their oppressors. However, as the Gabriel Revelation suggests, others had a very different idea of who the messiah was and what he would do. Some even seemed to expect a savior who would suffer, die, and, perhaps, even rise again. Israel Knohl, the Israeli biblical scholar, has convinced me that Jesus almost certainly saw his destiny in this way—and that the early followers of Jesus did not fabricate the idea of a suffering messiah to explain away the humiliation of the crucifixion. The kingdom of God that Jesus proclaimed would come, not through military might—not by fighting the Romans with Roman weapons—but through the countless acts of mercy, aid, and comfort that Jesus taught his disciples to put into practice.

While there is much in Jesus' teaching, as Jewish scholars note, that reflects ideas then current in the Jewish world, Jesus' unique way of expressing these ideas and focusing them struck his hearers as something radical and new. Throughout the New Testament, Jesus' hearers expressed astonishment at his teaching, asking, "What is this? A new teaching—with authority!" (Mark 1:27 NRSV). And the gospel, the "good news," that Jesus proclaimed was this: All people, rich and poor, Jew and Gentile, fall within the circle of God's concern. "Even the hairs of your head are all counted," Jesus said (Matt. 10:30 NRSV). All people, no matter how egregious their sins, are offered forgiveness. All are welcome in the kingdom.

Jesus vividly demonstrated this subversive teaching through the disturbing stories he told—his parables—but most dramatically through symbolic acts of mercy that amazed all who saw them. His followers were forever changed by what they saw Jesus do: cleansing lepers and those possessed by demons . . . intervening with a mob about to stone an adulteress to death . . . chatting with hated Samaritans and Romans . . . organizing great public banquets in which the guests of honor were the homeless and the destitute . . . eating and drinking with tax collectors and sinners. These were vivid demonstrations of what the kingdom Jesus was proclaiming was all about, and they amazed and delighted thousands.

Whether intentionally or not, Jesus ignited a worldwide crusade. In just three years or less, he gathered together a group of followers that would, after his death, create the largest, most influential, most enduring social movement in history. While Jesus' followers have never been perfect (one betrayed him to death, another denied even knowing him), only those blinded by ideology or hatred can deny what Jesus' message and example have achieved. For two thousand years, the followers of Jesus of Nazareth have built and staffed orphanages, created hospitals, founded universities, abolished slavery, resisted tyranny, fed the hungry, educated the illiterate, championed human rights, and carried the good news of salvation to every corner of the globe. Whoever you may think Jesus of Nazareth was—whether you think he was an ordinary man, or, as Christians believe, the Son of God—he changed the world more than anyone before or since.

FOR FURTHER STUDY

Bird, Michael F., Craig A. Evans, Simon J. Gathercole, Charles E. Hill, and Chris Tilling. *How God Became Jesus*. Grand Rapids, MI: Zondervan, 2014.

Brown, Raymond E. *An Introduction to New Testament Christology*. Mahwah, NJ: Paulist Press, 1994.

Dunn, James D. G. *Did the First Christians Worship Jesus?* London: SPCK, 2014.

Ehrman, Bart D. *How Jesus Became God*. New York: HarperOne, 2014.

Hurtado, Larry W. *How on Earth Did Jesus Become a God?* Grand Rapids, MI: Eerdmans, 2005.

Schäfer, Peter. *The Jewish Jesus: How Judaism and Christianity Shaped Each Other.* Princeton, NJ: Princeton University Press, 2012.

EPILOGUE

*"When the Son of Man comes, will
he find faith on earth?"*

—LUKE 18:8 NRSV

It's a cold, sunny Sunday in early February, and I am standing outside the parish church of Saint Andreas, located about two blocks from the Rhine River in the small German village of Bad Godesberg, waiting for the French-language service to begin. I'm here on business but speak only a few words of German, so I attend the French liturgy instead. Outside the church, a small group of francophone parishioners has gathered, despite the cold. An elderly, very elegant French woman is trying to help me light a white candle, but the icy wind rushing up from the Rhine keeps blowing it out. Finally, my candle is lit, and a young French teenager comes up to me to light his own candle. He's a bit too eager, however, and only succeeds in extinguishing mine. As a result, we both go back to the elderly woman and she lights both of our candles. We cup our hands around *les bougies* and shield them from the wind with our bodies, trying to keep the flames from going out. Of course, the candles symbolize Christian faith, with the light of Christ passed on from one person to another, one generation to another, across the ages. As the icy wind blows out someone's candle, another person steps up and helps to relight it. Finally, when all our candles are lit, an African priest from the Cameroon blesses our small group with holy water, and then we process into the brick church.

I love coming to this ordinary German parish. It symbolizes for me the global interconnectedness of the Christian community. The common belief in the United States is that Europe is utterly secularized and that few people go to church, and while that may be true statistically, I have my doubts. One reason is that Saint Andreas is packed full on Sunday mornings—young and old, black and white, rich and poor. The French congregation is much smaller than the German one but just as lively. It's mostly locals with French spouses, African immigrants and their families, and a few tourists like myself. But I feel immediately at home here. It's like attending a wedding of cousins I have never met but have heard about all my life. The Africans are particularly friendly and devout, their French crisp, precise, and easy to understand. They shake my hand, say, "*Paix du Christ*," and show me where to sit.

Today is the feast of the Presentation of the Lord, recounted in the gospel of Luke, and the theme is "Christ as the light of the world" (hence the candles). While waiting for the liturgy to begin, I search for the gospel reading on my iPhone. The passage in Luke follows immediately after the shepherds' arrival at Jesus' birth and a one-sentence mention of Jesus' ritual circumcision, the ancient sign of the covenant between the Jewish people and the Eternal God. The text reads simply that "when the time came for their purification according to the law of Moses, they brought him up to Jerusalem to present him to the Lord (as it is written in the law of the Lord, 'Every firstborn male shall be designated as holy to the Lord'), and they offered a sacrifice according to what is stated in the law of the Lord, 'a pair of turtledoves or two young pigeons'" (Luke 2:22–24 NRSV).

Of course, this being the New Testament, nothing is straightforward. Luke appears to conflate, or jumble together, two related but distinct commandments (*mitzvot*) of the Torah: the *mitzvah* of Pidyon ha-Ben, when Jewish parents "redeem," or buy back, their firstborn son from God; and the *mitzvah* that a mother be ritually purified after giving birth (requiring the sacrifice of a lamb or at least two doves or two young pigeons). According to the law of Moses, every firstborn son was to be consecrated to God as a priest. But after the Exodus from Egypt, the Torah says, the Israelites turned away from God and worshiped the golden calf instead—with only the tribe of Levi refusing to participate. As a result, God decreed that henceforth only Levites would be priests and that all other firstborn sons would need to be symbolically "bought back" from God. The Torah even sets the price: five shekels (Num. 3:47).

Luke complicates all this by not mentioning shekels at all, referring instead to the sacrifice of pigeons required of a mother after giving birth. Did Luke, presumably a Gentile with only secondhand knowledge of Jewish practice, get all this mixed up? Or did he just intentionally jumble everything together for the sake of brevity, assuming that his Gentile readers wouldn't know or care about the details of Jewish ritual law? We don't know.

And reading all this on my iPhone, I had to laugh: of course there is a text-critical issue as well! In our oldest Greek manuscripts, Luke says that "when the time came for *their* purification according to the law of Moses, they brought him up to Jerusalem to present him to the Lord" (2:22). The problem is, the Torah doesn't mention any purification requirement for *them*, only for her. As far as we know, neither the father nor the newborn son required any ritual purification—only the mother. Some Western scribes appeared to have mistakenly changed the Greek from "their" to "his" purification, meaning Jesus' purification, even though the requirement is for the mother's purification. Some English translations, such as the NIV, deliberately evade this issue altogether with creative syntax and/or the avoidance of pronouns. The NIV cleverly says, "When the time came for the purification rites required by the Law of Moses" (no pronouns at all!), while the King James Bible says "her" purification: "And when the days of her purification according to the law of Moses were accomplished." The King James version is incorrect from the point of view of what the most ancient Greek manuscripts say but correct from the point of view of what the Torah requires. These are the kinds of muddy "discrepancies" that drive text-critical scholars to distraction, and sometimes to lose their Christian faith altogether.

But not being a textual critic, I can shrug all this off and instead get to the point of Luke's story: the prophetic recognition by the *tzaddik* Simeon that Jesus is the messiah, the "consolation of Israel." This is the actual gospel passage read during the liturgy:

Now there was a man in Jerusalem whose name was Simeon. This man was righteous and devout, awaiting the consolation of Israel, and the holy Spirit was upon him. It had been revealed to him by the holy Spirit that he should not see death before he had seen the Messiah of the Lord. He came in the Spirit into the temple; and when the parents brought in the child Jesus to perform the custom of the law in regard to him, he took him in his arms and blessed God, saying: "Now, Master, you may let your servant go in peace, according to your word, for my eyes have seen your salvation, which you prepared in the sight of all the peoples, a light for revelation to the Gentiles, and glory for your people Israel." (Luke 2:25–32)

In just a few sentences, Luke presents one of the primary themes of his gospel and, indeed, of the entire New Testament: that Jesus is the Messiah, a "light" for the Gentiles and the glory of God's people, Israel.

Looking up from my iPhone and at the international group of worshipers gathered for this feast day—people from various European and African countries, speaking many different languages—I couldn't help but marvel at how Simeon's prophecy had literally come true. Whatever Jesus "really" was—and as we've seen in this book, after two hundred years of relentless scholarly digging, no one can agree what this is—whether Jesus was God incarnate or three quarters God or just a little God—it is literally true that he is and has been a "light of revelation" for untold billions of people throughout history. For those who believe in him, skeptic or not, Jesus is nothing less than the human face of God. And while individually each follower of Jesus might not reflect much of his light—not much goodness, not much wisdom, not much human decency—when combined with the lights carried by hundreds of millions or even billions of other followers, then the light is actually far more substantial. In the vast darkness that surrounds the earth, both literally and figuratively, this collective light is what allows humanity to see its way forward into the future God has planned.

FOR FURTHER STUDY

Dawes, Gregory W., ed. *The Historical Jesus Quest.* Louisville, KY: Westminster John Knox Press, 1999.

Johnson, Luke Timothy. *Living Jesus.* San Francisco: HarperSanFrancisco, 1999.

Kähler, Martin. *The So-Called Historical Jesus and the Historic, Biblical Christ.* Translated by Carl E. Braaten. Philadelphia: Fortress Press, 1964.

Wright, N. T. *The Challenge of Jesus.* Downers Grove, IL: InterVarsity Press, 1999.

ACKNOWLEDGMENTS

As I said earlier, I've been working on this book for most of my life in one way or another. As a result, the number of people I should thank is long indeed. My agent, Alexander Hoyt, believed in this project when no one else did—as did the generous editor Harry Crocker. The folks at Thomas Nelson, Joel Miller and Kristen Parrish, took a chance on this project without knowing exactly how it would turn out, and for that I am very grateful. I would also like to thank two tenacious and dedicated editors, Heather Skelton and Jennifer McNeil, who helped turn my often-murky, run-on sentences into something resembling English.

I had many, many teachers in my time on this earth, but a few really influenced me. L. John Topel, SJ, first introduced me to the academic study of the New Testament when I was still in college. The late lay theologian Louis G. Jeannot introduced me to Bernard Lonergan and the idea that you could be both philosophically astute and scripturally grounded at the same time. The theologian Scott Hahn inspired me to apply for admission to Fuller Theological Seminary in the mid-90s and told me that, as Jerome said, "Ignorance of Scripture is ignorance of Christ." At Fuller Seminary, I had many amazing teachers, including the legendary David Scholer. But the one I learned the most from was Dr. Mark Roberts, a Presbyterian minister and now a celebrated Christian author and blogger. (Mark would no doubt be shocked by many statements in this book and should not be held responsible for any of them.)

I would also like to thank the staff at the Tantur Institute in Jerusalem, especially Tony Pohlen and his lovely wife, Esther, who welcomed me so warmly and provided invaluable help as I researched parts of this book. I also gained many insights speaking with some of the scholars and ministers in residence at Tantur, including Shin Asami, Juanita Cordero, Ray Abella, Edna Mackintosh, Fred Negem, Kevin Burke, Michael Dooley, Margaret Ng, Lynn Holt, David and Liz Cannon, Florence Yu, Ian Dempsey, Miguel Lino Ferreira, Mervyn Tower, and Paul Howard. In addition, I should mention three other scholars who patiently answered my many questions and were very generous with their time: Israel Knohl, professor of Bible at the Hebrew University; Georg Gäbel of the Institute for New Testament Textual Research in Münster, Germany; and Daniel Wallace of the Center for the Study of New Testament Manuscripts at Dallas Theological Seminary.

Finally, I would like to thank my family. My parents, Mary Jane and A'lan Hutchinson, raised me in a large, easygoing Catholic household in which study and church were just taken as a given. My children—Robert, James, Kelly, Mary, Jane, and now Katerina—helped me with this book by all the questions they asked and by the vigorous skepticism they showed over the years. My beautiful and talented wife, Glenn Ellen, read every word of the manuscript many times and helped to sharpen and clarify points I did not express clearly. I could not have finished this book without her help.

SELECTED BIBLIOGRAPHY

Aland, Kurt and Barbara Aland. *The Text of the New Testament*. Grand Rapids, MI: Wm. B. Eerdmans, 1987.

Arav, Rami and John J. Rousseau. *Jesus and His World: An Archaeological and Cultural Dictionary*. Minneapolis, MN: Augsburg Fortress Press, 1995.

Aslan, Reza. *Zealot: The Life and Times of Jesus of Nazareth*. New York: Random House, 2013.

Barnet, Paul. *Jesus and the Rise of Early Christianity: A History of New Testament Times*. Downers Grove, IL: InterVarsity Press, 1999.

Bauckham, Richard. *God Crucified: Monotheism and Christology in the New Testament*. Grand Rapids, MI: Wm. B. Eerdmans, 1998.

———. *Jesus and the Eyewitnesses*. Grand Rapids, MI: Wm. B. Eerdmans, 2006.

Beilby, James K. and Paul Rhodes Eddy, eds. *The Historical Jesus: Five Views*. Downers Grove, IL: InterVarsity Press, 2009.

Bird, Michael F., Craig A. Evans, Simon J. Gathercole, Charles E. Hill, and Chris Tilling. *How God Became Jesus*. Grand Rapids, MI: Zondervan, 2014.

Blomberg, Craig. *The Historical Reliability of the Gospels*, 2nd ed. Downers Grove, IL: IVP Academic, 2007.

Borg, Marcus J. *Jesus: The Life, Teachings, and Relevance of a Religious Revolutionary*. New York: HarperOne, 2006.

Boteach, Shmuley. *Kosher Jesus*. Jerusalem: Gefen Publishing, 2012.

Boyarin, Daniel. *The Jewish Gospels*. New York: The New Press, 2012.

Brandon, S. G. F. *Jesus and the Zealots*. New York: Charles Scribner's, 1967.

Brown, Michael. *The Real Kosher Jesus*. Lake Mary, FL: Frontline, 2012.

Brown, Raymond E. *An Introduction to New Testament Christology*. Mahwah, NJ: Paulist Press, 1994.

———. *Birth of the Messiah*. New York: Doubleday, 1992.

———. *Death of the Messiah*. New York: Doubleday, 1994.

Bruce, F. F. *The Hard Sayings of Jesus*. Downers Grove, IL: InterVarsity Press, 1983.

Chilton, Bruce. *Rabbi Jesus: An Intimate Biography*. New York: Doubleday, 2000.

Comfort, Philip. *Encountering the Manuscripts: An Introduction to New Testament Paleography and Textual Criticism*. Nashville: Broadman and Holman, 2005.

Craig, William Lane. *Reasonable Faith: Christian Truth and Apologetics*, 3rd ed. Wheaton, IL: Crossway Books, 2008.

Crossan, John Dominic and Jonathan L. Reed. *Excavating Jesus: Beneath the Stones, Behind the Texts*. San Francisco: HarperSanFrancisco, 2001.

Crossan, John Dominic. *Jesus: A Revolutionary Biography*. New York: HarperCollins, 2009.

———. *The Historical Jesus: The Life of a Mediterranean Jewish Peasant*. San Francisco: HarperSanFrancisco, 1991.

———. *God and Empire: Jesus Against Rome, Then and Now*. San Francisco: HarperSanFrancisco, 2007.

———. *Who Killed Jesus?* San Francisco: HarperSanFrancisco, 1996.

Crossley, James G. *The Date of Mark's Gospel*. London: T&T Clark, 2004.

———. *Why Christianity Happened: A Sociohistorical Account of Christian Origins 26–50 CE*. Louisville, KY: Westminster John Knox Press, 2006.

Dark, Ken. "Early Roman Period Nazareth and the Sisters of Nazareth Convent." *Antiquaries Journal* 92 (2012).

———. "Has Jesus' Nazareth House Been Found?" *Biblical Archaeological Review* 41:02, March/April 2015.

Dawes, Gregory W., ed. *The Historical Jesus Quest*. Louisville, KY: Westminster John Knox Press, 1999.

Demarest, Bruce. *The Cross and Salvation*. Wheaton, IL: Crossway Books, 1997.

Dunn, James D. G. *Did the First Christians Worship Jesus?* London: SPCK, 2014.

———. *Jesus Remembered*. Grand Rapids, MI: Wm. B. Eerdmans, 2003.

Ehrman, Bart D. *How Jesus Became God*. New York: HarperOne, 2014.

———. *Did Jesus Exist?* New York: HarperOne, 2012.

———. *Forged*. New York: HarperOne, 2011.

———. *Misquoting Jesus: The Story Behind Who Changed the Bible and Why*. New York: HarperOne, 2007.

———. *Jesus: Apocalyptic Prophet of the New Millennium*. London: Oxford University Press, 1999.

Ehrman, Bart, ed. *Lost Scriptures: Books that Did Not Make It Into the New Testament*. London: Oxford University Press, 2003.

Evans, Craig. *From Jesus to the Church: The First Christian Generation*. Louisville, KY: Westminster John Knox Press, 2014.

Evans, Craig A. "Jewish Burial Traditions and the Resurrection of Jesus," *Journal for the Study of the Historical Jesus* 3 (2005).

Fredriksen, Paula. *Jesus of Nazareth: King of the Jews*. New York: Random House, 1999.

Freund, Richard A. *Digging Through the Bible.* Lanham, MD: Roman & Littlefield, 2009.

Fuller, Reginald H. *The Formation of the Resurrection Narratives.* New York: Macmillan, 1971.

Geisler, Norman and Joseph M. Holden. *The Popular Handbook of Archaeology and the Bible.* Eugene, OR: Harvest House, 2013.

Grant, Michael. *An Historian's Review of the Gospels.* New York: Charles Scribner's Sons, 1977.

Green, Joel B. and Mark D. Baker. *Recovering the Scandal of the Cross: Atonement in New Testament and Contemporary Contexts.* Downers Grove, IL: InterVarsity Press, 2000.

Haight, Roger. *Jesus: Symbol of God.* Maryknoll, NY: Orbis Books, 1999.

Hanson, K. C. and Douglas E. Oakman. *Palestine in the Time of Jesus: Social Structures and Social Conflicts.* Minneapolis, MN: Augsburg, 1998.

Hengel, Martin. *The Atonement: The Origins of the Doctrine in the New Testament.* Translated by John Bowden. Eugene, OR: Wipf and Stock Publishers, 1981.

Horsley, Richard A. and Neil Asher Silberman. *The Message and the Kingdom.* New York: Putnam, 1997.

Hurtado, Larry W. *How on Earth Did Jesus Become a God?* Grand Rapids, MI: Wm. B. Eerdmans, 2005.

Jeremias, Joachim. *The Parables of Jesus.* New York: Scribner's, 1954.

Johnson, Luke Timothy. *Living Jesus.* San Francisco: HarperSanFrancisco, 1999.

———. *The Real Jesus.* San Francisco: HarperSanFrancisco, 1996.

Jones, Timothy Paul "Is It Possible that Jesus' Body Was Left on the Cross?" *Timothy Paul Jones* (blog), April 6, 2012, http://www.timothypauljones.com/2012/04/06/is-it-possible-that-jesus-body-was-left-on-the-cross/.

Kähler, Martin. *The So-Called Historical Jesus and the Historic Biblical Christ.* Translated by Carl E. Braaten. Philadelphia: Fortress Press, 1964.

Kaiser, Walter, et al. *Hard Sayings of the Bible.* Downers Grove, IL: InterVarsity Press, 1996.

Klinghoffer, David. *Why the Jews Rejected Jesus.* New York: Doubleday, 2005.

Kloppenborg Verbin, John S. *Excavating Q: The History and Setting of the Sayings Gospel.* Minneapolis, MN: Fortress Press, 2000.

Knohl, Israel. *The Messiah before Jesus: The Suffering Servant of the Dead Sea Scrolls.* Berkeley: University of California Press, 2000.

———, "The Messiah Son of Joseph: 'Gabriel's Revelation' and the Birth of a New Messianic Model," *Biblical Archaeology Review* 34:05, September/October 2008.

Krosney, Herbert. *The Lost Gospel: The Quest for the Gospel of Judas Iscariot.* Washington, DC: National Geographic, 2006.

Küng, Hans. *On Being a Christian*. New York: Doubleday, 1976.

Levine, Amy-Jill. *The Misunderstood Jew: The Church and the Scandal of the Jewish Jesus*. New York: HarperCollins, 2007.

Mack, Burton L. *Who Wrote the New Testament: The Making of the Christian Myth*. San Francisco: HarperSanFrancisco, 1995.

Magness, Jodi. "Jodi Magness Responds to the 'New Jesus Discovery.'" ASORblog.org. http://asorblog.org/2012/02/28/1654/.

———. *Stone and Dung, Oil and Spit: Jewish Daily Life in the Time of Jesus*. Grand Rapids, MI: Wm. B. Eerdmans, 2011.

———. "The Burial of Jesus in Light of Archaeology and the Gospels." In *Eretz Israel* 28, Teddy Kollek Volume. Jerusalem: Israel Exploration Society.

McLaren, Brian. *The Secret Message of Jesus*. Nashville, TN: Thomas Nelson, 2006.

Meier, John P. *A Marginal Jew: Rethinking the Historical Jesus*. New York: Doubleday, 1994.

Meyer, Margin. *Judas: The Definitive Collection of Gospels and Legends About the Infamous Apostle of Jesus*. New York: HarperCollins, 2007.

Miller, Robert J., ed. *The Complete Gospels: Annotated Scholars Version*. San Francisco: HarperSanFrancisco, 1992.

Murphy-O'Connor, Jerome. *The Holy Land: An Oxford Archaeological Guide*, 5th ed. Oxford: Oxford University Press, 2008.

Neusner, Jacob. *A Rabbi Talks with Jesus*. New York: Doubleday, 1993.

O'Collins, Gerald. *Jesus Risen*. New York: Paulist Press, 1987.

Pagels, Elaine. *The Gnostic Gospels*. New York: Vintage Books, 1979.

Roberts, Mark D. *Can We Trust the Gospels? Investigating the Reliability of Matthew, Mark, Luke, and John*. Wheaton, IL: Crossway, 2007.

Robinson, John A. T. *Redating the New Testament*. London: SCM Press, 1976.

Sanders, E. P. *The Historical Figure of Jesus*. New York: Penguin Books, 1993.

Schäfer, Peter. *The Jewish Jesus: How Judaism and Christianity Shaped Each Other*. Princeton, NJ: Princeton University Press, 2012.

Silver, Abba Hillel. *Where Judaism Differed*. New York: Macmillian, 1956.

Spong, John Shelby. *Resurrection: Myth or Reality*. San Francisco: HarperSanFrancisco, 1994.

Stark, Rodney. *The Rise of Christianity*. New York: HarperCollins, 1996.

Stein, Robert H. *Jesus the Messiah*. Downers Grove, IL: IVP Academic, 1996.

Tabor, James D. and Simcha Jacobovici. *The Jesus Discovery*. New York: Simon & Schuster, 2012.

———. *The Jesus Dynasty*. New York: Simon and Schuster, 2006.

Theissen, Gerd. *The Shadow of the Galilean*, rev. ed. Minneapolis, MN: Fortress Press, 2007.

Theissen, Gerd and Annette Merz. *The Historical Jesus: A Comprehensive Guide.* Minneapolis, MN: Fortress Press, 1998.

Vermes, Geza. *The Religion of Jesus the Jew.* Minneapolis, MN: Fortress Press, 1993.

Wallace, Daniel B., ed. *Revisiting the Corruption of the New Testament.* Grand Rapids, MI: Kregel Publications, 2011.

Ware, James. "Paul's Understanding of the Resurrection in 1 Corinthians 15: 36–54." *Journal of Biblical Literature* 133 no. 4 (2014): 808.

Wills, Garry. *What Jesus Meant.* New York: Penguin, 2006.

Witherington III, Ben. *The Jesus Quest: The Third Search for the Jew of Nazareth.* Downers Grove, IL: InterVarsity Press, 1995.

Wright, N. T. *Jesus and the Victory of God.* Minneapolis, MN: Fortress Press, 1996.

———. *The Resurrection of the Son of God.* Minneapolis, MN: Fortress Press, 2003.

Yoder, John Howard. *The Politics of Jesus*, 2nd ed. Grand Rapids, MI: Wm. B. Eerdmans, 1994.

NOTES

Introduction

1. For example, see Kyle R. Hughes, "The Lukan Special Material and the Tradition History of the Pericope Adulterae," *Novum Testamentum* 55.3 (2013), 232–51.
2. Cf. Rudolf Bultmann, et al., *Kerygma and Myth* (New York: Harper & Row, 1961), 34–55.
3. For example, see Robert J. Hutchinson, "The Jesus Seminar Unmasked," *Christianity Today,* April 29, 1996.
4. See Robert J. Hutchinson, "What the Rabbi Taught Me About Jesus," *Christianity Today,* September 13, 1993, 28.

Prologue

1. One of the most passionate advocates of this position is the agnostic New Testament scholar Bart Ehrman. Like Albert Schweitzer, Ehrman argues that Jesus believed the world was about to end in his lifetime with the coming of a cosmic figure known as the Son of Man (a different figure from Jesus), when God would destroy all those opposed to Jesus and his message and appoint Jesus king of Israel; but, Erhman says, this harsh and frightening message was quickly toned down by the time the gospels of Luke and John came to be written. See *Jesus: Apocalyptic Prophet of the New Millennium* (London: Oxford University Press, 1999), 130–35.
2. Joseph Atwell, *Caesar's Messiah: The Roman Conspiracy to Invent Jesus* (Charleston, SC: CreateSpace, 2011).
3. "The commission in Matthew is expressed in Matthew's language and reflects the evangelist's idea of the world mission of the church," write members of the skeptical Jesus Seminar. "Jesus probably had no idea of launching a world

mission and certainly was not an institution builder." Robert W. Funk, Roy W. Hoover, et al., *The Five Gospels: The Search for the Authentic Words of Jesus* (New York: Macmillan, 1993), 270.

4. "The author of Matthew was an unknown Jewish Christian of the second generation writing around AD 90 in or near Antioch in Syria," Reginald H. Fuller, "Matthew," *Harper's Bible Commentary* (San Francisco: Harper & Row, 1988), 951.

5. Rodney Stark, *The Rise of Christianity* (New York: HarperCollins, 1996), 7.

6. "A comprehensive demographic study of more than 200 countries finds that there are 2.18 billion Christians of all ages around the world, representing nearly a third of the estimated 2010 global population of 6.9 billion. Christians are also geographically widespread—so far-flung, in fact, that no single continent or region can indisputably claim to be the center of global Christianity." Pew Research Center, "Global Christianity—A Report on the Size and Distribution of the World's Christian Population," December 19, 2011, http://www.pewforum.org/2011/12/19/global-christianity-exec/.

7. "As a Messianic movement Christianity failed, as have all such movements in Jewish history and in the history of other peoples," writes Abba Hillel Silver in *Where Judaism Differed* (New York: Macmillan, 1956), 96. David Klinghoffer, in *Why the Jews Rejected Jesus,* agrees. "Jesus never raised an army, fought the Romans, returned any Jewish exiles, ruled over any population, or did anything else a king messiah would do," he explains (New York: Harmony, 2006), 63.

Chapter 1: Is There Eyewitness Testimony in the Gospels?

1. Mishnah, Sabbath, VII, 2. According to the 1906 *Jewish Encyclopedia*, the thirty-nine categories of forbidden work are: sowing, plowing, reaping, gathering into sheaves, thrashing, winnowing, cleansing, grinding, sifting, kneading, and baking; shearing, bleaching, beating, and dyeing wool; spinning, making a warp, making two thrum-threads, weaving two threads, splitting two threads, tying, untying, sewing two stitches, tearing in order to sew two stitches; hunting deer, slaughtering, skinning, and salting it (its hide), tanning, scraping off the hair, cutting up (the hide); writing two letters, erasing for the purpose of writing two letters; building, pulling down; extinguishing fire, kindling fire; beating with a hammer; and carrying from one premise into another. See "Sabbath," *The Jewish Encyclopedia,* available online: http://www.jewishencyclopedia.com/articles/12962-sabbath.

2. James D. G. Dunn, *Jesus Remembered: Christianity in the Making,* Vol. 1 (Grand Rapids, MI: Eerdman's, 2003), 41.

3. Jerome Murphy-O'Connor, *The Holy Land: An Oxford Archaeological Guide*, 5th ed. (Oxford: Oxford University Press, 2008), 29–32.

4. Ibid, 29.

5. Saint Jerome, *De situ et nominibus Hebraicorum locurm*, vol. 23, cited in John J. Rousseau and Rami Arav, *Jesus and His World: An Archaeological and Cultural Dictionary* (Minneapolis: Fortress Press, 1995), 155.

6. Ibid., 157, emphasis added.

7. The most notable Roman historians who mention Jesus include Tacitus (AD 56–117), Pliny the Younger (AD 61–112), and Suetonius (AD 70–130). Perhaps the most informative is Tacitus's report in his *Annals* (15.44): "Consequently, to get rid of the report, Nero fastened the guilt and inflicted the most exquisite tortures on a class hated for their abominations, called Christians by the populace. Christus, from whom the name had its origin, suffered the extreme penalty during the reign of Tiberius at the hands of one of our procurators, Pontius Pilatus, and a most mischievous superstition, thus checked for the moment, again broke out not only in Judæa, the first source of the evil, but even in Rome, where all things hideous and shameful from every part of the world find their centre and become popular. Accordingly, an arrest was first made of all who pleaded guilty; then, upon their information, an immense multitude was convicted, not so much of the crime of firing the city, as of hatred against mankind." Tacitus, *The Annals* (From the Passing of the Divine Augustus), trans. Alfred John Church and William Jackson Brodribb (1876), https://en.wikisource.org/wiki/The_Annals_%28Tacitus%29/Book_15#44.

8. One of the most famous passages is from the Babylonian Talmud, Sanhedrin, 43a–b: "On (Sabbath eve and) the eve of Passover Jesus the Nazarene was hanged and a herald went forth before him forty days heralding, 'Jesus the Nazarene is going forth to be stoned because he practiced sorcery and instigated and seduced Israel to idolatry. Whoever knows anything in defense may come and state it.' But since they did not find anything in his defense they hanged him on (Sabbath eve and) the eve of Passover. Ulla said: Do you suppose that Jesus the Nazarene was one for whom a defense could be made? He was a mesit (someone who instigated Israel to idolatry), concerning whom the Merciful [God] says: Show him no compassion and do not shield him (Deut. 13:9). With Jesus the Nazarene it was different. For he was close to the government." Found in Peter Schäfer, *Jesus in the Talmud* (Princeton: Princeton University Press, 2007), 64–65.

9. John P. Meier, in the first volume of his encyclopedic series on the historical Jesus, *A Marginal Jew*, discusses the passages in Josephus in detail. He

concludes, along with many other scholars, that most of what is now found in Josephus's works about Jesus came from the author himself but that later Christian scribes did add a few phrases to enhance the text. Meier's translation of the key passage, known as the Testimonium Flavianum, follows. The italicized portions are those that Meier and others judge to be later Christian additions: "At this time there appeared Jesus, a wise man, *if indeed one should call him a man.* For he was a doer of startling deeds, a teacher of people who receive the truth with pleasure. And he gained a following both among many Jews and among many of Greek origin. *He was the Messiah.* And when Pilate, because of an accusation made by the leading men among us, condemned him to the cross, those who had loved him previously did not cease to do so. *For he appeared to them on the third day, living again, just as the divine prophets had spoken of these and countless other wondrous things about him.* And up until this very day the tribe of Christians, named after him, has not died out." John P. Meier, *A Marginal Jew: Rethinking the Historical Jesus*, Vol. 1 (New York: Doubleday, 1991), 60–61.

10. Charles W. Hedrick, "The 34 Gospels: Diversity and Division Among the Earliest Christians," *Bible Review* 18.3 (June 2002): 20–31.

11. Robert J. Miller, ed., *The Complete Gospels* (San Francisco: HarperSanFrancisco, 1994), 301–424.

12. Christian apologists often go to elaborate lengths to harmonize these factual divergences in order to maintain the doctrine that the Bible is inerrant down to the last detail. For example, some apologists contend that Quirinius may have had *two* periods as a governor in Syria and, if so, Luke could be referring to the earlier period. "Being the meticulous historian that he was, Luke demonstrated his awareness of a separate provincial census during Quirinius' governorship beginning in A.D. 6 (Acts 5:37)," writes David Miller. "In view of this familiarity, he surely would not have confused this census with one taken ten or more years earlier. Hence, Luke claimed that a prior census was, indeed, taken at the command of Caesar Augustus sometime prior to 4 B.C. He flagged this earlier census by using the expression *prote egeneto* ("first took place")—which assumes a later one (cf. Nicoll, n.d., 1:471). To question the authenticity of this claim, simply because no explicit reference has yet been found, is unwarranted and prejudicial." David Miller, "Luke, Quirinius, and the Census," available online at: http://www.apologeticspress.org/apcontent .aspx?category=6&article=907. However, other Christian scholars, even those who, like Daniel Wallace of Dallas Theological Seminary, affirm the inerrancy of the Bible, find these arguments based on Greek grammar to be

unconvincing for a variety of reasons. They simply insist that the difficulty has yet to be resolved. See Daniel Wallace, "The Problem of Luke 2:2: 'This was the first census taken when Quirinius was governor of Syria,'" available online at: https://bible.org/article/problem-luke-22-ithis-was-first-census -taken-when-quirinius-was-governor-syriai. Still other New Testament scholars, such as Raymond Brown, say that Luke simply made a minor mistake in chronology and concludes that "this information is dubious on almost every score, despite the elaborate attempts by scholars to defend Lucan accuracy." See Raymond Brown, *The Birth of the Messiah* (New York: Doubleday, 1999), 413.

13. See Boyarin's discussion of Jesus' conflicts with the Pharisees, which many critical scholars believe was made up by the early church, *The Jewish Gospels: The Story of the Jewish Christ* (New York: The New Press, 2012), 102 ff.

14. Earl Doherty, *Jesus: Neither God Nor Man, The Case for a Mythical Jesus* (Ottawa: Age of Reason Publications, 2009), 246.

15. Joseph Atwell, *Caesar's Messiah: The Roman Conspiracy to Invent Jesus* (Charleston, SC: CreateSpace, 2011).

16. Robert M. Price, "Jesus at the Vanishing Point," in *The Historical Jesus: Five Views*, eds. James K. Beilby and Paul Rhodes Eddy (Downers Grove, IL: InterVarsity Press, 2009), 62.

17. Bart D. Ehrman, *Did Jesus Exist?* (New York: HarperOne, 2012), 44.

18. Ibid., 45.

19. The New Testament scholar Larry Hurtado points out, however, that the notion of a pre-Christian gnostic redeemer myth was once common among "liberal," especially German, New Testament scholars, including Rudolf Bultmann, Ernst Käsemann, Helmut Koester, and James Robinson. See L. W. Hurtado, "Fashions, Fallacies and Future Prospects in New Testament Studies," available online at: http://larryhurtado.files.wordpress.com/2010/07 /fashions-fallacies-and-futures-in-nt-studies.pdf. He cites Edwin Yamauchi, *Pre-Christian Gnosticism: A Survey of the Proposed Evidences* (London: Tyndale Press, 1973), 24.

20. Ehrman, *Did Jesus Exist?*, 222.

21. Ibid., 208.

22. "Apollonius . . . really was a historical person, a Pythagorean philosopher who lived some fifty years after Jesus," Ehrman, *Did Jesus Exist?*, 209. See also, "Apollonius Of Tyana," *The New Encyclopedia Britannica*, vol. 1, 15th ed. (Chicago: Encyclopedia Britannica, 1987), 485.

23. "Many scholars assign II Thess, Col, Eph, and the Pastoral Letters (I and II

Tim and Titus) to this category of 'deuteroPauline' writings, composed in the period 70–100 (or even later), after Paul's death," Raymond E. Brown, *An Introduction to the New Testament* (New York: Doubleday, 1997), 6.

24. "According to the south Galatian theory (i.e., in its most popular form), the terminus ad quem of this epistle must be before the Council of Acts 15 and the terminus a quo must be after Paul's visit to Jerusalem in Acts 11:30. In other words, Galatians must have been written between autumn, 46 CE and autumn, 48 CE," Daniel Wallace, "Galatians: Introduction, Argument, and Outline," available online at: https://bible.org/seriespage/9-galatians-introduction-argument-and-outline#_ftn16. Wallace is discussing the chronology proposed by H. W. Hoehner, *Chronology of the Apostolic Age* (ThD Dissertation, Dallas Seminary, 1965), 382. Wallace himself argues that "this letter was written shortly before the Council of Jerusalem in Acts 15—that is, in late summer/fall of 48 CE (or 49 CE)." Other evangelical scholars, such as Ralph P. Martin, agree. See Ralph P. Martin, *New Testament Foundations,* vol. 2 (Grand Rapids, MI: Eerdmans, 1978), 152. Raymond Brown prefers a date in the mid-50s but insists that "the evidence leaves the question open." See Brown, *An Introduction to the New Testament,* 477.

25. Even the agnostic scholar Bart Ehrman concedes that the Gospels contain hymns, creeds, formulas, and Aramaic expressions that date back at least to the years immediately after the crucifixion. See Ehrman, *How Jesus Became God* (San Francisco: HarperOne, 2014), 218–20.

26. Burton L. Mack, *Who Wrote the New Testament: The Making of the Christian Myth* (San Francisco: HarperSanFrancisco, 1995), 64.

27. The nonhealing miracles are: 1. Calming the storm (Matt. 8:23–27; Mark 4:37–41; Luke 8:22–25); 2. Feeding the five thousand (Matt. 14:14–21; Mark 6:30–44; Luke 9:10–17; John 6:1–14); 3. Walking on water (Matt. 14:22–32; Mark 6:47–52; John 6:16–21); 4. Feeding four thousand (Matt. 15:32–39; Mark 8:1–9); 5. Fish with coin (Matt. 17:24–27); 6. Withered fig tree (Matt. 21:18–22; Mark 11:12–14, 20–25); 7. First miraculous catch of fish (Luke 5:4–11; John 21:1–11); 8. Water into wine (John 2:1–11); 9. Jairus's daughter (Matt. 9:18–26; Mark 5:21–43, Luke 8:40–56); 10. Widow's son at Nain (Luke 7:11–17); 11. Raising of Lazarus (John 11:1–44); 12. Second miraculous catch of fish.

28. Mark Roberts, *Can We Trust the Gospels?* (Wheaton, IL: Crossway Books, 2007), 128.

29. Reza Aslan, *Zealot* (New York: Random House, 2013), xix.

30. I take most of this analysis from Craig L. Blomberg's *The Historical Reliability of the Gospels,* 2nd ed. (Downers Grove, IL: IVP Academic, 2007), 152–94.

The topics are all discussed by Blomberg in great detail, but, for simplicity's sake, I rearrange here the order in which Blomberg takes up each topic.

31. Mark 16:1, Matthew 28:1, John 20:1, and Luke 24:1–10. Luke 24:10 says, "Now it was Mary Magdalene, Joanna, Mary the mother of James, and the other women with them who told this to the apostles" (NRSV). If "women" means at least two, then there were at least five women, according to Luke.

32. Blomberg, *The Historical Reliability of the Gospels*, 157.

33. Ibid., 190.

34. Richard A. Horsley and Neil Asher Silverman, *The Message and the Kingdom* (New York: Grosset/Putnam, 1997), 57.

35. See the discussion of this issue in detail later in this chapter.

36. "Then he went home; and the crowd came together again, so that they could not even eat. When his family heard it, they went out to restrain him, for people were saying, 'He has gone out of his mind.' And the scribes who came down from Jerusalem said, 'He has Beelzebul, and by the ruler of the demons he casts out demons'" (Mark 3:19–22 NRSV).

37. Robert M. Price, "Jesus at the Vanishing Point," in *The Historical Jesus: Five Views*, eds. James K. Beilby and Paul Rhodes Eddy (Downers Grove, IL: InterVarsity Press, 2009), 67–74.

38. Charles Foster, *The Jesus Inquest* (Nashville, TN: Thomas Nelson, 2010).

39. In the late nineteenth century, scholars began searching the texts of the Hebrew Bible in an effort to identify sources that lay behind what was claimed to be a final, composite, edited text of the Torah or the first five books of the Hebrew Bible. The theory, developed by the German Bible scholar Julius Wellhausen (1844–1918), was known as the Documentary Hypothesis. Scholars thought they could see four major documents or historical sources woven together in the final text of the Torah as it exists today. They dubbed these hypothetical sources *J* for Yahwist (or Jahwist), *E* for Elohist, *D* for Deuteronomist, and *P* for Priestly. Eventually, New Testament scholars began looking for similar sources "behind" or within the texts of the New Testament. The most famous of these is the hypothetical Jesus sayings source scholars now call *Q*.

40. Daniel B. Wallace, "The Synoptic Problem," bible.org, June 2, 2004, https://bible .org/article/synoptic-problem.

41. See also John S. Kloppenborg Verbin, *Excavating Q: The History and Setting of the Sayings Gospel* (Minneapolis: Fortress Press, 2000), 39–48.

42. The basic design of this map came from Jacob Prahlow (http://jprahlow.blogspot .com/2014/02/thinking-about-q.html) but is no longer accessible. Felix Just, SJ

has the same diagram, however, available at http://catholic-resources.org/Bible
/Synoptic_Problem.htm.

43. These are what are known as the "hard readings" in Mark, phrases or
incidents that Matthew and Luke either "soften" or delete altogether. For
example, Mark 6:5–6 says that Jesus could not work a miracle on some
occasions: "He could do no deed of power there, except that he laid his
hands on a few sick people and cured them. And he was amazed at their
unbelief" (NRSV). Matthew changes that to read that Jesus "did not do many
deeds of power there, because of their unbelief" (Matt. 13:58 NRSV). Luke
deletes any mention of Jesus not doing miracles (4:16–30).

44. We know about the writings of Papias (AD 70–163), which are now lost,
because they are quoted in the Christian historian Eusebius's major work,
Ecclesiastical History. Eusebius quotes from Papias the following passage:
"And John the Presbyter also said this, Mark being the interpreter of Peter
whatsoever he recorded he wrote with great accuracy but not however, in the
order in which it was spoken or done by our Lord, for he neither heard nor
followed our Lord, but as before said, he was in company with Peter, who
gave him such instruction as was necessary, but not to give a history of our
Lord's discources: wherefore Mark has not erred in any thing, by writing
some things as he has recorded them; for he was carefully attentive to one
thing, not to pass by any thing that he heard, or to state any thing falsely in
these accounts." Eusebius, *Ecclesiastical History*, trans. C. F. Cruse (Peabody,
MA: Hendrickson Publishers, 1998), 105–6.

45. I've always been fascinated by the Aramaic words in the Gospels. They seemed
to me when I was young, and still today, to be a living link to Jesus across the
ages. When I was a child, my family had a harmonization of the Gospels that
used the old Douai-Rheims translation of the New Testament, the forerunner
of the New American Bible (NAB) and now the New American Bible Revised
Edition (NABRE). I loved the archaic translation used in this book (despite the
thees and thous) because it kept a lot of the grittiness of Jesus' everyday speech
and the semiticisms that were stripped out of modern English translations, such
as the Revised Standard Version (RSV) or the later New International Version
(NIV). Even then, I particularly liked the Aramaic words—*raka, talitha kumi,
Golgotha, Gehenna, hosanna, maranatha, mammon, ephpgatha*. For some reason,
the Aramaic word *raka* (ריקה), pronounced *ray-ka,* in particular resonated
with me: the sound of the word echoed through the millennia, and I could
almost hear Jesus saying it himself. This was a carpenter talking, after all! He
didn't say if you "insult" your "brother or sister"; he said, "whoever says to

his brother, Raka!" I would later learn that this word is actually quite strong, meaning "empty(-headed)" but the equivalent of the English word "bastard," and my twelve-year-old male brain could somehow sense this. It was little clues like this, seemingly trivial or insignificant details, that hinted to me that Jesus was something other than the effeminate caricature I saw on Christmas cards, something far more interesting and even dangerous, someone worth listening to and perhaps even emulating. Here is the text of Matthew 5:21–22 from the NABRE that keeps in the Aramaic words found in the original Greek text: "You have heard that it was said to your ancestors, 'You shall not kill; and whoever kills will be liable to judgment.' But I say to you, whoever is angry with his brother will be liable to judgment, and whoever says to his brother, 'Raqa,' will be answerable to the Sanhedrin, and whoever says, 'You fool,' will be liable to fiery Gehenna." Now, here is how this same passage is translated in the NRSV: "But I say to you that if you are angry with a brother or sister, you will be liable to judgment; and if you insult a brother or sister, you will be liable to the council; and if you say, 'You fool,' you will be liable to the hell of fire."

46. The Biblical scholar Heinrich Julius Holtzmann (1832–1910) first proposed, in 1861, that Matthew and Luke had based their gospels on Mark and an unknown collection of Jesus' sayings. Apparently, the first scholar to nickname this hypothetical source *Q* was another German scholar, Johannes Weiss (1863–1914), in 1890. For a full discussion of the debate over *Q*, see the article "Q" in *Dictionary of Jesus and the Gospels*, eds. Joel B. Green, Scot McKnight and I. Howard Marshall (Downers Grove, IL: InterVarsity Press, 1992), 644–50.

47. Verbin, *Excavating Q*, 56.

48. "[T]here is wide scholarly agreement that Mark was written in the late 60s or just after 70." Raymond E. Brown, *An Introduction to the New Testament* (New York: Doubleday, 1997), 164.

49. "The best date [for Luke] would seem to be 85, *give or take five to ten years*." Ibid., 274.

50. "[T]his makes AD 80–90 the most plausible dating [for Matthew]; but the arguments are not precise, and so at least a decade in either direction must be allowed." Ibid., 217.

51. "Those who think that the Gospel was redacted (edited) by another hand after the main writer composed it may place the body of the Gospel in the 90s and the additions of the redactor ca. 100–110 . . ." Ibid., 334.

52. Josephus, *The Antiquities of the Jews*, 20.9.200, in *The Works of Josephus*, trans. William Whiston (Peabody, MA: Hendrickson Publishers, 1987), 538.

53. *Jewish War*, 6.9.414–18.

54. "A reasonable estimate would be something like 350,000 deaths all told, which would be around one third if the original population was 1 million, or one-half if it was 700,000, or one-fourth if it was 1.4 million." Matthew White, *The Great Big Book of Horrible Things* (New York: WW Norton & Co., 2012), 52. For a fuller account of the Jews' decades-long battle against the Romans, see George C. Brauer, Jr., *Judaea Weeping* (New York: Thomas Y. Crowell Company, 1970).

55. Tacitus, *The Histories*, 5.13.

56. "Now the number of those that were carried captive during this whole war was collected to be ninety-seven thousand; as was the number of those that perished during the whole siege eleven hundred thousand . . ." *Jewish War*, 6.9.420.

57. "But Pilate undertook to bring a current of water to Jerusalem, and did it with the sacred money [from the temple treasury], and derived the origin of the stream from the distance of two hundred furlongs. However the Jews were not pleased with what had been done about this water; and many ten thousands of the people got together, and made a clamor against him, and insisted that he should leave off that design. Some of them also used reproaches, and abused the man, as crowds of such people usually do. So he habited a great number of his soldiers in their habit, who carried daggers under their garments, and sent them to a place where they might surround them. So he bade the Jews himself go away; but they boldly casting reproaches upon him, he gave the soldiers that signal which had been beforehand agreed on; who laid upon them much greater blows than Pilate had commanded them, and equally punished those that were tumultuous, and those that were not, nor did they spare them in the least; and since the people were unwarned, and were caught by men prepared for what they were about, there were a great number of them slain by this means . . ." Josephus, *The Antiquities of the Jews*, 18.2, 60.

58. John A. T. Robinson, *Redating the New Testament* (London: SCM Press, 1976), 13.

59. James G. Crossley, *The Date of Mark's Gospel* (London: T&T Clark International, 2004), 22–24.

60. N. H. Taylor, "Palestinian Christianity and the Caligula Crisis. Part II. The Markan Eschatological Discourse," *Journal for the Study of the New Testament* 18, no. 62 (October 1996): 13–40.

61. Crossley, *The Date of Mark's Gospel*, 22–24.

62. Ibid., 81.

63. Bart Ehrman, *Jesus, Interrupted* (New York: HarperOne, 2009), 103. In this

passage, at least, Ehrman ignores the famous ending of John's gospel where the author at least hints that he was an eyewitness: "This is the disciple who is testifying to these things and has written them, and we know that his testimony is true" (21:24 NRSV).

64. Bart Ehrman, *How Jesus Became God* (New York: HarperOne, 2014), 92.

65. Mark D. Roberts, *Can We Trust the Gospels?* (Wheaton, IL: Crossway Books, 2007), 40.

66. James M. Arlandson, "Did Some Disciples Take Notes During Jesus' Ministry?" bible.org, https://bible.org/seriespage/8-did-some-disciples-take-notes-during -jesus-ministry.

67. Alan Millard, *Reading and Writing in the Time of Jesus* (London: Sheffield Academic Press, 2001), 223. Quoted by Arlandson, "Did Some Disciples Take Notes During Jesus' Ministry?"

68. Robert J. Miller, ed., *The Complete Gospels* (San Francisco: HarperSanFrancisco, 1994), 305–22.

69. "Mark was probably the first gospel to be written. Scholars have long thought it was produced about thirty-five or forty years after Jesus' death, possibly around 65 or 70 CE." Ehrman, *Jesus, Interrupted,* 23.

70. Richard Bauckham, *Jesus and the Eyewitnesses* (Grand Rapids, MI: Eerdmans Publishing, 2006), 433.

71. Ibid., 240.

72. Ibid., 241.

73. Eusebius, *Ecclesiastical History* 3.39.15–16, as quoted and translated by Bauckham, *Jesus and the Eyewitnesses,* 203.

74. Irenaeus, *Letter to Florinus,* in Eusebius, *Ecclesiastical History* 5.20.5–6, quoted and translated by Bauckham, *Jesus and the Eyewitnesses,* 35.

75. Bauckham, *Jesus and the Eyewitnesses,* 264.

76. Ibid., 266.

77. Ibid., 472.

78. Some experts in John's gospel, such as Raymond Brown, argue that John the apostle may have been a primary *source* for the gospel but that it may have been put into its final form by a later editor. According to Brown, the gospel text itself appears to point to an eyewitness source. "This testimony has been given by an eyewitness, and his testimony is true" (John 19:35). Translation in Brown, *An Introduction to the New Testament,* 369.

79. Some famous New Testament scholars, however, such as F. F. Bruce and John A. T. Robinson, do believe that John the apostle likely wrote at least parts of the gospel that bears his name. See F. F. Bruce, *The New Testament*

Documents: Are They Reliable? (Grand Rapids, MI: William B. Eerdmans, 1981), 46–7; and John A. T. Robinson, *Redating the New Testament* (Eugene, OR: Wipf and Stock, 1976), 310.

80. F. F. Bruce, *The New Testament Documents: Are They Reliable?* (Grand Rapids, MI: William B. Eerdmans, 1981), 46–7.

81. David Flusser, *The Sage from Galilee: Rediscovering Jesus' Genius* (Grand Rapids, MI: Wm. B. Eerdmans, 2007), 2–3. First English edition originally published as *Jesus* (Jerusalem: Magnes Press, 1997).

Chapter 2: Liar, Lunatic . . . or Legend?

1. James Tabor in particular speculates that, after the sudden and brutal execution of John the Baptist by Herod Antipas, Jesus knew that his life was in danger—and thus decided to seek a temporary haven in the pagan cultic areas to the north, "surely the last place anyone would think to look for him." See James D. Tabor, *The Jesus Dynasty* (New York: Simon & Schuster, 2006), 177.

2. *The Anchor Bible Dictionary,* vol. 2, s.v. "Ebionites" (New York: Doubleday, 1992), 260–61.

3. "Trypho: But if some one, knowing that this is so, after he recognises that this man is Christ, and has believed in and obeys Him, wishes, however, to observe these [institutions], will he be saved?

"Justin: In my opinion, Trypho, such an one will be saved, if he does not strive in every way to persuade other men—I mean those Gentiles who have been circumcised from error by Christ, to observe the same things as himself, telling them that they will not be saved unless they do so. This you did yourself at the commencement of the discourse, when you declared that I would not be saved unless I observe these institutions.

"Trypho: Why then have you said, 'In my opinion, such an one will be saved,' unless there are some who affirm that such will not be saved?

"Justin: There are such people, Trypho, and these do not venture to have any intercourse with or to extend hospitality to such persons; but I do not agree with them. But if some, through weak-mindedness, wish to observe such institutions as were given by Moses, from which they expect some virtue, but which we believe were appointed by reason of the hardness of the people's hearts, along with their hope in this Christ, and [wish to perform] the eternal and natural acts of righteousness and piety, yet choose to live with the Christians and the faithful, as I said before, not inducing them either to be circumcised like themselves, or to keep the Sabbath, or to observe any other such ceremonies, then I hold that we ought to join ourselves to such, and associate with them in all things as kinsmen and brethren. But if, Trypho, some of your race, who say they believe in this Christ, compel those Gentiles who believe in this Christ to live in all respects according to the law given by Moses, or choose not to associate so intimately with them, I in like manner do not approve of them. But I believe that even those, who have been persuaded by them to observe the legal dispensation along with their confession of God in Christ, shall probably be saved."

Justin Martyr, "Chapter 47. Justin communicates with Christians who observe the law. Not a few Catholics do otherwise," *Dialogue with Trypho*, trans. Marcus Dods and George Reith. From *Ante-Nicene Fathers*, vol. 1, eds. Alexander Roberts, James Donaldson, and A. Cleveland Coxe (Buffalo, NY: Christian Literature Publishing Co., 1885). Rev. and ed. Kevin Knight for New Advent, newadvent.org, http://www.newadvent.org/fathers/01283.htm.

4. Irenaeus, *Adversus haereses*, 1.26, trans. Alexander Roberts and William Rambaut. From *Ante-Nicene Fathers*, vol. 1, eds. Alexander Roberts, James Donaldson, and A. Cleveland Coxe (Buffalo, NY: Christian Literature Publishing Co., 1885). Rev. and ed. Kevin Knight for New Advent, newadvent.org, http://www.newadvent.org/fathers/0103126.htm.

5. Contemporary scholars who have written extensively on unorthodox or alternative versions of Christianity in the early centuries of the first millennium include Elaine Pagels, Bart Ehrman, James M. Robinson, and Robert Funk.

6. A good example is John P. Meier's discussion of the historical value of apocryphal gospels. "I have spent so much time on [John Dominic] Crossan's claim of independent, early tradition in the *Gospel of Peter* because it is perhaps the best-argued case for a large piece of pre-Synoptic tradition in an apocryphal gospel. If the claim fails, as I think it does, not much should be expected from the other apocryphal gospels." John P. Meier, *A Marginal Jew*, vol. 1 (New York: Doubleday, 1991), 118.

7. John Dominic Crossan, *The Historical Jesus* (San Francisco: HarperSanFrancisco, 1991), 427–34.

8. Thomas Spidlik, trans., *Drinking from the Hidden Fountain: A Patristic Breviary* (Kalamazoo, MI: Cistercian Publications, 1994), found at http://www.rc.net /wcc/readings/fathers7.htm.

9. Augustine, *On Christian Doctrine*, 3.5, trans. D. W. Robertson, Jr. (Indianapolis: The Bobbs-Merrill Company, 1958), 83–84.

10. "Letters of Jerome" (no. 112) in *A Select Library of Nicene and Post-Nicene Fathers of the Christian Church*, trans. Henry Wace and Philip Schaff (Oxford: Parker; New York: Christian Literature Co., 1890–1900).

11. *Summa Theologica*, 1.1.10., *The Summa Theologica of St. Thomas Aquinas*, 2nd ed., trans. Fathers of the English Dominican Province (1920). Available online at: http://www.newadvent.org/summa/1001.htm#article10.

12. The problem with harmonization, from the point of view of biblical scholars, is that it can miss the richness of the individual gospels themselves—and the emphases and details that the individual authors were actually trying to communicate. Looking at each gospel individually, for example, reveals unique understandings of who Jesus was and what he was trying to achieve. In other words, you can gain a fuller understanding of Jesus by studying the individual gospels—especially because they emphasize different aspects of Jesus' mission and teaching—than you might reading a harmonization such as the *Diatessaron* or *The Life of Christ in Stereo*.

13. One of the best Christian authors on this topic is Mike Licona, associate professor of theology at Houston Baptist University and author of many books on Christian apologetics. He touches on the issues involving discrepancies in the gospel accounts in his book on the resurrection, Gary Habermas and Mike Licona, *The Case for the Resurrection of Jesus* (Grand Rapids, MI: Kregel Publications, 2004).

14. Bart Ehrman, *Jesus, Interrupted* (New York: HarperOne, 2009), 23–52.

15. "Should we, therefore, accept the opposite opinion . . . that all the contents of the Gospels must be assumed fictitious until they are proven genuine? No, that also is too extreme a viewpoint and would not be applied in other fields. When, for example, one tries to build up facts from the accounts of pagan historians, judgment often has to be given not in the light of any external confirmation—which is sometimes, but by no means always, available—but on the basis of historical deductions and arguments which attain nothing better than probability. The same applies to the Gospels. Their contents need not be assumed fictitious until they are proved authentic. But they have to be subjected to the usual standards of historical persuasiveness." Michael Grant, *Jesus: An Historian's Review of the Gospels* (New York: Charles Scribner's Sons, 1977), 201.

16. "It is now some years since I detected how many were the false beliefs that I had from my earliest youth admitted as true, and how doubtful was everything I had since constructed on this basis; and from that time I was convinced that I must once for all seriously undertake to rid myself of all the opinions which I had formerly accepted, and commence to build anew from the foundation, if I wanted to establish any firm and permanent structure in the sciences." René Descartes, *Meditations on the First Philosophy*, 1, trans.

Elizabeth S. Haldane and G.R.T. Ross, Great Books of the Western World, vol. 31 (Chicago: Encyclopedia Britannica, 1952), 75.

17. "We distinguish by the name *evangelical mythus* a narrative relating directly or indirectly to Jesus, which may be considered not as the expression of a fact, but as the product of an idea of his earliest followers; such a narrative being mythical in proportion as it exhibits this character." David Friedrich Strauss, *The Life of Jesus, Critically Examined,* trans. George Eliot (New York: Cosimo Classics, 2009), 86. This influential book was originally published in Germany in 1840.

18. Reimarus believed that, after the execution of Jesus, the apostles, impoverished and ignorant but ambitious peasants, decided to perpetrate an elaborate fraud in order to convince Jesus' gullible followers that he had been raised from the dead: the apostles simply stole the body from the tomb and disposed of it in an unknown location. "Above all things, it was necessary to get rid of the body of Jesus as speedily as possible, in order that they might say he had arisen and ascended into heaven, and would promptly return from thence with great power and glory . . . when it became known that the body of Jesus was gone, they pretended to be full of astonishment, and ignorant of any resurrection, and proceeded with others to the spot in order to survey the empty tomb. And yet, it was too soon to make their assertion. They wait full fifty days before they attempt it, so that by-and-by the time might be past for an examination of the body, and for requiring them to produce openly the Jesus who had arisen. They wait fifty days that they may be able the more confidently to insist that they have seen him here and there, that he had been with them, had spoken to them, had eaten with them, and, lastly, had parted from them, and had ascended into heaven that he might soon return in glory." Hermann Samuel Reimarus, *Fragments,* English translator unknown (London: Forgotten Books, 2012), 94–5.

19. "The work went through 13 editions in the year following its publication, reaching its 61st edition by 1921." Jennifer Stevens, *The Historical Jesus and the Literary Imagination, 1860–1920* (Liverpool, UK: Liverpool University Press, 2010), 74.

20. "In the late 19th century, Ernest Renan and others proposed that the Ashkenazi Jews of Europe had fled from Khazaria. This theory has been used by anti-Semites to suggest that European Jews stem from a barbaric Asiatic race, and to disprove their ancestral connection to the land of Israel." Yori Yanover, "Study Finds No Evidence of Khazar Origin for Ashkenazi Jews," *The Jewish Press,* February 23, 2014, http://www.jewishpress.com/news/breaking-news/study -finds-no-evidence-of-khazar-origin-for-ashkenazi-jews/2014/02/23/.

21. Ernest Renan, *The Life of Jesus* (Cleveland: World Publishing Company, 1941), 117.

22. Ibid., 210.

23. Ibid.

24. Susannah Heschel, *The Aryan Jesus: Christian Theologians and the Bible in Nazi Germany* (Princeton: Princeton University Press, 2008), 35.

25. Renan, *The Life of Jesus,* 210.

26. Ibid., 209.

27. Ibid., 201.

28. Ibid., 209.

29. Ibid., 206–7.

30. Ibid., 205.

31. Albrecht Ritschl, "Instruction in the Christian Religion," *Albert Ritschl: Three Essays,* trans. Philip Hefner (Philadelphia: Fortress, 1972), 222; in Gregory Dawes, ed., *The Historical Jesus Quest* (Louisville: Westminster John Knox Press, 1999), 154.

32. William Temple, *Readings in St. John's Gospel* (London: Macmillan, 1945), xxiv; quoted in James D. G. Dunn, *Jesus Remembered* (Grand Rapids, MI: Eerdmans, 2003), 49.

33. Johannes Weiss, *Jesus' Proclamation of the Kingdom of God* (1892), trans. Richard H. Hiers and David L. Holland, Lives of Jesus Series (Philadelphia: Fortress, 1971); reprinted in Dawes, *The Historical Jesus Quest,* 180.

34. Albert Schweitzer, *The Quest of the Historical Jesus,* trans. W. Montgomery (London: Adam and Charles Black, 1911), 658.

35. Martin Kähler, *The So-Called Historical Jesus and the Historic Biblical Christ,* trans. Carl E. Braaten (Philadelphia: Fortress, 1964), 46.

36. James D. G. Dunn, *Jesus Remembered* (Grand Rapids: Eerdmans, 2003), 72.

37. Karl Barth, *Epistle to the Romans,* quoted in Dunn, *Jesus Remembered,* 73.

38. Rudolf Bultmann, *Jesus and the Word* (New York: Scribner, 1935), 8, quoted in Dunn, 75.

39. I am grateful to the Early Christian Writings website (www. earlychristianwritings.com), created by the entertaining agnostic scholar Peter Kirby, for its typology of historical Jesus research. I follow it quite closely here, even though I changed the names of some of the models. I also am grateful for the discussion of these scholars in Ben Witherington III's magisterial history of the third quest, *The Jesus Quest: The Third Search for the Jew of Nazareth* (Downers Grove, IL: InterVarsity Press, 1995). Some of the scholars mentioned can actually be placed in more than one of the categories.

40. Ehrman, *Did Jesus Exist?,* 313.

41. Ibid., 331, emphasis added.

42. Paula Fredriksen, *Jesus of Nazareth: King of the Jews* (New York: Random House, 1999), 266.

43. Hermann Samuel Reimarus, *Fragments,* English translator unknown (London: Forgotten Books, 2012).

44. Joel Carmichael, *The Death of Jesus* (New York: Horizon Press, 1982).

45. Brandon was one of the first scholars to propose that Jesus was really a violent revolutionary. His book on the subject is still considered a classic in the field, albeit dated. S. G. F. Brandon, *Jesus and the Zealots* (New York: Charles Scribner's, 1967).

46. Robert Eisenman is the author of a large study of James entitled *James: The Brother of Jesus* (New York: Penguin, 1997).

47. Reza Aslan, *Zealot: The Life and Times of Jesus of Nazareth* (New York: Random House, 2013).

48. Brandon, *Jesus and the Zealots*, 283.

49. Richard A. Horsley and Neil Asher Silberman, *The Message and the Kingdom* (New York: Putnam, 1997), 57.

50. Horsley doesn't use the term "community organizer," but that appears to be what he has in mind: "Thus through healings, preachings, and banquets, Jesus began to catalyze a movement that envisioned the independence of Israel in its village communities." Horsley and Silberman, *The Message and the Kingdom*, 57.

51. Ibid., 58.

52. Ibid., 57.

53. "For many churches, the Roman Empire was no longer the main enemy but rather the early environment in which Christianity would have to exist peacefully until the second coming of Christ. Indeed, so pervasive was the eventual acceptance of empire that the image of Christ was slowly transformed from that of an alternative king to that of a model emperor—presiding over a shadow government in heaven and showing by example how things should be done on earth." Ibid., 225.

54. Brandon, *Jesus and the Zealots*, 283.

55. Ibid., 226.

56. The Jesus Seminar was organized by Robert Funk and John Dominic Crossan, under the auspices of the Westar Institute. The summary of the Jesus Seminar conclusions can be found at the Westar Institute's website, http://www.westarinstitute.org/projects/the-jesus-seminar/.

57. John Dominic Crossan, *The Historical Jesus: The Life of a Mediterranean Jewish Peasant* (San Francisco: HarperSanFrancisco, 1991), 421.

58. Ibid., 422.

59. Geza Vermes, *Jesus the Jew: An Historian's Reading of the Gospels* (Minneapolis: Fortress Press, 1981), 35.

60. Shmuley Boteach, *Kosher Jesus* (Jerusalem: Gefen Publishing, 2012).

61. Marcus J. Borg, *Jesus: The Life, Teachings, and Relevance of a Religious Revolutionary* (New York: HarperOne, 2006), 127.

62. N. T. Wright, *Jesus and the Victory of God* (Minneapolis: Fortress Press, 1996), 593.

63. Ibid., 594.

64. Ibid, 595.

65. Ibid.

66. Ibid., 596.

67. Ibid.

68. N. T. Wright, *The Challenge of Jesus* (Downers Grove, IL: InterVarsity Press, 1999), 92.

69. Ibid., 90.

70. There is a significant body of scholarly debate on the meaning of the Greek word *hilasterion* and its cognates, whether it refers to a "propitiation" or appeasement of an angry deity or an "expiation" or cleansing of sins. Interested readers should refer to Millard J. Erickson's summary of the debate in his *Christian Theology*, 2nd ed., (Grand Rapids, MI: Baker Books, 1998), 827–40.

71. "If it be necessary, therefore, as it appears, that the heavenly kingdom be made up of men, and this cannot be effected unless the aforesaid satisfaction be made, which none but God can make and none but man ought to make, it is necessary for the God-man to make it." *Cur Deus Homo?* 2.6.

72. "Few other doctrines go to the heart of the Christian faith like the Atonement. Congregations sing at the top of their lungs: 'My sin, not in part but the whole, has been nailed to the cross, so I bear it no more, praise the Lord, praise the Lord, O my soul!' ("It Is Well with My Soul"). The priestly work of Christ separates Christianity from Judaism and Islam. Not surprisingly, the Cross has become the symbol for our faith. Still, God's work on the Cross leaves us with plenty of questions. In fact, there have always been a few Christians who question whether we need the Atonement, including, in recent years, some evangelicals who have challenged the dominant understanding of Christ's death on the Cross as the substitute for our sins. *At stake is nothing less than the essence of Christianity.* Historically understood, Christ's Atonement gives hope to Christians in their sin and in their suffering. If we have any assurance of salvation, it is because of Christ's Atonement; if any joy, it flows from Christ's work on the Cross. The

Atonement protects us from our native tendency to replace religion with morality and God's grace with legalism. Apart from Christ's atoning work, we would be forever guilty, ashamed, and condemned before God." Mark Dever, "Nothing But the Blood," *Christianity Today,* May 1, 2006, http://www.christianitytoday .com/ct/2006/may/9.29.html, emphasis added.

73. See David Neff, "Your Atonement Is Too Small," *Christianity Today,* May 20, 2008, http://www.christianitytoday.com/ct/2008/may/27.69.html.

74. E. P. Sanders, as summarized by Ben Witherington III, *The Jesus Quest* (Downers Grove, IL: InterVarsity Press, 1995), 126. See also E. P. Sanders, *The Historical Figure of Jesus* (New York: Penguin Books, 1993), 213.

75. New Testament scholars disagree about whether Jesus intended his new community to be a reform movement within Judaism or to include Gentiles from the beginning. Evangelical scholar Craig Evans puts it this way: "Did Jesus intend to found the Christian church? This interesting question can be answered in the affirmative and in the negative. It depends on what precisely is being asked. If by church one means an organization and a people that stand outside of Israel, the answer is no. If by a community of disciples committed to the restoration of Israel and the conversion and instruction of the Gentiles, then the answer is yes. . . . Jesus did not wish to lead his disciples out of Israel, but to train followers who will lead Israel, who will bring renewal to Israel, and who will instruct Gentiles in the way of the Lord. Jesus longed for the fulfillment of the promises and the prophecies, a fulfillment that would bless Israel and the nations alike. . . . The estrangement of the church from Israel was not the result of Jesus' teaching or Paul's teaching. Rather, the parting of the ways, as it has been called in recent years, was the result of a long process." Craig Evans, *From Jesus to the Church: The First Christian Generation* (Louisville, KY: Westminster John Knox Press, 2014), 18, 36.

76. See Martin Luther's comments on the role of the Christian community for salvation: Martin Luther, "Sermon for the Early Christmas Service; Luke 2:15–20," in *Luther's Works,* American ed., eds. Hans J. Hillerbrand and Helmut T. Lehmann (Philadelphia: Concordia Publishing House/Fortress Press, 1974), 52:39–40.

Chapter 3: Are the Gospels Forgeries?

1. Daniel Wallace, "Earliest Manuscript of the New Testament Discovered?" Dallas Theological Seminary, February 9, 2012, http://www.dts.edu/read /wallace-new-testament-manscript-first-century/.

2. "History of Codex Sinaiticus," Codexsinaiticus.org, accessed March 27, 2015, http://codexsinaiticus.org/en/codex/history.aspx.

3. Herman C. Hoskier, *Codex B and Its Allies: A Study and an Indictment, Part II* (London: Bernard Quaritch, 1914), 1. Available online at: http://catalog.hathitrust.org/Record/001930884.

4. Kurt Aland and Barbara Aland, *The Text of the New Testament,* 2nd ed., trans. Erroll F. Rhodes (Grand Rapids, MI: William B. Eerdmans, 1989), 87.

5. View the manuscript as scanned by the Codex Sinaiticus Project, http://codex sinaiticus.org/en/manuscript.aspx.

6. Kurt Aland, Matthew Black, Carlo M. Martini, Bruce M. Metzger and Allen Wikgren, eds. *The Greek New Testament,* 3rd ed. (Stuttgart, Germany: United Bible Societies, 1983), xix.

7. Ibid., xxxii.

8. Kurt Aland and Barbara Aland, *The Text of the New Testament,* 163.

9. Aland, et al., *The Greek New Testament,* xii.

10. The editors actually say, "D shows that there is a very high degree of doubt concerning the reading selected for the text," Ibid., xiii.

11. Readers interested in exploring the fascinating world of textual criticism are referred to two books that are classics: Kurt Aland and Barbara Aland, *The Text of the New Testament,* 2nd ed., trans. Erroll F. Rhodes (Grand Rapids, MI: William B. Eerdmans, 1989); and Bruce M. Metzger, *The Text of the New Testament,* 3rd ed. (New York: Oxford University Press, 1992). One of the nice features of the Alands' book is that it has many more photographs of the manuscripts.

12. For a fuller list of the dates of manuscripts for ancient documents, see Joseph M. Holden and Norman Geisler, *The Popular Handbook of Archaeology and the Bible* (Eugene, OR: Harvest House, 2013), 129.

13. Ibid., 118–19.

14. Bart Ehrman, *Misquoting Jesus: The Story Behind Who Changed the Bible and Why* (New York: HarperOne, 2007), 10. Quoted in Daniel B. Wallace, ed., *Revisiting the Corruption of the New Testament* (Grand Rapids, MI: Kregel Publications, 2011), 24.

15. I got the idea for this table from a list of New Testament textual variants in *Wikipedia. Wikipedia,* s.v. "Textual variants in the New Testament," last modified April 6, 2015, https://en.wikipedia.org/wiki/Textual_variants_in_the _New_Testament.

16. Bart D. Ehrman, *Misquoting Jesus* (New York: HarperOne, 2007), 208.

17. Daniel Wallace, transcribed interview with author, January 29, 2014.

18. Georg Gäbel, interview with author, February 10, 2014.

19. Bart Ehrman, *The New Testament: An Historical Introduction to the Early Christian Writings* (New York: Oxford University Press, 2003), 481. Cited in Daniel B. Wallace, ed., *Revisiting the Corruption of the New Testament* (Grand Rapids, MI: Kregel, 2011), 24.

20. Ehrman, *Misquoting Jesus*, 10, quoted in Wallace, *Revisiting the Corruption of the New Testament*, 24.

21. Daniel Wallace, transcribed interview with author, January 29, 2014.

22. "The vast majority of these mistakes are completely insignificant, showing us nothing more than that scribes in antiquity could spell no better than most people today." Ehrman, *Jesus, Interrupted* (New York: HarperOne, 2009), 184.

23. Ibid., 185.

Chapter 4: Have Archaeologists Found Jesus' House?

1. I am grateful to James Tabor's controversial but fascinating book, *The Jesus Dynasty: The Hidden History of Jesus, His Royal Family, and the Birth of Christianity* (New York: Simon & Schuster, 2006), for making me think about this episode in the writings of Josephus and how it related to life in Nazareth around the time of Jesus' birth.

2. The history of the struggle between devout Jews and their pagan rulers is recounted in 1 and 2 Maccabees, historical books that are part of the Roman Catholic and Eastern Orthodox canon but considered apocryphal books in most Protestant Bibles. In 164 BC, a Greek ruler of the Seleucid empire, Antiochus IV Epiphanes, decreed that all Jewish religious observances were to be banned, possession of the Torah a capital crime, and insisted that the Jews must sacrifice to Greek idols. An elderly priest named Mattathias, from the village of Modi'in near Jerusalem, triggered a national revolt when he killed a Hellenistic Jew who volunteered to perform the sacrifice in Mattathias's village. Mattathias and his five sons, who became known as the Maccabees, were eventually victorious and established an independent Jewish state, ruled by high priests, that lasted a century until the Roman general Pompey invaded in 63 BC.

3. Josephus, *Jewish War* 4.55, *The Works of Josephus*, trans. William Whiston (Peabody, MA: Hendrickson Publishers, 1987).

4. Josephus, *Jewish Antiquities* 17:285–98 and *Jewish War* 2.66–75.

5. The fourth century Christian writer Epiphanius of Salamis (310–403) mentions a pre-Christian Jewish sect called the Nasaraioi. "Next I shall undertake to describe the sect after the Hemerobaptists, called the sect of

the Nasaraeans. They are Jews by nationality, from Gileaditis, Bashanitis and the Transjordan as I have been told, but descendants of Israel himself. This sect practices Judaism in all respects and have scarcely any beliefs beyond the ones that I have mentioned." Epiphanius of Salamis, *The Panarion* 1.18, trans. Frank Williams, http://www.masseiana.org/panarion _bk1.htm#18. See also *The Anchor Bible Dictionary*, s.v. "Nazarenes," vol. 1, ed. David Noel Freedman (New York: Doubleday, 1992), 1049.

6. See the Itinerarium Burdigalense online at http://www.christusrex.org/www1 /ofm/pilgr/bord/10Bord01Lat.html.

7. Bargil Pixner, *With Jesus Through Galilee According to the Fifth Gospel* (Rosh Pina, Israel: Corazin Publishing, 1992), 15.

8. The photographs are available online at www.BiblePlaces.com.

9. Mark Twain, *The Innocents Abroad* (Connecticut: American Publishing Co., 1869), 538.

10. Bellarmino Bagatti, *Excavations in Nazareth. I: From the Beginning Till the XII Century. II: From the XII Century until Today,* trans. E. Hoad (Jerusalem: Franciscan Printing Press, 1969), 74, cited by Gregory C. Jenks, "The Quest for the Historical Nazareth," academia.edu (School of Theology, Charles Sturt University, 2013), http://www.academia.edu/3988852/The_Quest_for _the_Historical_Nazareth, 7.

11. This quote from Frank R. Zindler appears as an endorsement on the back cover of René Salm's *The Myth of Nazareth: The Invented Town of Jesus* (Cranford, NJ: American Atheist Press, 2008).

12. "The Tel Dan Inscription: The First Historical Evidence of King David from the Bible," Bible History Daily, September 17, 2014, http://www .biblicalarchaeology.org/daily/biblical-artifacts/artifacts-and-the-bible /the-tel-dan-inscription-the-first-historical-evidence-of-the-king-david -bible-story/.

13. Yardenna Alexandre, "The Archaeological Finds in the Property of the Chemin Neuf Mary of Nazareth International Centre: Preliminary Report," Israel Antiquities Authority, unpublished manuscript, 3. See also "For the Very First Time: A Residential Building from the Time of Jesus was Exposed in the Heart of Nazareth," Israel Antiquities Authority, December 21, 2009, http://www .antiquities.org.il/article_eng.aspx?sec_id=25&subj_id=240&id=1638.

14. Ibid., 4.

15. Ibid., 5.

16. "In the Early Roman period the village of Nazareth was located at the heart of the Jewish settlement in the Lower Galilee, with the large city of Sepphoris

lying 5 km to the west, whilst the new city of Tiberias lay about 25 km to the north-east. Around Nazareth were several villages, including Cana, Iksal, and Yafia. This fact can explain why Nazareth was not mentioned by Josephus in the description of preparations and the events of the Great Revolt." Ibid., 5.

17. Ken Dark, "Has Jesus' Nazareth House Been Found?" *Biblical Archaeological Review* 41:02, March/April 2015, http://members.bib-arch.org/publication.asp ?PubID=BSBA&Volume=41&Issue=2&ArticleID=7.

18. Ibid.

19. Arculfus, *The Pilgrimage of Arculfus in the Holy Land: About the Year A.D. 670*, trans. James Rose MacPherson (London: Palestine Pilgrims' Text Society, 1889), 83.

20. Larry W. Hurtado, "The Nazareth Home of Jesus?" Larry Hurtado's Blog, February 19, 2005, https://larryhurtado.wordpress.com/2015/02/19/the -nazareth-home-of-jesus/.

21. "The artifacts found in the first-century house include broken cooking pots, a spindle whorl (used in spinning thread) and limestone vessels, suggesting possibly a family lived there, the archaeologists said. The limestone vessels suggest a Jewish family lived in the house, because Jewish beliefs held that limestone could not become impure. If a Jewish family lived here it would support the idea that this could have been Jesus' house." Owen Jarus, "Jesus' House? 1st-Century Structure May Be Where He Grew Up," March 1, 2015, http://www.livescience.com/49997-jesus-house-possibly-found-nazareth.html.

22. Dark, "Has Jesus' Nazareth House Been Found?" *Biblical Archaeological Review*.

23. Israel Finkelstein and Neil Asher Silberman, *The Bible Unearthed: Archaeology's New Vision of Ancient Israel and the Origins of Its Sacred Texts* (New York: Simon & Schuster, 2001), 62.

24. For a more conservative response to Finkelstein and Silberman, see K. A. Kitchen, *On the Reliability of the Old Testament* (Grand Rapids, MI: William B. Eerdmans, 2003).

25. Lawrence Mykytiuk, "Archaeology Confirms 50 Real People in the Bible," *Biblical Archaeology Review*, March/April 2014, http://www.biblicalarchaeology .org/daily/people-cultures-in-the-bible/people-in-the-bible/50-people-in-the-bible -confirmed-archaeologically/, 46–47.

26. Ken Dark, "Early Roman-Period Nazareth and the Sisters of Nazareth Convent," *Antiquaries Journal* 92 (2012): 37–64.

27. Dark, "Early Roman-Period Nazareth," 1–28.

28. See Ofira Koopmans, "Synagogue Where Jesus Likely Preached Uncovered in Israel," *Haaretz,* December 22, 2014, http://www.haaretz.com/life/ archaeology/1.633141.

29. Dina Avshalom-Gorni and Arfan Najar, "Preliminary Report," Israel Antiquities Authority, June 8, 2013, http://www.hadashot-esi.org.il/report_detail_eng.aspx ?id=2304.

30. Ronny Reich, "Caiaphas Name Inscribed on Bone Boxes," *Biblical Archaeology Review* 18:05, September/October 1992, http://members.bib-arch.org /publication.asp?PubID=BSBA&Volume=18&Issue=5&ArticleID=2.

31. British barrister Charles Foster provides an excellent summary of the history of Roman crucifixion practices and the various controversies over whether Jesus was tied and/or nailed to a stake or a cross. See Charles Foster, *The Jesus Inquest* (Nashville: Thomas Nelson, 2010), 813–91.

32. "The story of Jesus' trial and crucifixion is a pastiche of verses from scripture, and has nothing to do with 'history remembered,'" Earl Doherty, *Jesus: Neither God Nor Man* (Ottawa: Age of Reason Publications, 2009), 388.

33. Hershel Shanks, "New Analysis of the Crucified Man," *Biblical Archaeology Review* 11:6, November/December (1985): 20–21. See also Vassilios Tzaferis, "Crucifixion—The Archaeological Evidence," *Biblical Archaeological Review* 11:1 (1985): 44–53.

34. Rami Arav and John J. Rousseau, *Jesus and His World: An Archaeological and Cultural Dictionary* (Minneapolis, MN: Augsburg Fortress Press, 1995), 27.

35. Ibid., 25–29.

36. Jerome Murphy-O'Connor, OP, "Capernaum," *The Holy Land: An Oxford Archaeological Guide from Earlier Times to 1700,* 5th ed. (New York: Oxford University Press, 2008), 4663–763.

37. Richard Bailey, *Jesus & the Forgotten City* (Grand Rapids, MI: Baker Book House, 1991), 70–71.

38. Joseph M. Holden and Norman Geisler, *The Popular Handbook of Archaeology and the Bible* (Eugene, OR: Harvest House, 2013), 347.

39. Arav and Rousseau, *Jesus and His World*, 225–27.

40. Holden and Geisler, *The Popular Handbook of Archaeology and the Bible*, 358.

41. John Dominic Crossan and Jonathan L. Reed, *Excavating Jesus: Beneath the Stones, Behind the Texts* (San Francisco: HarperSanFrancisco, 2001), 108–117.

42. Arav and Rousseau, *Jesus and His World*, 170–71.

43. Richard A. Horsley and Neil Asher Silberman, *The Message and the Kingdom* (New York: Putnam, 1997), 76.

44. James D. Tabor, *The Jesus Dynasty* (New York: Simon & Schuster, 2006), 195.

45. Arav and Rousseau, *Jesus and His World*, 170.

46. John Dominic Crossan, *Who Killed Jesus?* (San Francisco: HarperSanFrancisco, 1996), 64.

47. Crossan and Reed, *Excavating Jesus*, 211.

48. Crossan, *Who Killed Jesus?*, 65.

49. S. G. F. Brandon, *Jesus and the Zealots* (New York: Charles Scribner's Sons, 1967), 338.

Chapter 5: Did the Church Invent the Idea of a Suffering Messiah?

1. "The tablet, probably found near the Dead Sea in Jordan according to some scholars who have studied it, is a rare example of a stone with ink writings from that era—in essence, a Dead Sea Scroll on stone. . . . [I]ts authenticity has so far faced no challenge, so its role in helping to understand the roots of Christianity in the devastating political crisis faced by the Jews of the time seems likely to increase." Ethan Bronner, "Ancient Tablet Ignites Debate on Messiah and Resurrection," *New York Times*, July 6, 2008.

2. Israel Knohl, "The Messiah Son of Joseph: 'Gabriel's Revelation' and the Birth of a New Messianic Model," *Biblical Archaeology Review* 34:05, September/October 2008, 58–62.

3. Hillel Halkin, "Blurry 'Vision of Gabriel,'" *New York Sun*, July 8, 2008, http://www.nysun.com/opinion/blurry-vision-of-gabriel/81384/.

4. Rudolf Karl Bultmann, "Jesus and the Eschatological Kingdom," in Roger A. Johnson, ed., *Rudolf Bultmann: Interpreting Faith for the Modern Era* (Minneapolis: Augsburg Fortress Press, 1991), 127, emphasis added.

5. David Klinghoffer, *Why the Jews Rejected Jesus* (New York: Doubleday, 2005), 63.

6. Reza Aslan, *Zealot: The Life and Times of Jesus of Nazareth* (New York: Random House, 2013), 166.

7. Bart D. Ehrman, *How Jesus Became God: The Exaltation of a Jewish Preacher from Galilee* (New York: HarperOne, 2014), 115.

8. Interview with the author, June 5, 2014. Also see Israel Knohl, *The Messiah before Jesus: The Suffering Servant of the Dead Sea Scrolls* (Berkeley: University of California Press, 2000), 2.

9. Knohl, *The Messiah before Jesus*, 2.

10. Ibid.

11. "The [sensus plenior] is the deeper meaning, intended by God but not clearly intended by the human author, that is seen to exist in the words of Scripture when they are studied in the light of further revelation or of development in the understanding of revelation." Raymond E. Brown and Sandra M. Schneiders, "Hermeneutics," *The New Jerome Biblical Commentary*, eds. Raymond E. Brown, SS; Joseph A. Fitzmyer, SJ; and Roland E. Murphy, O.Carm. (Englewood Cliffs, NJ: Prentice Hall, 1990), 1157.

12. Klinghoffer, *Why the Jews Rejected Jesus*, 36.

13. "The story of Jesus's triumphal entry into Jerusalem has long been recognized by scholars as historically problematic." Ehrman, *Did Jesus Exist?*, 201.

14. Ehrman, *Did Jesus Exist?*, 202.

15. Ibid.

16. Ibid., 202–3.

17. The phrase "Son of God" is not found in many early Greek manuscripts and is therefore often put in brackets in many modern translations.

18. The three predictions are: (1) "Then he began to teach them that the Son of Man must undergo great suffering, and be rejected by the elders, the chief priests, and the scribes, and be killed, and after three days rise again" (Mark 8:31 = Matt. 16:21–28 = Luke 9:22–27); (2) "They went on from there and passed through Galilee. He did not want anyone to know it; for he was teaching his disciples, saying to them, 'The Son of Man is to be betrayed into human hands, and they will kill him, and three days after being killed, he will rise again'" (Mark 9:30–31 = Matt. 17:22–23); and (3) "While Jesus was going up to Jerusalem, he took the twelve disciples aside by themselves, and said to them on the way, 'See, we are going up to Jerusalem, and the Son of Man will be handed over to the chief priests and scribes, and they will condemn him to death; then they will hand him over to the Gentiles to be mocked and flogged and crucified; and on the third day he will be raised.'" (Matt. 20:17–19).

19. Knohl says that the first version of these hymns are found in three different Qumran manuscripts: 4QHe, 4QHa frag. 7 and 1QHa col 16. See Knohl, *The Messiah before Jesus*, 153.

20. Ibid., 24.

21. Ibid., 26.

22. Quoted in Knohl, *The Messiah before Jesus*, emphasis added.

23. Knohl, *The Messiah before Jesus*, 40.

24. Ibid., 48–49.

25. Joseph Cedar, *Footnote ("Hearat Shulayim")*, directed by Joseph Cedar (Sony Pictures Classics, 2012), DVD.

26. Daniel Boyarin, *The Jewish Gospels* (New York: The New Press, 2012), 47–52.

27. Ibid., 129–31.

28. Ibid., 130.

29. Ibid., 133.

30. Ibid., 132.

31. Ibid.

32. Ibid., 153. The passage in the Talmud is Sanhedrin 98b.

33. Ibid.

34. Ibid., 157.

35. Ibid., 158.

36. Peter Schäfer, "The Jew Who Would Be God," *The New Republic*, May 18, 2012, http://www.newrepublic.com/article/103373/books-and-arts/magazine/jewish-gospels-christ-boyarin.

37. In a private e-mail to me, February 26, 2015, Boyarin wrote: "It is a gross distortion to portray me as holding that Judaism gave birth to Christianity; I reject such metaphors explicitly. If anything, I would suggest that Judaism and Christianity grew together."

Chapter 6: Just How Kosher Was Jesus?

1. Flavius Josephus, *Antiquities of the Jews*, 18.2–6.

2. Ibid., 18.3.

3. Ibid., 18.6.

4. As we saw in an earlier chapter, in *Jewish War*, 6.9.420, Josephus claimed that 1.1 million were killed, but contemporary historians believe the number may have been closer to 350,000.

5. See Hyam Maccoby, *Jesus the Pharisee* (London: SCM Press, 2003).

6. "'Sure, I love promoting God and Judaism,' Boteach told an interviewer in 1999, 'but let's call a spade a spade: The main reason I'm on TV is because I want to be a celebrity.'" Batya Ungar-Sargon, "Celebrity Rabbi, Heal Thyself," *Tablet*, July 23, 2014, http://tabletmag.com/jewish-news-and-politics/179882/shmuley-boteach.

7. Shmuley Boteach, *Kosher Jesus* (Jerusalem: Gefen Publishing, 2012), x.

8. Among the messianic claimants mentioned by Josephus are Simon of Peraea ca. 4 BC (*Antiquities*, 17.10.6), Athronges ca. 4–2 BC (*Antiquities*, 17.10.7), Judas of Galilee ca. AD 6 (*Wars*, 2.8.1), Menahem ben Judah (*Wars*, 2.17.8), Theudas ca. AD 44–46 (*Antiquities*, 20.5.1), and the Egyptian ca. AD 52–54 (*Wars*, 2.13.5).

9. Boteach, *Kosher Jesus*, x.

10. Ibid., 126.

11. Shmuley Boteach, "The Ferocious Battle over 'Kosher Jesus,'" *Jerusalem Post*, January 16, 2012, http://www.jpost.com/Opinion/Columnists/The-ferocious-battle-over-Kosher-Jesus.

12. Hyam Maccoby, *Revolution in Judaea: Jesus and the Jewish Resistance* (New York: Taplinger Publishing Company, 1981).

13. Joseph Klausner, *Jesus of Nazareth: His Life, Times, and Teaching* (New York: Bloch Publishing Company, 1997).

14. "On the eve of the Passover Yeshu was hanged. For forty days before the execution took place, a herald went forth and cried, 'He is going forth to be stoned because he has practised sorcery and enticed Israel to apostasy. Any one who can say anything in his favour, let him come forward and plead on his behalf.' But since nothing was brought forward in his favour he was hanged on the eve of the Passover." Sanhedrin 43a, trans. Jacob Shachter and H. Freedman, in I. Epstein, ed., *Soncino Babylonian Talmud* (London: Socino Press, 1935–1948), http://www.come-and-hear.com/sanhedrin/sanhedrin_43.html.

15. Josephus, *Antiquities of the Jews*, 18:3, 3. This is the controversial *Testimonium Flavium* which many scholars, including Daniel Boyarin in an e-mail to me, believe is a forgery added later to the text of Josephus. However, according to James Dunn, "there is a broad consensus" that, while the text contains later Christian additions or interpolations, the core of the Testimonium is largely authentic. According to Dunn, that authentic core was something like this: "At this time there appeared Jesus, a wise man. For he was a doer of startling deeds, a teacher of people who received the truth with pleasure. And he gained a following both among many Jews and among many of Greek origin. And when Pilate, because of an accusation made by the leading men among us, condemned him to the cross, those who had loved him previously did not cease to do so. And up until this very day the tribe of Christians (named after him) has not died out." James Dunn, *Jesus Remembered* (Grand Rapids, MI: Eerdmans, 2003), 141.

16. Boteach, *Kosher Jesus*, 219–23.

17. Leonard B. Glick, *Abraham's Heirs: Jews and Christians in Medieval Europe* (Syracuse, NY: Syracuse University Press, 1999), 199–203. Apparently Yechiel conceded that one of the references to "Yeshu" in the Talmud likely did refer to the Jesus of Nazareth of Christianity, that which said he practiced magic, but that other references in the Talmud referred to other individuals with the same name.

18. See Hyam Maccoby, *The Mythmaker: Paul and the Invention of Christianity* (New York: Barnes & Noble Books, 1998).

19. Boteach, *Kosher Jesus,* 118.

20. Ibid., 23.

21. Ibid., 27. Boteach relies upon the analysis of David Biven, "Principles of Rabbinic Interpretation: Kal va-Homer," Jerusalem Perspective Online, http://jerusalemperspective.com/Default.aspx?tabid=27andArticleID=1495.

22. Ibid., 27–28.

23. Ibid., 29.

24. Yoma 85b, quoted in Boteach, *Kosher Jesus*, 31.

25. "The Romans used the term *tekton* as slang for any uneducated or illiterate peasant, and Jesus was very likely both." Reza Aslan, *Zealot* (New York: Random house, 2013), 34.

26. Ibid.

27. "Shliach Condemns Boteach Book," Community New Service, January 10, 2012, http://www.collive.com/show_news.rtx?id=18084.

28. See Mitchell Landsberg, "Rabbi's 'Kosher Jesus' Book is Denounced as Heresy," *Los Angeles Times*, February 5, 2012, http://articles.latimes.com/2012 /feb/05/local/la-me-kosher-jesus-20120206.

29. Nir Hasson and Yair Ettinger, "Secular Activists: Police Ignoring Ultra-Orthodox Attacks on Sabbath Traffic in Jerusalem," *Haaretz,* July 10, 2011, http://www.haaretz.com/news/national/secular-activists-police-ignoring-ultra -orthodox-attacks-on-sabbath-traffic-in-jerusalem-1.372493.

30. See Nir Hasson, "Jerusalem Christians Are Latest Targets in Recent Spate of 'Price Tag' Attacks," *Haaretz*, February 21, 2012, http://www.haaretz.com /print-edition/news/jerusalem-christians-are-latest-targets-in-recent-spate-of -price-tag-attacks-1.413848.

31. Boteach, "The Ferocious Battle Over 'Kosher Jesus,'" http://www.jpost.com /Opinion/Columnists/The-ferocious-battle-over-Kosher-Jesus.

32. See Sarah J. Tanzer, "Judaisms of the First Century CE," eds. Bruce Metzger and Michael David Coogan, *The Oxford Companion to the Bible* (New York: Oxford University Press, 1993), 391–94.

33. "The Pharisees sought to convert other Jews to their way of thinking about God and the Torah, a way of thinking that incorporated seeming changes in the written Torah's practices that were mandated by what the Pharisees called 'the tradition of the Elders.' The justification of these reforms in the name of an oral Torah, a tradition passed down by the Elders from Sinai on, would have been experienced by many traditional Jews as a radical change, especially when it involved changing the traditional ways that they and their ancestors had kept the Torah for generations immemorial. At least some of these pharisaic innovations may very well have represented changes in religious practice that took place during the Babylonian Exile, while the Jews who remained 'in the land' continued their ancient practices. It is quite plausible, therefore, that other Jews, such as the Galilean Jesus, would reject angrily such ideas as an affront to the Torah and a sacrilege." Daniel Boyarin, *The Jewish Gospels* (New York: The New Press, 2012), 104.

34. Ibid., 105.

35. Ibid.

36. Ibid., 116.

37. Ibid., 117.

38. Ibid.

39. Ibid.

40. Ibid., 118.

41. Ibid., 118–19. Boyarin cites and follows Yair Furstenberg, "Defilement Penetrating the Body: A New Understanding of Contamination in Mark 7.15," *New Testament Studies* 54 (2008): 178.

42. "Moses received the Torah from Sinai and transmitted it to Joshua; Joshua to the Elders; the Elders to the Prophets; and the Prophets transmitted it to the Men of the Great Assembly. They [the Men of the Great Assembly] said three things: Be deliberate in judgment; develop many disciples; and make a fence for the Torah." Pirkei Avot, *Pirkei Avos: Ethics of the Fathers*, 1.1 (Brooklyn, NY: Mesorah Publications, 1984). The *Pirkei Avot* is part of the Mishnah, the compendium of debates on biblical law compiled by Rabbi Yehudah ha-Nasi around AD 217 in Sepphoris, about three miles from Nazareth.

43. Ibid., 125–26.

44. "The anti-Semitic claim that the Jews killed Jesus became the wellspring from which Christian anti-Semitism flowed, and its root is in the text of the Gospel itself." Boteach, *Kosher Jesus,* 52.

45. "*Kosher Jesus* is the true story of Jesus' Jewish life—culled from early Christian and Jewish sources—that portrays Jesus as a Torah-observant teacher who instructed his followers to keep every letter of the Law, whose teachings quoted extensively from the Bible and rabbinical writings, who fought Roman paganism and persecution of the Jewish people, and was killed by Pontius Pilate for his rebellion against Rome, the Jews having had nothing whatsoever to do with his murder." Shmuley Boteach, "The Ferocious Battle over 'Kosher Jesus,'" *Jerusalem Post*, January 16, 2012, http://www.jpost.com /Opinion/Columnists/The-ferocious-battle-over-Kosher-Jesus.

46. Boteach believes that Jesus saw himself as the messiah of Israel, and that, as the messiah, his role was to lead his fellow Jews in a military rebellion against the Roman occupation authorities—thus making him guilty of being an insurrectionist. Jesus "inspires the wary Jews to overcome their fears of Rome. He broadcasts his call to arms far and wide, building a passionate and devoted following." Boteach, *Kosher Jesus,* 4.

47. David Klinghoffer, *Why the Jews Rejected Jesus* (New York: Doubleday, 2005), 72.

48. "Jesus of Nazareth who aspired to be the Mashiach and was executed by the

court was also alluded to in Daniel's prophecies, as ibid. 11:14 states: 'The vulgar among your people shall exalt themselves in an attempt to fulfill the vision, but they shall stumble.' Can there be a greater stumbling block than Christianity? All the prophets spoke of Mashiach as the redeemer of Israel and their savior who would gather their dispersed and strengthen their observance of the mitzvot. In contrast, Christianity caused the Jews to be slain by the sword, their remnants to be scattered and humbled, the Torah to be altered, and the majority of the world to err and serve a god other than the Lord." Moses Maimonides, *Mishneh Torah*, trans. Eliyahu Touger, chabad.org, http://www.chabad.org/library/article_cdo/aid/1188356/jewish /Melachim-uMilchamot-Chapter-11.htm.

49. Paula Fredriksen, *Jesus of Nazareth: King of the Jews* (New York: Random House, 1999), 254.

50. Josephus, as usual, put the number on the high side, around 2.7 million (*Jewish War*, 6.9.3: 422–27). The historian E. P. Sanders, on the other hand, is more conservative, estimating between 300,000 and 500,000 people crowded into the city during the Passover festival. E. P. Sanders, *Judaism: Practice and Belief 63 BCE–66 CE* (London: SCM Press, 1992), 126.

51. "We should think neither of a massive number of troops nor even of troops dispersed, however thinly, throughout the countryside. Rome did not occupy Judea the way that modern armies occupied conquered countries in World War II. The major concentration of troops was in Syria, under the Roman legate. He commanded four legions—approximately twenty thousand men—and about five thousand cavalry; in time of emergency, should he need more, he could count on contributions of auxiliary troops from the local clients of Rome (such as Agrippa or Philip; see BH 2.500–503). The Judea prefect, by contrast, had approximately three thousand troops garrisoned with him on the coast at Caesarea." Fredriksen, *Jesus of Nazareth,* 169.

52. Josephus, *Jewish War*, 17.2.7 and 17.2.10.

53. Boteach, *Kosher Jesus,* 86.

54. Fredriksen, *Jesus of Nazareth,* 256.

55. "Now the number of those that were crucified on this account were two thousand." Josephus, *Antiquities*, 17.10.1.

56. In 1964, the General Convention of the Episcopal Church in the United States issued a statement that declared, "We reject the charge of deicide against the Jews and condemn anti-Semitism." Cf. General Convention of the Episcopal Church (USA), "A Resolution of the 1964 General Convention: Deicide and the Jews," October 26, 1964, http://www.ccjr.us/dialogika

-resources/documents-and-statements/protestant-churches/na/episcopalian/685
-ecusa64oct.

57. The statement continues: "True, the Jewish authorities and those who followed their lead pressed for the death of Christ; still, what happened in His passion cannot be charged against all the Jews, without distinction, then alive, nor against the Jews of today. Although the Church is the new people of God, the Jews should not be presented as rejected or accursed by God, as if this followed from the Holy Scriptures. All should see to it, then, that in catechetical work or in the preaching of the word of God they do not teach anything that does not conform to the truth of the Gospel and the spirit of Christ." Pope Paul VI, *Nostra Aetate: Declaration on the Relationship of the Church to Non-Christian Religions*, Second Vatican Council, October 28, 1965, Section 4.

58. As we saw in earlier chapters, Epiphanius (ca. 315–403), bishop of Salamis in Cyprus, wrote about groups of Jewish Christians in the fourth century AD.

59. Boteach, *Kosher Jesus*, 111.

60. "Amy-Jill Levine to Discuss Jesus' Parables in March 11 Lecture at American Bible Society," *America*, January 8, 2015, http://americamagazine.org/content /all-things/amy-jill-levine-discuss-jesus-parables-march-11-lecture-american -bible-society.

61. Amy-Jill Levine, *The Misunderstood Jew: The Church and the Scandal of the Jewish Jesus* (New York: HarperCollins, 2007), 1.

62. Caitlin Yoshiko Kandil, "The Gospel of Amy-Jill Levine: The Life and Times of a Jewish New Testament Scholar," Moment, November-December 2013, http://www.momentmag.com/gospel-amy-jill-levine/.

63. Levine, *The Misunderstood Jew*, 124.

64. Ibid., 131.

65. Ibid., 127.

66. Ibid.

67. In an e-mail, Professor Levine kindly clarified to me that, in her view, "Jesus did not 'void the sabbath' (and I have no gospel evidence that he did; to the contrary, I have lots of evidence that he did not); Jesus did not 'declare all foods clean' (as I note, if he had, no one got the message, as Galatians and Acts 10, 15 indicate); Jesus did not 'dismiss' the Torah, as he frequently appeals to it. Disputes of course happened; how they play out in the gospels, e.g, with Mark's apparent conclusion that Jesus declared all foods clean, is another issue."

68. Levine, *The Misunderstood Jew*, 224.

69. Ibid., 220.

70. Ibid., 224.

71. Ibid., 228.

Chapter 7: Did Jesus Have a Secret Message?

1. The Hebrew word for "harp" is *kinor*. The Sea of Galilee was thought to be shaped like a biblical harp.
2. In her diary, Egeria refers to a cave in the hillside at the Seven Springs "and the Lord ascending above it preached the Beatitudes." This text is not found in Egeria's extant diary, the beginning and parts of the middle of which have been lost, but are quoted in a work by a Benedictine monk Peter the Deacon of the famous monastery of Monte Cassino. Bargil Pixner quotes this text in his book, *With Jesus Through Galilee According to the Fifth Gospel* (Rosh Pina, Israel: Corazin Publishing, 1992), 36–37. Pixner quotes from D. baldi, Enchiridion Locorum Sanctorum, Jerusalem (1982), 281, nr 412 and 290, nr 443. For those interested in Egeria's diary, one contemporary edition is *Egeria: Diary of a Pilgrimage*, trans. George E. Gingras (New York: The Newman Press, 1970).
3. When Pope John Paul II celebrated mass on this site in the year 2000, more than one hundred thousand people easily fit into the area.
4. Cynthia Astie, "Galilee in Jesus' Time Was a Center of Change," http://ancienthistory.about.com/od/biblearchaeology/a/041511-CW-Galilee-In-Jesus-Time-Was-A-Center-Of-Change.htm.
5. Frederick M. Strickert estimates between 1,500 and 2,500 people in the time of Jesus. See Frederick M. Strickert, *Philip's City: From Bethsaida to Julias* (Collegeville, MN: Liturgical Press, 2011).
6. Jonathan L. Reed, *Archaeology and the Galilean Jesus: A Re-Examination of the Evidence* (Harrisburg, PA: Trinity Press International, 2000), 82.
7. Ibid.
8. There have been many efforts to reconstruct what the hypothetical sayings source scholars call Q might have looked like. It is technically the sayings of Jesus found in both Matthew and Luke but not in Mark. One easy-to-read collection is found in Robert J. Miller, ed., *The Complete Gospels* (San Francisco: HarperSanFrancisco, 1992), 253–300.
9. James M. Arlandson, "Did Some Disciples Take Notes During Jesus' Ministry?" bible.org, https://bible.org/seriespage/8-did-some-disciples-take-notes-during-jesus-ministry.
10. Robert H. Stein, *Jesus the Messiah* (Downers Grove, IL: IVP Academic, 1996), 124.
11. "The historical Jesus was, then, a *peasant Jewish Cynic*." John Dominic Crossan, *The Historical Jesus* (San Francisco: HarperSanFrancisco, 1991), 421.

12. Richard A. Horsley with John S. Hanson, *Bandits, Prophets and Messiahs* (Harrisburg, PA: Trinity Press International, 1999), 64.

13. As mentioned in chapter 2, there is a text-critical issue with this famous verse, in which Jesus prays to God to show forgiveness to the men who crucified him: "Then Jesus said, 'Father, forgive them; for they do not know what they are doing.'" The line is missing from many of the oldest manuscripts.

14. "Through the wrath of the LORD of hosts the land was burned, and the people became like fuel for the fire" (Isa. 9:19 NRSV); "Therefore thus says the LORD GOD: My anger and my wrath shall be poured out on this place" (Jer. 7:20 NRSV); "Soon now I will pour out my wrath upon you; I will spend my anger against you (Ezek. 7:8 NRSV); "And in anger and wrath I will execute vengeance on the nations that did not obey" (Mic. 5:15 NRSV); "A jealous and avenging God is the LORD, the LORD is avenging and wrathful" (Nah. 1:2 NRSV); "That day will be a day of wrath, a day of distress and anguish, a day of ruin and devastation, a day of darkness and gloom, a day of clouds and thick darkness" (Zeph. 1:15 NRSV); "Thus says the LORD of hosts: I am jealous for Zion with great jealousy, and I am jealous for her with great wrath" (Zech. 8:2 NRSV). It goes without saying that the proclamation of God's wrath is not the sole, nor even the primary, message of the biblical prophets. They, too, frequently proclaim God's mercy, and some would even argue that God's wrath is how God's mercy is expressed. The point is only that Jesus emphasized God's mercy to such a degree that it amazed and, in some cases, shocked his contemporaries, as the Synoptic Gospels report: "They were all amazed, and they kept on asking one another, 'What is this? A new teaching—with authority!'" (Mark 1:27 NRSV).

15. "Complete texts" is a relative term. In Robert J. Miller's edited edition of *The Complete Gospels,* he presents the four apocryphal Gospels we possess more or less intact: (1) The Gospel of Thomas, (2) the Secret Book of James, (3) the Dialogue of the Savior and (4) the Gospel of Mary. Even these complete texts, however, are far shorter than the canonical Gospels and seem fragmentary. In addition to these four, Miller presents five more texts of which we have small manuscript fragments: the (1) Gospel of Peter, (2) the Secret Gospel of Mark, (3) the Egerton Gospel, (4) Gospel Oxyrhynchus 840, and (5) Gospel Oxyrhynchus 1224. Finally, there are two "infancy gospels" that provide legends about miraculous deeds of Jesus as a baby: (1) the Infancy Gospel of Thomas and (2) the Infancy Gospel of James. Robert J. Miller, ed., *The Complete Gospels* (San Francisco: HarperSanFrancisco, 1994), 301–424.

16. Saying 114, James M. Robinson, ed., *The Nag Hammadi Library in English* (San Francisco: Harper and Row, 1978), 138.

17. Elaine Pagels, *The Gnostic Gospels* (New York: Vintage Books, 1979; 1989), 102.

18. Bart D. Ehrman ed., *Lost Scriptures: Books that Did Not Make It Into the New Testament* (London: Oxford University Press, 2003), 40.

19. Ibid., 36.

20. Eusebius, *Ecclesiastical History*, 3.25.

21. Ibid.

22. The ancient Christian historian Bishop Eusebius of Caesarea (ca. 260–340) relates a tradition, widely believed to be legendary, that Jesus once wrote a letter to King Abgarus V of Edessa (ca. 4 BC–AD 13–50), expressing his regrets that he could not visit him in person as Abgarus had requested in an earlier letter. The texts of both letters are found in Eusebius's *Ecclesiastical History*, 1.13.

23. "Jesus did not invent parables, but he perfected the art to a celebrated standard." Peter Rhea Jones, *Studying the Parables of Jesus* (Macon, GA: Smyth & Helwys Publishing, 2015), 27.

24. There are many different lists of parables because New Testament experts disagree on what constitutes a parable. Some experts say there are as few as thirty parables; others say forty-six. For my purposes, however, I define a parable as a brief symbolic story that expresses a universal spiritual truth. Thus, if you count only those extended metaphors of Jesus that involve actual stories with characters, I agree with those scholars who count thirty-seven. They are in no particular order: (1) the Wedding Feast (Luke 14:7–14); (2) Two Debtors (Luke 7:41–43); (3) Lamp under a Bushel (Matt. 5:14–15, Mark 4:21–25, Luke 8:16–18); (4) Good Samaritan (Luke 10:25–37); (5) Friend at Night (Luke 11:5–8); (6) Wise and the Foolish Builders (Matt. 7:24–27, Luke 6:46–49); (7) Sheep and the Goats (Matt. 25:31–46); (8) the Talents (Matt. 25:14–30, Luke 19:12–27); (9) New Wine into Old Wineskins (Matt. 9:17, Mark 2:21–22, Luke 5:37–39); (10) The Growing Seed (Mark 4:26–29); (11) Rich Fool (Luke 12:16–21); (12) the Strong Man (Matt. 12:29, Mark 3:27, Luke 11:21–22); (13) Sower (Matt. 13:3–9, Mark 4:3–9, Luke 8:5–8); (14) Tares (Matt. 13:24–30); (15) Barren Fig Tree (Luke 13:6–9); (16) Mustard Seed (Matt. 13:31–32, Mark 4:30–32, Luke 13:18–19); (17) Leaven (Matt. 13:33, Luke 13:20–21); (18) Pearl (Matt. 13:45–46); (19) Pulling in the Net (Matt. 13:47–50); (20) Hidden Treasure (Matt. 13:44); (21) Lost Sheep (Matt. 18:10–14, Luke 15:4–6); (22) Counting the Cost (Luke 14:28–33); (23) Unforgiving Servant (Matt. 18:23–35); (24) Lost Coin (Luke 15:8–9); (25) Prodigal Son (Luke 15:11–32); (26) Unjust Steward (Luke 16:1–13); (27)

Lazarus and the Rich Man (Luke 16:19–31); (28) Master and Servant (Luke 17:7–10); (29) Unjust Judge (Luke 18:1–9); (30) Pharisee and the Publican (Luke 18:10–14); (31) Workers in the Vineyard (Matt. 20:1–16); (32) Two Sons (Matt. 21:28–32); (33) Wicked Husbandmen (Matt. 21:33–41, Mark 12:1–9, Luke 20:9–18); (34) Great Banquet (Matt. 22:1–14, Luke 14:15–24); (35) Budding Fig Tree (Matt. 24:32–35, Mark 13:28–31, Luke 21:29–33); (36) Faithful Servant (Matt. 24:42–51, Mark 13:34–37, Luke 12:35–48); and (37) Ten Virgins (Matt. 25:1–13).

25. *The Dictionary of Jesus and the Gospels*, s.v. "parable," eds. Joel B. Green, Scot McKnight, and I. Howard Marshall, (Downers Grove, IL: InterVarsity Press, 1992), 594.

26. See David M. Brown, *All the Parables of Jesus: A Guide to Discovery* (Nashville, TN: WestBow Press, 2012).

27. "Among these larger silver coins was the denarius which was the accepted salary for a day's work by a common laborer." *The Anchor Bible Dictionary*, s.v. "coinage," ed. David Noel Freedman, vol. 1 (New York: Doubleday, 1992), 1086.

28. Ehrman, *Did Jesus Exist?*, 312.

29. Brian McLaren, *The Secret Message of Jesus* (Nashville: Thomas Nelson, 2006), 17–18.

Chapter 8: Was Jesus a Zealot Revolutionary?

1. Charles Duke Yonge, trans., *On the Embassy to Gaius,* Early Christian Writings, http://www.earlychristianwritings.com/yonge/book40.html, 302.

2. Josephus, *Antiquities,* 18.3.1.

3. *Jewish War*, 2:175–77.

4. *Antiquities*, 18:60–62.

5. James S. Jeffers, *The Greco-Roman World of the New Testament Era* (Downers Grove, IL: InterVarsity Press, 1999), 130.

6. Albert Schweitzer, *The Quest of the Historical Jesus* (London: Adam and Charles Black, 1911), 25.

7. John P. Meier, a Catholic priest and author of the encyclopedic, multivolume series *A Marginal Jew,* writes that Jesus was an "eschatological prophet" whose preaching of the kingdom of God meant "the definitive coming of God in the near future to bring the present state of things to an end and to establish his full and unimpeded rule over the world in general and Israel in particular." John P. Meier, *A Marginal Jew: Rethinking the Historical Jesus,* vol. 2 (New York: Doubleday, 1994), 349.

8. Bart Ehrman is now a spokesman for this view of Jesus which, he claims, "appears to be the most widely held by critical scholars in the field . . ." Ehrman, *Did Jesus Exist?*, 298.

9. Ibid., 331, emphasis added.

10. Ibid., 301.

11. Ibid.

12. Ibid., 313.

13. James Tabor, "Jesus as a Pacifist? Apocalypticism, Non-resistance, and Violence," *JamesTabor.com* (blog), June 25, 2012, http://jamestabor.com/2012/06/25/jesus-as-a-pacifist-apocalypticism-non-resistance-and-violence/.

14. John Dominic Crossan and Jonathan Reed, *Excavating Jesus: Beneath the Stones, Behind the Texts* (New York: HarperCollins, 2003), 127.

15. Richard Horsley and Neil Asher Silberman, *The Message and the Kingdom* (New York: Putnam, 1997), 25.

16. Josephus, *Life*, 374–84, in Crossan and Reed, *Excavating Jesus*, 114.

17. Josephus recounts how Aristobulus, the reigning king of the bickering Hasmonean dynasty, sent to the Roman general Pompey, camped near Damascus, a gift of a golden vine worth five hundred talents. At the time, Aristobulus and his brother Hyrcanus were locked in a deadly conflict over who should be king. Emissaries from both sides arrived to plead the causes of their respective masters and urged the Roman general to intervene—which, eventually, he did, by invading the country and conquering Jerusalem. Josephus, *Antiquities*, 14.3.1 (34).

18. Crossan and Reed, *Excavating Jesus*, 22.

19. Hermann Samuel Reimarus, *Fragments*, English translator unknown (London: Forgotten Books, 2012), 86.

20. S. G. F. Brandon, *Jesus and the Zealots* (New York: Charles Scribner's, 1967), 1–13.

21. Ibid., 9–10.

22. Robert Eisenman, *James the Brother of Jesus* (New York: Penguin Books, 1997), xix.

23. "Whereas the Jesus of Scripture is anti-nationalist, cosmopolitan, antinomian—that is, against the direct application of Jewish Law—and accepting of foreigners and other persons of perceived impurities, the Historical James will turn out to be zealous for the Law, xenophobic, rejecting of foreigners and polluted persons generally, and apocalyptic." Eisenman, *James the Brother of Jesus*, xxxii. Eisenman's argument is that James, Jesus' "brother," knew Jesus far better and

understood his teaching far better than the apostle Paul, who never met Jesus at all—and that James's alleged Jewish zealotry was far closer to what Jesus taught than the Hellenistic religion of universal peace and love taught by Paul.

24. Reza Aslan, *Zealot: The Life and Times of Jesus of Nazareth* (New York: Random House, 2013), 216.

25. "The bedrock of evangelical Christianity, at least as it was taught to me, is the unconditional belief that every word of the Bible is God-breathed and true, literal and inerrant. The sudden realization that this belief is patently and irrefutably false, that the Bible is replete with the most blatant and obvious errors and contradictions—just as one would expect from a document written by hundreds of hands across thousands of years—left me confused and spiritually unmoored. And so, like many people in my situation, I angrily discarded my faith as if it were a costly forgery I had been duped into buying. I began to rethink the faith and culture of my forefathers, finding in them as an adult a deeper, more intimate familiarity than I ever had as a child, the kind that comes from reconnecting with an old friend after many years apart." Ibid., xix.

26. See transcript of Aslan's now-infamous interview with Fox News's Lauren Green in Erik Wemple, "Fox News Must Apologize to Reza Aslan," *Washington Post*, July 29, 2013, http://www.washingtonpost.com/blogs/erik-wemple/wp /2013/07/29/fox-news-must-apologize-to-reza-aslan/.

27. Aslan, *Zealot*, 11.

28. Ibid., 120.

29. Ibid., 212.

30. Ibid., 216.

31. Sanhedrin 107b, Sotah 47a.

32. Mark 14:47, Matthew 26:51, Luke 22:50, John 18:10.

33. "Since the Jews constantly made disturbances at the instigation of Chrestus, he expelled them from Rome." Suetonius, Claudius, *Lives of the Twelve Caesars*, 25.4, trans. Loeb Classical Library, 1914, http://penelope.uchicago. edu/Thayer/E/Roman/Texts/Suetonius/12Caesars/Claudius*.html.

34. Lucian, *On the Death of Perigrinus*, 11, trans. A. M. Harmon, Loeb Classical Library, 1936, http://www.tertullian.org/rpearse/lucian/peregrinus.htm.

35. Greg Myre, "Israeli Prisoners Dig Their Way to Early Christianity," *New York Times*, November 7, 2005, http://www.nytimes.com/2005/11/07 /international/middleeast/07mideast.html?_r=0.

36. *The Didache,* vol 6., trans. James A. Kleist, SJ (New York: Newman Press, 1948), 16.

37. Justin Martyr, *Dialogue with Trypho* CX, in Philip Schaff, ed., *Ante-Nicene*

Fathers, vol. 1 (1885), available on Christian Classics Ethereal Library, http://www.ccel.org/ccel/schaff/anf01.viii.iv.cx.html.

38. Irenaeus, *Proof of the Apostolic Preaching*, 96.

39. Tertullian, *De Corona Militis*, 2.2.91–93, as quoted in Cecil John Cadoux, *The Early Christian Attitude to War* (London: Headley Bros, 1919), 110–11.

40. Hippolytus, *The Apostolic Tradition*, 16.

41. Lactantius, *Divine Institutes*, trans. William Fletcher, 6.20, in Alexander Roberts, James Donaldson, and A. Cleveland Coxe, eds., *Ante-Nicene Fathers*, vol. 7., rev. and ed. Kevin Knight for newadvent.org, http://www.newadvent.org /fathers/07016.htm. I was alerted to this passage by Scot McKnight in his *Jesus Creed* blog, an excerpt from Preston Sprinkle's book: *Fight: A Christian Case for Non-Violence* (Colorado Springs: David C. Cook, 2013), http://www.patheos .com/blogs/jesuscreed/2013/07/08/the-early-church-and-military-service/.

42. N. T. Wright, *Jesus and the Victory of God* (Minneapolis: Fortress Press, 1996), 594.

43. Ibid., 594–95.

44. Josephus, *Antiquities*, 20.9. See also "Why Was Jesus Crucified?" in Joel B. Green and Scot McKnight, eds., *Dictionary of Jesus and the Gospels* (Downers Grove, IL: InterVarsity Press, 1992), 153.

45. Josephus, *Antiquities*, 17: 285–98 and *Jewish War* 2.66–75.

Chapter 9: Did Jesus Plan His Own Execution?

1. Irenaeus, *Against Heresies*, trans. Alexander Roberts and William Rambaut, 1.31.1, in Alexander Roberts, James Donaldson, and A. Cleveland Coxe, eds., *Ante-Nicene Fathers*, vol. 1, http://www.newadvent.org/fathers/0103131.htm.

2. "Gospel of Judas Copied," *The Lost Gospel of Judas*, nationalgeographic.com, http://www.nationalgeographic.com/lostgospel/timeline_11.html.

3. "Because the Gospel of Judas was hidden in the Egyptian desert for more than 1,600 years, the papyrus remained intact. However, the document severely deteriorated when it was kept in a safe-deposit box on Long Island, New York, for 16 years. As a result, the conservation process to rescue and preserve the manuscript has been an enormous undertaking, as Rodolphe Kasser and his team worked to piece the document back together by reassembling nearly a thousand broken fragments of papyrus." "Frequently Asked Questions," *The Lost Gospel of Judas*, http://www.nationalgeographic.com/lostgospel/about_faq.html.

4. For a book-length treatment of the discovery and translation of the Gospel of Judas Iscariot, see Herbert Krosney, *The Lost Gospel: The Quest for the Gospel of Judas Iscariot* (Washington, DC: National Geographic, 2006).

5. Bart Ehrman, *The Lost Gospel of Judas* (New York: Oxford University Press, 2006), 87. Marvin Meyer translates this verse, "The secret revelatory discourse that Jesus spoke with Judas Iscariot in the course of a week, three days before his passion." Marvin Meyer, *Judas: The Definitive Collection of Gospels and Legends About the Infamous Apostle of Jesus* (New York: HarperOne, 2007), 53.

6. Meyer, *Judas*, 54.

7. Ibid.

8. Ibid., 60.

9. Ibid., 61.

10. Ibid., 62.

11. David Ian Miller, "Religious Scholar Elaine Pagels on How the Newly Discovered Gospel of Judas Sheds New Light on the Dawn of Christianity," sfgate.com, April 2, 2007, http://www.sfgate.com/news/article/FINDING -MY-RELIGION-Religious-scholar-Elaine-2605086.php.

12. Meyer, *Judas*, 65.

13. Ibid., 60.

14. Ibid., 66.

15. Ibid.

16. Meyer's version has the apparently correct translation and reads, "In the last days they will . . . to you, that you may not ascend up to the holy [generation]." *Judas*, 60.

17. April D. DeConick, "What the Gospel of Judas Really Says," *New York Times*, December 2, 2007, http://www.nytimes.com/2007/12/02/opinion/02iht-edeconick .1.8558749.html?_r=0.

18. Ibid.

19. Ibid.

20. Miller, "Religious Scholar Elaine Pagels . . ." sfgate.com.

21. Ibid.

22. Hugh J. Schonfield, *The Passover Plot* (New York: Bernard Geis, 1965), 165.

23. See M. M. H. Nuri-Rabwah, "Jesus Christ Did Not Die on the Cross—A Cardiologist's Perspective," *The Review of Religions*, March 2012, http://www .reviewofreligions.org/11445/jesus-christ-did-not-die-on-the-cross-a-cardiologists -perspective-2/.

24. For a summary presentation of this perspective, see "Could Jesus Have Survived the Crucifixion?" excerpted from Michael Baigent, *The Jesus Papers* (New York: HarperOne, 2007), http://www.beliefnet.com/Faiths /Christianity/2006/04/Could-Jesus-Have-Survived-The-Crucifixion .aspx?p=2.

25. Michael Baigent, Richard Leigh, and Henry Lincoln, *Holy Blood, Holy Grail* (New York: Dell Publishing, 1982), 358.

26. For example, see Sylvia Browne and Lindsay Harrison, *The Two Marys: The Hidden History of the Mother and Wife of Jesus* (New York: Penguin, 2007).

27. "On the night before the final confrontation, the rabbi [Jesus] gathers his disciples together. He orders them to collect swords. They must prepare to seize the Temple by force. They will demonstrate to the people of Jerusalem their teacher's courage and fearlessness in the face of Rome. When the people see, they will follow him, sparking a massive rebellion. The Romans will have no choice but to retreat." Shmuley Boteach, *Kosher Jesus* (Jerusalem: Gefen Publishing, 2012), 6.

28. John Dominic Crossan, *Who Killed Jesus?* (New York: HarperCollins, 1996), 67.

29. Geza Vermes, *The Religion of Jesus the Jew* (Minneapolis: Fortress Press, 1993), x.

30. R. C. Sproul, "Forsaken—Jesus Became A Curse," *Ligonier Ministries* (blog), April 4, 2012, http://www.ligonier.org/blog/forsaken-jesus-became-curse/.

31. "[S]ince all have sinned and fall short of the glory of God; they are now justified by his grace as a gift, through the redemption that is in Christ Jesus, whom God put forward as a sacrifice of atonement by his blood, effective through faith." (Rom. 3:23–25).

32. Marcus Borg, *The Heart of Christianity: Rediscovering a Life of Faith* (New York: HarperOne, 2004), 92.

33. "The apostle Paul is the principal spokesman (in our surviving records) for these atonement concepts. He communicates them through cultic and social metaphors he uses at key moments in his arguments." Stephen Finlan, *Options on Atonement in Christian Thought* (Collegeville, MN: Liturgical Press, 2007), 1.

34. Borg, *The Heart of Christianity*, 95.

35. "The God that holds you over the pit of hell, much as one holds a spider, or some loathsome insect over the fire, abhors you, and is dreadfully provoked: his wrath towards you burns like fire; he looks upon you as worthy of nothing else, but to be cast into the fire; he is of purer eyes than to bear to have you in his sight; you are ten thousand times more abominable in his eyes, than the most hateful venomous serpent is in ours." Jonathan Edwards, "Sinners in the Hands of an Angry God," Christian Classics, http://www.ccel.org/ccel/edwards/sermons.sinners.html.

36. "Luke 7:47 is difficult in that Jesus seems to say the woman was forgiven much because she loved much, rather than the reverse. Surely the meaning is that she must have been forgiven much since it is evident she loves much. The conclusion of the story (vv. 49–50) could possibly have been originally in

another context. After all, the issue has not been Jesus' authority to forgive sins; nor has the praiseworthy quality in the woman been her faith. It was her love that had been abundantly demonstrated." Fred B. Craddock, "Luke," *Harper's Bible Commentary* (San Francisco: Harper & Row, 1988), 1024. For a more technical discussion of the Greek grammar involved, see John Nolland, Luke 1–9:20, *Word Biblical Commentary* (Dallas, TX: Word Books, 1989), 357–59.

37. "[I]t is an unworthy concept of God to imagine a God who demands the slaughter of his Son to pacify his wrath," wrote Pope Benedict XVI. ". . . [I]ndeed, God must not be thought of in this way . . . [S]uch a concept of God has nothing to do with the idea of God to be found in the New Testament." Joseph Ratzinger, *Introduction to Christianity* (San Francisco: Ignatius Press, 2004), 222.

38. "We as Christians participate in the only major religious tradition whose founder was executed by established authority," concludes Borg. "And if we ask the historical question, 'Why was he killed?' the historical answer is because he was a social prophet and movement initiator, a passionate advocate of God's justice, and radical critic of the domination system who had attracted a following. If Jesus had been only a mystic, healer, and wisdom teacher, he almost certainly would not have been executed. Rather, he was killed because of his politics—because of his passion for God's justice." Borg, *The Heart of Christianity*, 91.

39. Nadia Bolz-Weber, *Pastrix: The Cranky, Beautiful Faith of a Sinner & Saint* (Nashville, TN: Jericho Books, 2013), 150.

Chapter 10: Do We Have Proof for the Resurrection?

1. Martin Biddle, *The Tomb of Christ* (London: Sutton Publishing, 1999), 1.
2. Ibid.
3. The archaeologist Jerome Murphy-O'Conner of the École Biblique in Jerusalem believes that the Church of the Holy Sepulchre has a solid claim to being the actual location of Golgotha. "Is this the place where Christ died and was buried?" he asks. "Yes, very probably." See Jerome Murphy-O'Conner, *The Holy Land: An Oxford Archaeological Guide* (New York: Oxford University Press, 2008), 49–57. The Israeli archaeologist Shimon Gibson also accepts that the Church of the Holy Sepulchre is the likely location of Golgotha, although he argues that the raised hill venerated in the current church was more a "marker" of the general area rather than the actual spot of the crucifixion. Shimon Gibson, *The Final Days of Jesus: The Archaeological Evidence* (New York: HarperOne, 2009), 122.

4. "The overall conclusion is that there is no evidence that the Garden Tomb was that of Joseph of Arimathea in which Jesus was temporarily buried," note archaeologists John J. Rousseau and Rami Arav in their marvelous survey of New Testament archaeology, *Jesus and His World* (Minneapolis: Fortress Press, 1995), 109. Rousseau and Arav are also somewhat skeptical of the Church of the Holy Sepulchre site, insisting that it has not been proven that it lay *outside* the city walls in the late AD 20s and early 30s.

5. William Lane Craig, "Did Jesus Rise From the Dead?," in Michael J. Wilkins and J. P. Moreland, *Jesus Under Fire: Modern Scholarship Reinvents the Historical Jesus* (Zondervan, 2010), 159.

6. Frank Tipler, *The Physics of Christianity* (New York: Doubleday, 2007), 194–224.

7. James D. Tabor, *The Jesus Dynasty* (New York: Simon & Schuster, 2006), 236.

8. Ibid.

9. Ibid., 213.

10. In Aramaic: *"Ya'akov bar-Yosef akhui diYeshua"*

11. "We, members of the committee for examination of the content and script in the Yehoash inscription and the James Ossuary ('James son of Joseph brother of Jesus') conclude that to the best of our scientific judgement: A) the Yehoash inscription is a forgery; B) The James Ossuary inscription is a forgery." Uzi Dahari, "Final Report Of The Examining Committees For the Yehoash Inscription and James Ossuary," Israel Antiquities Authority, http ://www.antiquities.org.il/article_eng.aspx?sec_id=17&sub_subj_id=185.

12. "A limestone box bearing the inscription 'James, son of Joseph, brother of Jesus' in Aramaic appears to be genuine, the prestigious *Biblical Archaeology Review* said Wednesday in a long story written by editor Hershel Shanks. The ossuary, dating from AD 63, has been highly controversial, with Israeli authorities claiming it is a forgery and prosecuting antiquities dealer Oded Golan, who originally sold it. That trial ended in March when a judge dismissed the charges, saying that the prosecutor had not proved claims that the ossuary was a fake. Shanks has provided no new evidence of the ossuary's authenticity, but he does refute some of the government's key arguments in that trial." Thomas H. Maugh II, "Archaeology Journal Says Burial Box of Jesus' Brother is Genuine," *Los Angeles Times,* June 13, 2012, http://articles.latimes.com/2012/jun/13/science/la-sci-sn-jesus-brother -ossuary-20120613. Shanks himself commented on the case in a video lecture: "It [the James Ossuary] was declared genuine by prominent experts on ancient writing, as well as by geologists. But shortly after I published a story on the ossuary in *Biblical Archaeology Review*, the Israel Antiquities

Authority declared it a forgery. Many people now think it's a forgery simply because the Israel Antiquities Authority said so. But the IAA never really made its case—and scholars I have challenged on the matter have been unable to defend the IAA decision. The ossuary needs to be studied by a new set of international experts so the truth can finally be learned." "Video: Hershel Shanks Explores the Evidence Before the James Ossuary Trial," *Bible History Daily*, March 13, 2013, http://www.biblicalarchaeology.org /daily/biblical-artifacts/artifacts-and-the-bible/video-hershel-shanks-explores -the-evidence-before-the-james-ossuary-trial/.

13. Gordon Govier, "James Ossuary Verdict Not Set In Stone," *Christianity Today*, June 13, 2012, http://www.christianitytoday.com/ct/2012/juneweb-only/james -ossuary-verdict.html.

14. Graeme Ball and Simcha Jacobovici, *The Lost Tomb of Jesus*, directed by Simcha Jacobovici (Entertainment One, 2007), DVD.

15. "Jesus was temporarily placed in this new tomb, with the entrance blocked with a stone, to protect his body from exposure and from predators." James D. Tabor and Simcha Jacobovici, *The Jesus Discovery* (New York: Simon & Schuster, 2012), 36.

16. "Discovering remains of the body of Jesus is no threat to the original resurrection faith of Jesus' followers; it is actually an affirmation of that faith. Paul knows nothing of that first empty tomb. He knows that Jesus died and was *buried* and on the third day he was *raised up*. He then appeared to his followers not as a resuscitated corpse, but in Paul's words, as a 'life-giving spirit' (1 Corinthians 15:3–8)." Tabor and Jacobovici, *The Jesus Discovery*, 194.

17. Ibid., 196–98.

18. Ibid., 201.

19. Ibid., 199–202.

20. Ibid., 91.

21. Mati Milstein, "Jesus' Tomb Claim Slammed By Scholars," *National Geographic News*, February 28, 2007, http://news.nationalgeographic.com/news/2007/02 /070228-jesus-tomb.html.

22. "All of the names on these ossuaries were extremely common names among Jews in Palestine at this period. We have a great deal evidence about this (the data is collected in the enormously useful reference book: *Tal Ilan, Lexicon of Jewish Names in Late Antiquity, Part 1* [Mohr-Siebeck, 2002], and also analysed in chapter 4 of my recent book *Jesus and the Eyewitnesses* [Eerdmans, 2006])." Richard Bauckham, "The Alleged 'Jesus Family Tomb,'" http://www.leaderu.com/jesus/alleged_tomb.html.

23. "The most common response to my hypothesis is the assertion that 'The names in this tomb are extremely common.' The implication is that this particular 'Jesus,' namely 'Yeshua son of Yehosef,' is simply one of many of the time, and he, along with his family members: Yoseh, Mariah, Mariamene/Mara, Matyah, and Yehudah could be any one of dozen of families with names like these. Accordingly, we are told, there is no good argument that this particular Jesus was our own Jesus of Nazareth . . . In fact, the growing body of evidence that has emerged as a result of academic discussions of the Talpiot tomb shows quite the opposite—namely, that the majority of these six names are not only uncommon they are actually rare—with several of them associated uniquely with the family of Jesus of Nazareth." James Tabor, "The Names in the Talpiot 'Jesus Tomb' Are Not Common: The Latest on Yoseh," *TaborBlog*, October 20, 2012, http://jamestabor.com/2012/10/20/the-names-in-the-talpiot-jesus-tomb-are-not-common-the-latest-on-yoseh/.

24. Jodi Magness, "Jodi Magness Responds to the 'New Jesus Discovery,'" *ASORblog.org*, February 28, 2012, http://asorblog.org/2012/02/28/1654/.

25. Jodi Magness, *Stone and Dung, Oil and Spit: Jewish Daily Life in the Time of Jesus* (Grand Rapids, MI: Wm. B. Eerdmans, 2011), 174.

26. Tim McGirk, "Jesus 'Tomb' Controversy Reopened," *Time* magazine, January 16, 2008, http://content.time.com/time/world/article/0,8599,1704299,00.html.

27. It's worth reading the statement, available online at the Duke University religion department's blog: Marc Goodacre et. al., "The Talpiot Tomb Controversy Revisited," January 24, 2008, http://dukereligion.blogspot.com/2008/01/talpiot-tomb-controversy-revisited.html. "A statistical analysis of the names engraved on the ossuaries leaves no doubt that the probability of the Talpiot tomb belonging to Jesus' family is virtually nil if the Mariamene named on one of the ossuaries is not Mary Magdalene. . . . Moreover, the DNA evidence from the tomb, which has been used to suggest that Jesus had a wife, was dismissed by the Hebrew University team that devised such procedures and has conducted such research all over the world."

28. Michael Posner, "Filmmaker Simcha Jacobovici Sues Academic for Libel," *Times of Israel*, April 1, 2014, http://www.timesofisrael.com/filmmaker-simcha-jacobovici-sues-academic-for-libel/.

29. John Dominic Crossan, *The Historical Jesus: The Life of a Mediterranean Jewish Peasant* (San Francisco: HarperSanFrancisco, 1991), 391. See also V. Tzaferis, "Crucifixion—The Archaeological Evidence: Remains of a Jewish Victim of Crucifixion Found in Jerusalem," *Biblical Archaeology Review*, 11 (January—February 1985): 44–53.

30. Crossan, *The Historical Jesus*, 392.

31. Bart D. Ehrman, *How Jesus Became God: The Exaltation of a Jewish Preacher from Galilee* (New York: HarperOne, 2014), 157.

32. Ibid.

33. Ibid., 158. Ehrman is correct that Josephus portrays Pilate as a particularly harsh and stubborn ruler. See *Antiquities,* 18.3.

34. Josephus, *Jewish War*, 4.5 (59).

35. Timothy Paul Jones, "Is It Possible that Jesus' Body Was Left on the Cross?" *Timothy Paul Jones* (blog), April 6, 2012, http://www.timothypauljones.com/2012/04/06/is-it-possible-that-jesus-body-was-left-on-the-cross/.

36. Quoted in Ibid.

37. "Pilate was the first who brought those images to Jerusalem, and set them up there; which was done without the knowledge of the people, because it was done in the nighttime; but as soon as they knew it, they came in multitudes to Cesarea, and interceded with Pilate many days, that he would remove the images; and when he would not grant their requests, because it would tend to the injury of Caesar, while yet they perservered in their request, on the sixth day he ordered his soldiers to have their weapons privately, while he came and sat upon his judgment seat, which seat was so prepared in the open place of the city, that it concealed the army that lay ready to oppress them; and when the Jews petitioned him again, he gave a signal to the soldiers to encompass them around, and threatened that their punishment should be no less than immediate death, unless they would leave off disturbing him, and go their ways home. But they threw themselves upon the ground, and laid their necks bare, and said they would take their death very willingly, rather than the wisdom of their laws should be transgressed, upon which Pilate was deeply affected with their firm resolution to keep their laws inviolate, and presently commanded the images to be carried back from Jerusalem to Cesarea." Josephus, *Antiquities*, 18.3.

38. Shimon Gibson, *The Final Days of Jesus: The Archaeological Evidence* (New York: HarperOne, 2009), 132.

39. Magness, *Stone and Dung, Oil and Spit*, 165.

40. "Some assume that Jesus' body would have been routinely disposed of by the authorities. But the tradition is firm that Jesus was given a proper burial (Mark 15:42–47 pars.), and there are good reasons why its testimony should be respected. The tradition of Jesus' burial is one of the oldest pieces of tradition we have (1 Cor. 15:4—*hoti etaphē*), and, unlike the preceding narrative, no detail is drawn from scripture." James D. G. Dunn, *Jesus Remembered* (Grand Rapids, MI: William B. Eerdmans, 2003), 783.

41. "From all these reasons I conclude that the historian, of whatever persuasion, has no option but to affirm both the empty tomb and the 'meetings' with Jesus as 'historical events' . . ." N. T. Wright, *The Resurrection of the Son of God* (Minneapolis: Fortress Press, 2003), 707.

42. Raymond E. Brown, SS, *The Death of the Messiah,* vol. 2 (New York: Doubleday, 1994), 1240.

43. "After a relatively short period of suffering he [Jesus] died, and some of his followers and sympathizers hastily buried him." E. P. Sanders, *The Historical Figure of Jesus* (New York: Penguin, 1993), 275.

44. "It is commonly assumed that the tomb in which they placed Jesus that late afternoon belonged to Joseph of Arimathea," James D. Tabor, *The Jesus Dynasty* (New York: Simon & Schuster, 2006), 224.

45. "Even if the historian chooses to regard the youthful apparition as extra-historical, he cannot justifiably deny the empty tomb." Michael Grant, *Jesus: An Historian's Review of the Gospels* (New York: Charles Scribner's Sons, 1977), 176.

46. Craig A. Evans, "Jewish Burial Traditions and the Resurrection of Jesus," *Journal for the Study of the Historical Jesus*, 3 (2005), 233–48. Also available at *CraigEvans.com* (blog), http://craigaevans.com/Burial_Traditions.pdf, 7.

47. Ibid.

48. "The chief priests and the scribes were looking for a way to arrest Jesus by stealth and kill him" (Mark 14:1).

49. ". . . and when Pilate, at the suggestion of the principal men amongst us, had condemned him to the cross, those that loved him at the first did not forsake him . . ." Josephus, *Antiquities*, 18.3 (63). The authenticity of this passage, the famous Testimonium Flavianum, is questioned by many contemporary scholars but accepted by others as genuine.

50. Brown, *The Death of the Messiah,* vol. 2, 1240.

51. Jodi Magness, "The Burial of Jesus in Light of Archaeology and the Gospels," *Eretz Israel*, 28 (Teddy Kollek volume) (Jerusalem: Israel Exploration Society, 2007), 1–7.

52. Gibson, *The Final Days of Jesus*, 132.

53. William Lane Craig presents these facts in more detail in his magnum opus, *Reasonable Faith: Christian Truth and Apologetics,* 3rd ed. (Wheaton, IL: Crossway Books, 2008), 360–75. He also includes a detailed analysis of the philosophical presuppositions of both proponents and opponents of the bodily resurrection. Transcripts of Craig's fascinating debate with Bart Ehrman can be found on Dr. Craig's website, ReasonableFaith.org, under "Is There Historical Evidence for the Resurrection of Jesus?" March 28, 2006, http://www.reason

ablefaith.org/is-there-historical-evidence-for-the-resurrection-of-jesus-the-craig
-ehrman.

54. John A. T. Robinson, *The Human Face of God* (Philadelphia: Westminster, 1973), 131, quoted in William Lane Craig, "The Resurrection of Jesus," ReasonableFaith.org, accessed March 31, 2015, http://www.reasonablefaith .org/the-resurrection-of-jesus#_edn1.

55. Gerd Lüdemann, *What Really Happened to Jesus?*, trans. John Bowden (Louisville, KY: Westminster John Knox Press, 1995), 80, quoted by Craig, "The Resurrection of Jesus," http://www.reasonablefaith.org/the-resurrection -of-jesus#_edn1.

56. Luke Timothy Johnson, *The Real Jesus* (San Francisco: HarperSanFrancisco, 1996), 136, quoted in Craig, "The Resurrection of Jesus," http://www.reason ablefaith.org/the-resurrection-of-jesus#_edn1.

57. Gary R. Habermas and Michael Licona, *The Case for the Resurrection of Jesus* (Grand Rapids, MI: Kregel Publications, 2004), 206–10.

58. "The proposal that Jesus was bodily raised from the dead possesses unrivalled power to explain the historical data at the heart of early Christianity." Wright, *The Resurrection of the Son of God*, 718.

59. Tabor and Jacobivici, *The Jesus Discovery*, 154.

60. Ibid., 210.

61. In later writings, Tabor asserts that Luke and John represent what he terms "a major departure from early Christian resurrection faith" that occurred when the original Jesus community in Jerusalem was cut off from the wider Christian world after the Jewish War of AD 70. For Tabor, the belief of Jesus' earliest, true disciples was in the "spiritual" resurrection he describes, completely harmonious with a knowledge of where Jesus' body lay buried. John and Luke's accounts, according to him, are "secondary and legendary" and were written "for *apologetic* purposes against pagan critics like Celsus who charged that the 'appearances' of Jesus to his followers were merely based on hysteria and delusion." See James Tabor, "Why People are Confused About the Earliest Christian View of Resurrection of the Dead?" *TaborBlog*, April 14, 2012, http://jamestabor.com/2012/04/14/why-people-are-confused-about-the -earliest-christian-view-of-resurrection-of-the-dead/.

62. *Catechism of the Catholic Church*, Profession of Faith, 646, Vatican.va, http ://www.vatican.va/archive/ccc_css/archive/catechism/p122a5p2.htm.

63. Ibid., 1017, http://www.vatican.va/archive/ccc_css/archive/catechism/p123a11 .htm.

64. Biblical scholars count at least eight examples in the Bible of people being

raised to life after having died: three in the Hebrew Bible (the son of Zarephath's widow in 1 Kings 17:17–24, the son of the Shunammite woman in 2 Kings 4:8–36, and a dead man coming back to life when he touches Elisha's bones in 2 Kings 13:21) and between five and seven in the New Testament (Jesus raising Lazarus in John 11:43–44, many "saints" in Matthew 27:52–53, a female disciple named Tabitha raised by Peter in Acts 9:36–42, and Eutychus raised by Paul in Acts 20:9–12). In addition, two other possibly contestable examples are the widow's son at Nain in Luke 7:13–15 and Jairus's daughter in Mark 5:42, Luke 8:55, and Matthew 9:25. The text for the latter, however, is ambiguous, as Jesus says, "Why do you make a commotion and weep? The child is not dead but sleeping" (Mark 5:39).

65. One classic statement of this type of approach was made by Robert Funk, the late cofounder of the Jesus Seminar. In his 1998 essay, "The Coming Radical Reformation," Funk summarized what the resurrection of Jesus meant for him: "Jesus did not rise from the dead, except perhaps in some metaphorical sense. The meaning of the resurrection is that a few of his followers—probably no more than two or three—finally came to understand what he was all about. When the significance of his words and deeds dawned on them, they knew of no other terms in which to express their amazement than to claim that they had seen him alive." The paper is available online on the website of the Westar Institute: http://www.westarinstitute.org/resources/the-fourth-r/the-coming-radical-reformation/.

66. Hans Küng, *On Being a Christian* (New York: Doubleday, 1976), 350.

67. Ibid., 360.

68. Bart D. Ehrman, *The New Testament: A Historical Introduction to the Early Christian Writings*, 3rd. ed. (New York, Oxford: Oxford University Press, 2004), 276.

69. Robert Funk, *Honest to Jesus* (San Francisco: HarperSanFrancisco, 1996), 40, 266.

70. "The followers of Jesus had experiences of him after his death that convinced them that he continued to be a figure of the present." Marcus Borg, *Jesus: The Life, Teachings, and Relevance of a Religious Revolutionary* (New York: HarperOne, 2006), 278–87.

71. Some writers include John Dominic Crossan among those skeptics who affirm the reality of at least the resurrection appearances, however they are understood, but I cannot find that affirmation in any of Crossan's works. In his book *Who Killed Jesus?* Crossan insists that "the risen apparitions are not historical events in the sense of trances or ecstasies, except in the case

of Paul." Instead, Crossan appears to say that the early Christians "did not lose their faith and quit" but rather "they found, even after his execution . . . that the empowering Kingdom was still present, was still operative, was still there." Thus, while Crossan affirms that Christian faith is "the experience of Jesus' continued empowering presence," he denies that the early disciples had encounters with Jesus alive in any meaningful sense. As best as I can tell, for Crossan Jesus died and stayed dead, just like every other human being, but his *movement* and influence continued on. See John Dominic Crossan, *Who Killed Jesus?* (San Francisco: HarperSanFrancisco, 1996), 208–10.

72. Bart D. Ehrman, *How Jesus Became God* (New York: HarperOne, 2014), 174.

73. William Lane Craig, "The Bodily Resurrection of Jesus," *Gospel Perspectives I*, eds. R. T. France and D. Wenham (Sheffield, England: JSOT Press, 1980), 47–74. Also available online at http://www.leaderu.com/offices/billcraig/docs /bodily.html.

74. E. P. Sanders, *The Historical Figure of Jesus* (New York: Penguin Books, 1993), 279–80.

75. Ibid., 280.

76. See James Ware, "Paul's Understanding of the Resurrection in 1 Corinthians 15:36–54," *Journal of Biblical Literature* 133, no. 4 (2014): 809–35. Ware concludes that an analysis of Paul's syntax and the structure of his argument in this passage means that Paul's understanding of a "spiritual body" (*soma pneumatikos*) is not that of a "replacement" for the physical with some sort of ethereal substance but rather "reflects the mainstream Jewish concept of the resurrection of the body of flesh and bones from the tomb . . . the miraculous reconstitution of the mortal body of flesh and bones and its transformation so as to be imperishable" (835).

Chapter 11: Jesus, God and Man

1. Strangely, Bart Ehrman claims in his book *How Jesus Became God* that the exalted claims about Jesus as the revelation of God "appear only in John, our latest and most theologically oriented Gospel" (New York: HarperOne, 2014), 125. He doesn't appear to consider these texts from *Q*, cited by Dunn, which also stress a sentiment that "no one knows the Father except the Son and anyone to whom the Son chooses to reveal him" (11:27).

2. Daniel Boyarin, *The Jewish Gospels* (New York: The New Press, 2012), 54.

3. Burton L. Mack, *A Myth of Innocence: Mark and Christian Origins* (Philadelphia: Fortress Press, 1988), cited in Larry W. Hurtado, *How on Earth Did Jesus Become a God?* (Grand Rapids, MI: W.B. Eerdmans, 2005), 18.

4. "In the judgment of a wide range of biblical scholars, these views [that Jesus had been exalted to heaven] are quite ancient. In fact, they may represent the oldest views of the very earliest Christians, views first reached when the followers of Jesus came to believe he had been raised from the dead," Ehrman, *How Jesus Became God*, 218.

5. Ibid., 222.

6. Ibid., 220–21.

7. Peter Schäfer, *The Jewish Jesus: How Judaism and Christianity Shaped Each Other* (Princeton: Princeton University Press, 2012), 103–59.

8. W. Sibley Towner, "Daniel," *Harper's Bible Commentary* (San Francisco: Harper & Row, 1988), 696.

9. Boyarin, *The Jewish Gospels*, 43.

10. Bart Ehrman argues that Jesus of Nazareth believed the Son of Man was someone other than himself, a celestial figure who would shortly come to inaugurate God's reign on earth, kill all the Romans, and establish Jesus as king of Israel. "Jesus appears to have talked about a future Son of Man who would bring in God's kingdom at the end of this age. Later Christians who thought that Jesus himself was that one took his sayings and manufactured traditions in which he spoke of himself in this way." Bart D. Ehrman, *Did Jesus Exist?* (New York: HarperOne, 2012), 306–07.

11. Boyarin, *The Jewish Gospels*, 47.

12. Ibid., 55.

13. Raymond E. Brown, *An Introduction to New Testament Christology* (Mahwah, NJ: Paulist Press, 1994), 90.

14. Martin Hengel, *Between Jesus and Paul* (London: SCM, 1983), 30–47. Quoted by Hurtado in "Early Devotion to Jesus: A Report, Reflections and Implications," *Expository Times* 122.4 (2010): 167–76. Available online at: http://larryhurtado.files.wordpress.com/2010/07/early-devotion-to-jesus2.pdf.

15. Hurtado points to Hengel's full treatment in his book, *Son of God: The Origin of Christology and the History of Jewish-Hellenistic Religion* (1975; ET 1976).

16. L. W. Hurtado, "Early Devotion to Jesus: A Report, Reflections and Implications," *Expository Times* 122.4 (2010): 167–76. Available online at: http://larryhurtado.files.wordpress.com/2010/07/early-devotion-to-jesus2.pdf.

17. Rabbi Schmuley Boteach, author of *Kosher Jesus*, makes this argument. "[T]he fact that Jesus thought of himself as the messiah shouldn't bother Jews," [Boteach] insists. "I could declare myself the messiah right now. There's nothing blasphemous about this," Boteach said. "I even encourage people to have a certain messianic tendency in their lives, a desire to redeem the

world." Raphael Ahren, "New Book by U.S. Rabbi Depicts Jesus as a Jewish Patriot," *Haaretz*, January 6, 2012, http://www.haaretz.com/weekend/anglo -file/new-book-by-u-s-rabbi-depicts-jesus-as-a-jewish-patriot-1.405735.

18. Ibid.

19. "A higher Christology than Paul already expresses in 1 Corinthians 8:6 is scarcely possible . . ." Richard Bauckham, *God Crucified: Monotheism & Christology in the New Testament* (Grand Rapids, MI: William B. Eerdmans, 1998), 40.

20. "If all the Jews—or even a substantial number—expected that the Messiah would be divine as well as human, then the belief in Jesus as God is not the point of departure on which some new religion came into being but simply another variant (and not a deviant one) of Judaism." Boyarin, *The Jewish Gospels*, 53.

21. Hurtado, "Early Devotion to Jesus," 172.

22. Hurtado, *How On Earth Did Jesus Become a God?*, 25.

23. Dunn's discussion of these issues is actually far more complex and nuanced than we have space for in this book because it goes beyond New Testament exegesis into the realms of early Trinitarian theology. Dunn argues that the early followers of Jesus did not make a simple identification of Jesus with God—and did not worship Jesus as such. "The New Testament writers are really quite careful at this point," he writes. "Jesus is not the God of Israel. He is not the Father. He is not Yahweh. An identification of Jesus with and as Yahweh was . . . labelled as 'Modalism' . . . and accounted a heresy." James D. G. Dunn, *Did the First Christians Worship Jesus?* (London: SPCK, 2014), 142. As for worship, Dunn is equally careful: "Worship language and practice at times do appear in the New Testament in reference to Christ. But on the whole, there is more reserve on the subject. Christ is the subject of praise and hymn-singing, the content of early Christian worship, more than the one to whom the worship and praise is offered" (150).

24. Hurtado, *How On Earth Did Jesus Become a God?*, 306.

25. David Flusser, *The Sage from Galilee: Rediscovering Jesus' Genius* (Grand Rapids, MI: Wm. B. Eerdmans, 2007), 2–3.

26. Jerome Murphy-O'Connor, *The Holy Land: An Oxford Archaeological Guide*, 5th ed. (Oxford: Oxford University Press, 2008), 117.

27. Ibid.

INDEX

A

Adomnán, 100
adultery, woman caught in, xxi, xxii
Aedicule, 221
Aland, Kurt, 20, 72, 78, 79
Aland-Nestle text, 72, 78, 81
  critical apparatus, 78
Alexandre, Yardenna, 98, 99
am ha-aretz (people of the land), 165
Anselm of Canterbury, 65
Antipas-Nabatean war, 30
anti-Semitism, 151, 154, 157, 159, 314n44,
  315n56
Apocryphon of James, 176–77
Apollonius of Tyana, 10
Aquinas, Thomas, 44
Aramaic, 10
  used by Jesus, 165
  used by Luke, 20
  used by Mark, 19–20
  used in early creedal statements, 256
Arav, Rami, 5, 106
archaeological finds
  evidence of people once considered
    fictional, 102
  importance of State of Israel to, 101
  in Nazareth, 96, 97, 98, 99
  See also under individual finds
Arculf, 100
Arlandson, James M., 32, 33
Aslan, Reza, xxiii, xxiv, 14, 58, 114, 120,
  143, 192–94
atonement, 62, 63–65, 66, 130, 211,
  213–14, 302–3n72, 325n31, 325n33

B

Augustine, 44

Bagatti, Bellarmino, 96, 99
Banias, 40
bar Kokhba, Simon, 220
Barth, Karl, 53, 54
Basilica of the Annunciation, 95, 96, 97,
  98, 99
Bauckham, Richard, 7, 34, 35, 36, 37, 258
  on early worship of Jesus, 263, 264
Bauer, Bruno, 8, 72
Beatitudes. *See* Sermon on the Mount
Beit She'arim, 95
ben Joseph, Yechiel, 142
ben Matityahu, Yosef. *See* Josephus, Titus
  Flavius
ben Perachyah, Yehoshua, 142
Benedict XVI, 73
Beth Zetha Valley, 5
Bethesda, Pool of, 2, 3, 4, 5
Bethsaida, 41, 110, 164
  excavation of, xix
Bethzatha, Pool of. *See* Bethesda, Pool of
Bible versions, 72, 74, 76
biblical minimalists, 74
Biven, David, 143
Blomberg, Craig L., 14–17
Bolz-Weber, Nadia, 217
Borg, Marcus, 60, 61, 68, 212, 213, 216,
  250, 267
Bornkamm, Günther, 54
Boteach, Shmuley
  about, 140, 311n6

against religious extremism, 146

approach to Jesus, 61, 135, 140, 141, 142, 147, 150, 154, 157, 159

Kosher Jesus, 140, 314n45

on Jesus as apostate, 142

on Jesus as highly trained rabbi, 143–45

on Jesus as messiah, 314n46, 325n27, 335n17

on Paul and Jesus, 143, 155

on Romans alone killing Jesus, 152, 153, 314n45

Boyarin, Daniel, 7, 258, 264, 265

and Jewish Gospels, The, 132–35

on Jesus as critic of the Pharisees, 154

on Jesus as the Son of Man, 259, 260

on Jesus as the suffering messiah, 120, 133–34

on Jesus' understanding of Jewish practices, 147, 148, 149, 150

Brandon, S. G. F., 57, 58, 59, 114, 115, 191, 192, 193

Brodie, Thomas, 8

Brown, Dan, 209

Brown, Raymond, 233, 234, 261, 289n12, 290n24, 295n78, 309n11

Bruce, F. F., 37

Bultmann, Rudolf, xxiii, 7, 25, 32, 37, 53, 54, 119, 120

burial

of Jesus, 232–36. *See also* Garden Tomb; *Lost Tomb of Jesus, The*; ossuary; Talpiot, tombs found at

C

Caesar, Augustus, 131

Caesar, Julius, 82

Caesarea Maritima, 96, 111, 181, 182, 188

Caesarea Philippi, xxi, 39, 40, 41, 109

Caiaphas, 152

ossuary, 104–5, 225

Caligula crisis, 30

Calvin, John, 45, 65

Cameron, James, 224, 228

Cana, 95

canon, biblical, 75

Capernaum, xix, xxv

ruins of, 107–8

Carmichael, Joel, 57

Carrier, Richard, 9

Carson, D. A., 32

Celsus, 46

Charlesworth, James, 229

Chorazin, xxi

Christ myth theory. *See* mythicism

Christianity and Judaism, birth of, 147

Christology

development of Jewish, 258

Jewish views of the Godhead, 259–60

low versus high, 255–57

Church of the Holy Sepulchre, 219–20, 221, 250

Church of St. Anne, 4, 5

Codex Alexandrinus, 78, 83, 84

See also manuscripts

Codex Bezae, 79, 84

See also manuscripts

Codex Ephraemi, 78, 84

See also manuscripts

Codex Sinaiticus, 76, 77, 78, 83, 84

See also manuscripts

Codex Vaticanus, 76, 77, 78, 83, 84

See also manuscripts

codices, 75

Coherence-Based Genealogical Method, 88

coins, discovery of ancient, 96

Colwell, E. C., 89

Constantine, xxxi–xxxii

Craig, William Lane, 29, 222, 234, 235, 236, 250

Crassus, 113

Cross Gospel, 44

Crossan, John Dominic, 43

approach to Jesus, 68, 199, 267

on Jesus as "Cynic philosopher," 60, 167, 210

on Jesus' acts of civil disobedience 12, 113, 114

on Jesus' burial and empty tomb, 230, 231, 232, 233, 234, 237

on harsh Roman rule, 198

on lavish Roman building projects, 111, 112, 188, 189

on value of Gnostic texts, 173–74

See also Jesus Seminar

Crossley, James, 7, 29, 30, 34

crucifixion, 154, 210, 223

of Jesus, xvii, 191, 209, 210
controversy over, 122, 230–31. *See
also* Jesus, death of; Jesus, killed
by whom
site of, 220, 221, 231
time of, 17
of Jesus' followers, 198–99
of 2,000 Jews by Quintilius Varus, 92,
131, 154, 198
of Yehochanan, 105–6
of Yehohanan, 230, 233, 234
Cullmann, Oscar, 54

D

Da Vinci Code, The (Brown), 209, 237
Dark, Ken, 99, 100, 102–3
David, King
evidence of, 102
House of, 92–93, 98
messiah, 123, 124
de Cisneros, Francisco Jiménez, 73
Dead Sea Scrolls, 117, 120, 129, 171, 192,
229, 258
messianic hopes in, 130–32
DeConick, April D., 207
Descartes, René, 49
Dever, Mark, 65
Dibelius, Martin, 7, 25
Dodd, C. H., 54
Doherty, Earl, 8, 9
Dunn, James D. G., 5, 53, 233, 255, 258,
264

E

Ebionites, 43, 155, 171
Egeria, 163, 221, 317n2
Ehrman, Bart, 120, 179, 210, 231, 232, 233,
234, 235, 238, 250, 257, 258
about, xxiii, xxiv
charges leveled against by Daniel
Wallace, 89–90
debate with Daniel Wallace, 69, 70
debate with William Lane Craig, 235
in defense of text-critical guild, 84
on belief in dying-rising gods in
antiquity, 10
on beliefs of Jesus' followers, 250, 257,
258

on Codex Vaticanus and Codex
Sinaiticus, 77
on early New Testament copies, 70, 83,
85, 86, 87
on Erasmus's Greek New Testament, 76
on evidence for existence of individuals
in ancient world, 9
on Gospel accounts, 32, 46, 47, 238
on Jesus as deluded apocalyptic prophet,
56, 67, 179, 186, 187, 210
on Jesus' dead body, 231, 232, 233,
234
on Jesus' Palm Sunday entrance into
Jerusalem, 126–27, 128
on Jewish view of messiah, 120
Eisenman, Robert, 57, 192
Elliott, J. K., 89
Erasmus, Desidarius, of Rotterdam, 48,
74, 76
eruv (artificial "household"), 3
Essenes, 120, 121, 131, 137, 138, 147, 192
Eusebius, 35, 95, 175, 182, 220, 221,
292n44
Evans, Craig, 232, 233
exodus, the, 102
extremist Jews, 145–46
eyewitness testimony
ages of eyewitnesses, 34–35
hidden in the Gospels, 31–34
in the Gospels, 4–5, 7, 18, 25, 31, 36
in Luke, 33
in Mark's Greek vocabulary, 147–49
of John, 4–5, 32, 33, 35, 37
of Peter in Mark, 35, 36

F

Fee, Gordon, 89
Fitzgerald, David, 9
Flusser, David, 37–38, 266
Fredriksen, Paula, 57, 152
form criticism, 32
Four-Source theory, 17
Franciscan order in Israel, 107–8
Funk, Robert, 60
Furstenberg, Yair, 147, 148, 149, 150

G

Gäbel, Georg, 74, 88

Gabriel Revelation, 117, 118, 119, 120, 122, 268

Galilee, Sea of, xix–xxi
discovery of Jesus Boat at, 106–7
fishing in, xx

Galileo, 48

Gandhi, Mahatma, 187, 212

Garden Tomb, 221

Gethsemane, Garden of, 201, 212
Jesus' travail and arrest in, 202, 203

Gibson, Shimon, 233, 234, 326n3

Ginosar, xx–xxi

Givat Hamivtar, 106

Gnostic gospels, 170–79
sexism in the, 173
See also Gospel of Judas

Gnosticism, 174

Golan Heights, xxi

Golgotha, 220

Gospel of Judas, 203–8
manuscript, 204–5
Gnosticism in, 206

Gospel of Mary, 175

Gospel of Philip, 174

Gospel of Thomas, 34, 171, 172, 173, 174, 175, 176, 318n15

Gospels
apocryphal, 6
as historical sources, 6–7
discrepancies in, 6–7, 14–18, 46–47
harmonizations of the, 45–46
late dating of, 29
reliability of, 37–38
sources, 49. *See also* Q sayings source
See also Gnostic gospels; John, Gospel of; Mark, Gospel of; Synoptic Gospels

Grant, Michael, 48, 233

Gratus, Valerius, 183

Gregory IX, 221

H

Habermas, Gary, 234, 236

halacha (way of the Jewish law), xxvi

Halkin, Hillel, 119

hallucination theory, 223, 237. *See also* resurrection

hand washing controversy in Mark, 147–49

Hengel, Martin, 261

Herod Agrippa I, 113

Herod Antipas, xix, 59

Herod Archelaus, 183

Herod the Great, 12, 39, 91, 92, 93, 131, 181

Herod Philip, 107

Herodotus, 81, 82

Hillel, 143

Hippolytus, on killing, 196

Holtzmann, Heinrich, 119

Holy Blood, Holy Grail (Baigent, Leigh, and Lincoln), 209

Holy Fire, 221, 222

Horsley, Richard, 16, 59, 60, 68, 112, 167, 188, 189, 199, 267

Hurtado, Larry, 257, 258, 261, 262, 263, 264, 265

hyraxes (*shafanim*), 40

I

infancy narratives
as *theologoumena*, xxiii

Institute for New Testament Textual Research, 72, 87

insula (connected townhouses), xxv, 108

International Mary of Nazareth Center, 98, 99

intertestamental works. *See* pseudepigrapha

ipsissima verba, 16

ipsissima vox, 16

Irenaeus, 35, 43, 171, 203
on peace, 196

Israel, State of, importance of to archaeological investigation, 101

Israel Antiquities Authority, 98

J

Jacobovici, Simcha, 224, 225, 226, 228, 229, 329n23, 329n27

James the Just, xvi, 11, 26, 42, 142, 187, 192, 194, 229, 321n23

Japha, 95

Jerome, 5, 44, 73, 75, 86, 277

Jerusalem, 25, 92, 93
excavations at, 111–12
fall of, not in Gospels, 28, 30–31
volatility of in Jesus' day, 152–54

Jerusalem Council, first, 42

Jesus
  anointing of, by woman at Bethany,
    21–17
  approach to Torah, 61, 140, 142, 144,
    147, 149, 150, 151, 160, 166–67, 168,
    179
  as apocalyptic prophet, 185–87, 198
  as divine, 259, 260, 261–66
  as God and man, 255–57. *See also*
    Christology
  as *hasid*, 61
  as kosher, 139–41
  as lamb of God, 154, 213
  as Messiah in the New Testament,
    129–30, 156
  as not kosher, 145–46
  as not a Pharisee, 146–47, 154
  as peacemaker, 194–95, 197–99
  as Pharisee, 139–41, 154
  as rabbi, 143–45
  as Son of Man, xv, 41, 56, 64, 122, 129,
    130, 260, 261, 271, 335n10. *See also*
    son of man
  as suffering messiah, 118–35, 157, 210,
    268
  as Zealot, 59, 142, 153, 190, 191, 193,
    201, 210, 267, 268
  "attack" on the temple, 114–15
  baptism of, 253–54
  burial of, 232–36. *See also* burial, of
    Jesus; Garden Tomb; *Lost Tomb of
    Jesus, The*; ossuary; Talpiot, tombs
    found at
  date of birth, 7
  death of, 208–14. *See also* crucifixion, of
    Jesus; Gethsemane, Garden of; Gospel
    of Judas; hallucination theory; *Passover
    Plot, The*; swoon theory
  disputes over identity of, 41–43, 55–68
      atoning sacrifice model, 63–65. *See
        also* atonement
      charismatic faith healer model,
        60–61
      deluded apocalyptic prophet model,
        56–57
      founder of a global movement
        model, 65–68
      Jewish messiah model, 61–63

    social reformer and community
      organizer, 58–60
    violent revolutionary model, 57–58
    wisdom sage model, 60
  existence of, xxx, 8–10
  fame of, 196–97
  first quest for, 49–54
  forgiveness offered by, seen as
    controversial, 215–17
  home of, 91
  killed by whom, 151–52, 153, 154
  literary devices used by, 165
  modern quest for, 48–49
  Palm Sunday entrance into Jerusalem,
    126–28
  politically correct, of the academics,
    159–61
  postresurrection appearances of, 239,
    241, 242, 243, 245. *See also* visions of
    Jesus
  quest for the historical, 44–48
  radicalizing of the Torah, 166–68
  rejection of by Jews, 154–57
  resurrection of, 219, 222–24. *See also*
    ossuary, alleged discovery of Jesus'
    family's; resurrection, of Jesus
  travail and arrest in Gethsemane, 202,
    203
  travels of, 2
  upholding the Law and the Prophets,
    149–51, 166, 169. *See also* Torah
  vocation of, 109–10
  See also kingdom of God; parables of
    Jesus; Sermon on the Mount
Jesus Boat, xxi, 106–7
Jesus Discovery, The (Jacobovici and Tabor),
  227, 228
Jesus Seminar, 5, 43, 60, 111, 173, 210, 230,
  250, 257
Jesus Trail, 94
Jewish Agency, xxiv
Jewish War of AD 66–70, 26, 27, 28, 30,
  58, 95, 99, 103, 107, 138, 153, 191
  assault of Sepphoris, 189
  nonparticipation of Sepphoris in, 109
  See also Zealots
Jews
  extremist. *See* extremist Jews

rejection of Jesus by, 154–56
John, Gospel of, 4–5
    author as eyewitness, 4–5, 32
John the Baptist, xxx
    arrest of, 15
    baptism of Jesus by, 253, 254. *See also*
        Qasr el Yahud
    death of, 296n1
    message of, 169
    message of, to Jesus, 57
Johnson, Luke Timothy, 62, 68, 236
Jones, Timothy Paul, on Roman burial laws,
    232
Joseph (stepfather of Jesus), 92
Joseph of Arimathea, 209, 226, 231, 233,
    235, 240
Josephus, Titus Flavius, 6, 9, 26, 27, 95, 99,
    137, 189, 232, 233
Judah ha-Nasi, 109
Judas the Galilean, xxxii, 26
Judas Iscariot, 203, 214–15
    his version of Jesus' death, 205–8
    See also Gospel of Judas
Justin Martyr, 43
    on peace, 196

K

Kabbalat Shabbat (welcoming of the
    Sabbath), xxv
Kähler, Martin, 53
kal ve-chomer ("light and heavy"), 143, 144
kepha (rock), xxi
kerygma (preaching), xxiii
kibbutz, xxiv
Kibbutz Ginosar, 106, 107
King, Martin Luther, Jr., 187, 212
kingdom of God
    as Jesus' central message, 52, 67, 168–69
    growth of, xxxi–xxxii
    Jesus' meaning of, 57
Kinneret. *See* Sea of Galilee
Klausner, Joseph, xxii, 133, 141, 150
Klinghoffer, David, 120, 125, 152
Kloner, Amos, 228
Knohl, Israel, 118, 120–21, 122, 130, 131,
    132, 268
Koine, 10
kokhim, 221

Küng, Hans, on Jesus' resurrection, 248–49

L

Lactantius, on killing, 196
Lectionary 150 (Codex Harleianus), 79
    See also manuscripts
Levine, Amy-Jill, 157–59, 160, 161, 177
Liberal Protestantism, 52, 54
Licona, Michael, 234, 236, 298n13
Life of Jesus, 50–52
Lion's Gate, 2, 4, 5, 202
literary devices used by Jesus, 165
Lost Tomb of Jesus, The (Cameron and
    Jacobovici), 224, 226
Lucian, 195
Lüdemann, Gerd, 56, 236
Luther, Martin, 48, 67, 160

M

Maccoby, Hyam, 58, 59, 141, 142, 143,
    150, 155
Mack, Burton, 11, 257
Magdala, xxi, 189
    discovery of first-century synagogue at,
        103–4
Magness, Jodi, 228–29, 233, 234
Maimonides, Moses, 152
Makarios, Bishop, 220
manuscripts, New Testament, 69–72, 73,
    74, 75, 76, 77
    accuracy rating system, 81
    ancient translations, 79–80
    lectionaries, 79
    majuscules (uncials), 78–79
    minuscules, 79
    papyri, 77
    passages not found in, 86–87
    quotations from church fathers, 80–82
    scribal changes, 82–85
Mark, Gospel of
    author of, 35
    dating of, 29, 30–31
    ending, 240–42
    manuscripts of gospel of, 71
Mary, mother of Jesus, 92, 93
Mary Magdalene, xxi, 46–47, 226, 227,
    235, 240, 241, 242, 329n27
Mary's Well, 95, 96, 99

Masada, 101, 102, 190
mashiach, 122–23
    See also *messiah*
McLaren, Brian, 179
Meier, John P., 56
Meir, Rabbi, 143
Menahem, 132
messiah
    diverse visions of a Jewish, 125–26
    in the Hebrew Bible, 122–25
    in Isaiah, 124
    in Jeremiah, 124
    in Micah, 123
    in the New Testament, 129–30
    in Zechariah, 126
    Jesus believing himself to be the, 142
    suffering, 117–20, 121, 122, 130, 131,
        132, 133, 134, 135, 157, 210, 268
    See also Gabriel Revelation; Jesus, as
        suffering messiah
messianic Jews, 43
    See also Ebionites
Metatron (Enoch), 259
Metz, Johann Baptist, 73
Metzger, Bruce, 89
midrash, 10, 18
Migdal, Battle of, 107. See also Magdala
Millard, Alan, 32, 33
miracles, historical problem of, 11–13
Mishnah, 147
mitzvot, xxv
Moo, Douglas, 32
moshav. See kibbutz.
Mount Hermon, 39, 40, 41
Mount of Beatitudes, xxi
Mount of Olives, 201, 202
Mount Sinai, 77
Mount Tabor, xxiv, 94, 202
mythicism, 8–10

N

Nag Hammadi, texts found at, 34, 171, 172,
    173, 258
    library 174
    See also Gospel of Thomas
Nash, John, 55
Nazarenes, 155, 171. See also Nazoreans
Nazareth, 91, 92, 94–100

archaeological discoveries at, 96, 102–3
stone house unearthed at, 96–100
Nazareth Village, 95
Nazoreans, 94
neoorthodoxy, 54
Nestle, Eberhard, 72
netzarim (branches), 94
Neusner, Jacob, xxvi
New Testament
    authors, 11
    first edition of Greek, 73–74
    key archaeological discoveries relating to
        the, 101–11
        Caiaphas ossuary, 104–5. See also
            ossuary, Caiaphas's
        crucified Yehochanan, 105–6, 230,
            233, 234
        first-century synagogue in
            Magdala, 103–4
        Jesus Boat, 106–7. See also Jesus Boat
        Nazareth excavations, 102–3
        Peter's house, 107–9
        Roman inscriptions, 110–11
        Sepphoris, 109–10. See also
            Sepphoris, ruins of
    manuscripts. See manuscripts, New
        Testament
    translations, 10–11, 72, 74, 75, 76
    trustworthiness of, 87–90
Nicodemus, 209
Nussberger-Tchacos, Frieda, 205

O

Oracle of Hystaspes, 131
Origen, 44, 75, 171
ossuary, 106
    alleged discovery of Jesus' family's,
        224–26, 227–28, 229, 230
    at Dominus Flevit
    Caiaphas's, 104–5, 225
    James's, 327n11, 327–28n12, 328n22,
        229n27

P

P45, 71
    See also manuscripts
P52 fragment, 26, 77, 78, 82
    See also manuscripts

P75, 78
  See also manuscripts
Pagels, Elaine, 172, 208
  on sexism in the Gnostic gospels, 173
Paine, Thomas, 46
palaces of Jerusalem aristocracy, 111–14
Palatial Mansion excavation, 112, 113
Palestine
  military occupation of, 189
  violence in first-century, 187–89
Pan, xxi, 40
  See also Banias
Paneas. *See* Banias
Papias, 20, 35, 292n44
papyri. *See* manuscripts
parables of Jesus, 175–79
  good Samaritan, 177–78
  prodigal son, 177
  reason for, 176
  sheep and the goats, 178–79
  two debtors, 178
  types of, 177–79
paradidomi (handing on [a tradition]), 36
paralambano (receiving [a tradition]), 36
Passover Plot, The (Schonfield), 208–10
Paul
  and alleged rivalry with messianic Jews,
    194
  as changer of Jesus' message, 192
  as founder of Christianity, 142
  as Pharisee, 155
  as tent maker, 143
  message of the cross, 170
  on the resurrection, 223, 238–39
Paulus, Heinrich, 209
Peter, 41
  home of, xx, 107–9
  proclamation of Jesus as Messiah, 41,
    129
Pharisees, 137, 138, 139
  belittling of by Christians, 158–59
  Jesus as a loyal Pharisee, 139–41
  Jesus not a Pharisee, 146–47
Philip the Tetrarch, 39
Philo, 120, 183
Pilate, Pontius
  burial of Jesus, 240
  condemned Jesus to death, 142, 153–54

evidence for his existence, 9, 110–11,
    183–85
  hater of Jews, 153, 233
  inscription, 111, 183–85
  "killer" of Jesus, 141
  questioned kingship of Jesus, 156–57
  refrained from massacre of unarmed
    Jews, 159, 330n37
  released Jesus' body, 240
  residence, 182
  slaughtered Jewish protestors, 184–85,
    294n57
  surprised at Jesus' quick death, 210, 240
pilgrim of Bordeaux, 95
Plato, 81, 82
Pliny the Younger, 82
Polycarp, 35
Pompey, General, 189
Pool of Bethesda. *See* Bethesda, Pool of
Postresurrection appearances of Jesus, 239,
    241, 242, 243, 245. *See also* visions of Jesus
Price, Robert, 8, 18
Protestant Reformation, 48, 75, 76, 160
pseudepigrapha, 132–33, 258

Q

Q sayings source, xxix, 23, 24, 30, 32, 165,
    171, 255
Qasr el Yahud, 253, 254
quest for the historical Jesus. *See* Jesus, quest
  for the historical
Qumran, 57, 120, 121, 130, 171. *See also*
  Essenes

R

Red Letter Christians, 168
Reed, Jonathan L., 111, 112
Reimarus, Hermann, 49, 57, 114, 190–91
Renan, Ernest, 50–52, 53
resurrection, of Jesus
  as compared with "raised," 237
  as foundation of Christianity, 222–24
  effect on lives of followers, 248–51
  four proven facts argument, 234–37
  Gospel accounts of, 237–44
  in the Apostles' and Nicene Creeds, 246
  in the catechism of the Roman Catholic
    Church, 246

See also postresurrection appearances of Jesus; visions of Jesus

Ritschl, Albrecht, 52

Roberts, C. H., 78

Roberts, Mark, 14, 32, 277

Roberty, Mario, 205

Robinson, James, 171, 173

Robinson, John A. T., 29, 235

Roman inscriptions, 110–11
  of Erastus, 111
  of Gallio, 111
  of Pontius Pilate, 111
  of Sergius Paulus, 111

Rousseau, John, 5

S

Sabbath
  Jesus' teaching on the, 144–45, 160
  Jewish observance of, 3–4, 146, 286n1
  Pharisees' observance of, 138

Sadducees, 137, 138

Saint Gabriel Church, 95, 99

Saint Joseph Church, 95

Salm, René, 9, 98

Sanders, E. P., 56, 66, 216, 233, 250, 251

Schäfer, Peter, 120, 132, 135, 258, 259, 260

Schochet, Jacob Immanuel, 145

Schonfield, Hugh, 208, 209

Schweitzer, Albert, 52, 53, 56, 62, 142, 186

Sea of Galilee. *See* Galilee, Sea of

Senès, Henri, 100

Sepphoris (Zippori), 93, 94, 164
  assault on, 189
  revolt in, 91–92
  ruins of, 109–10, 111–12, 188

Sermon on the Mount, 165–68

Sextus Julius Africanus, 95

shafanim. *See* hyraxes

Shanks, Hershel, 225

Sheep Gate, 2, 5
  See also Lion's Gate

Sicarii, 193

Silberman, Neil Asher, 16, 59, 188, 189

Simon bar Jonah. *See* Peter

Sisters of Nazareth, 99, 100
  archaeological discoveries at convent, 102–3

sola scriptura, 48

Son of man,
  in Daniel, 259, 260, 261
  Jesus' view of himself as the, xv, 41, 56, 64, 122, 129, 130, 260, 261, 271, 335n10
  meaning of the term, 259, 178
  use of the term by Stephen, 265
  use of the term in the Gospels, Romans, Hebrews, and Revelation, 259

St. Catherine's Monastery, 77

Stark, Rodney, xxxi

Stein, Robert, 62, 165

stone house, excavation of at Nazareth, 96–100

Strauss, David, 8, 49, 54, 72

Suetonius, 195

suffering messiah. *See* messiah, suffering

Suffering Servant passages, 121, 124, 130, 131, 133–34, 157
  See also messiah, suffering

swoon theory, 209, 237. *See also* resurrection

Synoptic Gospels
  definition of, 18
  discrepancies in, 6–7, 14–18
    apparent doublets, 16
    chronological divergences, 15
    omissions, 17
    paraphrases and composite speeches, 15–16
    true contradictions, 17
    variations in name and number, 15
  literary dependence of evangelists, 19–25
    Augustinian hypothesis, 19
    Farrer/Goulder hypothesis, 19
    Griesbach hypothesis, 19
    Holtzmann/Streeter hypothesis, 19, 20
  See also Four-Source theory

T

Tabor, James
  Jesus Discovery, The, 227
  on beliefs of early disciples regarding resurrection, 233, 237, 243, 245, 250
  on Dominus Flevit ossuaries, 225
  on Jesus as deluded apocalyptic prophet, 56, 67, 187

on poverty in Roman-occupied
Palestine, 112
on Talpiot tombs, 224, 228, 229
on temple commerce, 114, 243, 245, 250
Tacitus, 27, 82
Tag Mehir (Price Tag). *See* extremist Jews
Talmud
Babylonian, 147
on Jesus, 141–43
Palestinian, 147
Talpiot, tombs found at, 224, 225, 226,
228, 229, 329n23, 329n27
Taricheae. *See* Magdala
Taylor, N. H., 30
Tel Dan Nature Reserve, 40, 98
Temple, William, 52
Temple Mount, 12
Tertullian, on peace, 196
textual criticism, 82–84
Theissen, Gerd, 30, 58, 59
Theudas, xxxii
Thomas, "Doubting," 247–48. *See
also* postresurrection appearances of
Jesus
Thompson, Thomas, 8
Thucydides, 81, 82
Tiberias, xix, 104, 110, 164
Tiberius Caesar, 111, 183, 287n7
Tippler, Frank, 223
Titus, 27
Arch of, 27, 28
tomb. *See* ossuary; Talpiot, tombs found at
Torah
debates between Jesus and the Pharisees,
138–39, 143–45, 146–47, 151
Jesus' approach to, 61, 140, 142, 160,
166–67, 179
Jesus' radicalization of, 166–68
Jesus' upholding of, 149–51, 169
Pharisaical fence around the, 138, 147,
150, 179
Pharisees' approach to, 138
Sadducees' approach to, 138
Zealots' approach to, 138
Transfiguration, xxiv

U

ulpan, xxiv, xxv

uncials. See manuscripts, New Testament,
majuscules
Upper Room, traditional site of, 266–67

V

Varus, Publius Quintilius, 92
crucifixion of 2,000 Jewish rebels, 131,
198
Verbin, John S. Kloppenborg, 23
Vermes, Geza, xxii, 60, 61, 210–11, 267
Vespasian, 9, 39
violence, Christian opposition to, 196
visions of Jesus
by Ananias, 245
by Paul (Saul), 245
by Peter, 245
by Stephen, 245, 265
von Galen, Clemens August Graf, 73
von Harnack, Adolf, 52
von Tischendorf, Constantin, 76
Vulgate, 75, 76, 80, 87

W

Wadi Kerazeh, xxi
Wallace, Daniel
criticism of Bart Ehrman, 85, 89
debate with Bart Ehrman, 69, 70
in support of Gospel versions of Jesus'
burial, 232
on copiest accuracy, 87, 90
on discovery of seven New Testament
papyri, 70, 71, 78
on literary dependence in the Gospels,
19
Weiss, Johannes, 52, 119
White Fathers of France, 5
Witherington, Ben, III, 225
Wolf, Yitzchok, 145
Wrede, William, 156
Wright, N. T., 30, 62–63, 66, 68, 114, 199,
210, 267
on Jesus as peacemaker, 197–98
on Jesus' burial, 232, 233
on Jesus' resurrection, 234–35, 236, 249

Y

Yahad community, 121, 130
See also Essenes

Yehochanan, crucified, 105–6, 234
Yehohanan, crucified, 230, 233, 234
Yigal Alon Center, 107
Yochanan, 143

Z

Zealot (Aslan), 14, 58, 114, 120, 192, 193
Zealots, 114, 137, 138, 184, 193
　See also Jesus, as Zealot

Zias, Joe, 230
Zindler, Frank, 9, 96
Zippori. *See* Sepphoris
Zuntz, Günther, 89

ABOUT THE AUTHOR

Robert Hutchinson studied philosophy as an undergraduate, moved to Israel to learn Hebrew, and earned an MA in New Testament from Fuller Theological Seminary. He has been a professional writer his entire adult life, over the years writing both for Christian publications such as *Christianity Today* and for secular magazines and newspapers. Hutchinson's first paid article, in 1978, was about the children of the Hare Krishnas living in Seattle, and he has a lifelong interest in non-Christian religions. His book *The Politically Incorrect Guide to the Bible* demonstrates how the ideas embedded in the ancient biblical texts helped give rise to modern science, the development of democratic government, and the global recognition of human rights. Hutchinson's classic travelogue about the inner workings of the Vatican, *When in Rome: A Journal of Life in Vatican City,* was called a "*tour de force* that manages the rare and difficult feat of being at once ribald and reverent, informative and outrageous and, not least, very funny." Hutchinson lives with his wife and children in a small town on the West Coast. He blogs at www.RobertHutchinson.com.

STAY IN TOUCH

For more information about Robert Hutchinson and his upcoming books and presentations, visit his website, www.RobertHutchinson.com.

You'll find free resources that include:

- Book excerpts

- Exclusive features
- Downloads of audio and video presentations
- Special reports
- Free e-mail updates
- And more.

Robert J. Hutchinson

27525 Puerta Real #100–340
Mission Viejo, CA 92691
www.RobertHutchinson.com